Beat

VAMPIRE KNIGHT

Story & Art by
Matsuri
Hino

Vol. 10

The Story of VAMPIRE KNIGHT

1 Cross Academy, a private boarding school, is where the Day Class and the Night Class coexist. The Night Class—a group of beautiful elite students—are all vampires!

2 Four years ago, after turning his twin brother Ichiru against him, the pureblood Shizuka Hio bit Zero and turned him into a vampire. Kaname kills Shizuka, but the source may still exist. Meanwhile, Yuki suffers from her lost memories. When Kaname sinks his fangs into her neck, her memories return!

3 Yuki is the princess of the Kuran family—and a pureblood vampire!! Ten years ago, her mother exchanged her life to seal away Yuki's vampire nature. Yuki's Uncle Rido killed her father. Rido takes over Shiki's body and arrives at the Academy. He targets Yuki for her blood, so Kaname gives his own blood to resurrect Rido. Kaname confesses that he is the progenitor of the Kurans, and that Rido is the master who awakened him!

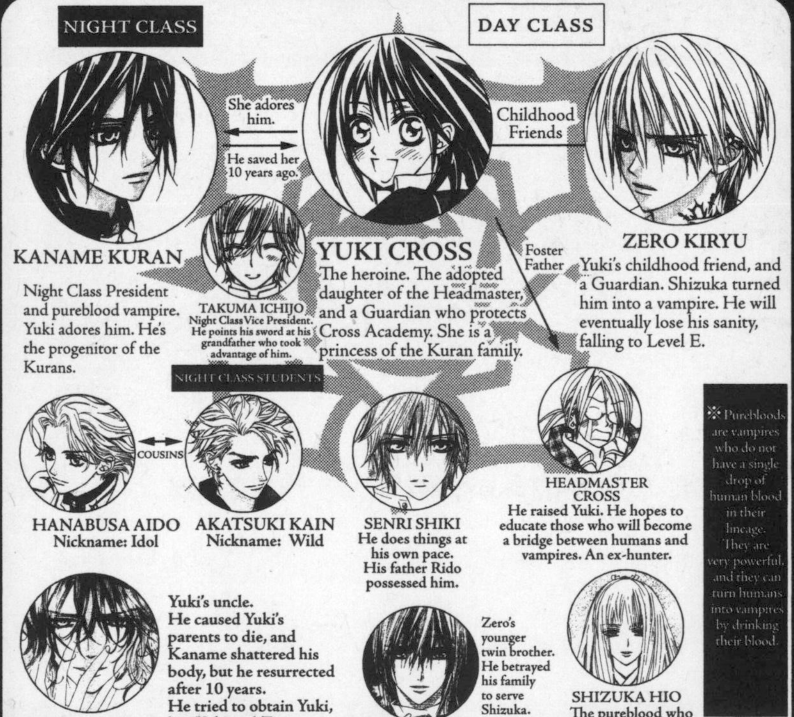

NIGHT CLASS
DAY CLASS
She adores him.
He saved her 10 years ago.
Childhood Friends
Foster Father
KANAME KURAN
Night Class President and pureblood vampire. Yuki adores him. He's the progenitor of the Kurans.
TAKUMA ICHIJO
Night Class Vice President. He points his sword at his grandfather who took advantage of him.
YUKI CROSS
The heroine. The adopted daughter of the Headmaster, and a Guardian who protects Cross Academy. She is a princess of the Kuran family.
ZERO KIRYU
Yuki's childhood friend, and a Guardian. Shizuka turned him into a vampire. He will eventually lose his sanity, falling to Level E.
NIGHT CLASS STUDENTS
COUSINS
HANABUSA AIDO
Nickname: Idol
AKATSUKI KAIN
Nickname: Wild
SENRI SHIKI
He does things at his own pace. His father Rido possessed him.
HEADMASTER CROSS
He raised Yuki. He hopes to educate those who will become a bridge between humans and vampires. An ex-hunter.
※Purebloods are vampires who do not have a single drop of human blood in their lineage. They are very powerful, and they can turn humans into vampires by drinking their blood.
Yuki's uncle. He caused Yuki's parents to die, and Kaname shattered his body, but he resurrected after 10 years. He tried to obtain Yuki, but Yuki and Zero killed him.
RIDO KURAN
Zero's younger twin brother. He betrayed his family to serve Shizuka.
ICHIRU
SHIZUKA HIO
The pureblood who robbed Zero of his family. Kaname killed her.

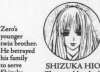

4 The truth about Yuki shatters Zero. Kaname tells Zero to kill Rido. After Zero refuses, Ichiru shoots Zero in the chest! Ichiru had wounded Rido to avenge Shizuka, and was himself fatally wounded in the process.

"Devour what remains of my life..." To become the strongest hunter of all and to make Ichiru's last wish come true, Zero is forced to make a decision while grieving.

The academy becomes a battlefield as Rido and his servant vampires attack. Yuki and the Night Class students fight to protect the academy. Then Zero appears. Yuki and Zero kill Rido after an intense battle, but then Zero points his gun at her!!

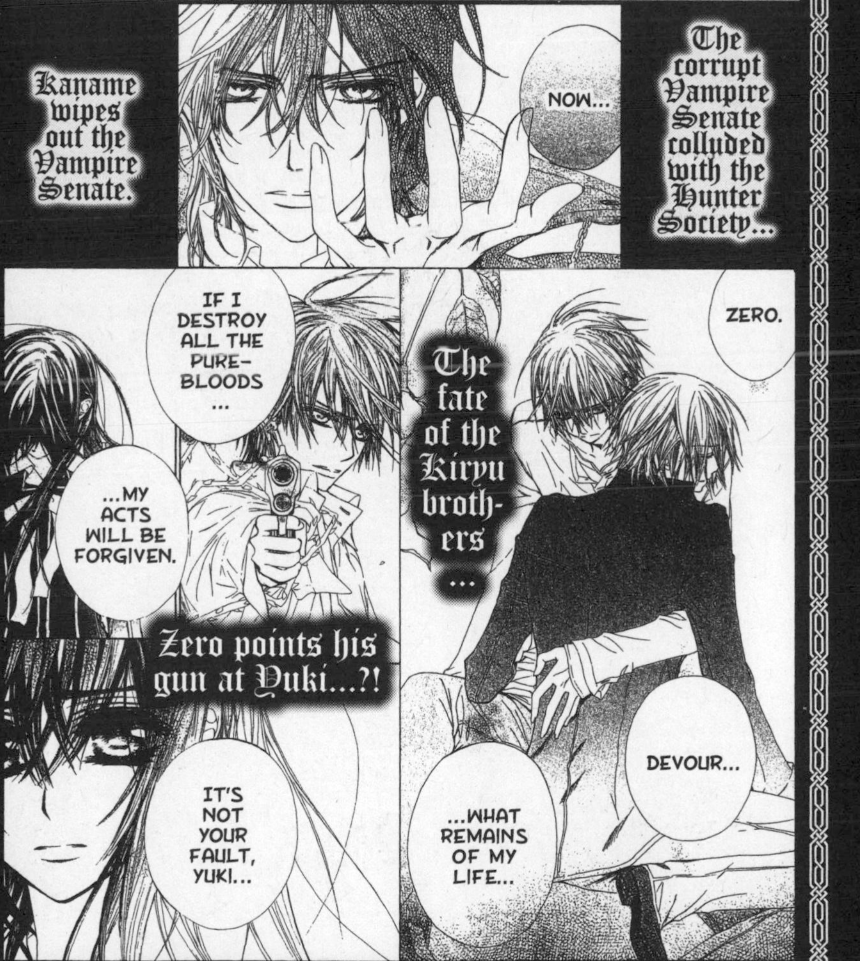
The corrupt Vampire Senate colluded with the Hunter Society...
NOW...
Kaname wipes out the Vampire Senate.
ZERO.
The fate of the Kiryu brothers...
DEVOUR...
...WHAT REMAINS OF MY LIFE...
IF I DESTROY ALL THE PUREBLOODS...
...MY ACTS WILL BE FORGIVEN.
Zero points his gun at Yuki...?!
IT'S NOT YOUR FAULT, YUKI...

VAMPIRE KNIGHT

Contents

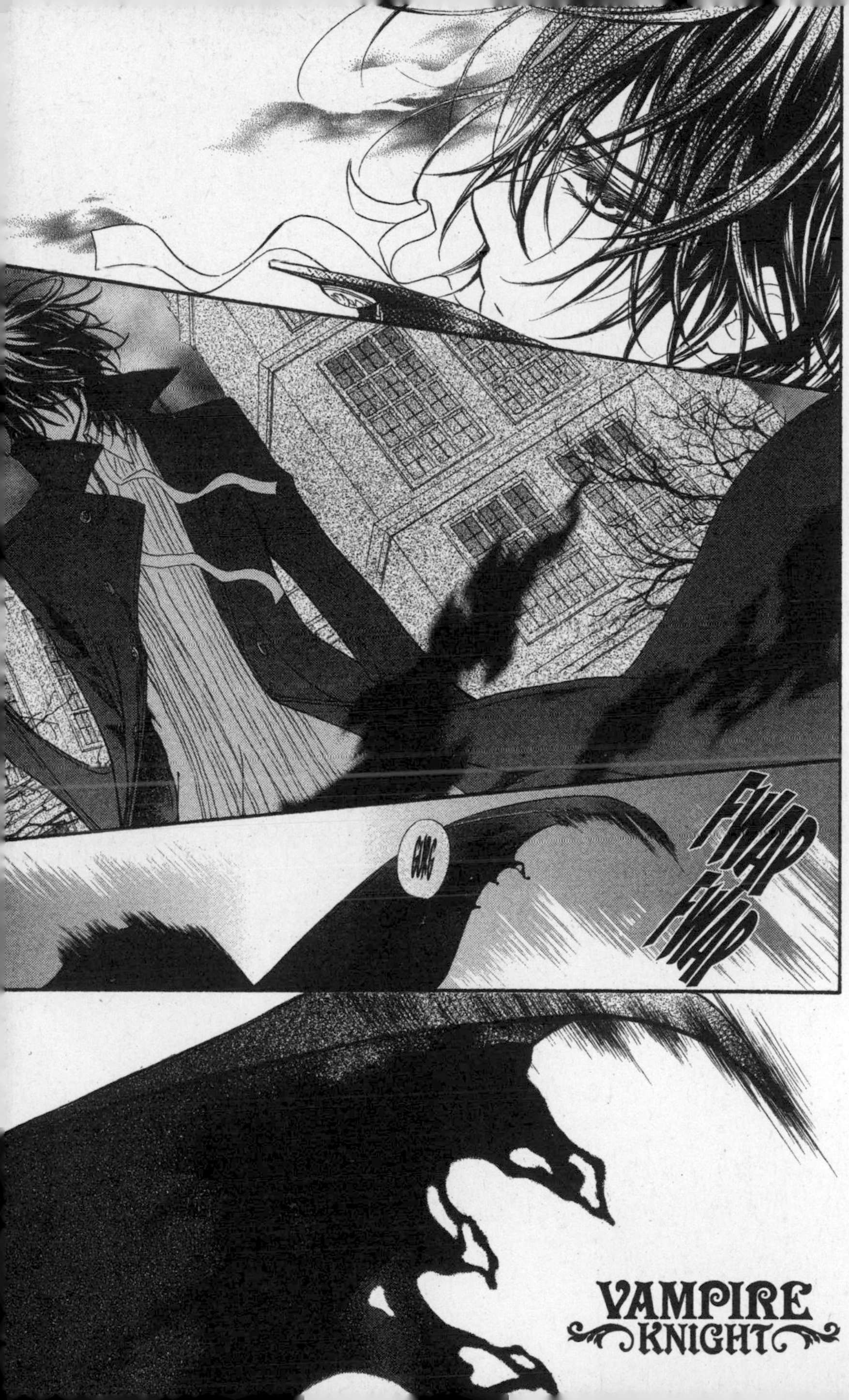
FWAP FWAP
VAMPIRE KNIGHT

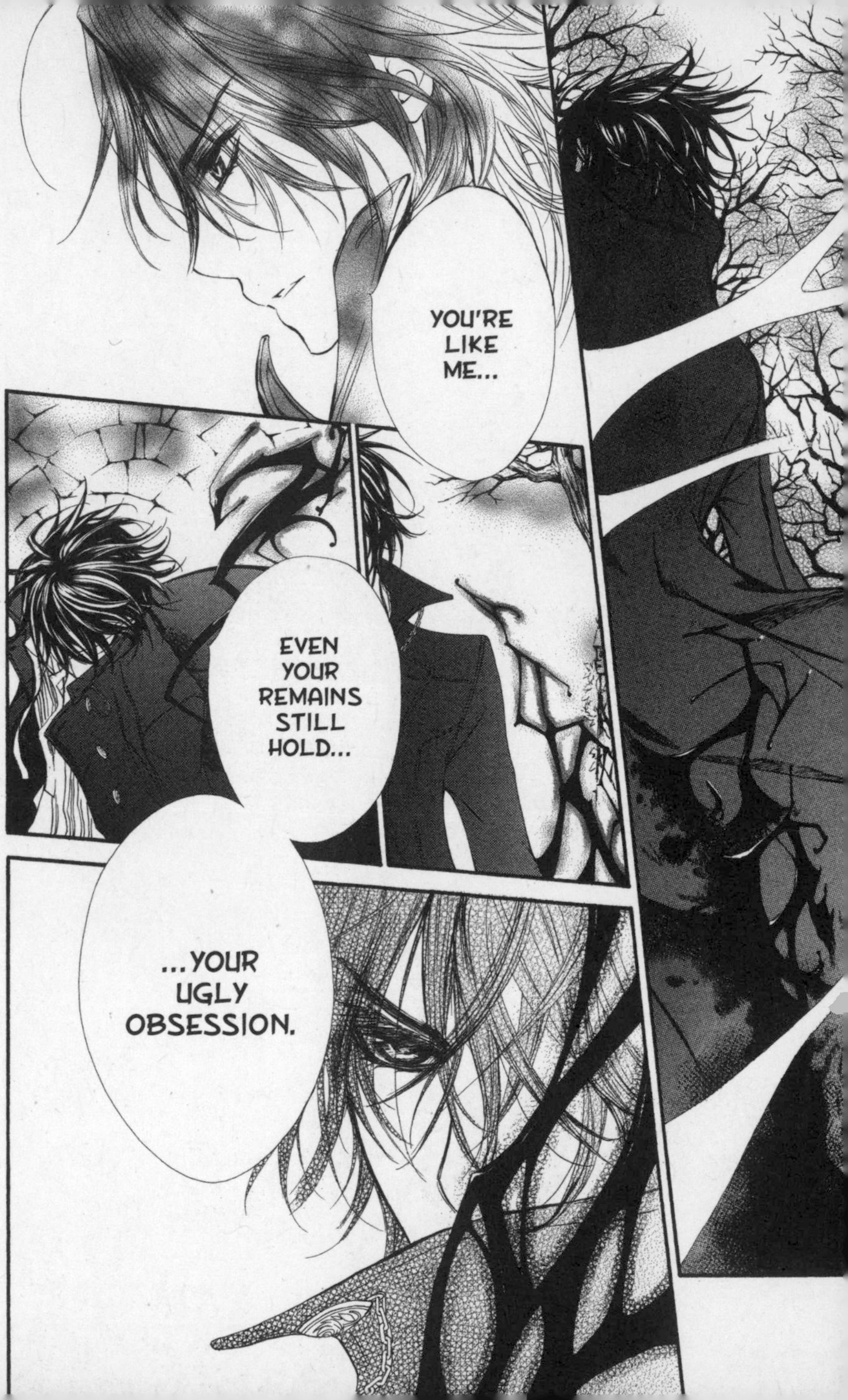
YOU'RE LIKE ME...
EVEN YOUR REMAINS STILL HOLD...
...YOUR UGLY OBSESSION.

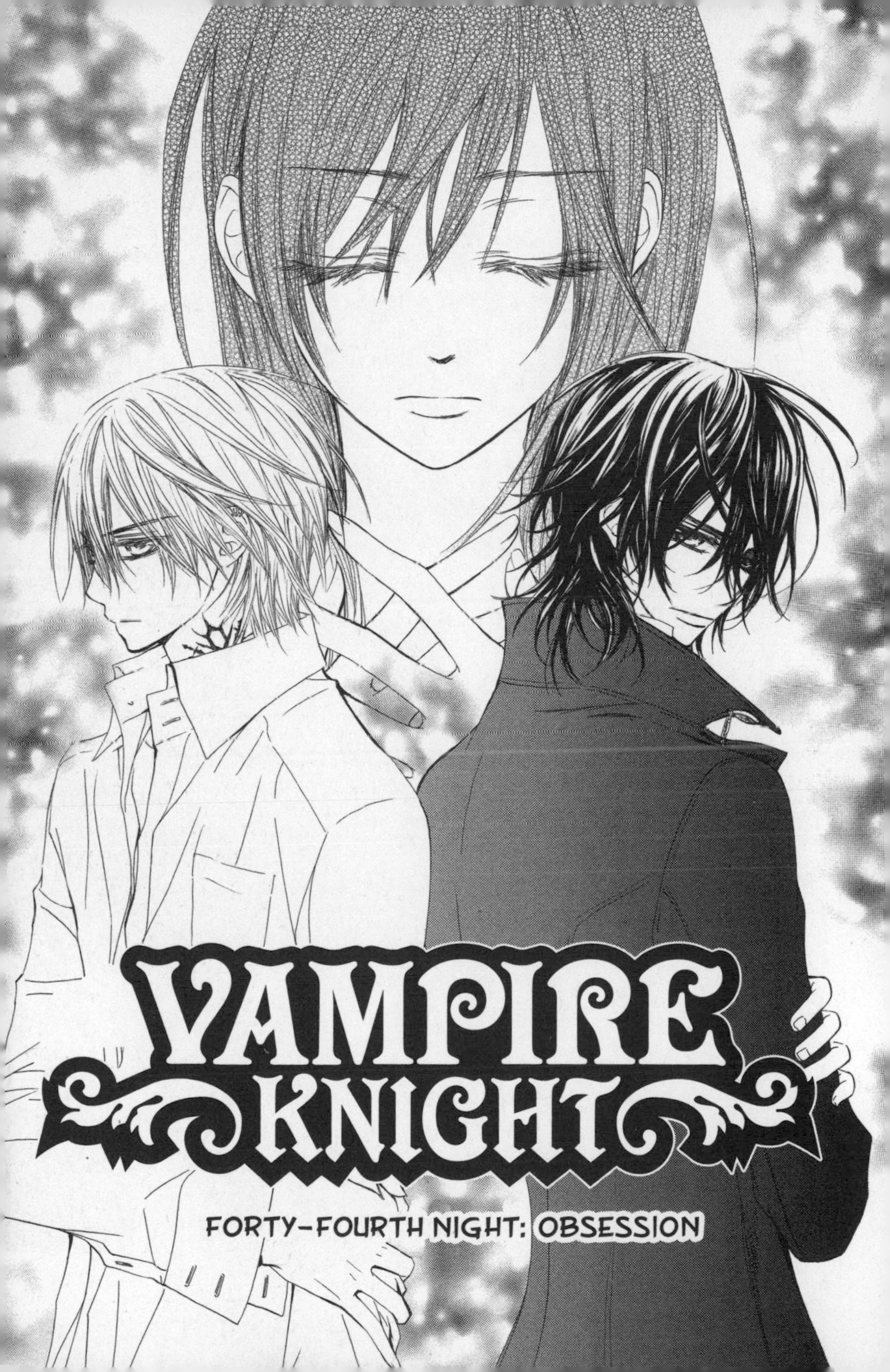
VAMPIRE KNIGHT
FORTY-FOURTH NIGHT: OBSESSION

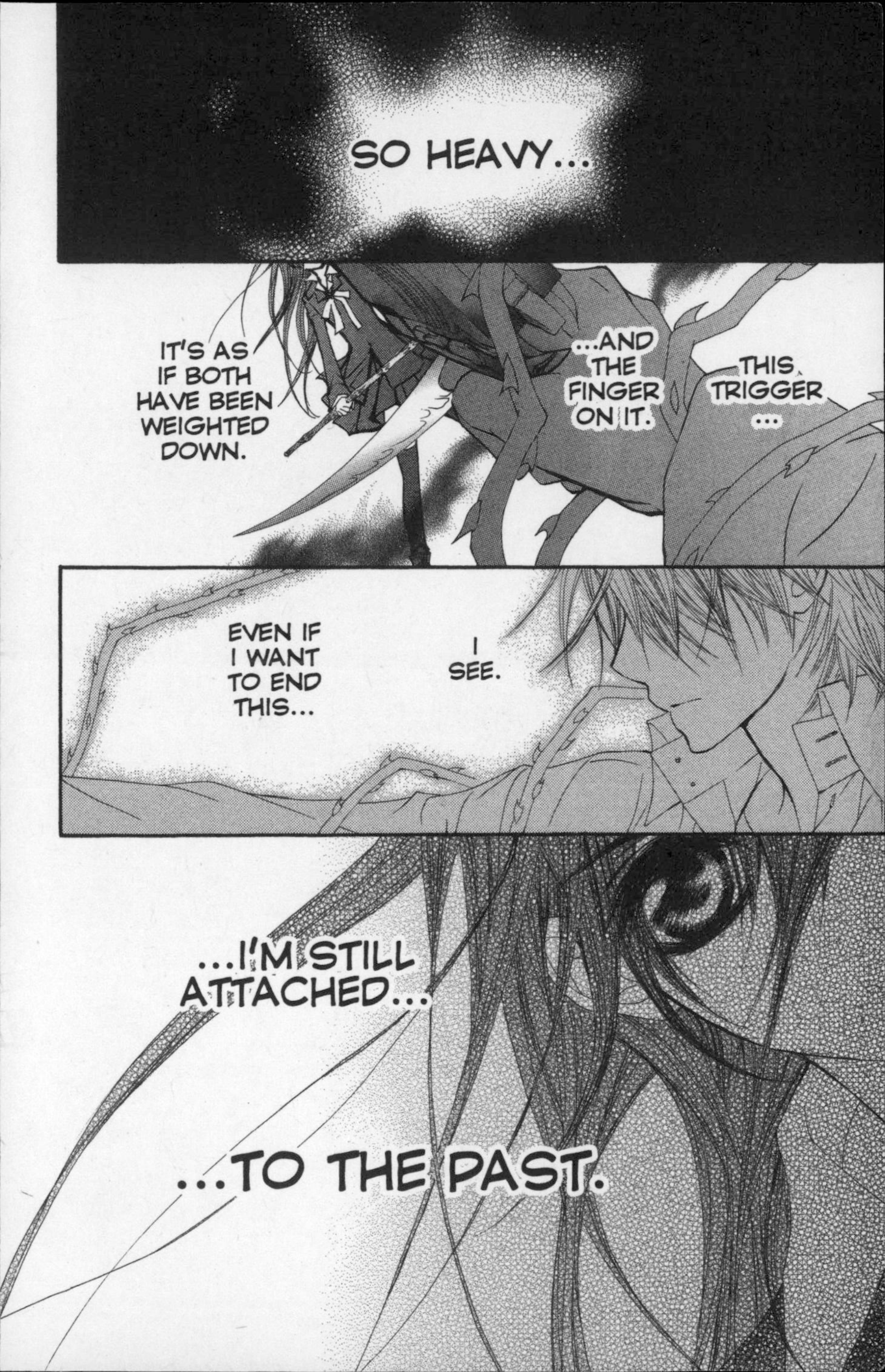
SO HEAVY...
THIS TRIGGER...
...AND THE FINGER ON IT.
IT'S AS IF BOTH HAVE BEEN WEIGHTED DOWN.
I SEE.
EVEN IF I WANT TO END THIS...
...I'M STILL ATTACHED...
...TO THE PAST.

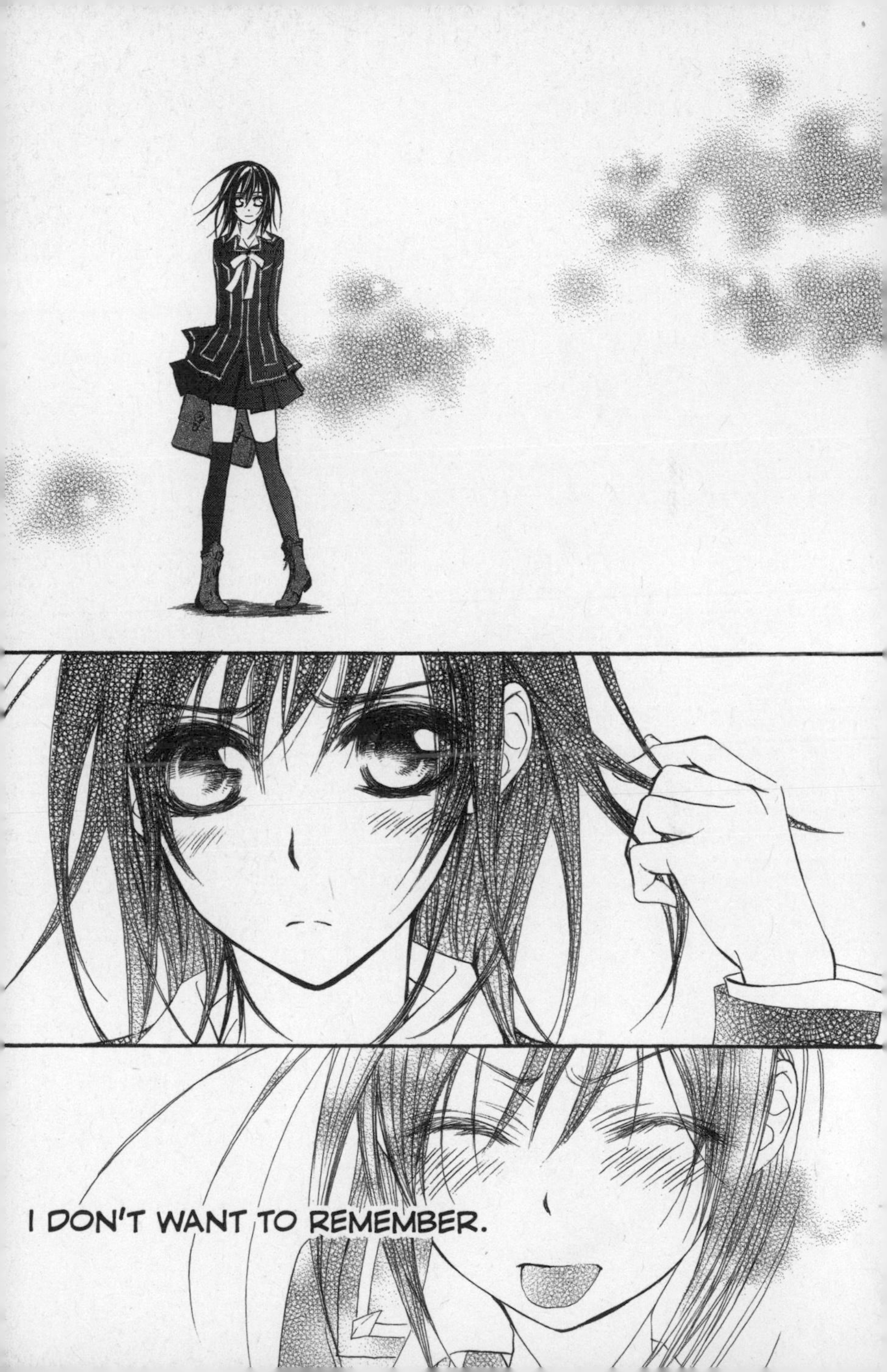
I DON'T WANT TO REMEMBER.

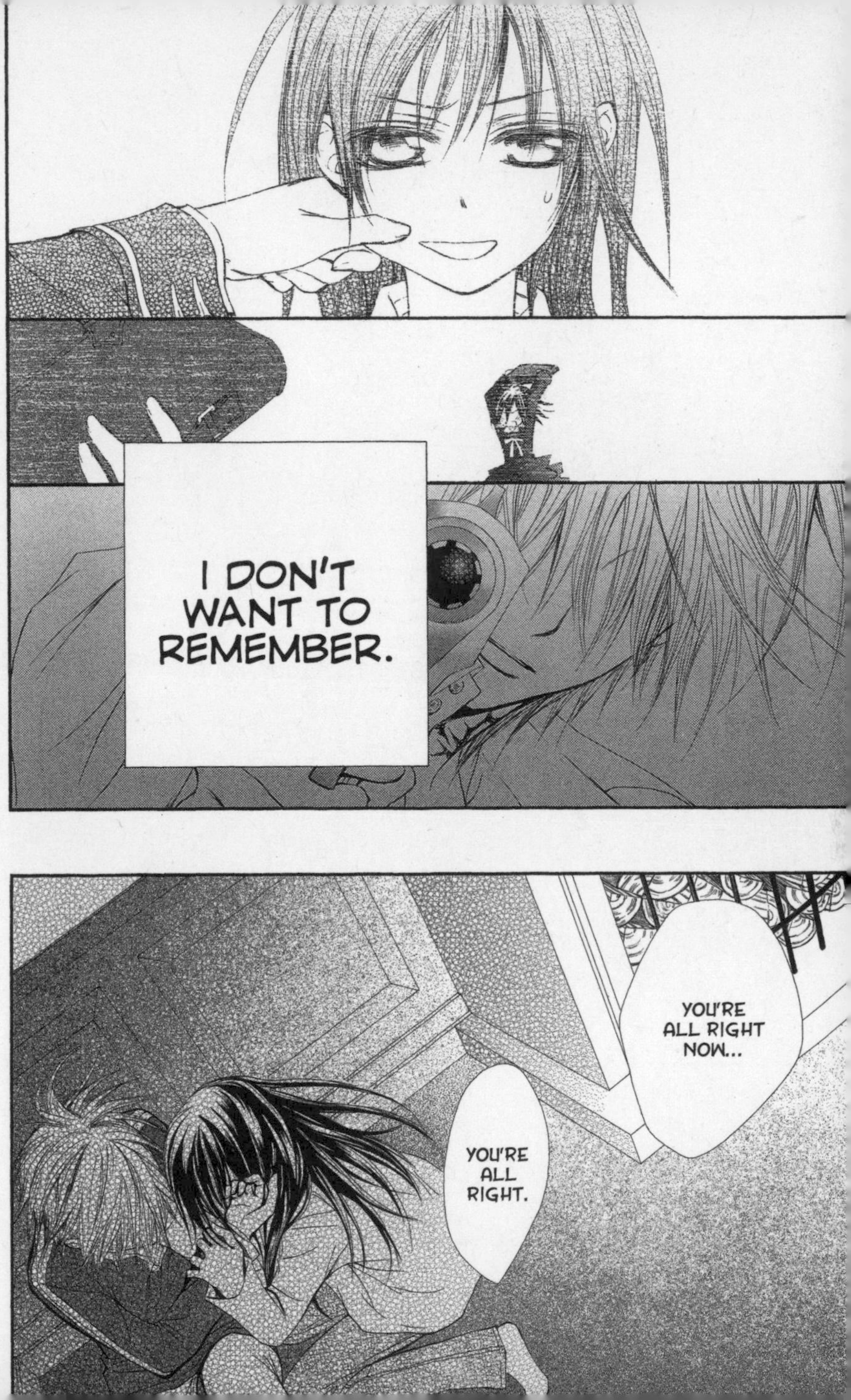
I DON'T WANT TO REMEMBER.
YOU'RE ALL RIGHT NOW...
YOU'RE ALL RIGHT.

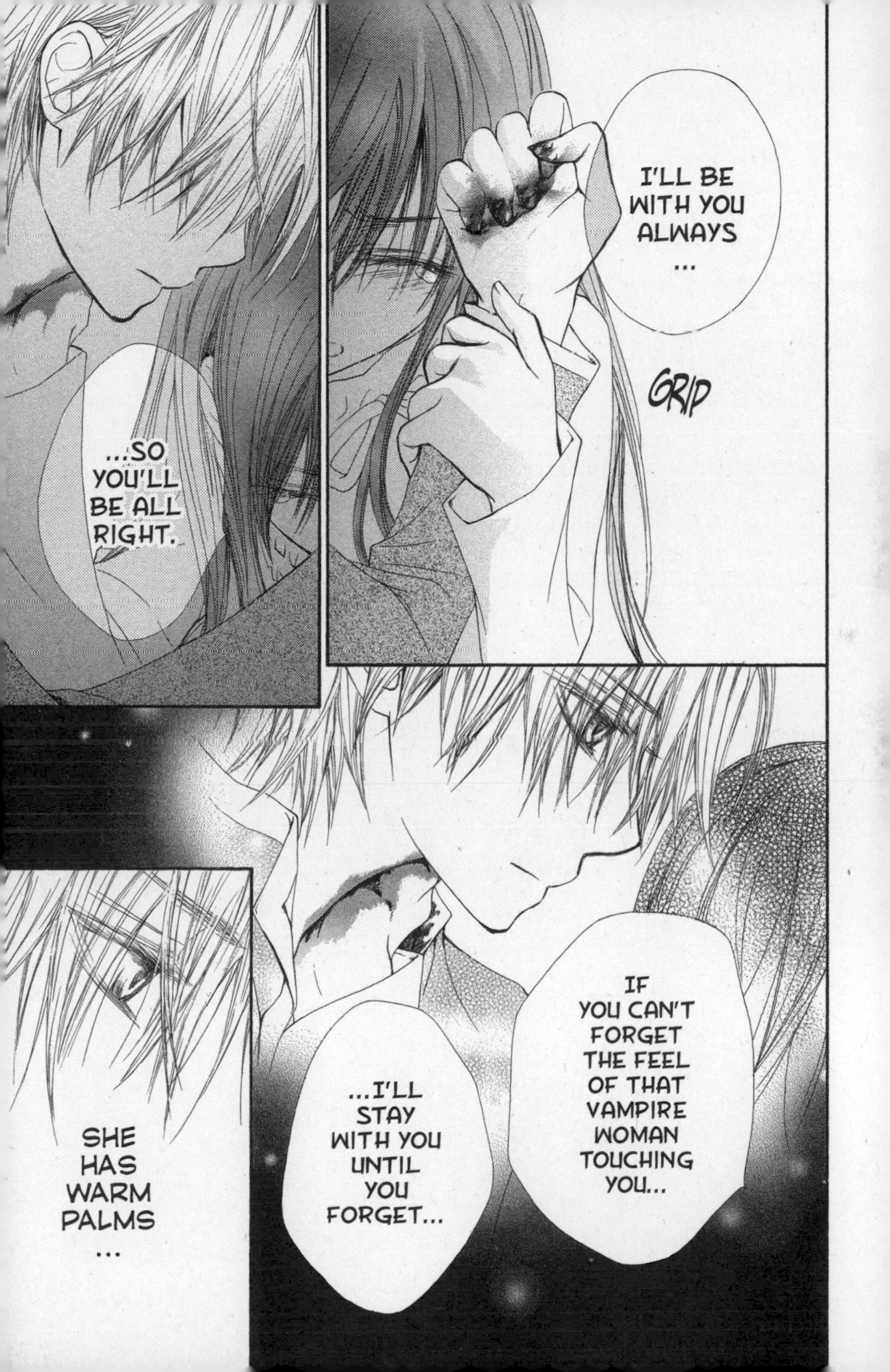
I'LL BE WITH YOU ALWAYS ...
GRIP
...SO YOU'LL BE ALL RIGHT.
IF YOU CAN'T FORGET THE FEEL OF THAT VAMPIRE WOMAN TOUCHING YOU...
...I'LL STAY WITH YOU UNTIL YOU FORGET...
SHE HAS WARM PALMS ...

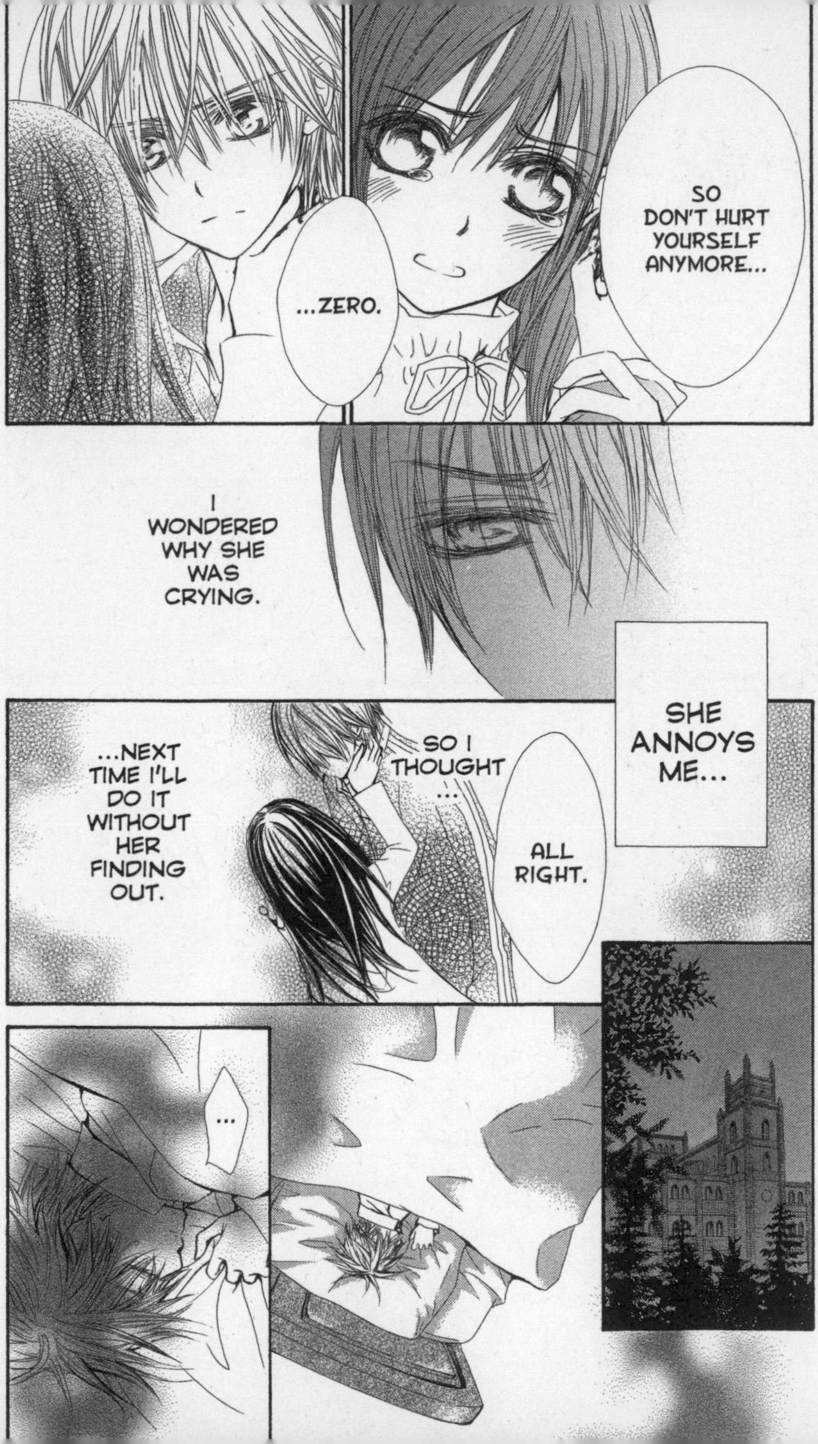
SO DON'T HURT YOURSELF ANYMORE...
...ZERO.
I WONDERED WHY SHE WAS CRYING.
SHE ANNOYS ME...
ALL RIGHT.
SO I THOUGHT ...
...NEXT TIME I'LL DO IT WITHOUT HER FINDING OUT.
...

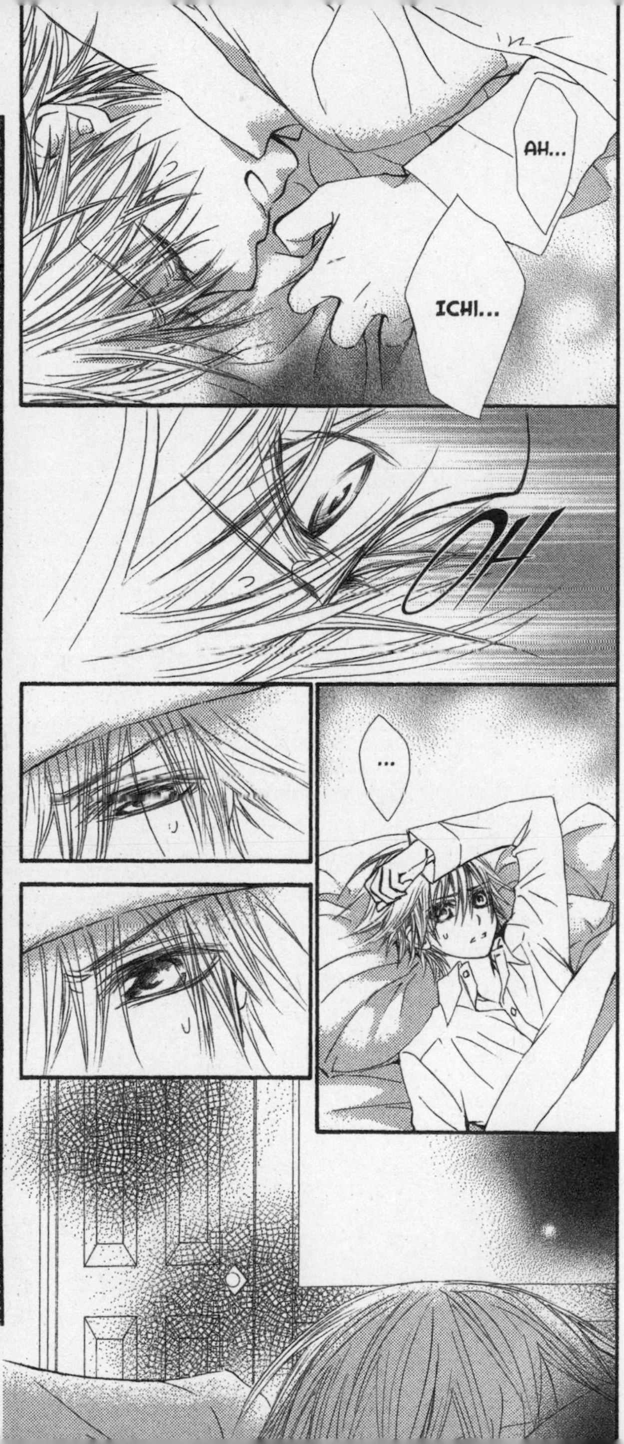
AH...
ICHI...
OH
...

Hello! Hino here!

Thanks to everyone, volume 10 is out. Thank you so much..

Because I spent more time than the previous volume for corrections and such, there's only one sidebar. I'm very sorry, and I'm really embarrassed. Regret...

In the next volume, I hope to write about Germany, where I was invited for an autograph session. I would like to write about how I was impressed that Kanon Wakeshima-san's song went well with the European atmosphere... and about German food, and about the people I met, etc.

Well, I hope to see you in the next volume as well!!

樋野まつり。
Matsuri Hino

Thank you for helping me in many ways! Mio-sama, Midori-sama, Asami-sama, my mother! And everyone involved...I'm sorry I keep inconveniencing you.

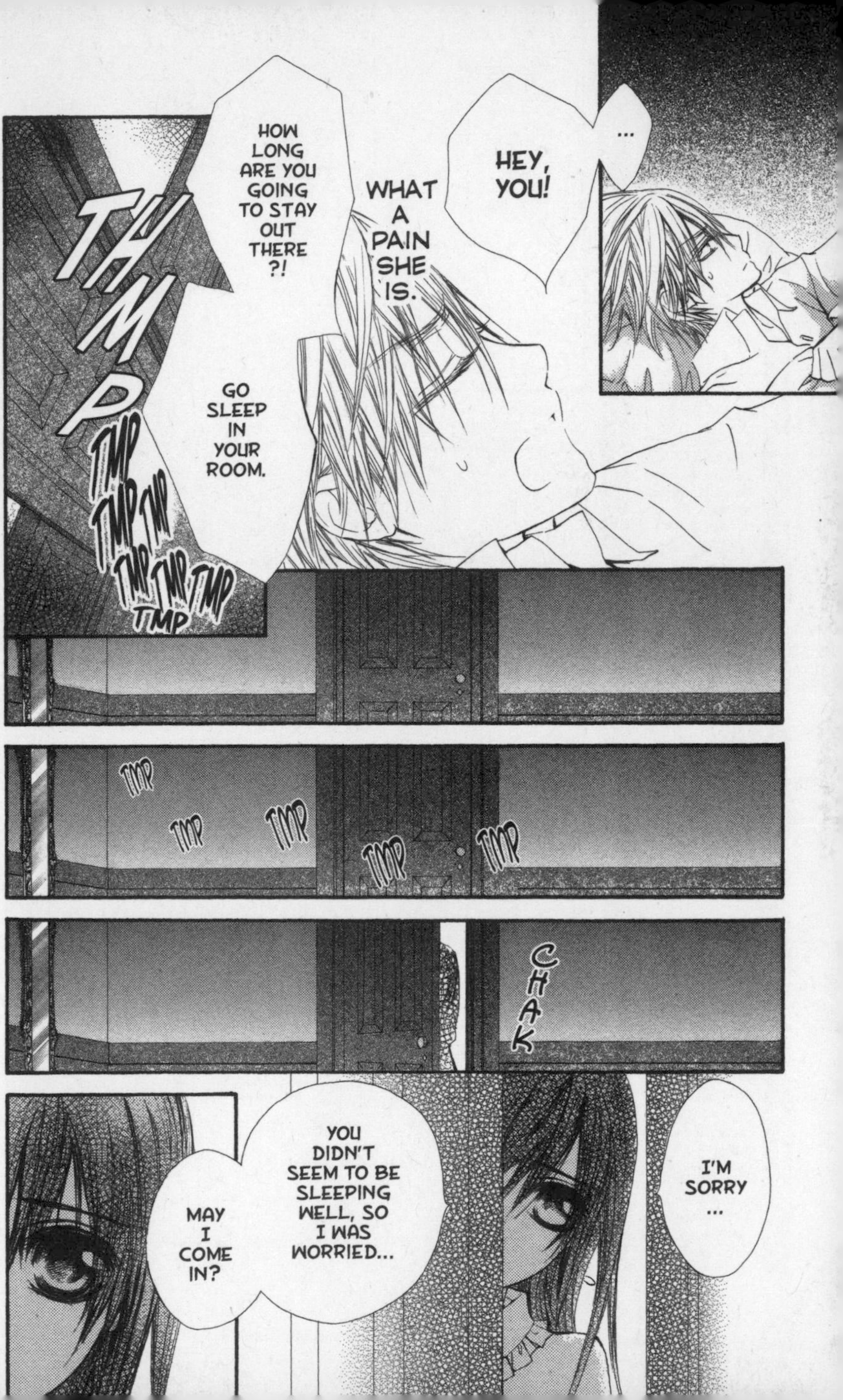
...
HEY, YOU!
WHAT A PAIN SHE IS.
HOW LONG ARE YOU GOING TO STAY OUT THERE?!
GO SLEEP IN YOUR ROOM.
THMP
TMP TMP TMP TMP TMP TMP TMP
TMP TMP TMP TMP TMP
CHAK
I'M SORRY...
YOU DIDN'T SEEM TO BE SLEEPING WELL, SO I WAS WORRIED...
MAY I COME IN?

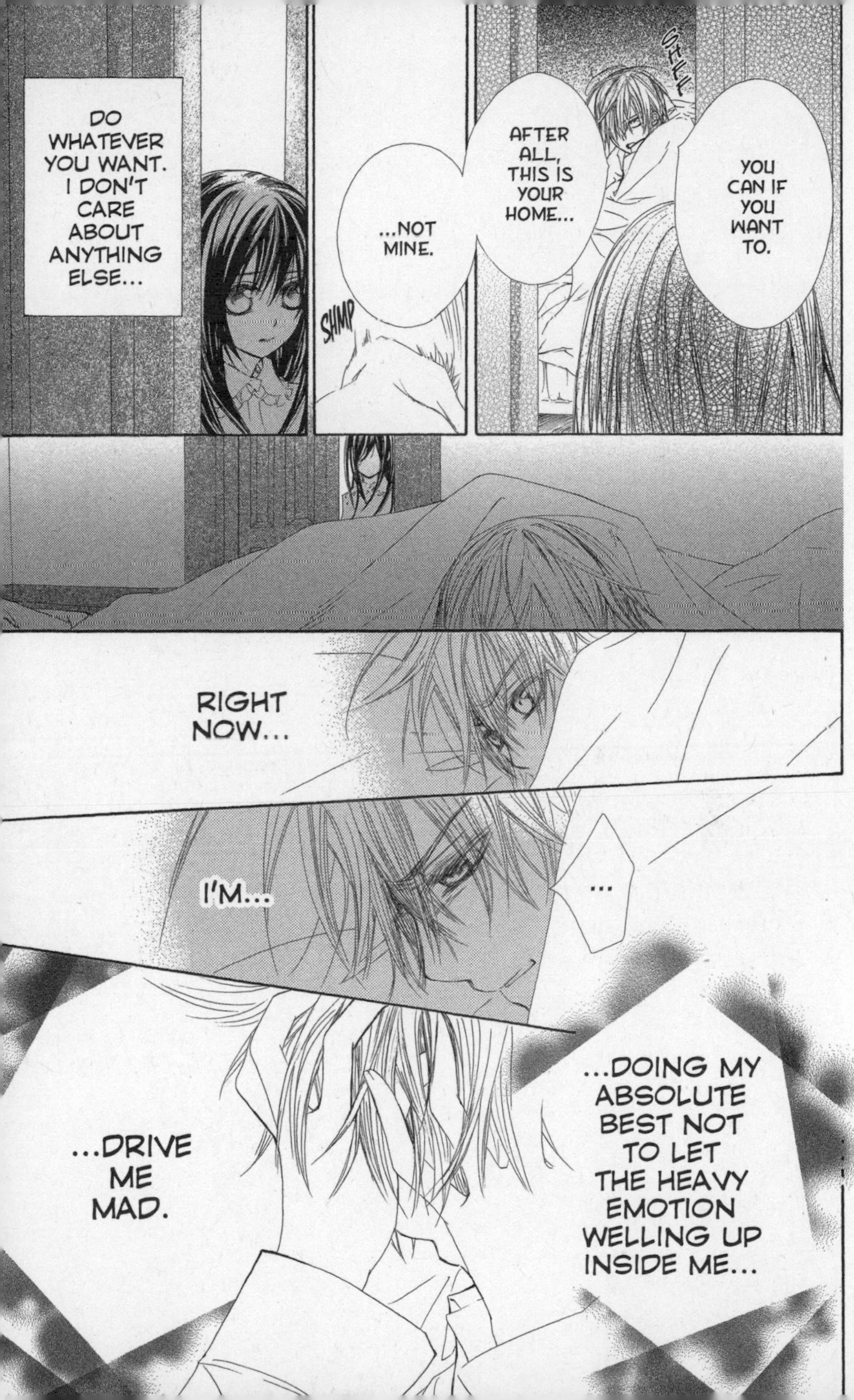
SHFF
YOU CAN IF YOU WANT TO.
AFTER ALL, THIS IS YOUR HOME...
...NOT MINE.
SHMP
DO WHATEVER YOU WANT. I DON'T CARE ABOUT ANYTHING ELSE...
RIGHT NOW...
...
I'M...
...DOING MY ABSOLUTE BEST NOT TO LET THE HEAVY EMOTION WELLING UP INSIDE ME...
...DRIVE ME MAD.

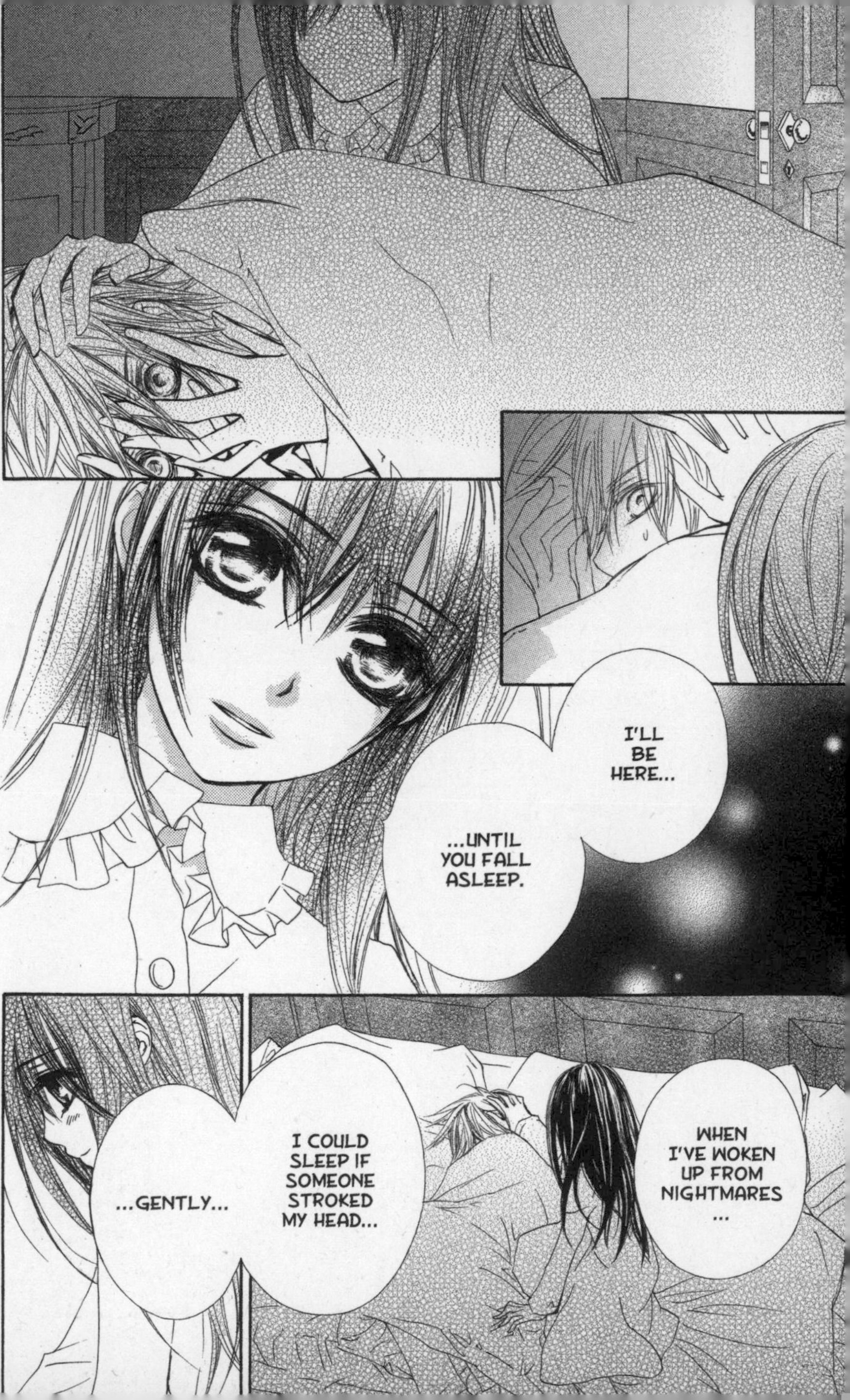
I'LL BE HERE...
...UNTIL YOU FALL ASLEEP.
WHEN I'VE WOKEN UP FROM NIGHTMARES ...
I COULD SLEEP IF SOMEONE STROKED MY HEAD...
...GENTLY...

SUFF

YOU'LL
BE ALL
RIGHT
...

SUFF

I
CLUNG...

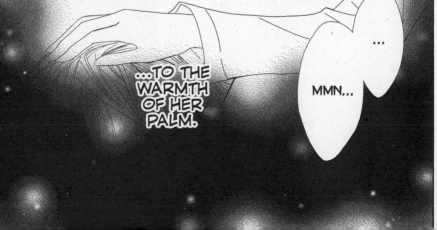

...TO THE
WARMTH
OF HER
PALM.

...

MMN...

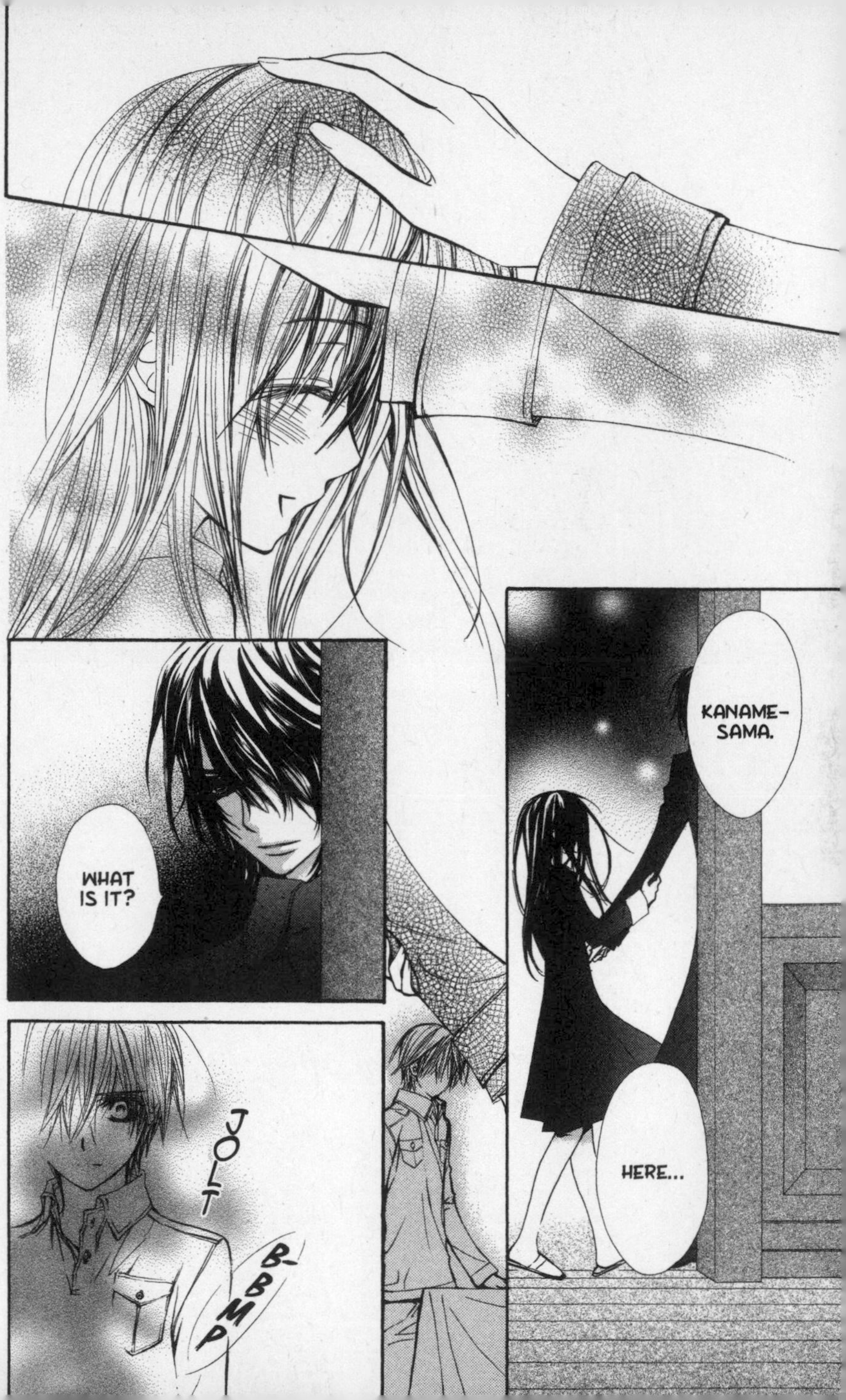
KANAME-SAMA.
HERE...
WHAT IS IT?
JOLT
B-BBMP

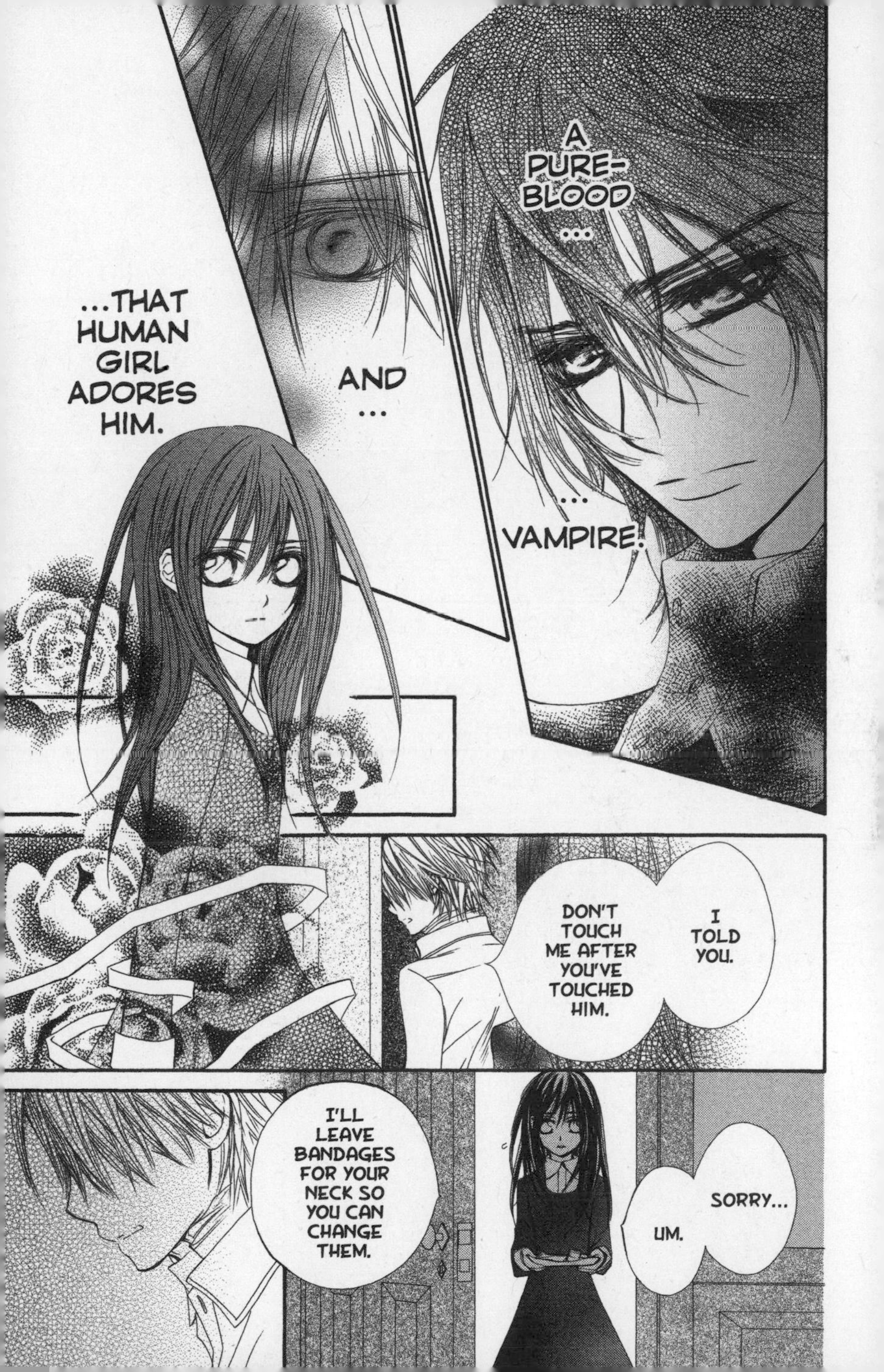
A PURE-BLOOD ...
... VAMPIRE.
AND ...
...THAT HUMAN GIRL ADORES HIM.
I TOLD YOU.
DON'T TOUCH ME AFTER YOU'VE TOUCHED HIM.
SORRY...
UM.
I'LL LEAVE BANDAGES FOR YOUR NECK SO YOU CAN CHANGE THEM.

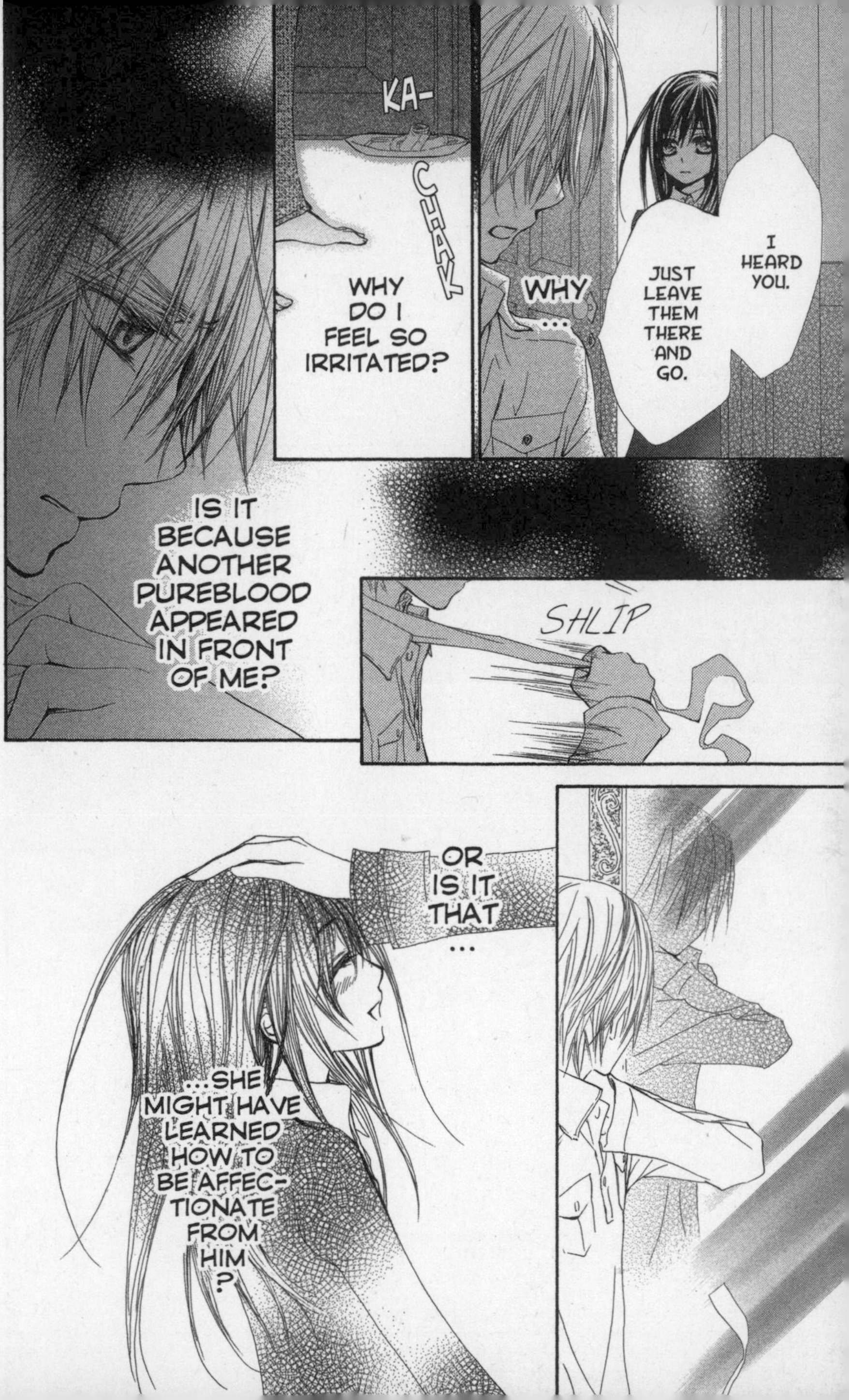
I HEARD YOU.
JUST LEAVE THEM THERE AND GO.
WHY ...
KA-CHAK
WHY DO I FEEL SO IRRITATED?
SHLIP
IS IT BECAUSE ANOTHER PUREBLOOD APPEARED IN FRONT OF ME?
OR IS IT THAT ...
...SHE MIGHT HAVE LEARNED HOW TO BE AFFEC-TIONATE FROM HIM?

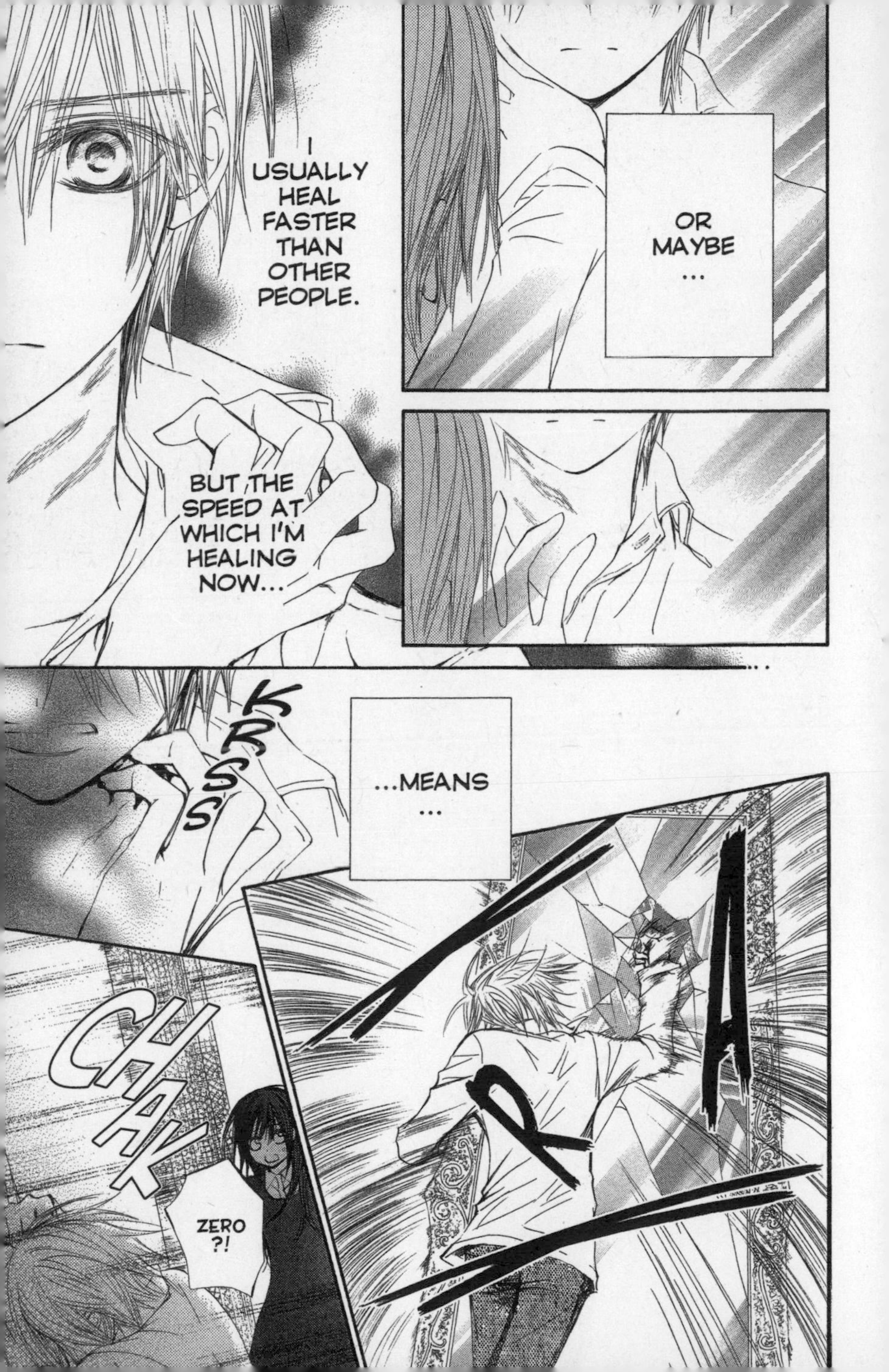

OR MAYBE ...
I USUALLY HEAL FASTER THAN OTHER PEOPLE.
BUT THE SPEED AT WHICH I'M HEALING NOW...
...MEANS ...
KRSSS
CHAK
ZERO ?!

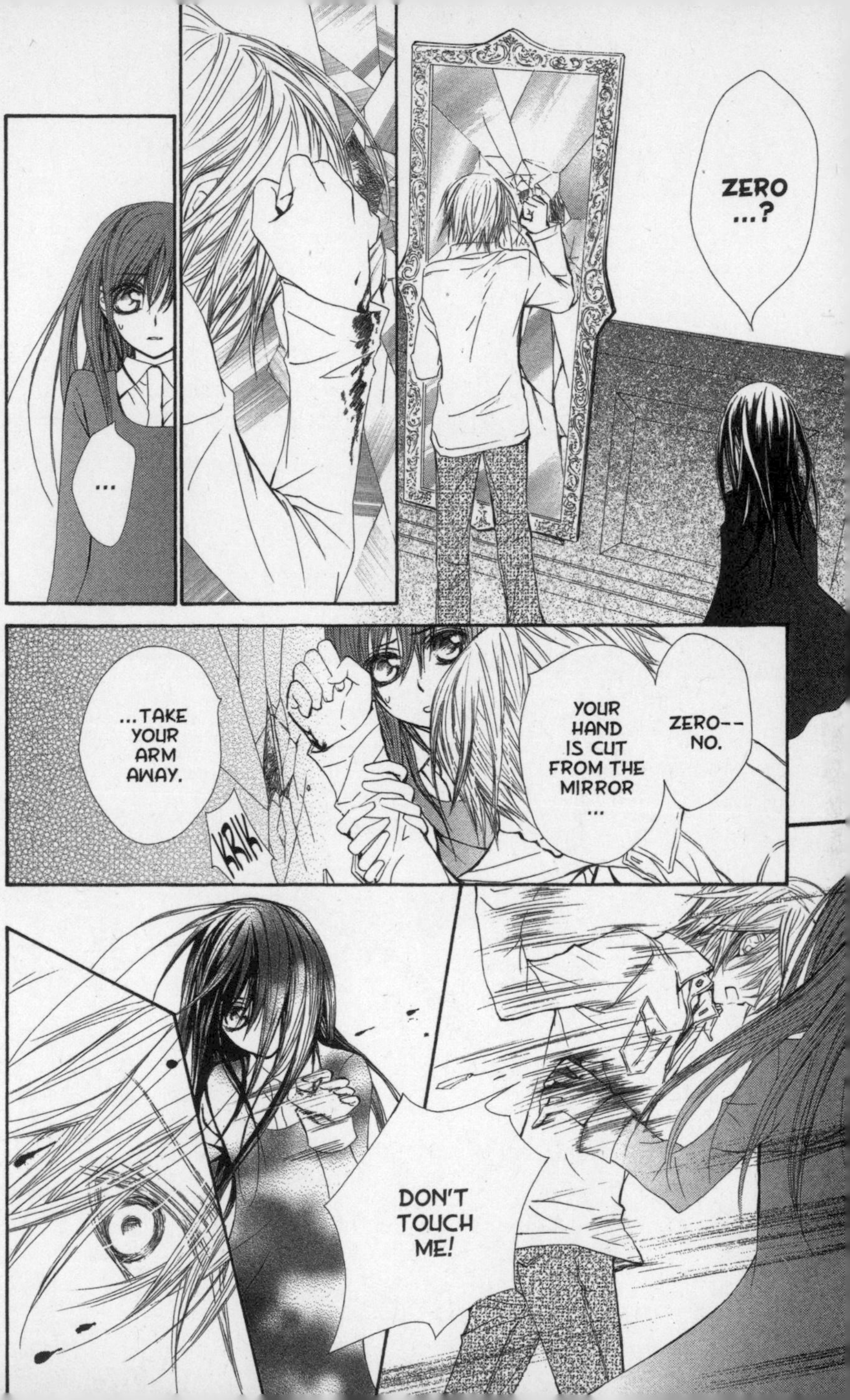
ZERO ...?
...
ZERO-- NO.
YOUR HAND IS CUT FROM THE MIRROR ...
KRIK
...TAKE YOUR ARM AWAY.
DON'T TOUCH ME!

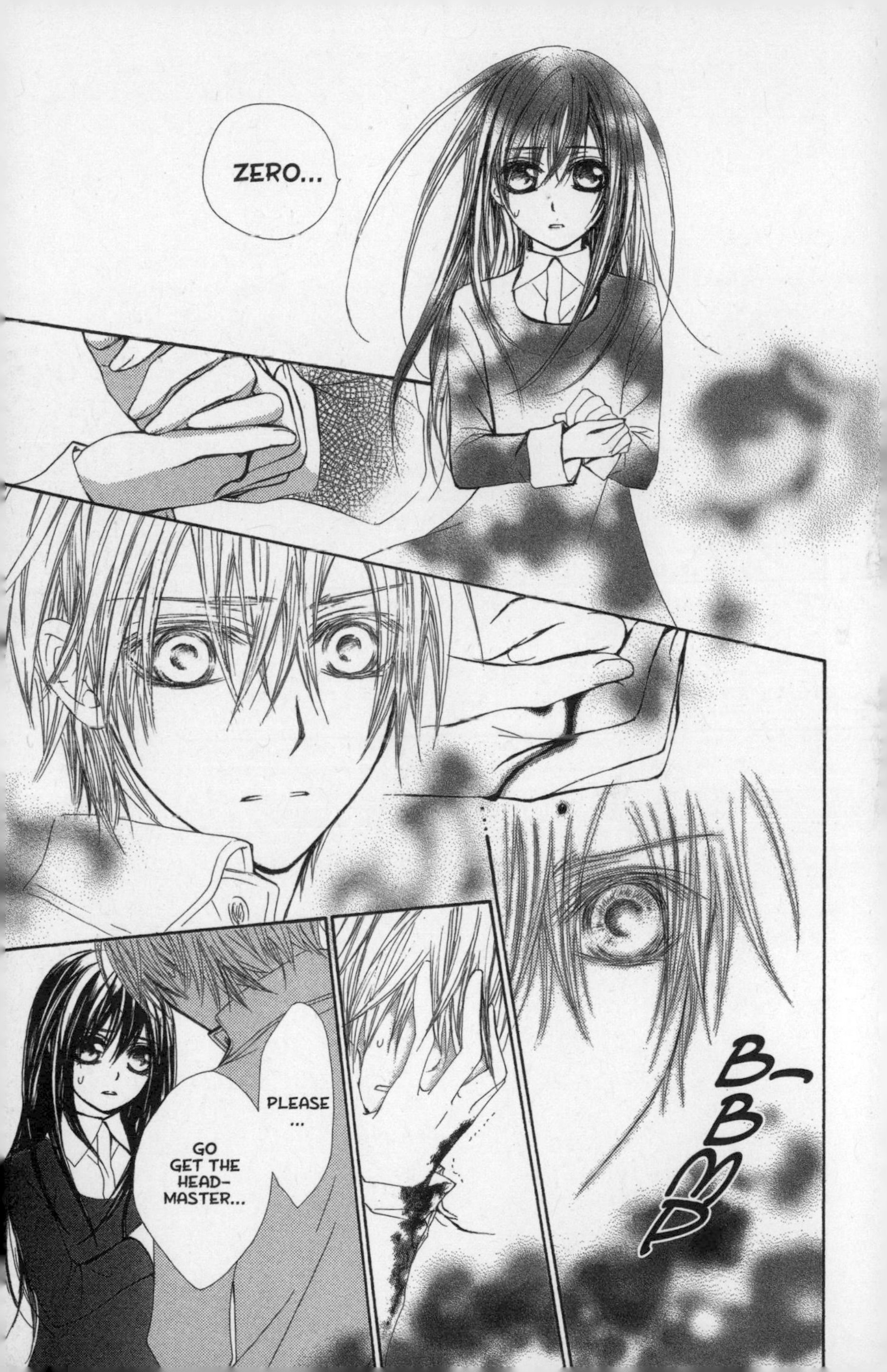
ZERO...
B-B-BMP
PLEASE ...
GO GET THE HEAD-MASTER...

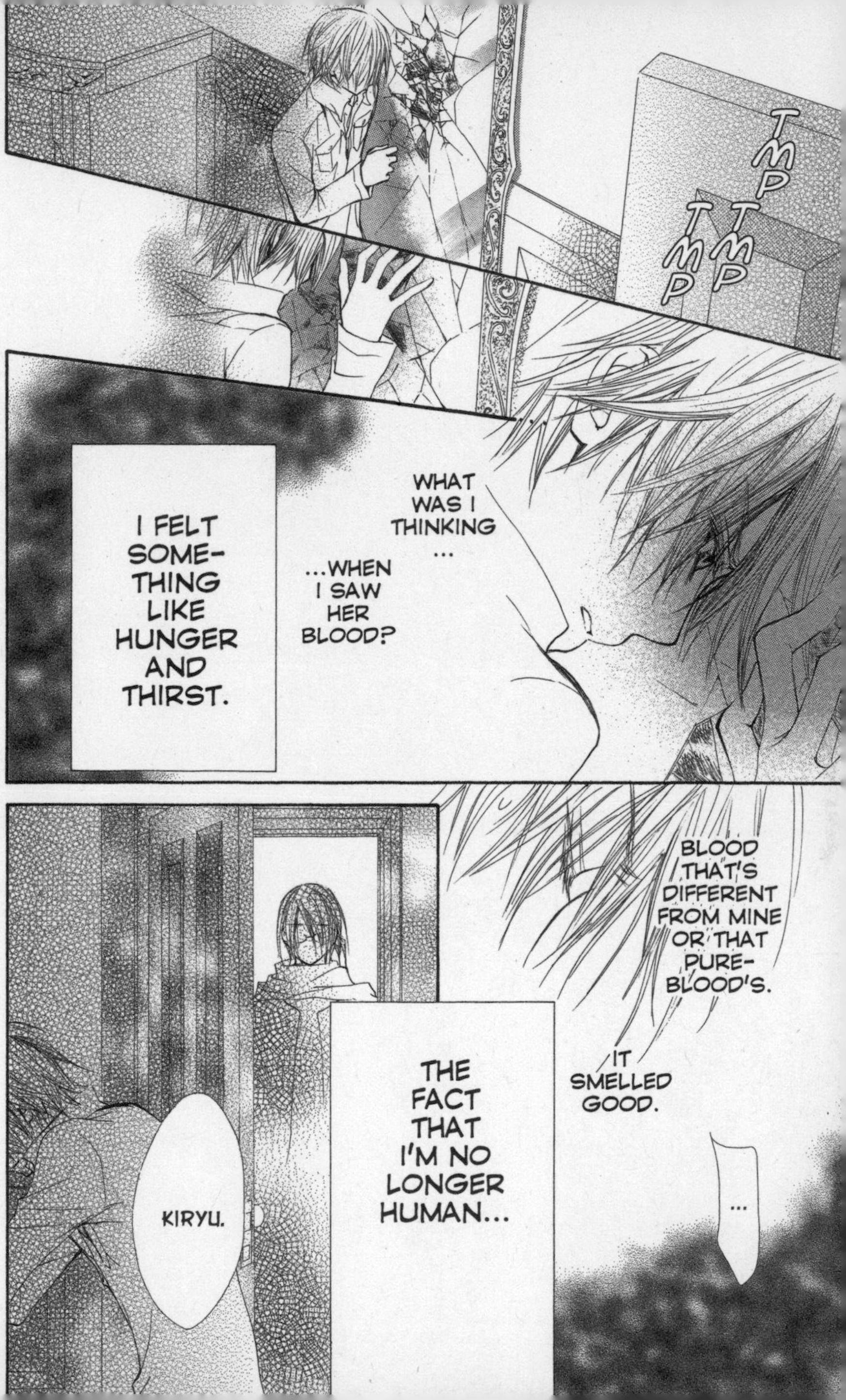
TMP TMP TMP
TMP
WHAT WAS I THINKING...
...WHEN I SAW HER BLOOD?
I FELT SOME-THING LIKE HUNGER AND THIRST.
BLOOD THAT'S DIFFERENT FROM MINE OR THAT PURE-BLOOD'S.
IT SMELLED GOOD.
...
THE FACT THAT I'M NO LONGER HUMAN...
KIRYU.

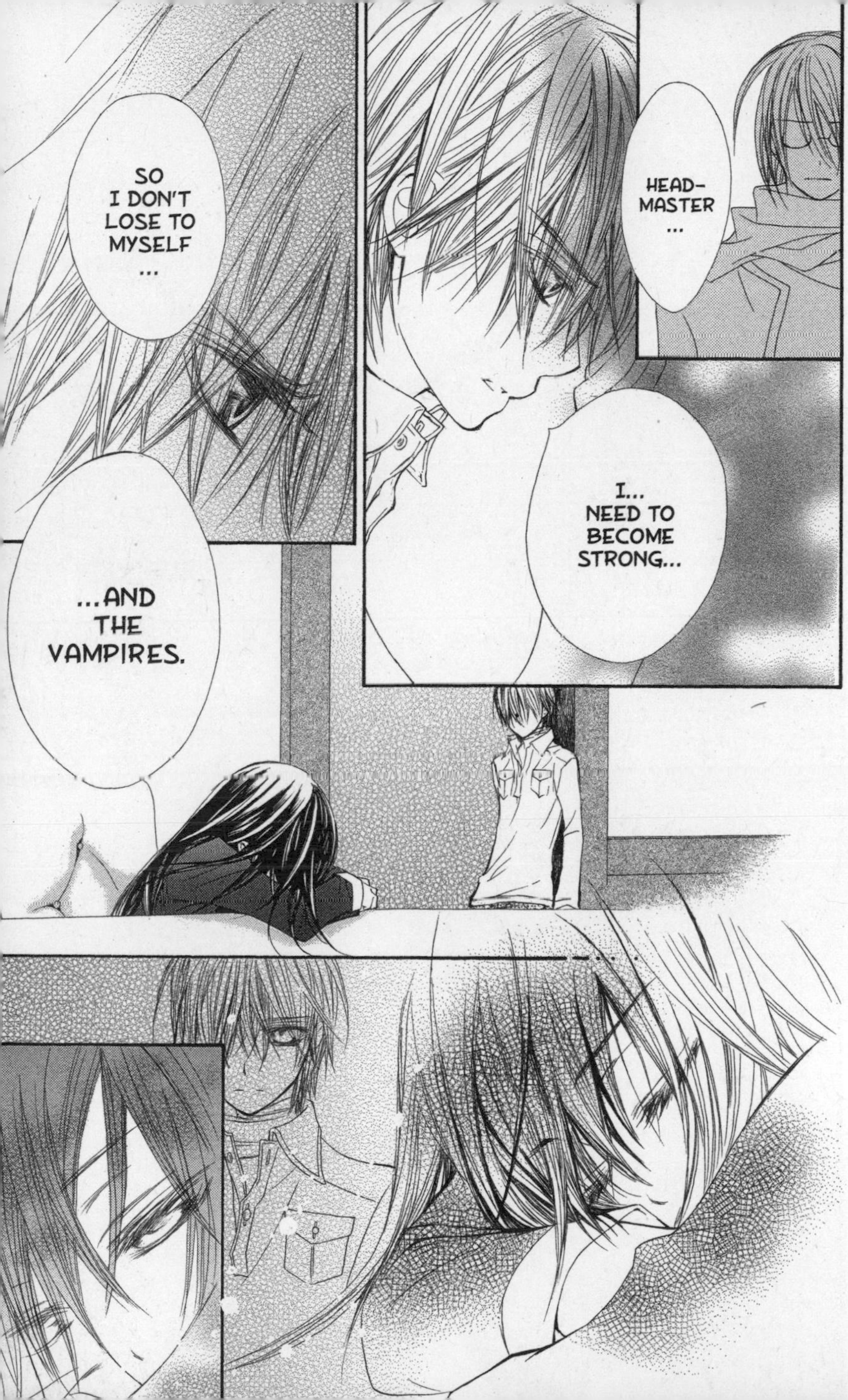
HEAD-MASTER ...
I... NEED TO BECOME STRONG...
SO I DON'T LOSE TO MYSELF ...
...AND THE VAMPIRES.

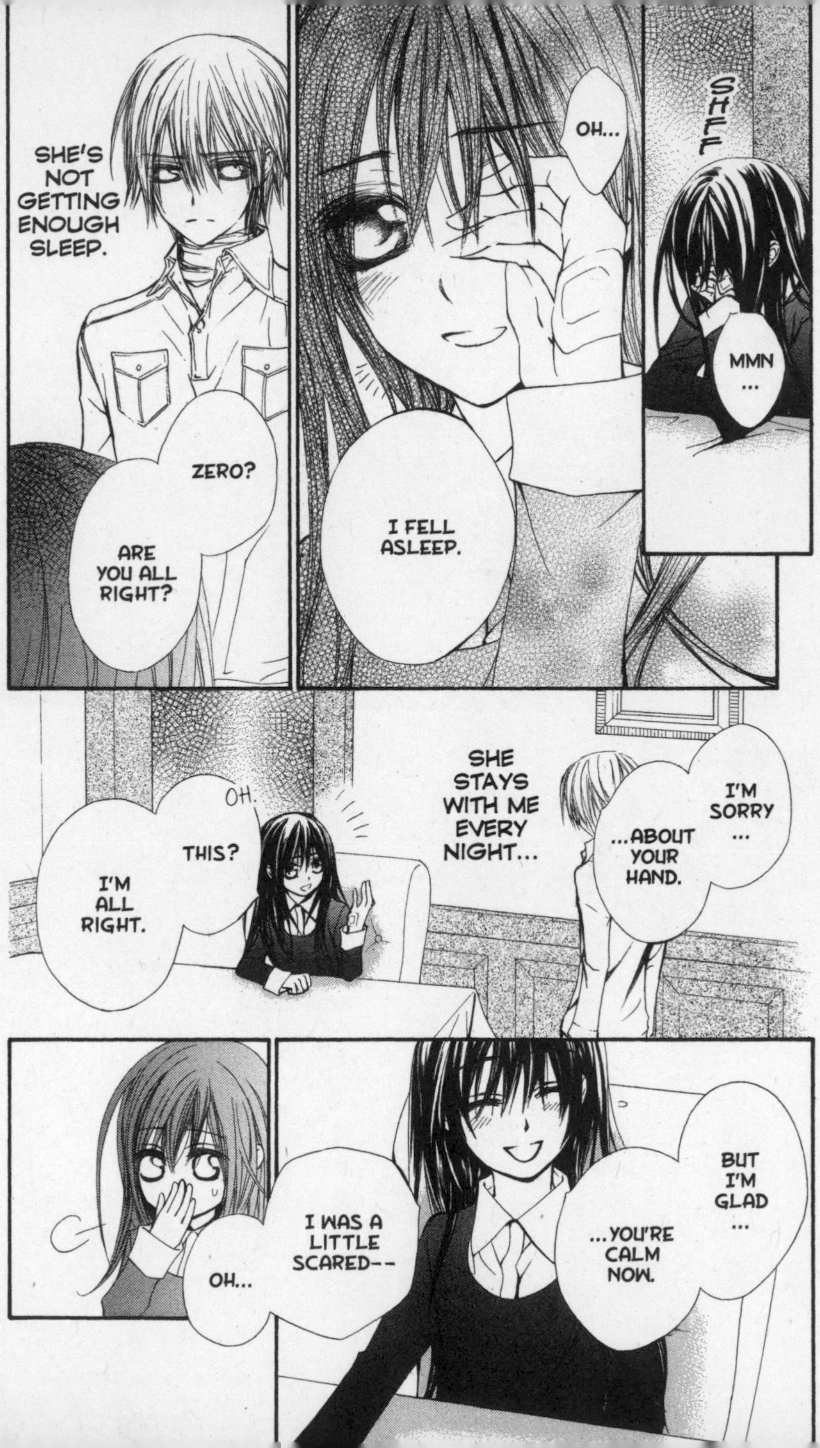
SHFF
MMN...
OH...
I FELL ASLEEP.
SHE'S NOT GETTING ENOUGH SLEEP.
ZERO? ARE YOU ALL RIGHT?
I'M SORRY... ...ABOUT YOUR HAND.
SHE STAYS WITH ME EVERY NIGHT...
OH. THIS? I'M ALL RIGHT.
BUT I'M GLAD... ...YOU'RE CALM NOW.
I WAS A LITTLE SCARED--
OH...

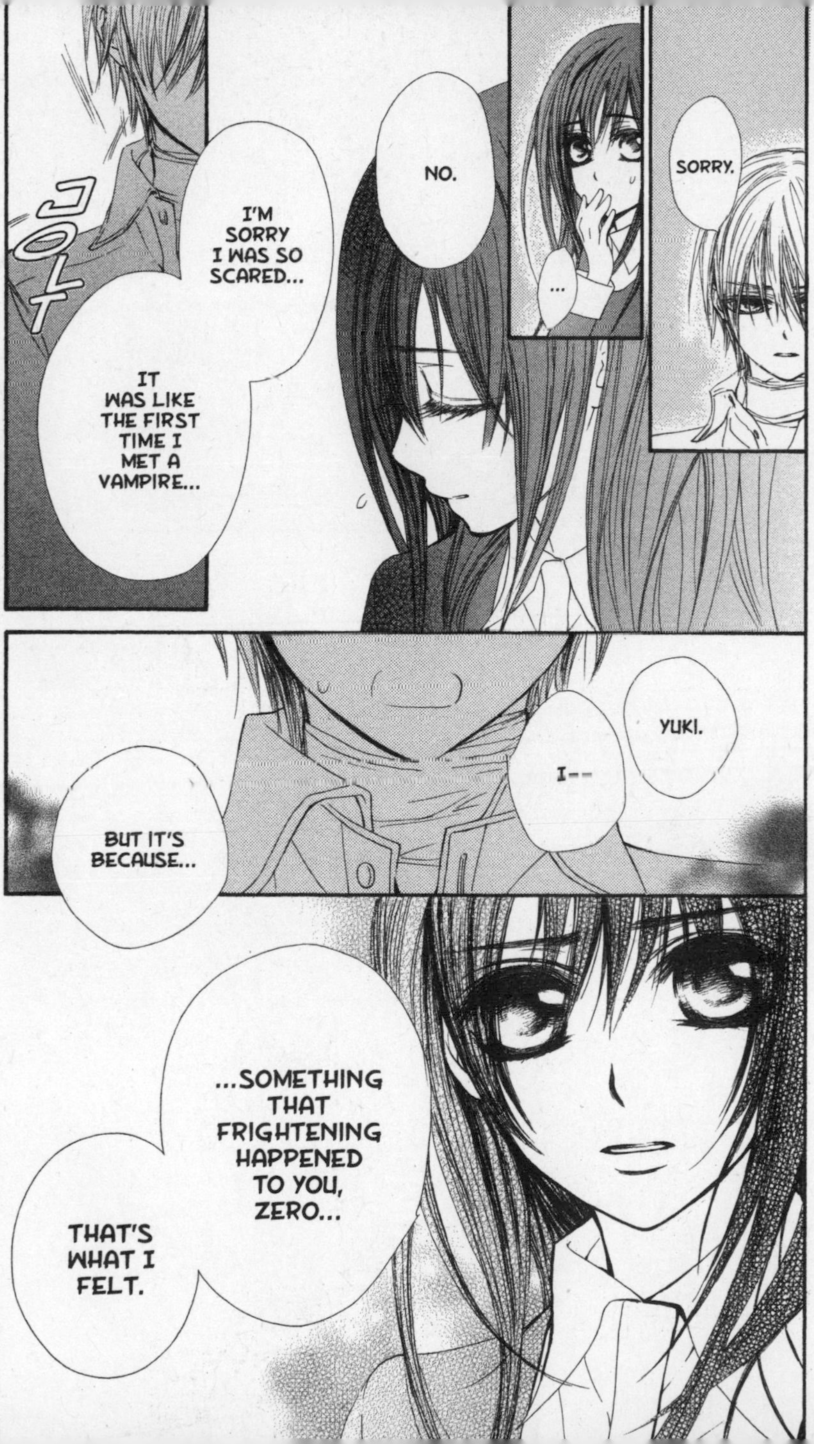
SORRY.
...
NO.
I'M SORRY I WAS SO SCARED...
IT WAS LIKE THE FIRST TIME I MET A VAMPIRE...
JOLT
YUKI.
I--
BUT IT'S BECAUSE...
...SOMETHING THAT FRIGHTENING HAPPENED TO YOU, ZERO...
THAT'S WHAT I FELT.

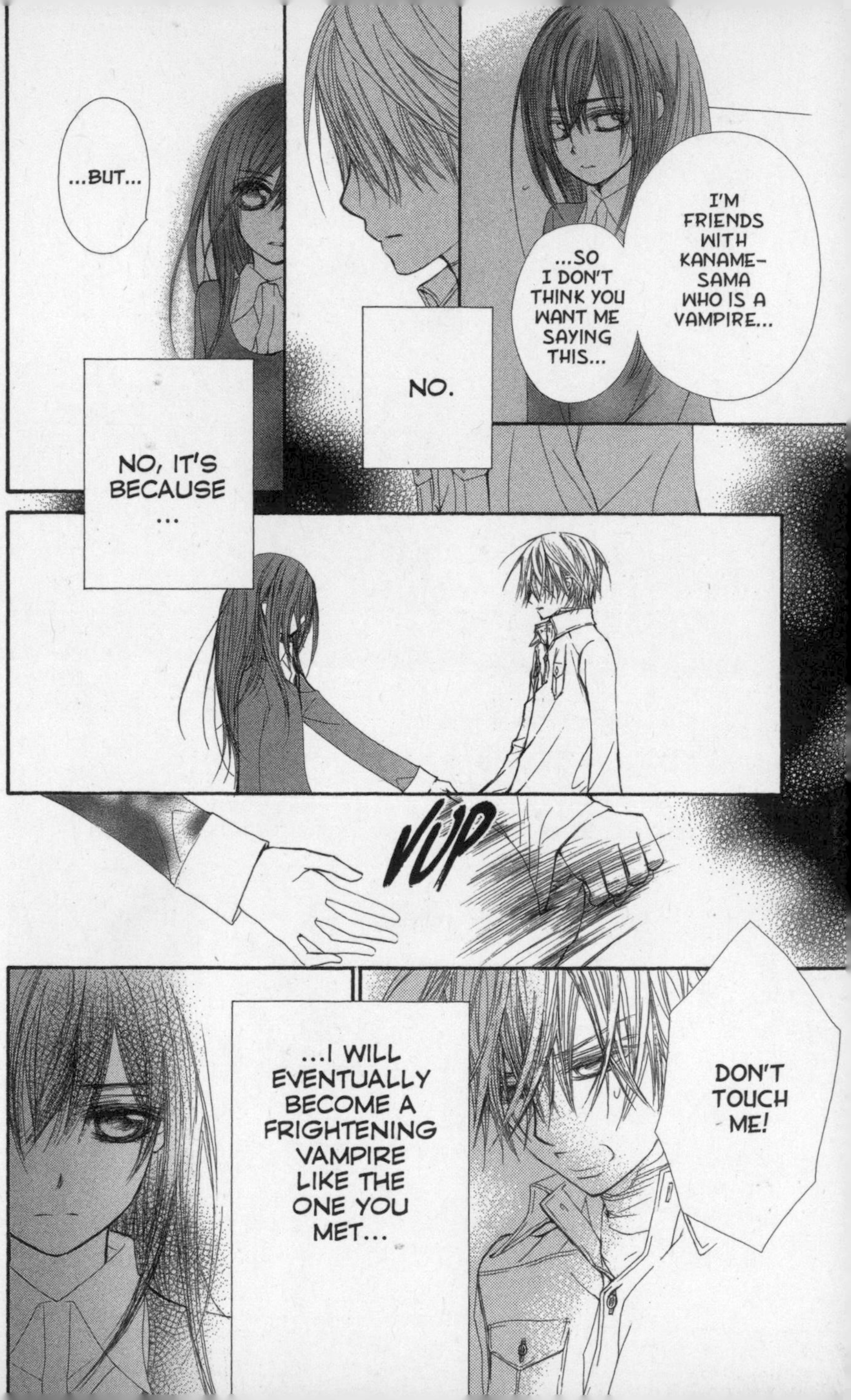
I'M FRIENDS WITH KANAME-SAMA WHO IS A VAMPIRE...
...SO I DON'T THINK YOU WANT ME SAYING THIS...
NO.
...BUT...
NO, IT'S BECAUSE ...
VOP
DON'T TOUCH ME!
...I WILL EVENTUALLY BECOME A FRIGHTENING VAMPIRE LIKE THE ONE YOU MET...

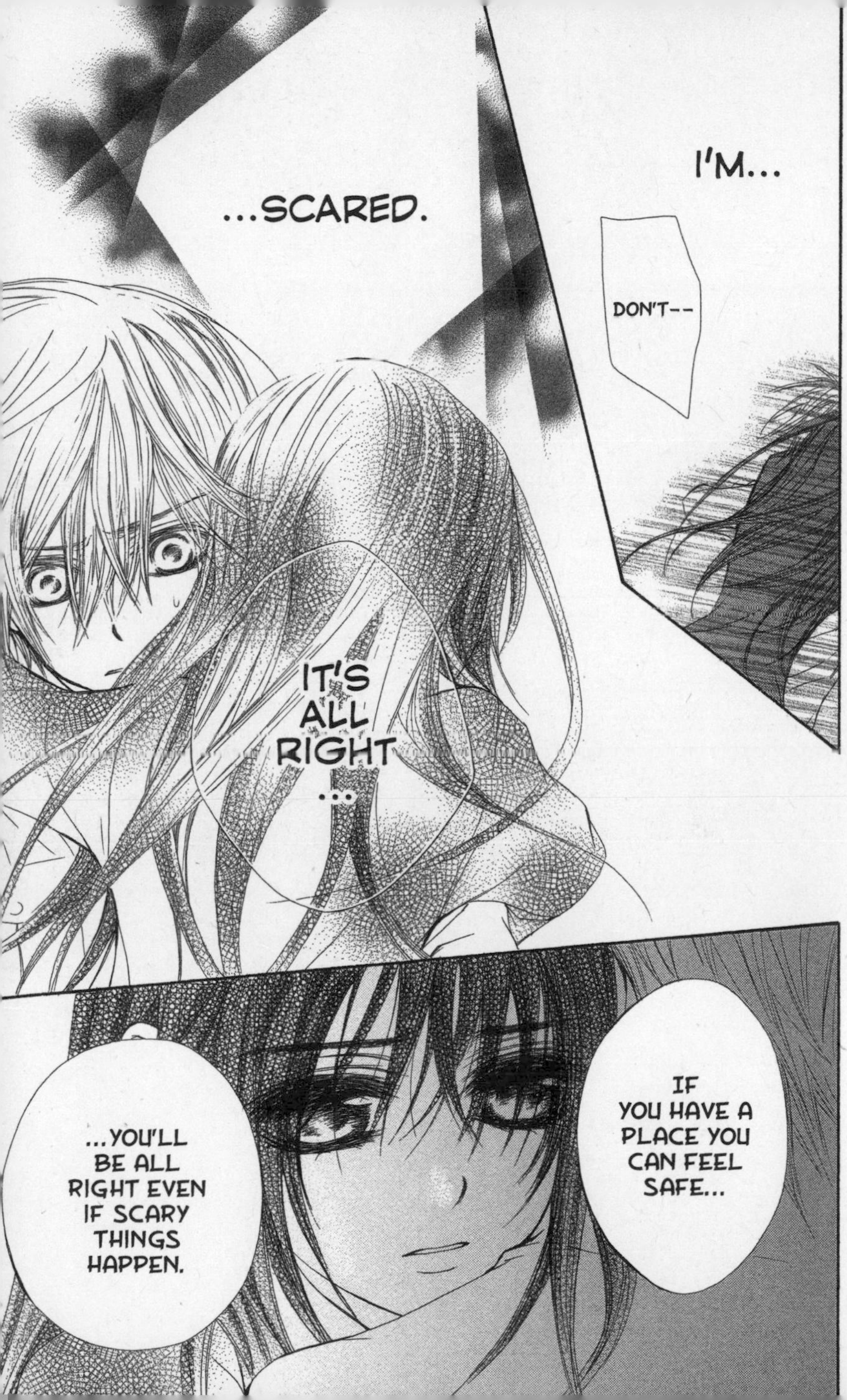

I'M...
DON'T--
...SCARED.
IT'S ALL RIGHT...
IF YOU HAVE A PLACE YOU CAN FEEL SAFE...
...YOU'LL BE ALL RIGHT EVEN IF SCARY THINGS HAPPEN.

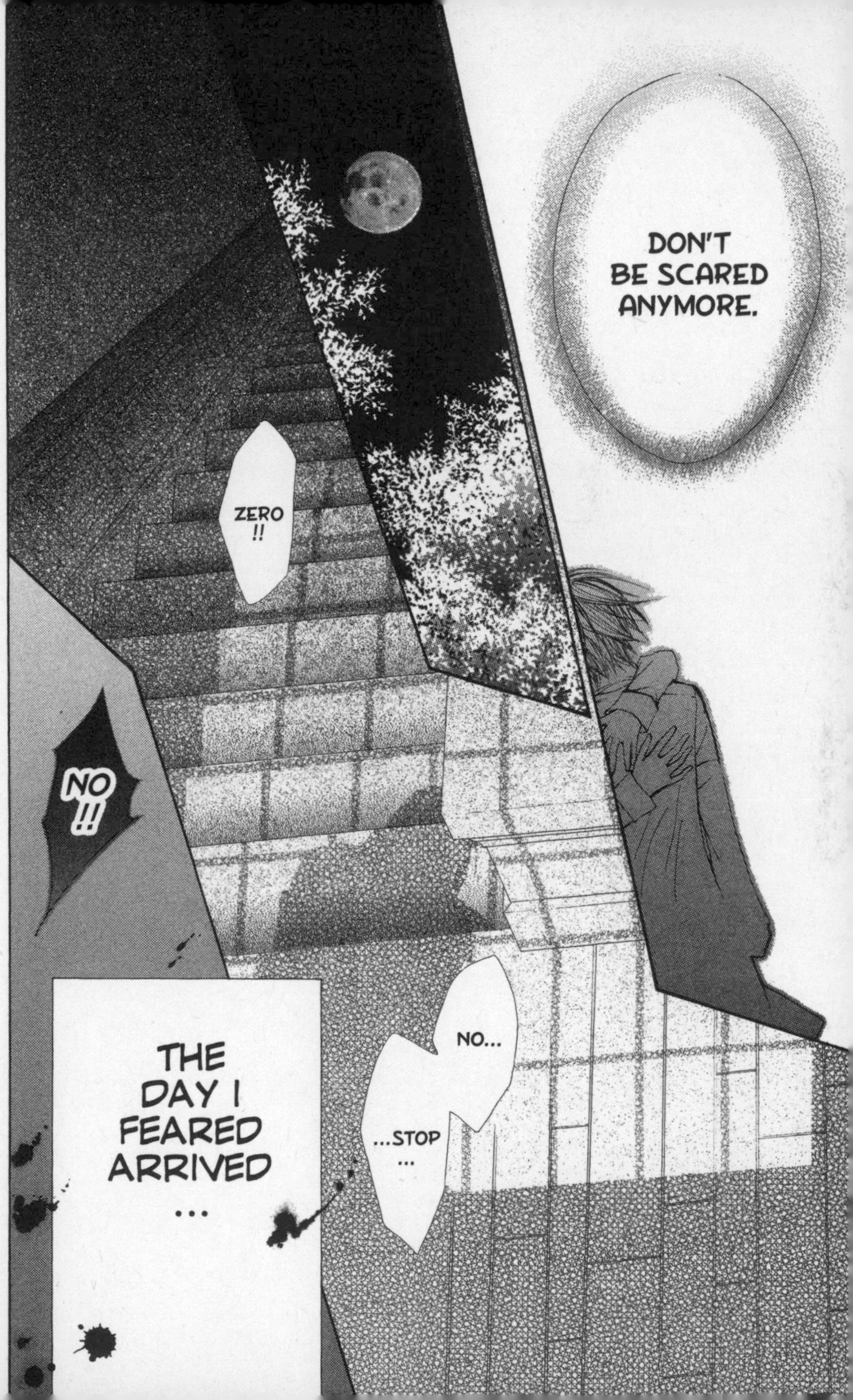
DON'T BE SCARED ANYMORE.
ZERO !!
NO !!
NO...
...STOP ...
THE DAY I FEARED ARRIVED ...

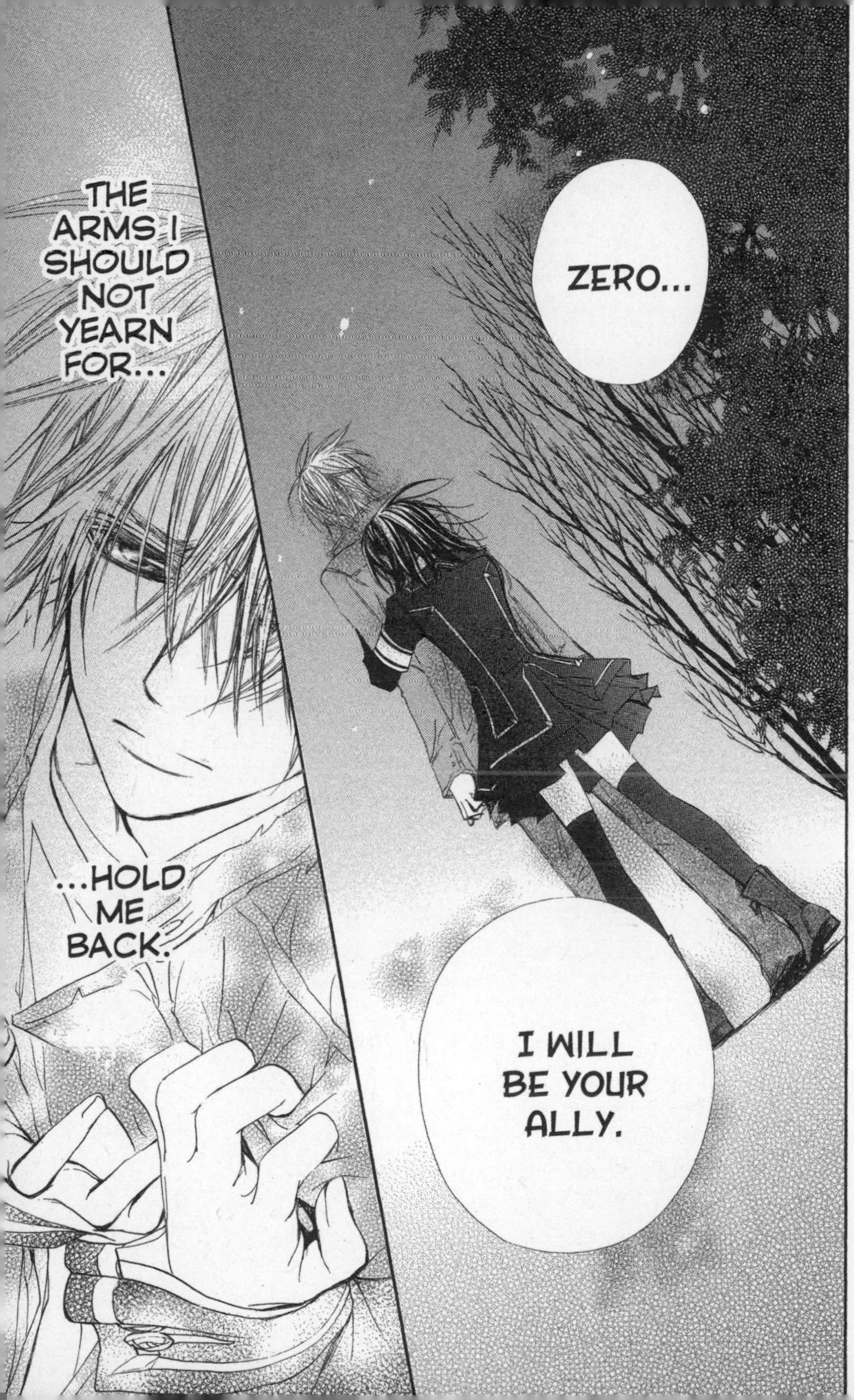
ZERO...
I WILL BE YOUR ALLY.
THE ARMS I SHOULD NOT YEARN FOR...
...HOLD ME BACK.

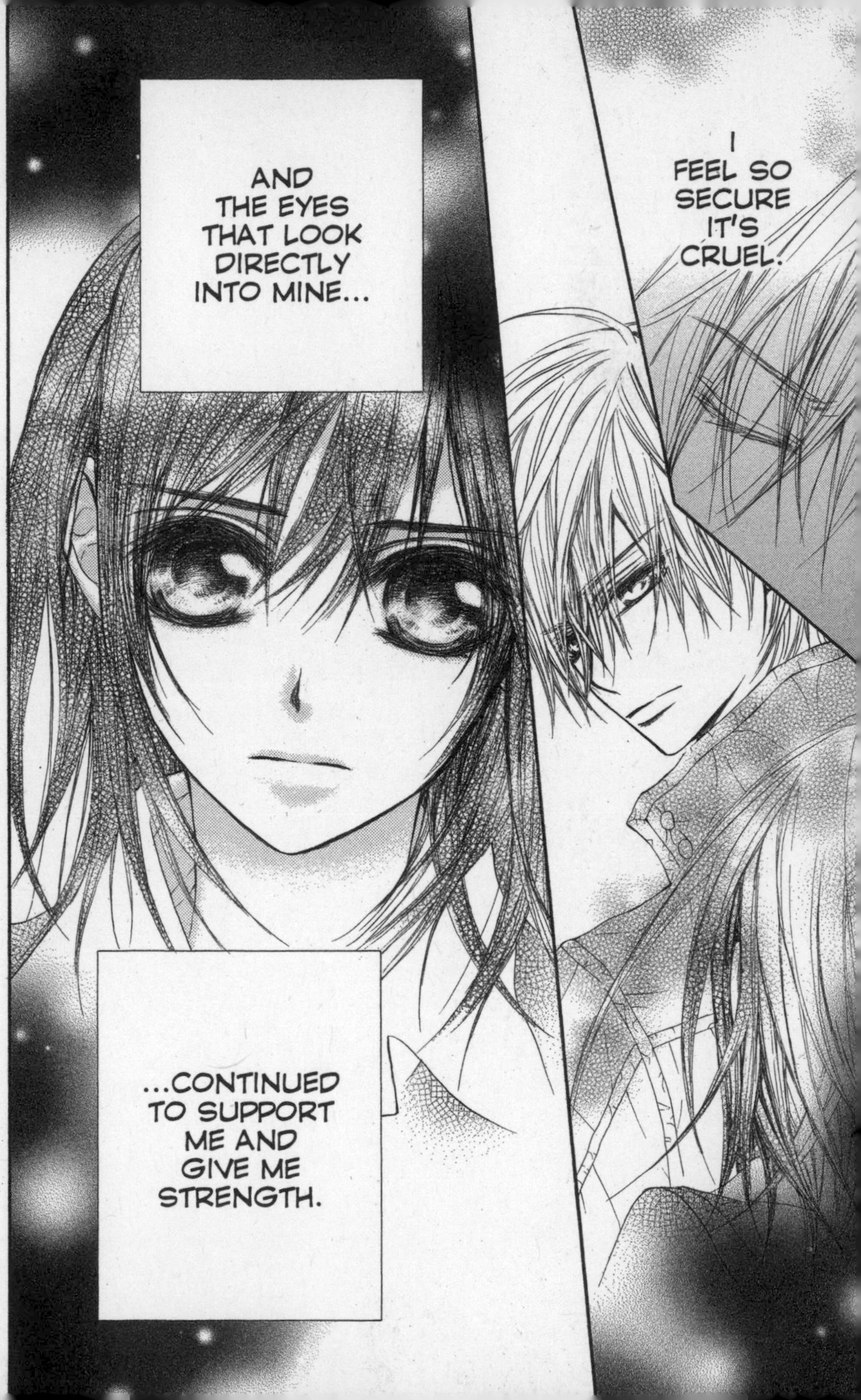
I FEEL SO SECURE IT'S CRUEL.
AND THE EYES THAT LOOK DIRECTLY INTO MINE...
...CONTINUED TO SUPPORT ME AND GIVE ME STRENGTH.

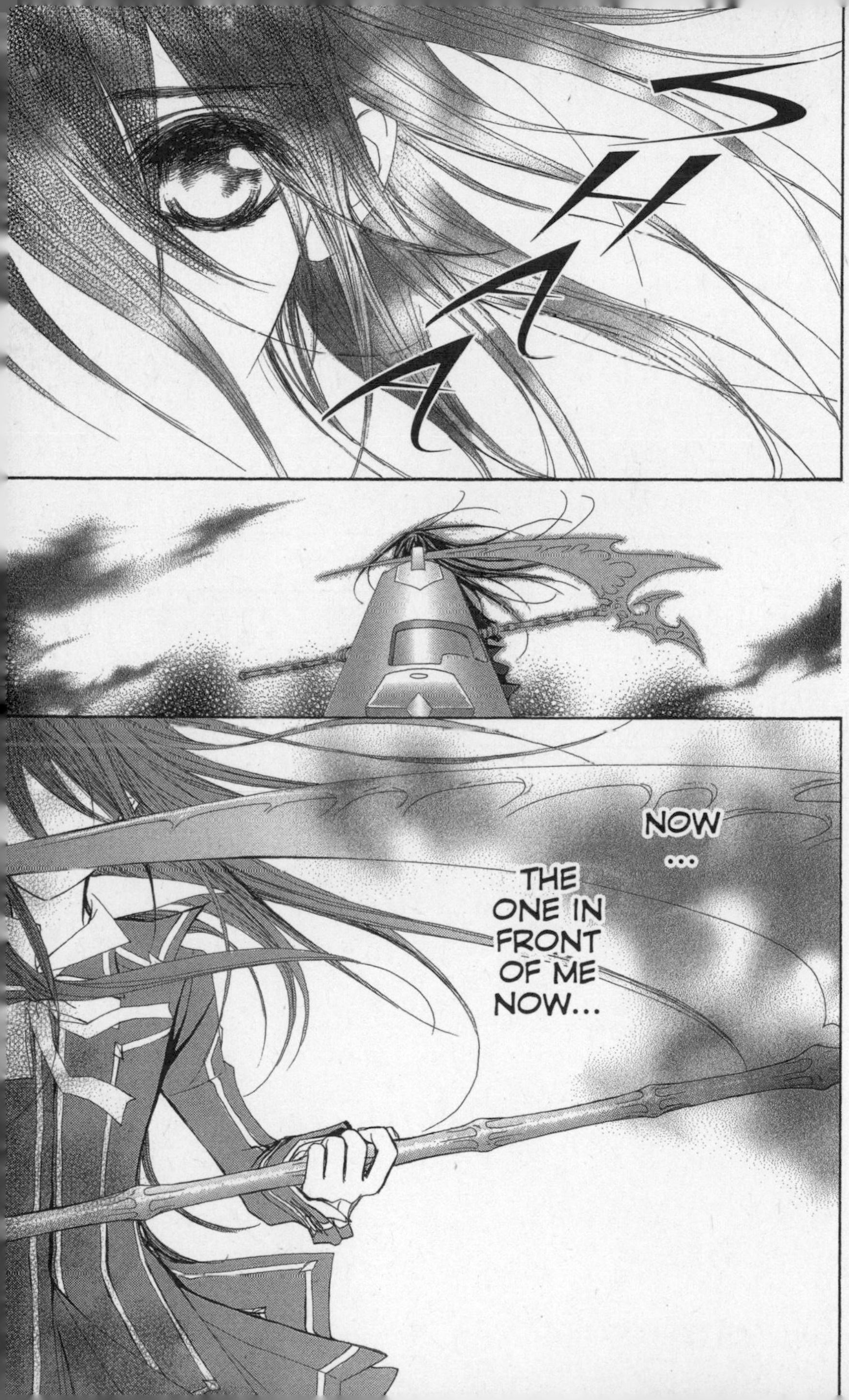
SHAA
NOW ...
THE ONE IN FRONT OF ME NOW...

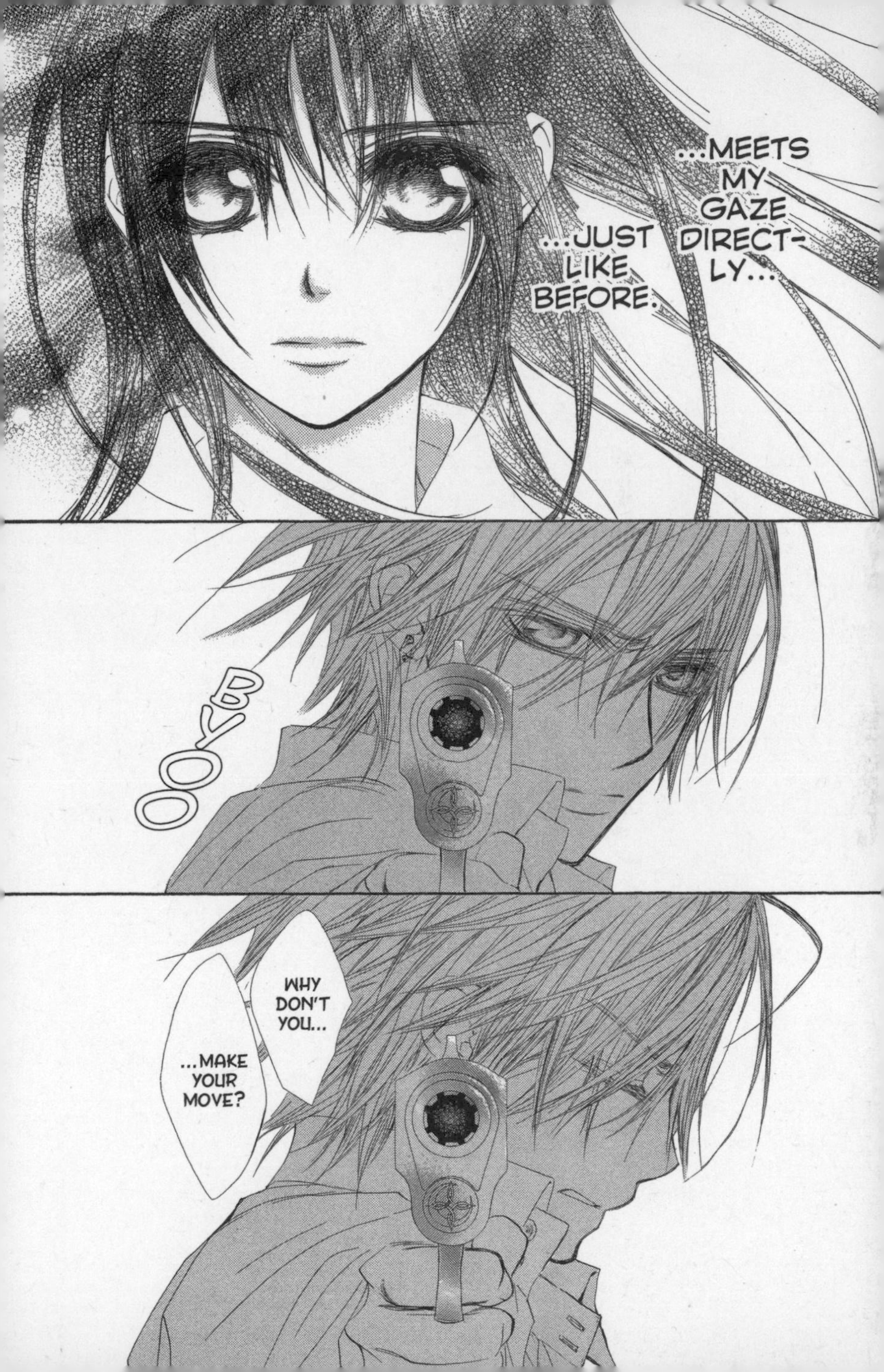
...MEETS MY GAZE DIRECT-LY...
...JUST LIKE BEFORE.
BYOO
WHY DON'T YOU...
...MAKE YOUR MOVE?

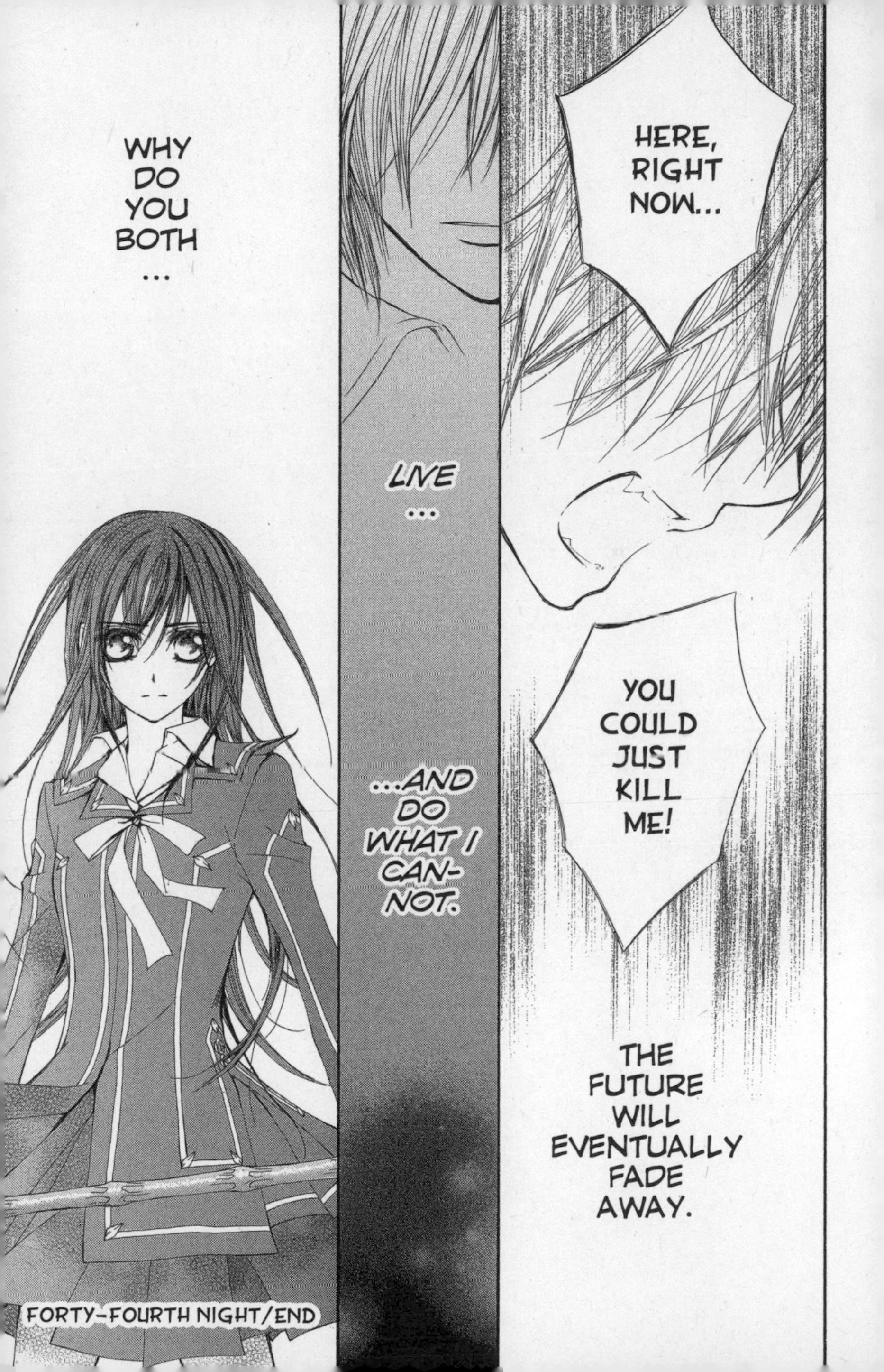
HERE, RIGHT NOW...
YOU COULD JUST KILL ME!
THE FUTURE WILL EVENTUALLY FADE AWAY.
LIVE ...
...AND DO WHAT I CAN-NOT.
WHY DO YOU BOTH ...
FORTY-FOURTH NIGHT/END

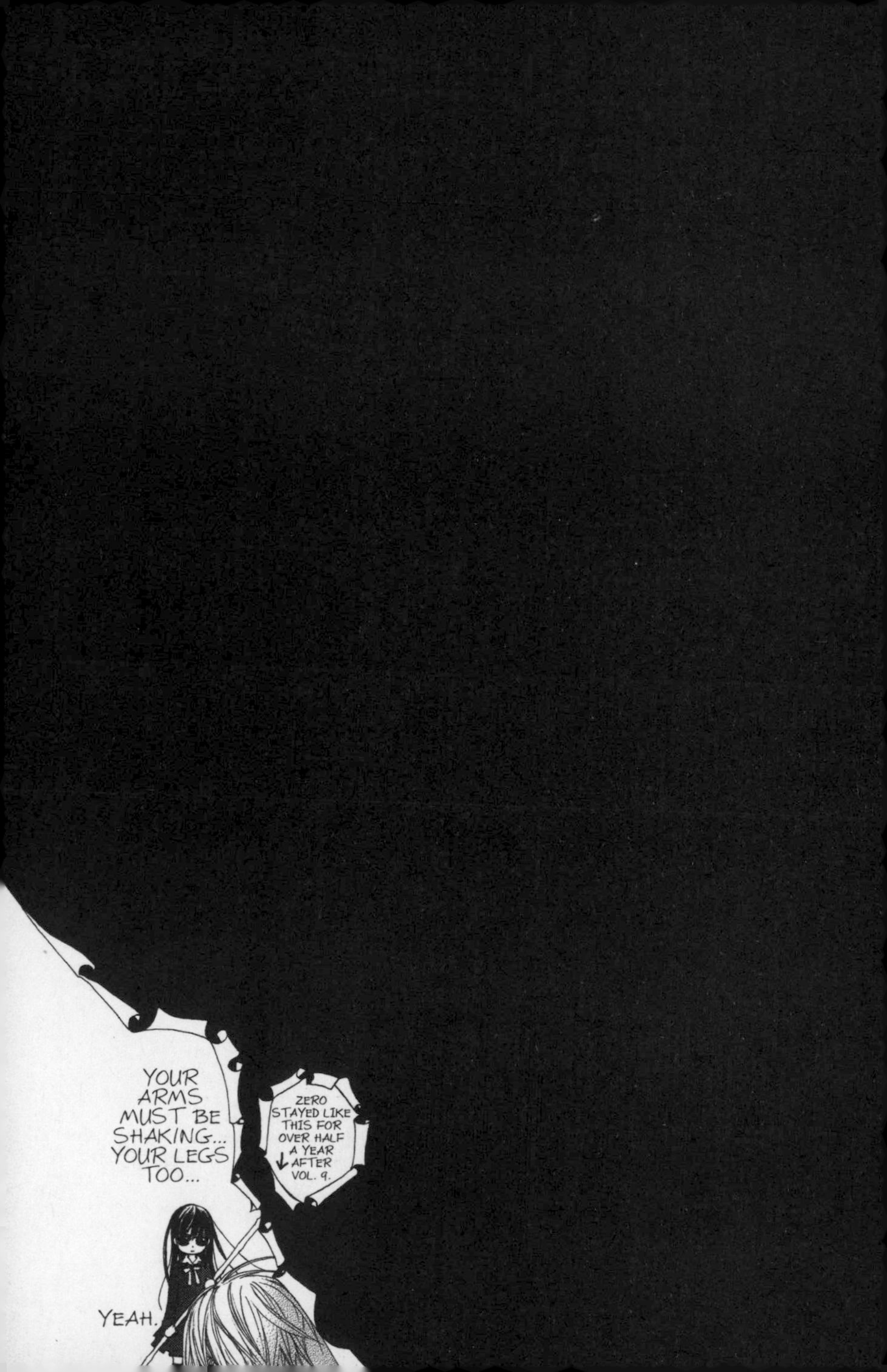
ZERO STAYED LIKE THIS FOR OVER HALF A YEAR AFTER VOL. 9.
YOUR ARMS MUST BE SHAKING... YOUR LEGS TOO...
YEAH.

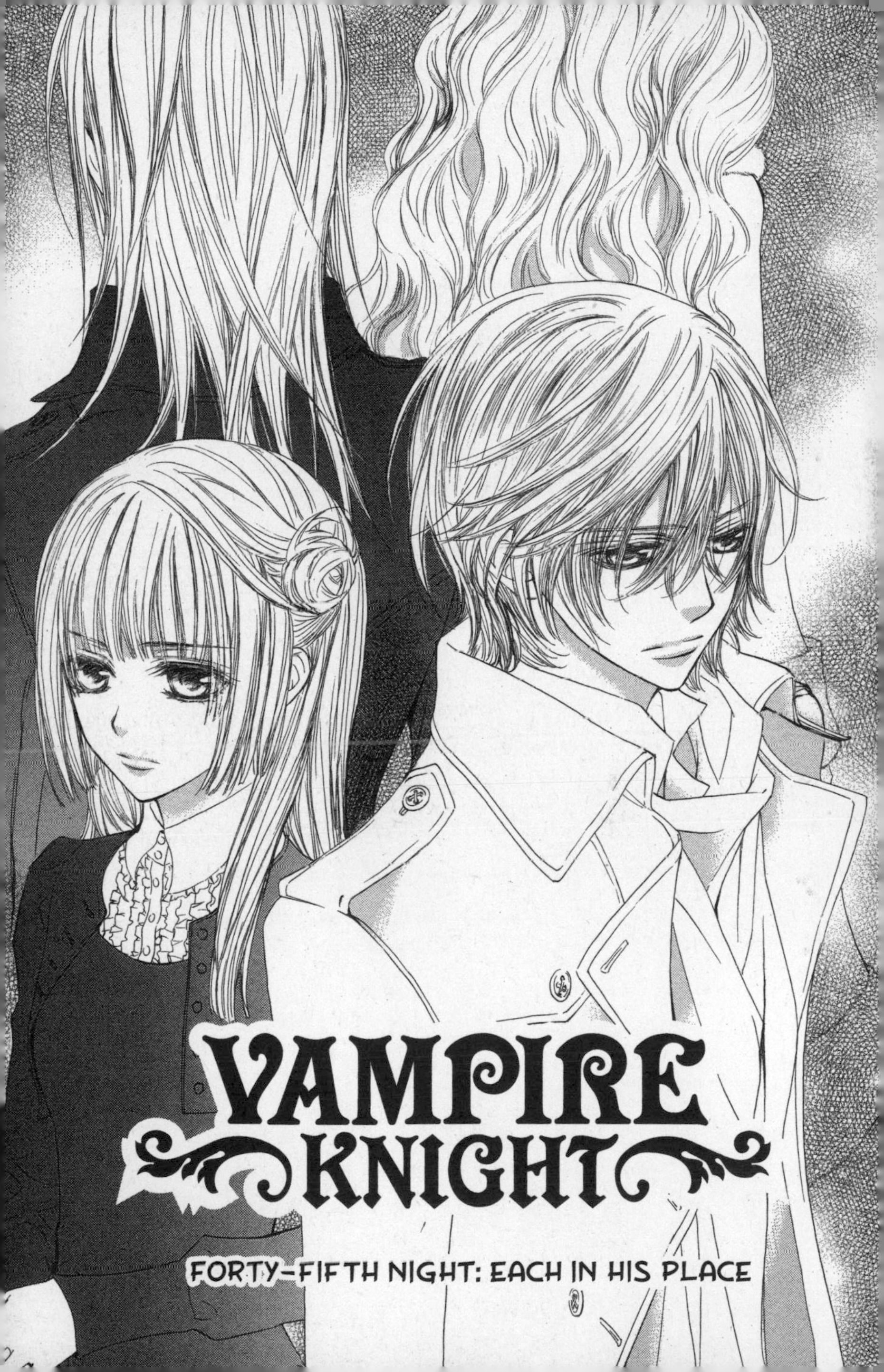
VAMPIRE KNIGHT
FORTY-FIFTH NIGHT: EACH IN HIS PLACE

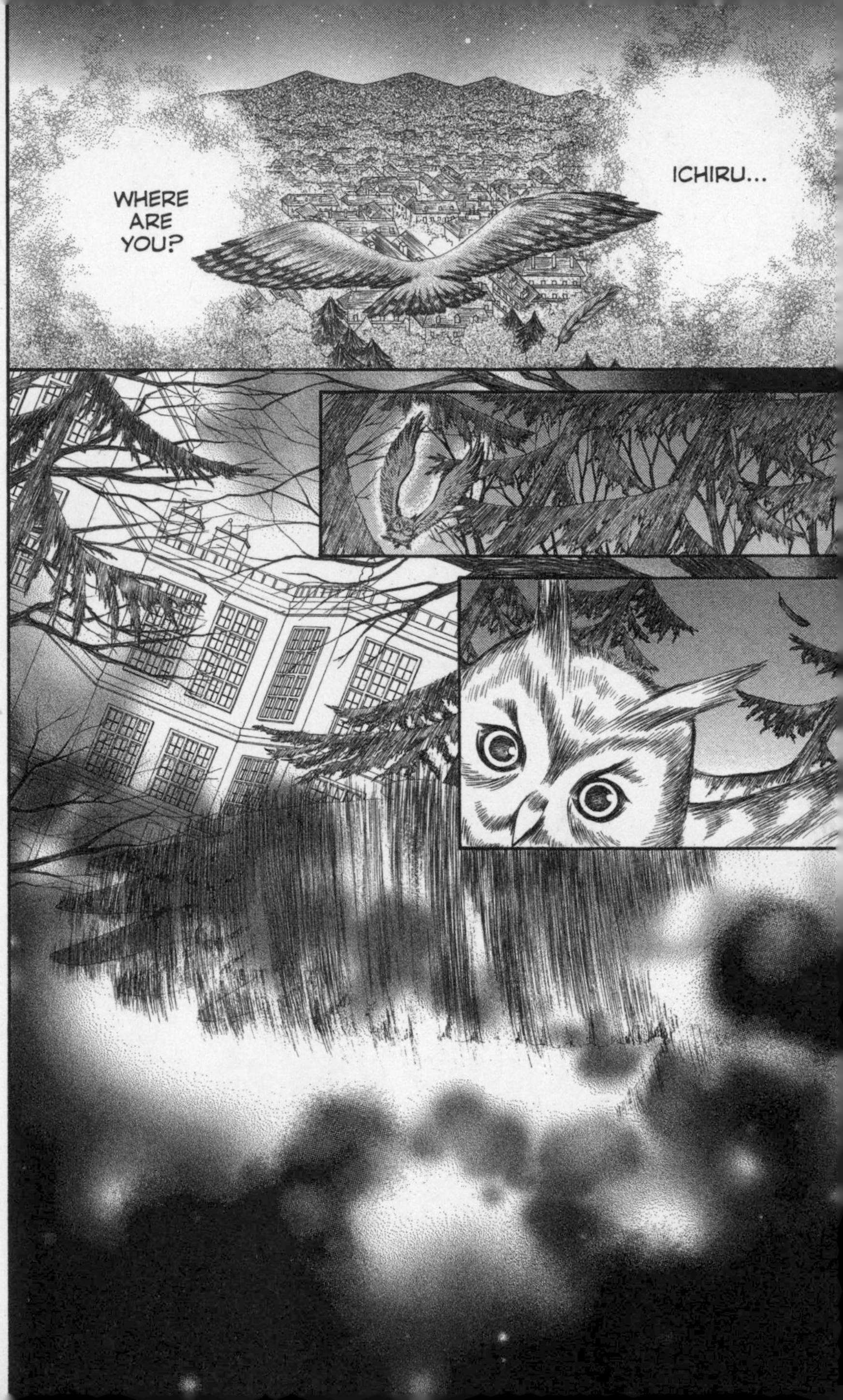
ICHIRU...
WHERE ARE YOU?

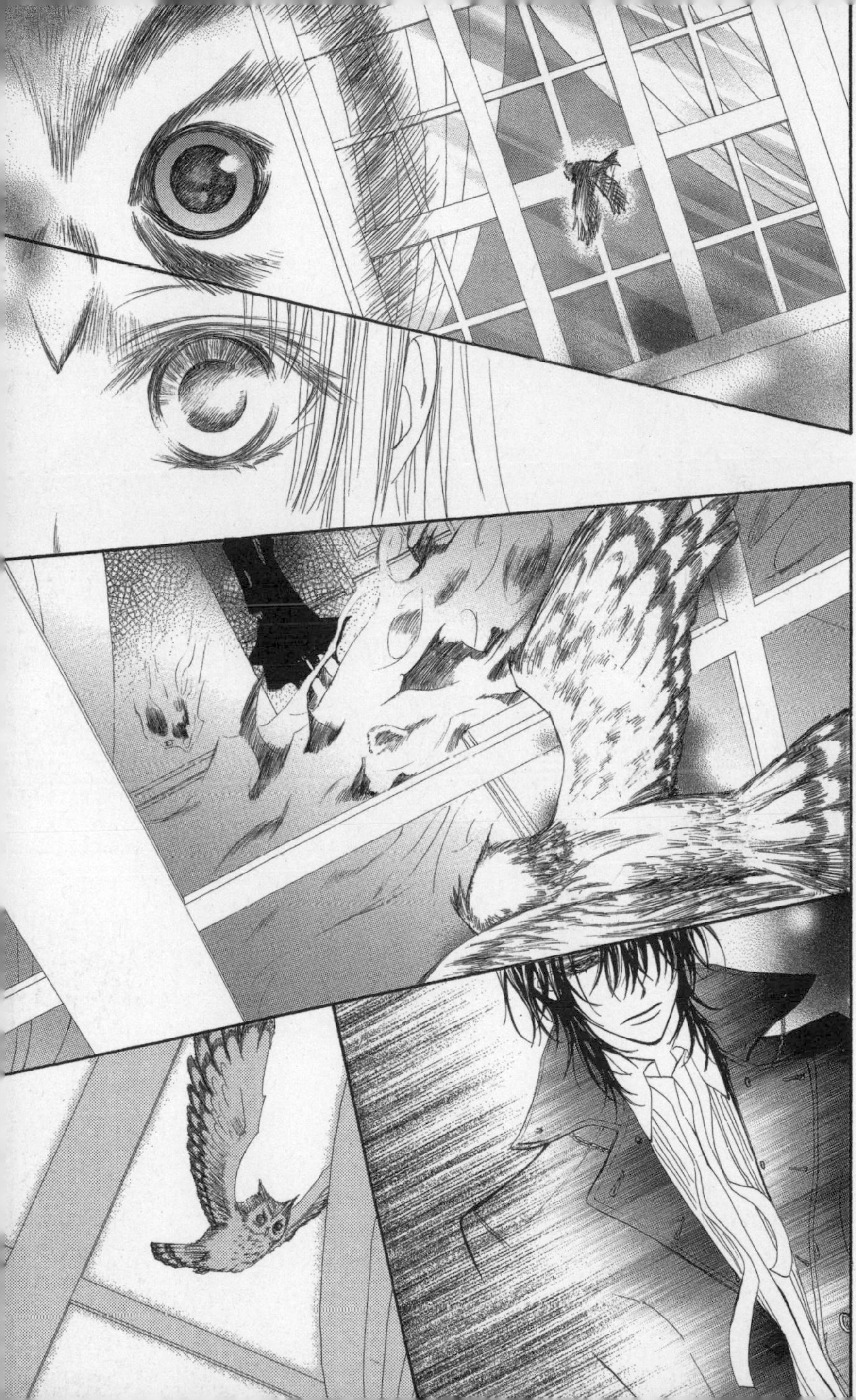

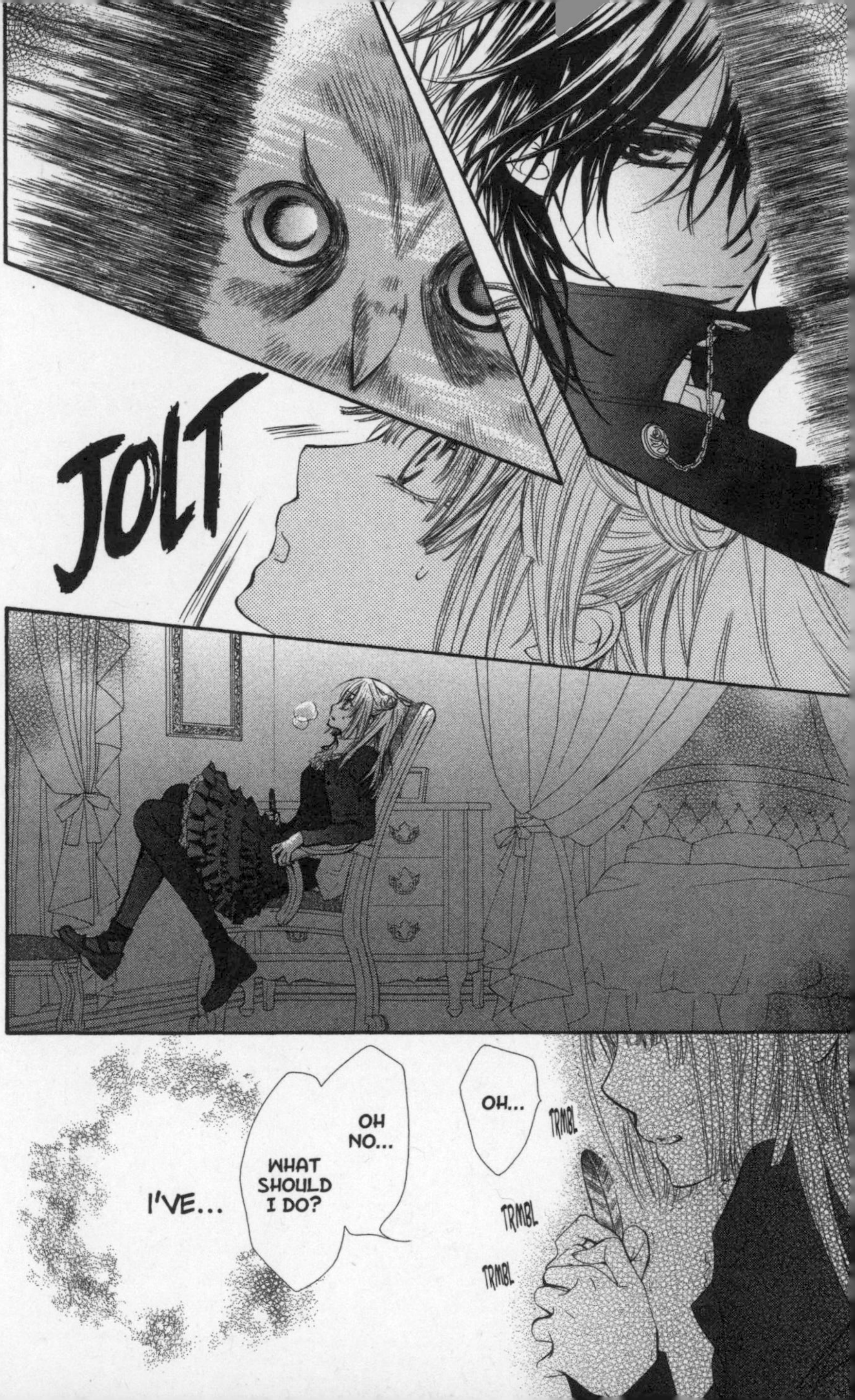
JOLT
OH...
TRMBL
TRMBL
TRMBL
OH NO... WHAT SHOULD I DO?
I'VE...

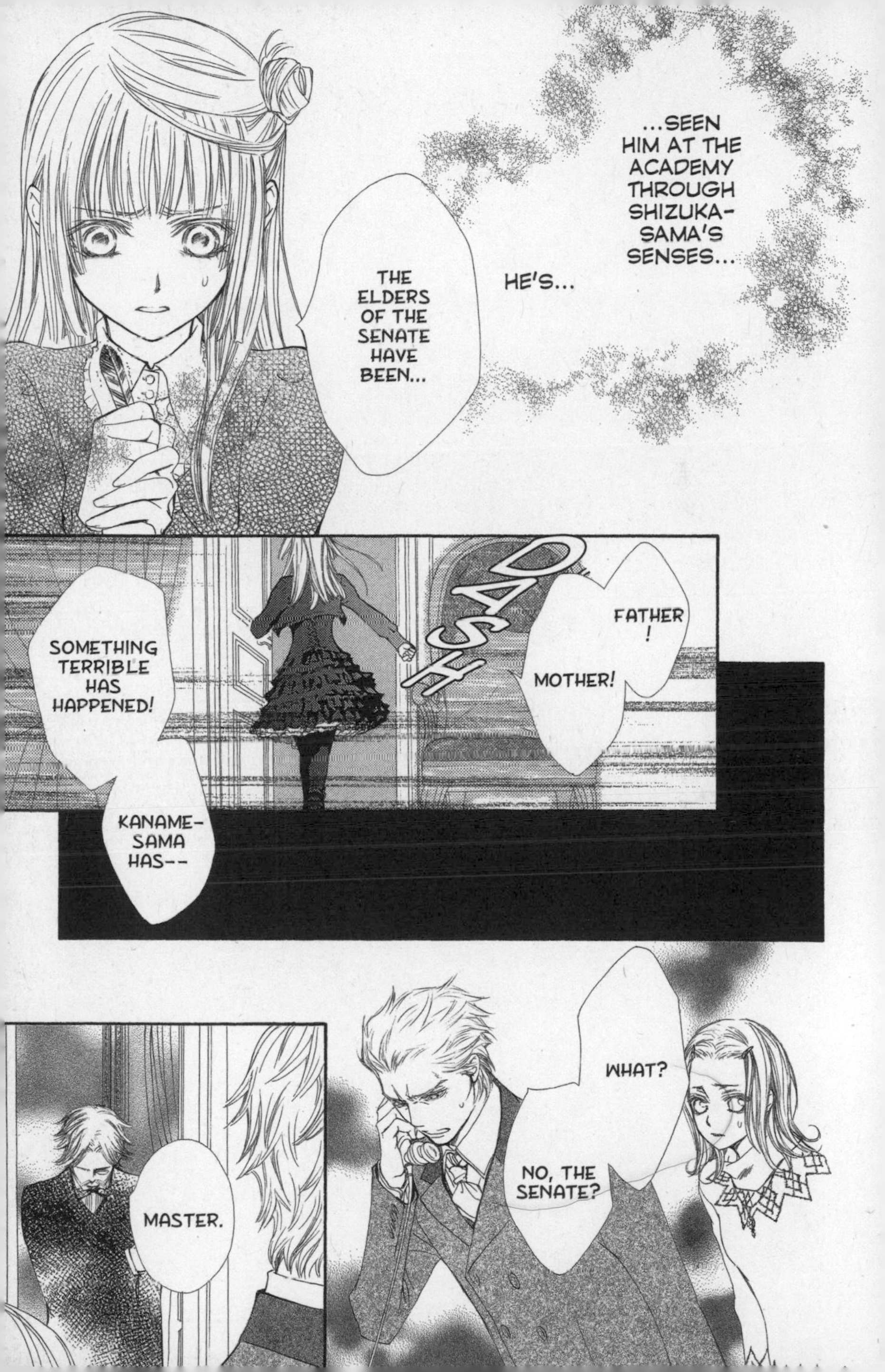
...SEEN HIM AT THE ACADEMY THROUGH SHIZUKA-SAMA'S SENSES...
HE'S...
THE ELDERS OF THE SENATE HAVE BEEN...
DASH
FATHER!
MOTHER!
SOMETHING TERRIBLE HAS HAPPENED!
KANAME-SAMA HAS--
WHAT?
NO, THE SENATE?
MASTER.

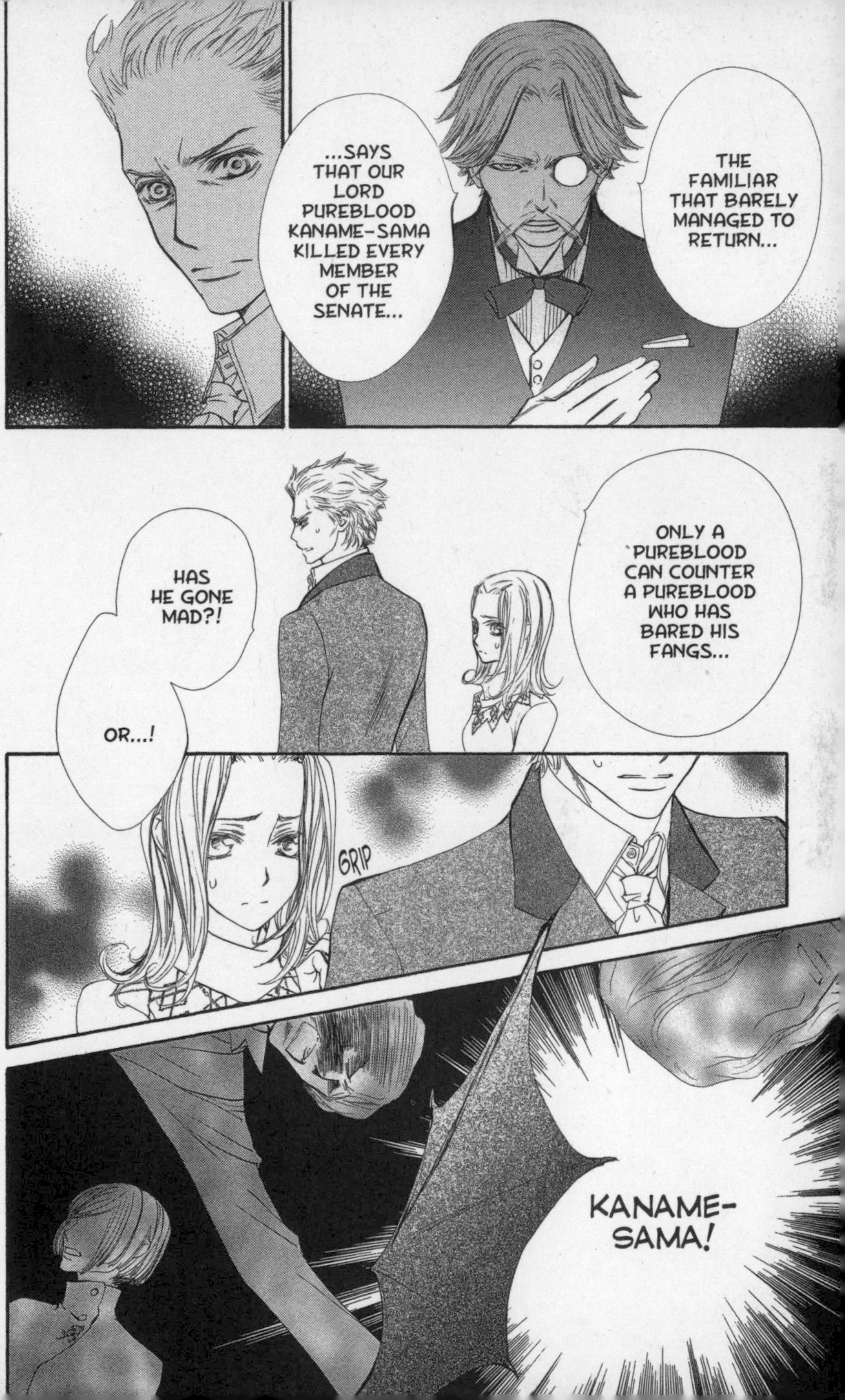
THE FAMILIAR THAT BARELY MANAGED TO RETURN...
...SAYS THAT OUR LORD PUREBLOOD KANAME-SAMA KILLED EVERY MEMBER OF THE SENATE...
ONLY A PUREBLOOD CAN COUNTER A PUREBLOOD WHO HAS BARED HIS FANGS...
HAS HE GONE MAD?!
OR...!
GRIP
KANAME-SAMA!

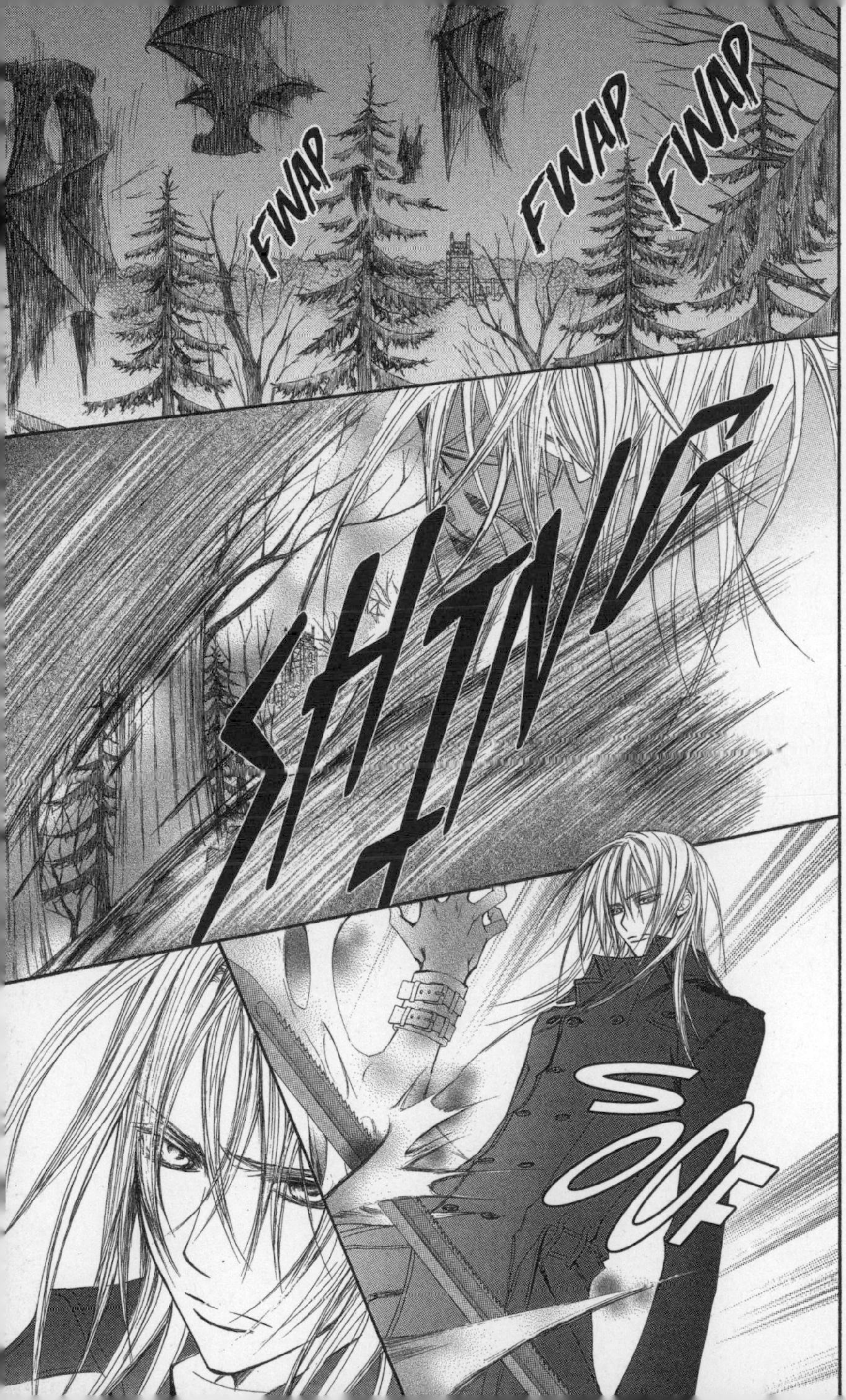
FWAP
FWAP
FWAP
SHING
SOOF

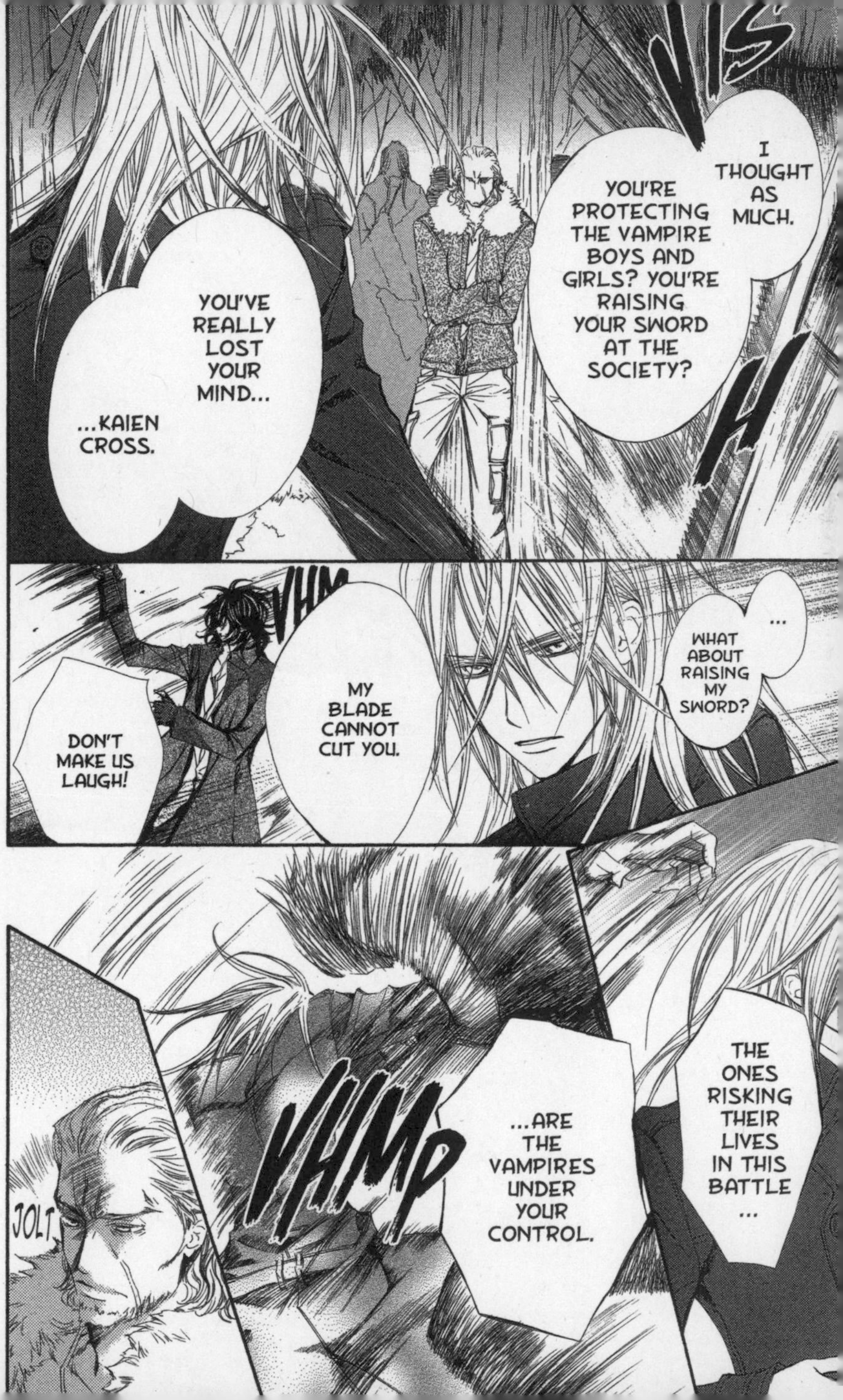
I THOUGHT AS MUCH.
YOU'RE PROTECTING THE VAMPIRE BOYS AND GIRLS? YOU'RE RAISING YOUR SWORD AT THE SOCIETY?
YOU'VE REALLY LOST YOUR MIND...
...KAIEN CROSS.
...
WHAT ABOUT RAISING MY SWORD?
MY BLADE CANNOT CUT YOU.
DON'T MAKE US LAUGH!
THE ONES RISKING THEIR LIVES IN THIS BATTLE...
...ARE THE VAMPIRES UNDER YOUR CONTROL.
VHMP
JOLT

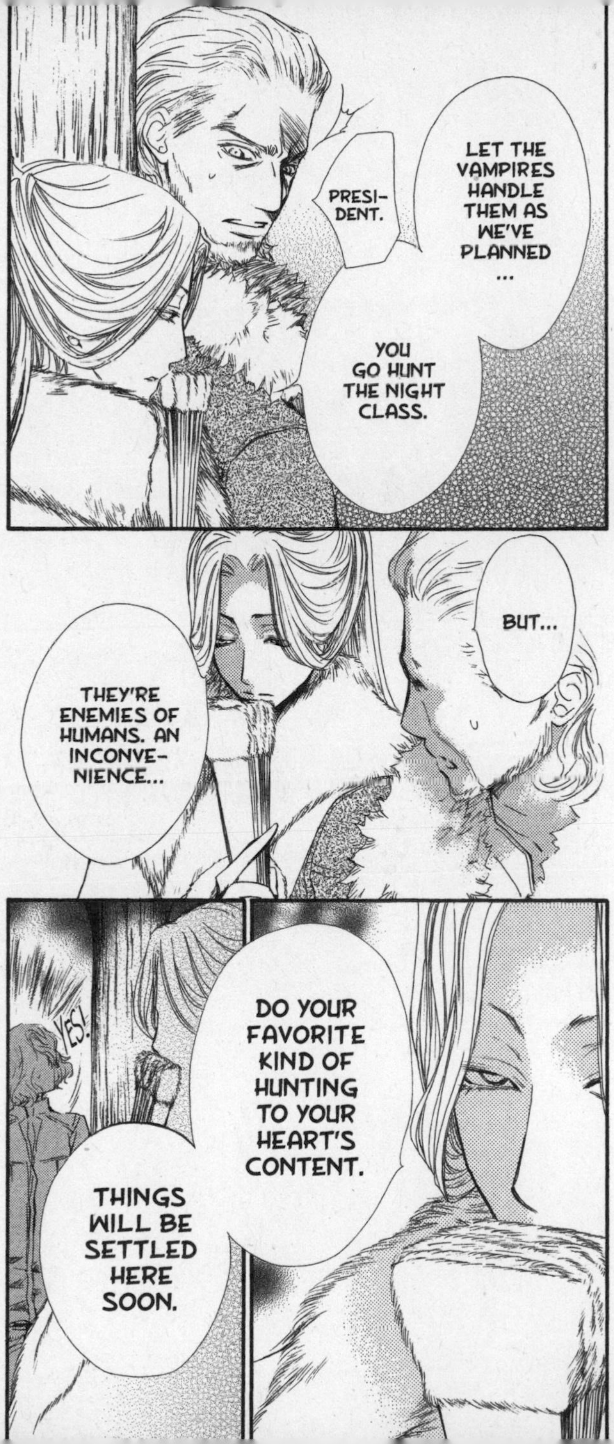
LET THE VAMPIRES HANDLE THEM AS WE'VE PLANNED ...
PRESI- DENT.
YOU GO HUNT THE NIGHT CLASS.
BUT...
THEY'RE ENEMIES OF HUMANS. AN INCONVE- NIENCE...
DO YOUR FAVORITE KIND OF HUNTING TO YOUR HEART'S CONTENT.
THINGS WILL BE SETTLED HERE SOON.
YES!

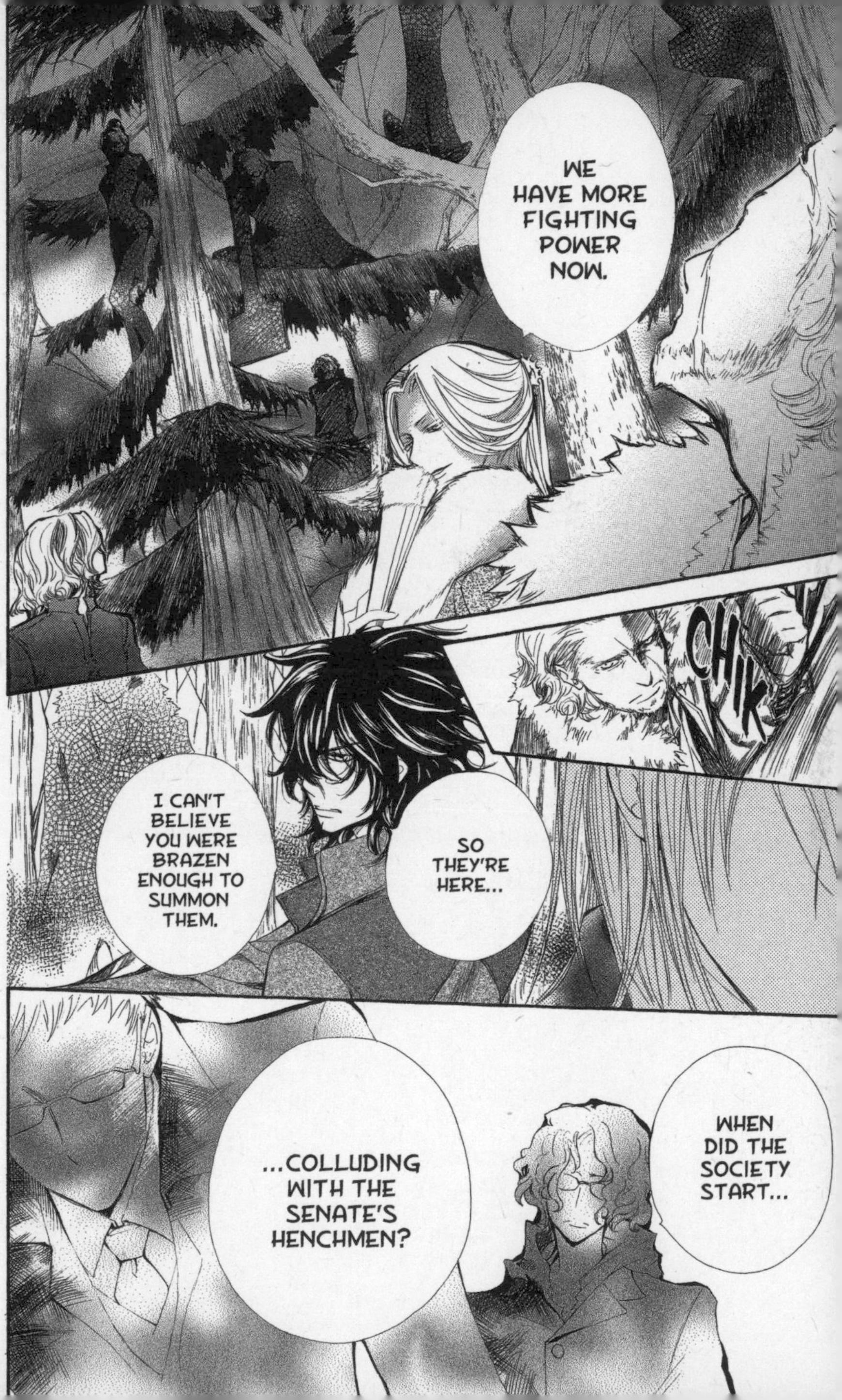
WE HAVE MORE FIGHTING POWER NOW.
CHIK
SO THEY'RE HERE...
I CAN'T BELIEVE YOU WERE BRAZEN ENOUGH TO SUMMON THEM.
WHEN DID THE SOCIETY START...
...COLLUDING WITH THE SENATE'S HENCHMEN?

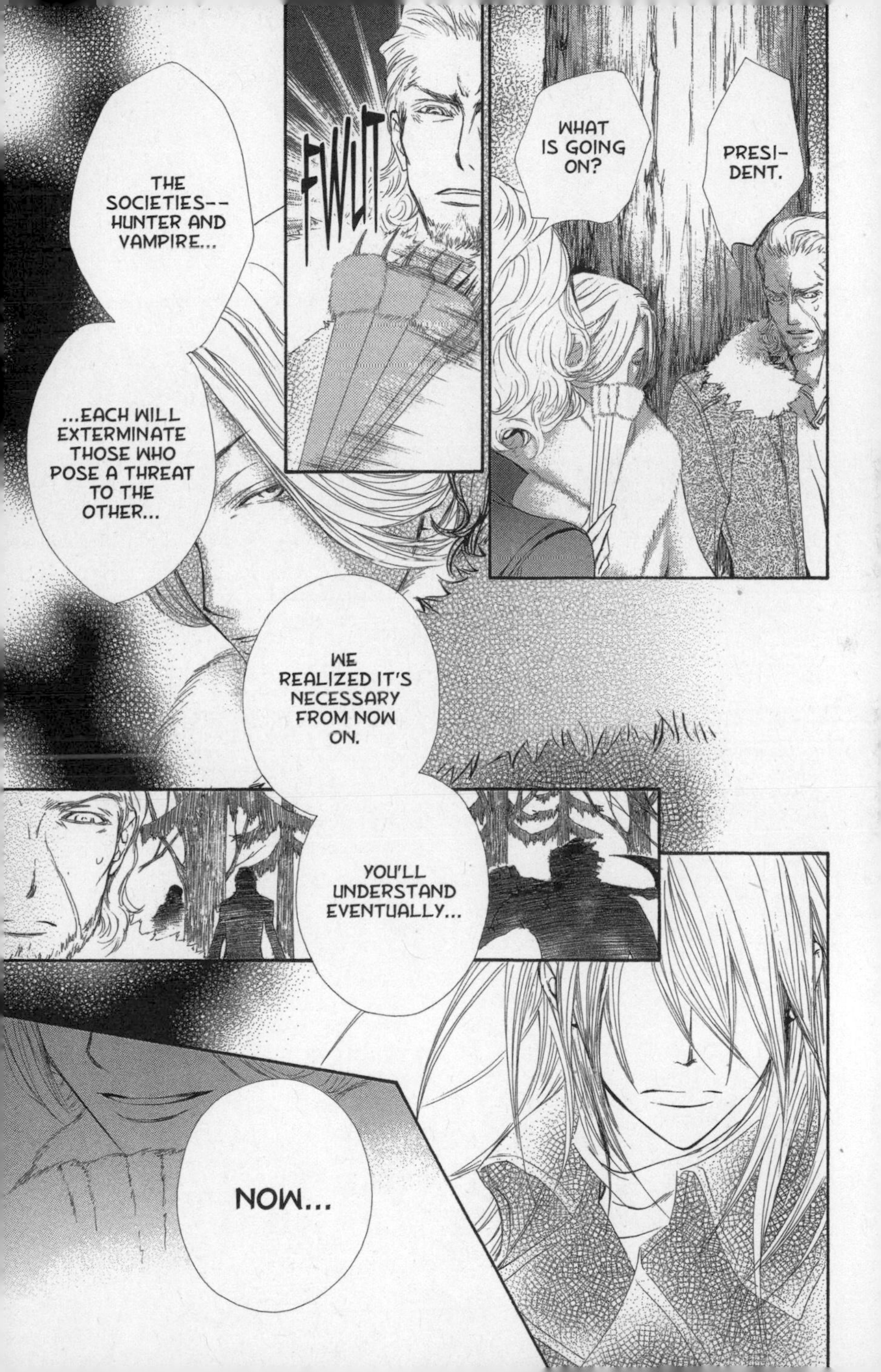
PRESI-DENT.
WHAT IS GOING ON?
FWUT
THE SOCIETIES--HUNTER AND VAMPIRE...
...EACH WILL EXTERMINATE THOSE WHO POSE A THREAT TO THE OTHER...
WE REALIZED IT'S NECESSARY FROM NOW ON.
YOU'LL UNDERSTAND EVENTUALLY...
NOW...

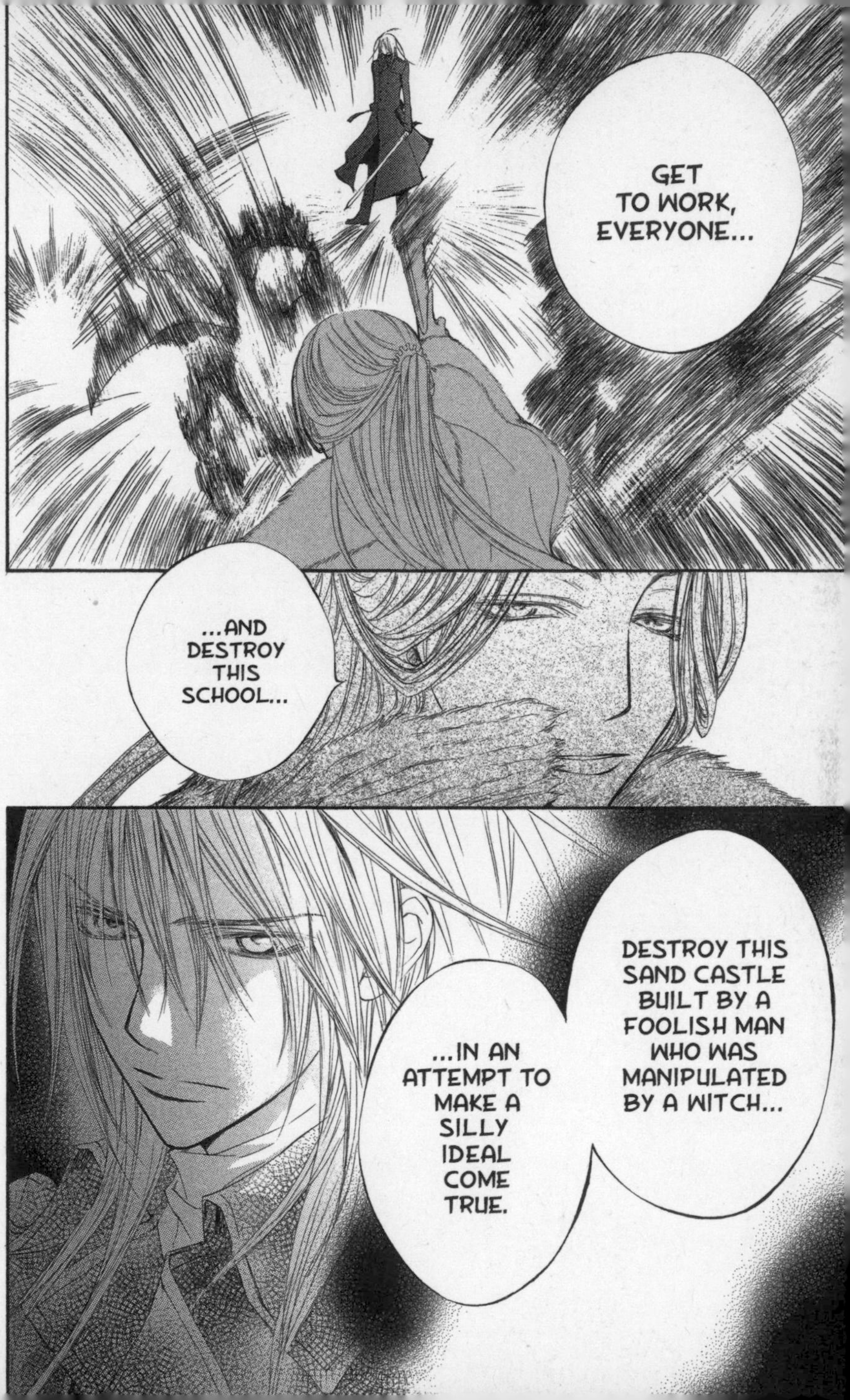
GET TO WORK, EVERYONE...
...AND DESTROY THIS SCHOOL...
DESTROY THIS SAND CASTLE BUILT BY A FOOLISH MAN WHO WAS MANIPULATED BY A WITCH...
...IN AN ATTEMPT TO MAKE A SILLY IDEAL COME TRUE.

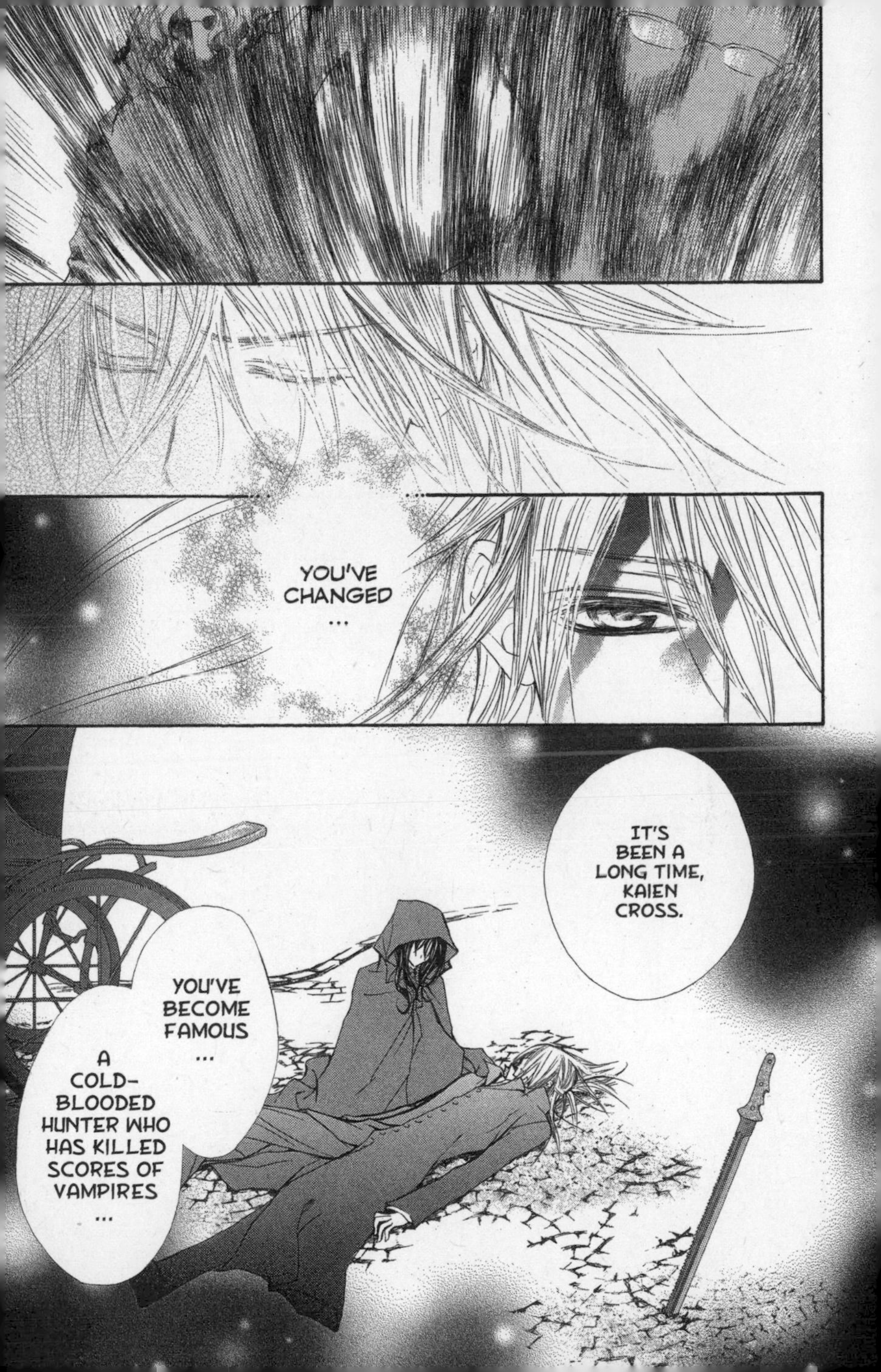
YOU'VE CHANGED ...
IT'S BEEN A LONG TIME, KAIEN CROSS.
YOU'VE BECOME FAMOUS ...
A COLD-BLOODED HUNTER WHO HAS KILLED SCORES OF VAMPIRES ...

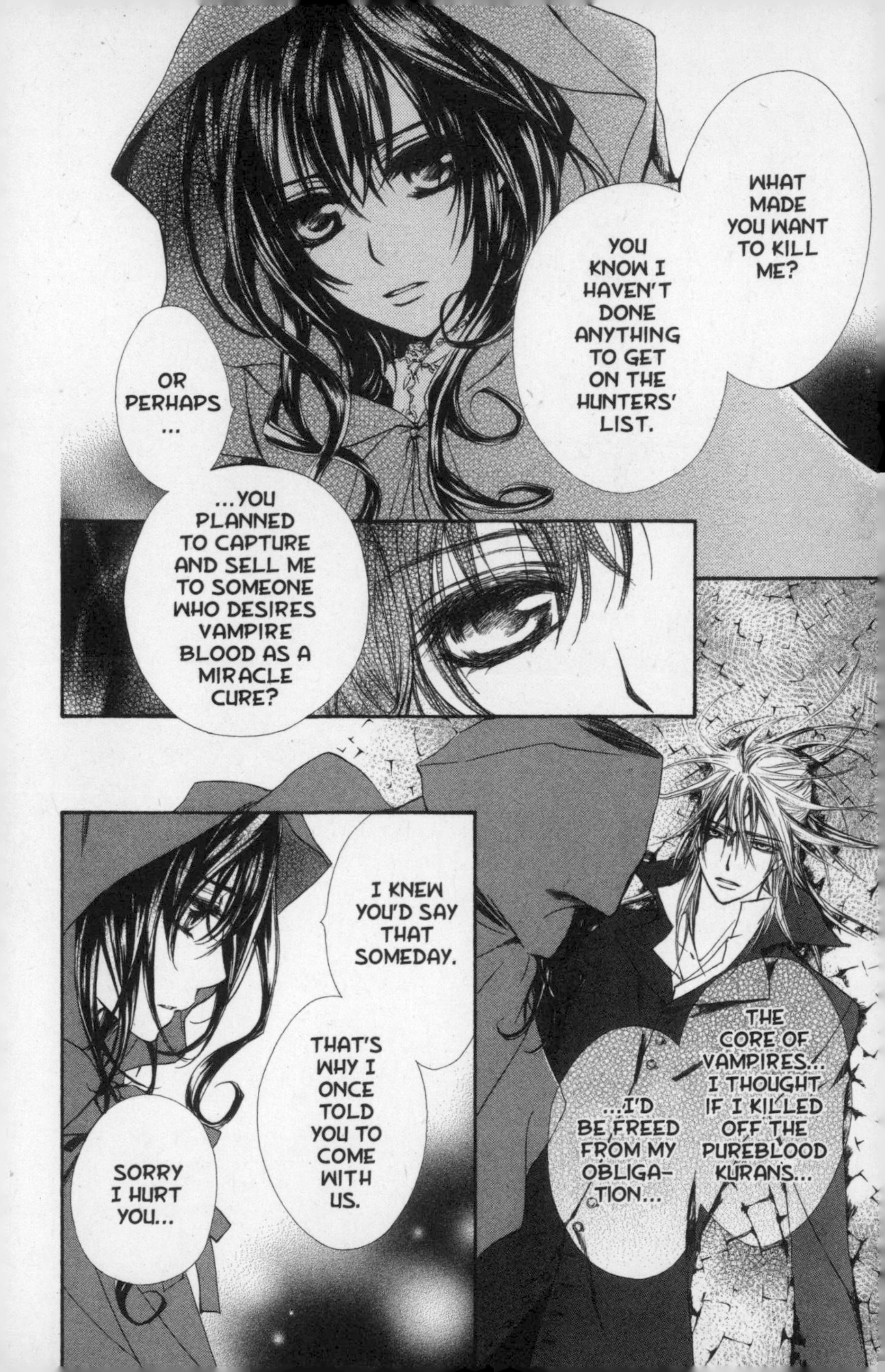
WHAT MADE YOU WANT TO KILL ME?
YOU KNOW I HAVEN'T DONE ANYTHING TO GET ON THE HUNTERS' LIST.
OR PERHAPS ...
...YOU PLANNED TO CAPTURE AND SELL ME TO SOMEONE WHO DESIRES VAMPIRE BLOOD AS A MIRACLE CURE?
THE CORE OF VAMPIRES... I THOUGHT IF I KILLED OFF THE PUREBLOOD KURANS...
...I'D BE FREED FROM MY OBLIGA-TION...
I KNEW YOU'D SAY THAT SOMEDAY.
THAT'S WHY I ONCE TOLD YOU TO COME WITH US.
SORRY I HURT YOU...

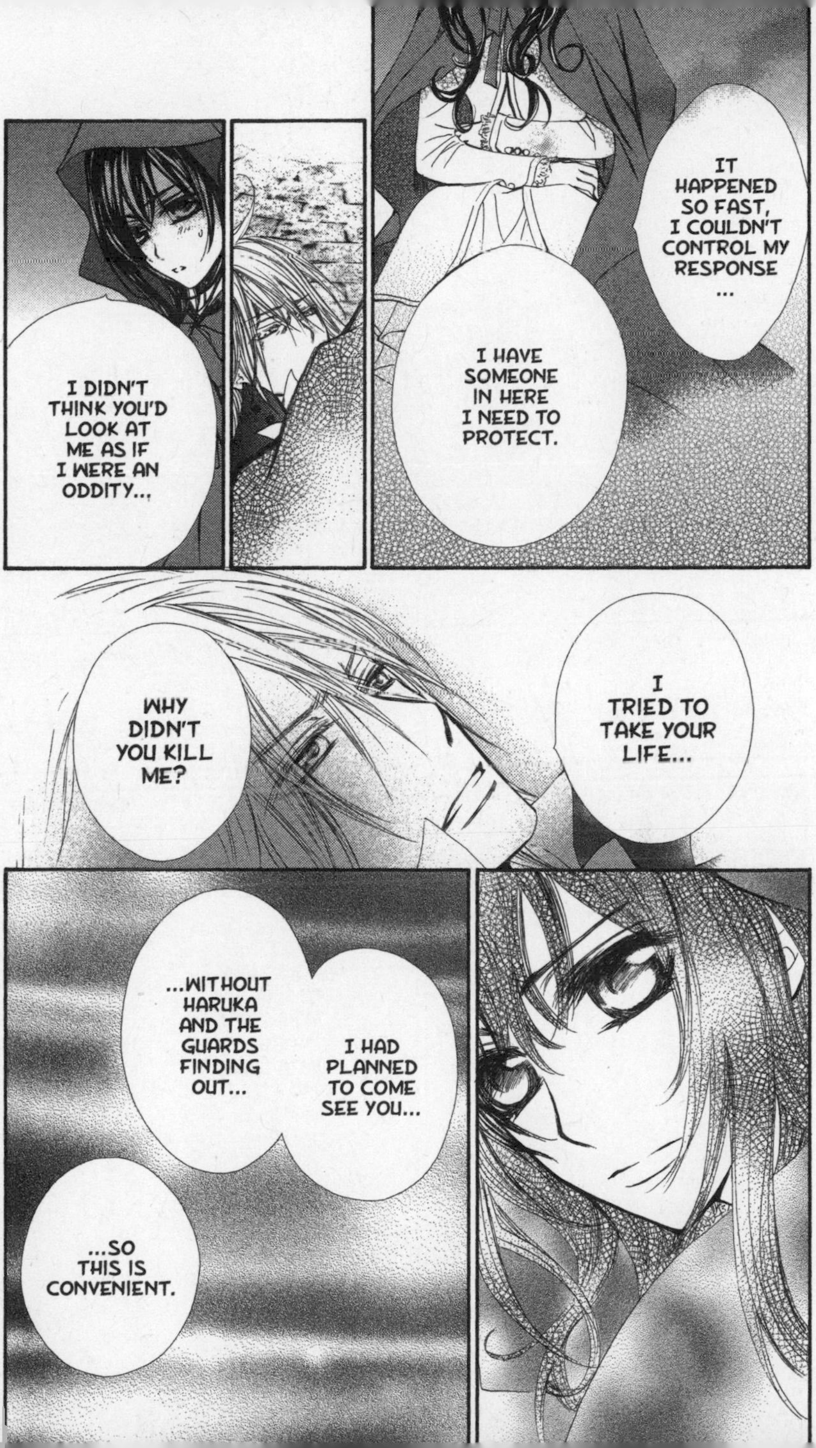
IT HAPPENED SO FAST, I COULDN'T CONTROL MY RESPONSE ...
I HAVE SOMEONE IN HERE I NEED TO PROTECT.
I DIDN'T THINK YOU'D LOOK AT ME AS IF I WERE AN ODDITY..,
I TRIED TO TAKE YOUR LIFE...
WHY DIDN'T YOU KILL ME?
I HAD PLANNED TO COME SEE YOU...
...WITHOUT HARUKA AND THE GUARDS FINDING OUT...
...SO THIS IS CONVENIENT.

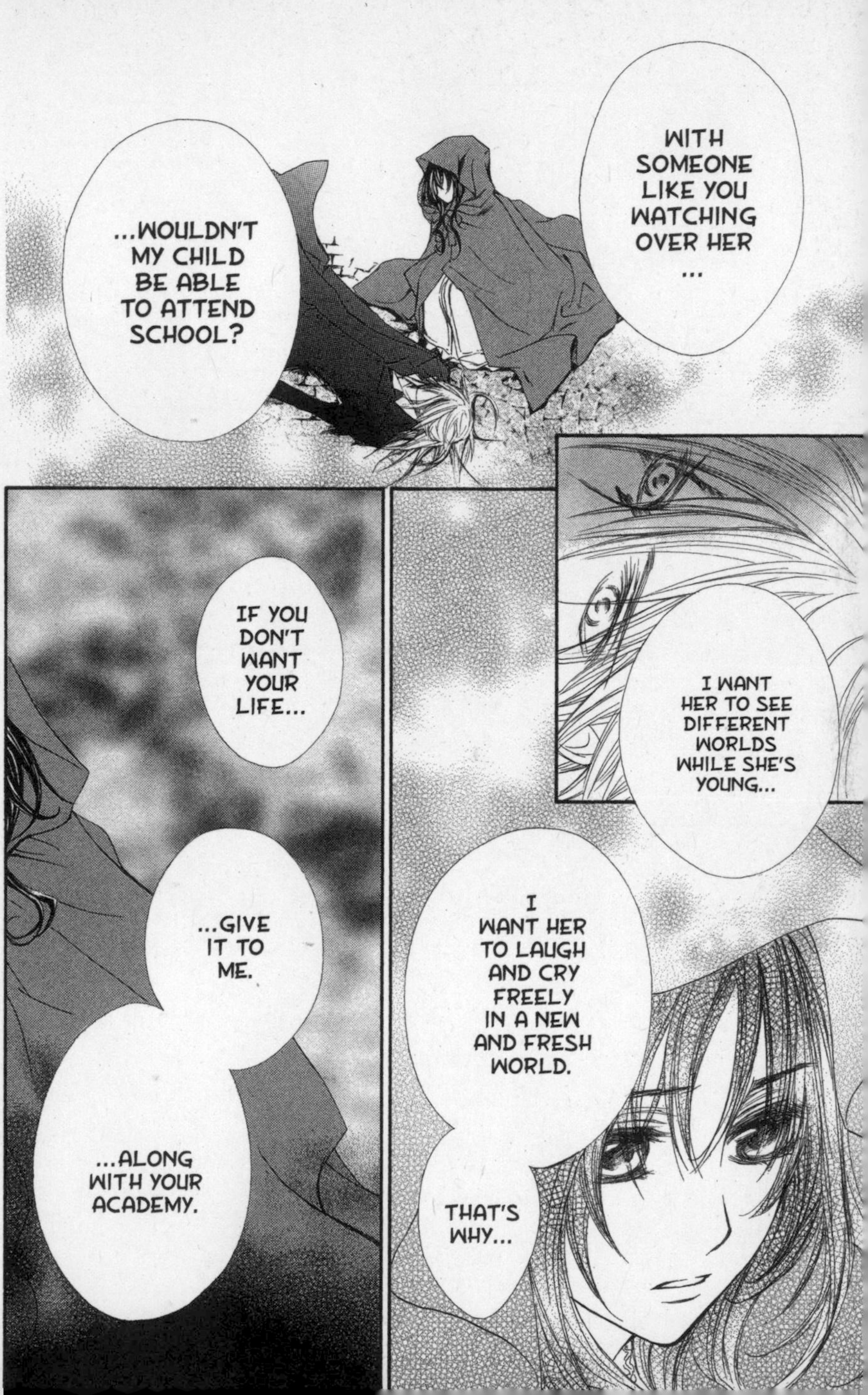
WITH SOMEONE LIKE YOU WATCHING OVER HER...
...WOULDN'T MY CHILD BE ABLE TO ATTEND SCHOOL?
I WANT HER TO SEE DIFFERENT WORLDS WHILE SHE'S YOUNG...
I WANT HER TO LAUGH AND CRY FREELY IN A NEW AND FRESH WORLD.
THAT'S WHY...
IF YOU DON'T WANT YOUR LIFE...
...GIVE IT TO ME.
...ALONG WITH YOUR ACADEMY.

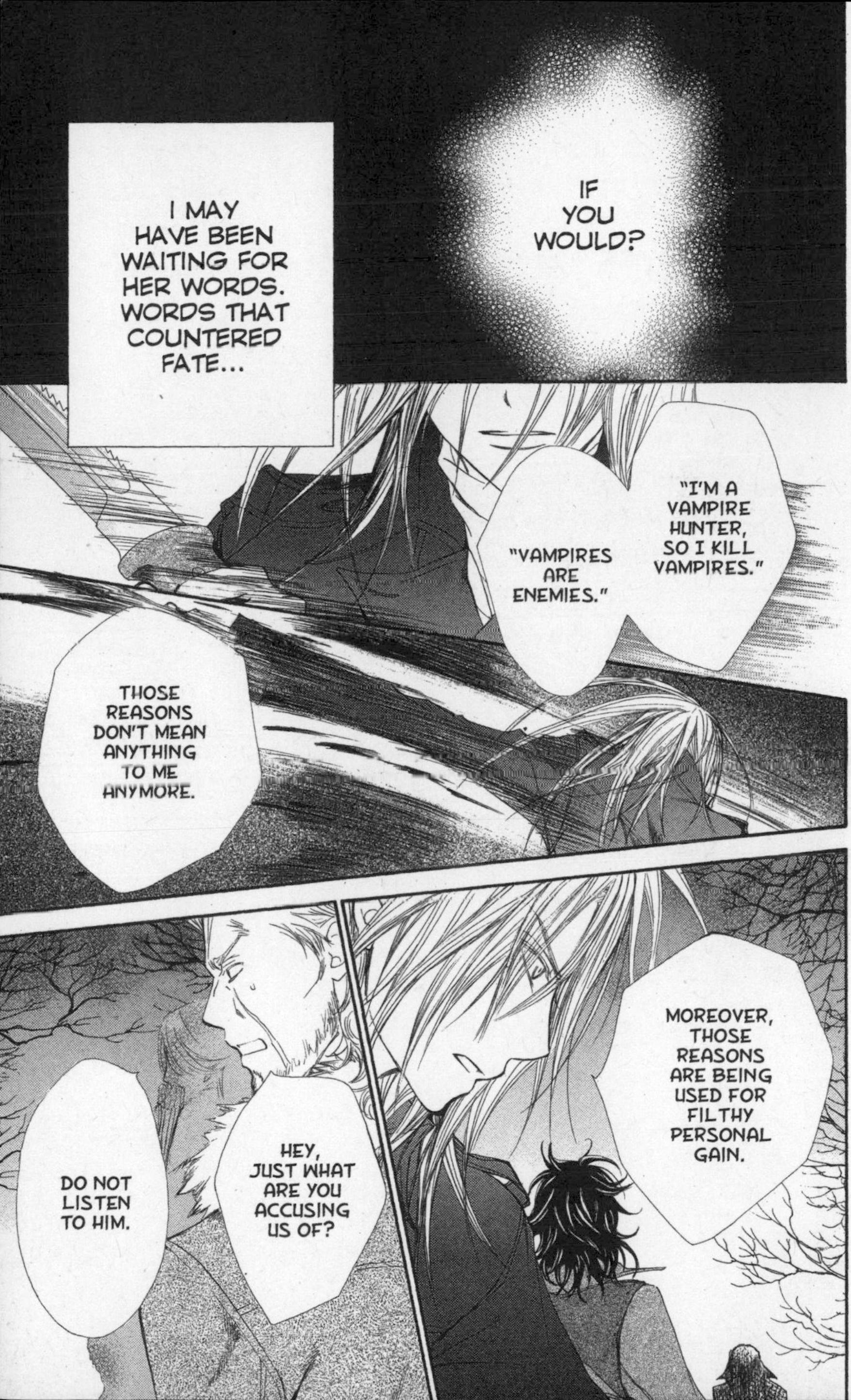
IF YOU WOULD?
I MAY HAVE BEEN WAITING FOR HER WORDS. WORDS THAT COUNTERED FATE...
"I'M A VAMPIRE HUNTER, SO I KILL VAMPIRES."
"VAMPIRES ARE ENEMIES."
THOSE REASONS DON'T MEAN ANYTHING TO ME ANYMORE.
MOREOVER, THOSE REASONS ARE BEING USED FOR FILTHY PERSONAL GAIN.
HEY, JUST WHAT ARE YOU ACCUSING US OF?
DO NOT LISTEN TO HIM.

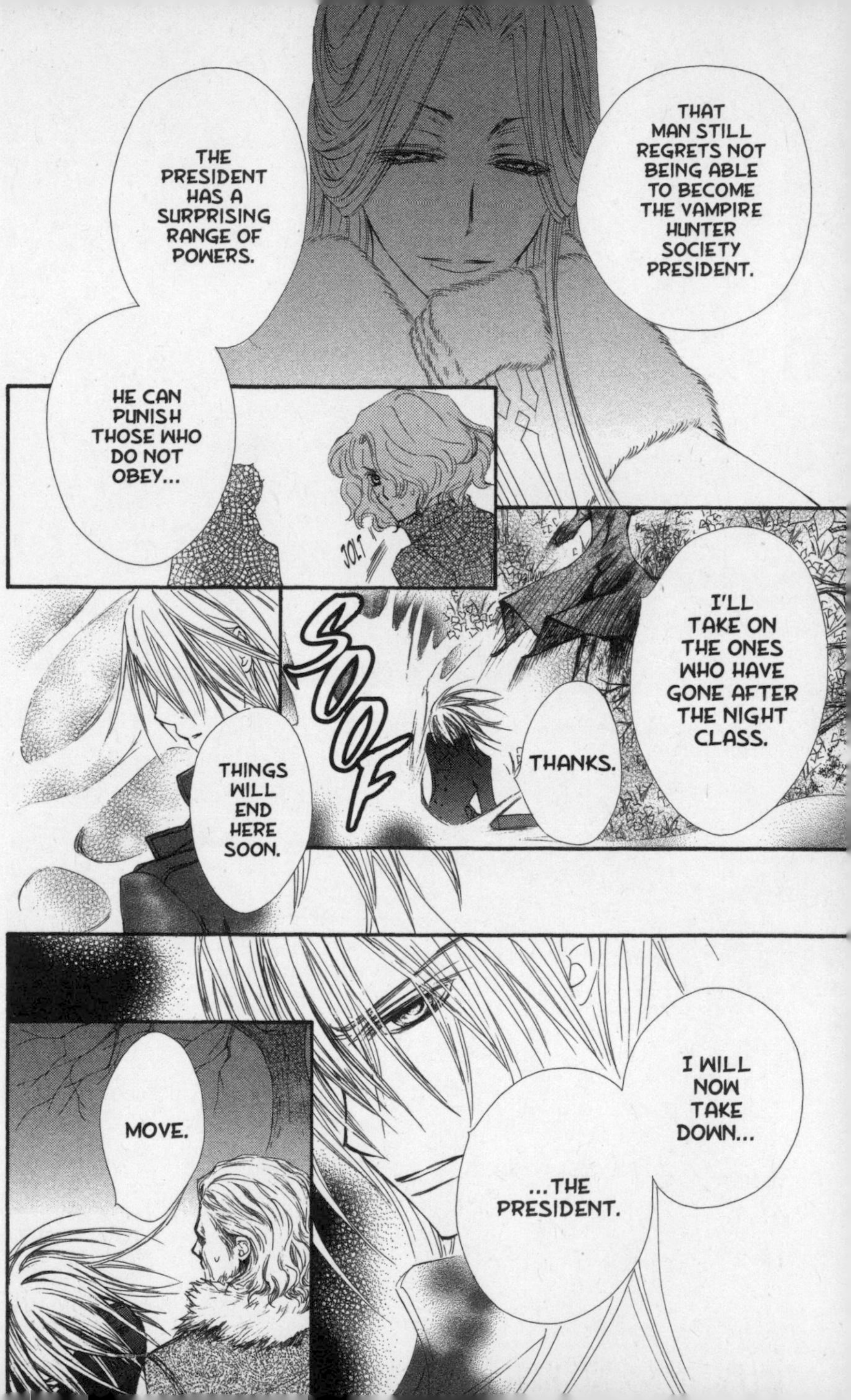
THAT MAN STILL REGRETS NOT BEING ABLE TO BECOME THE VAMPIRE HUNTER SOCIETY PRESIDENT.
THE PRESIDENT HAS A SURPRISING RANGE OF POWERS.
HE CAN PUNISH THOSE WHO DO NOT OBEY...
JOLT
I'LL TAKE ON THE ONES WHO HAVE GONE AFTER THE NIGHT CLASS.
THANKS.
SOOF
THINGS WILL END HERE SOON.
I WILL NOW TAKE DOWN...
...THE PRESIDENT.
MOVE.

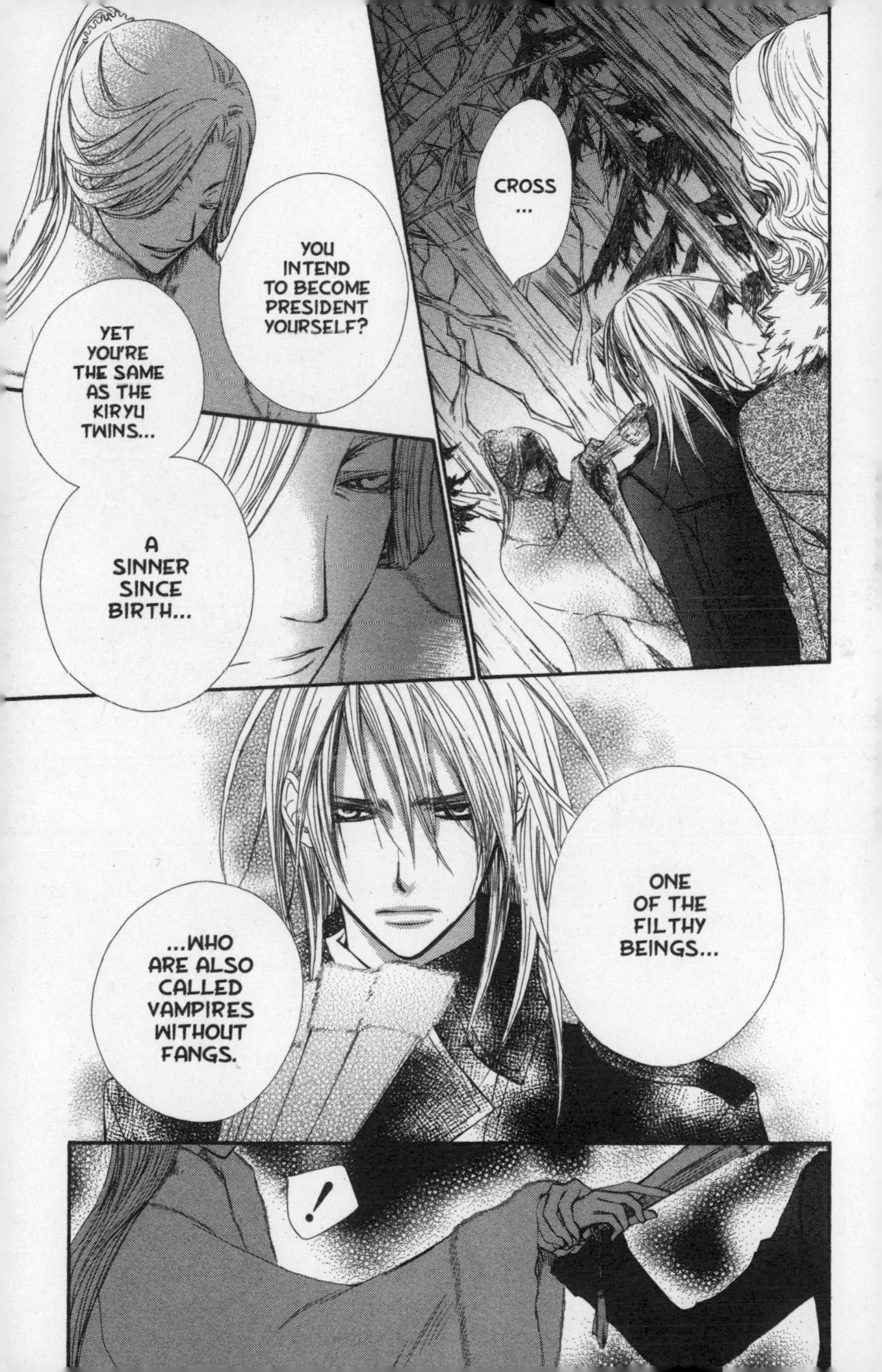
CROSS...
YOU INTEND TO BECOME PRESIDENT YOURSELF?
YET YOU'RE THE SAME AS THE KIRYU TWINS...
A SINNER SINCE BIRTH...
ONE OF THE FILTHY BEINGS...
...WHO ARE ALSO CALLED VAMPIRES WITHOUT FANGS.
!

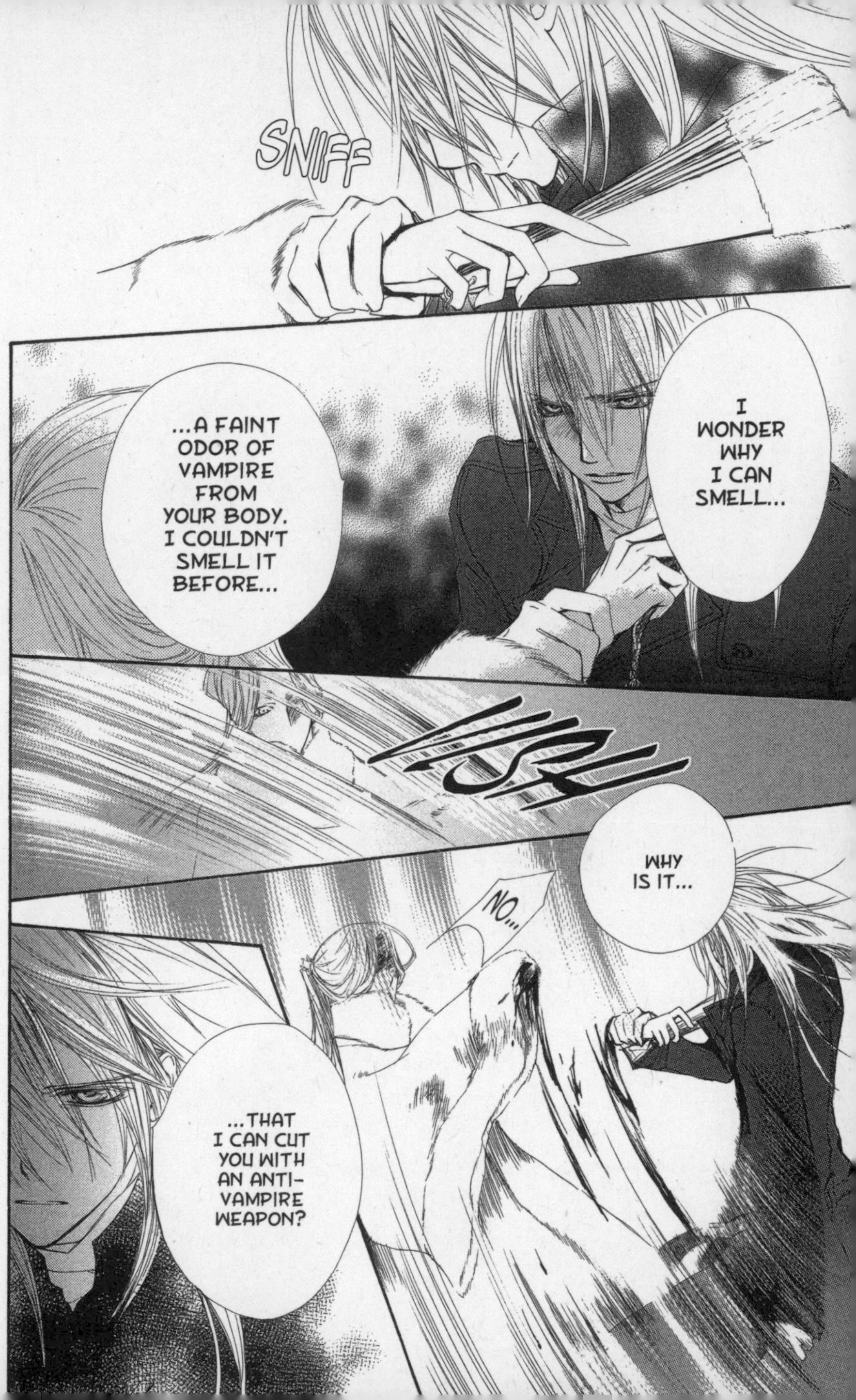
SNIFF
I WONDER WHY I CAN SMELL...
...A FAINT ODOR OF VAMPIRE FROM YOUR BODY. I COULDN'T SMELL IT BEFORE...
VISH
WHY IS IT...
NO...
...THAT I CAN CUT YOU WITH AN ANTI-VAMPIRE WEAPON?

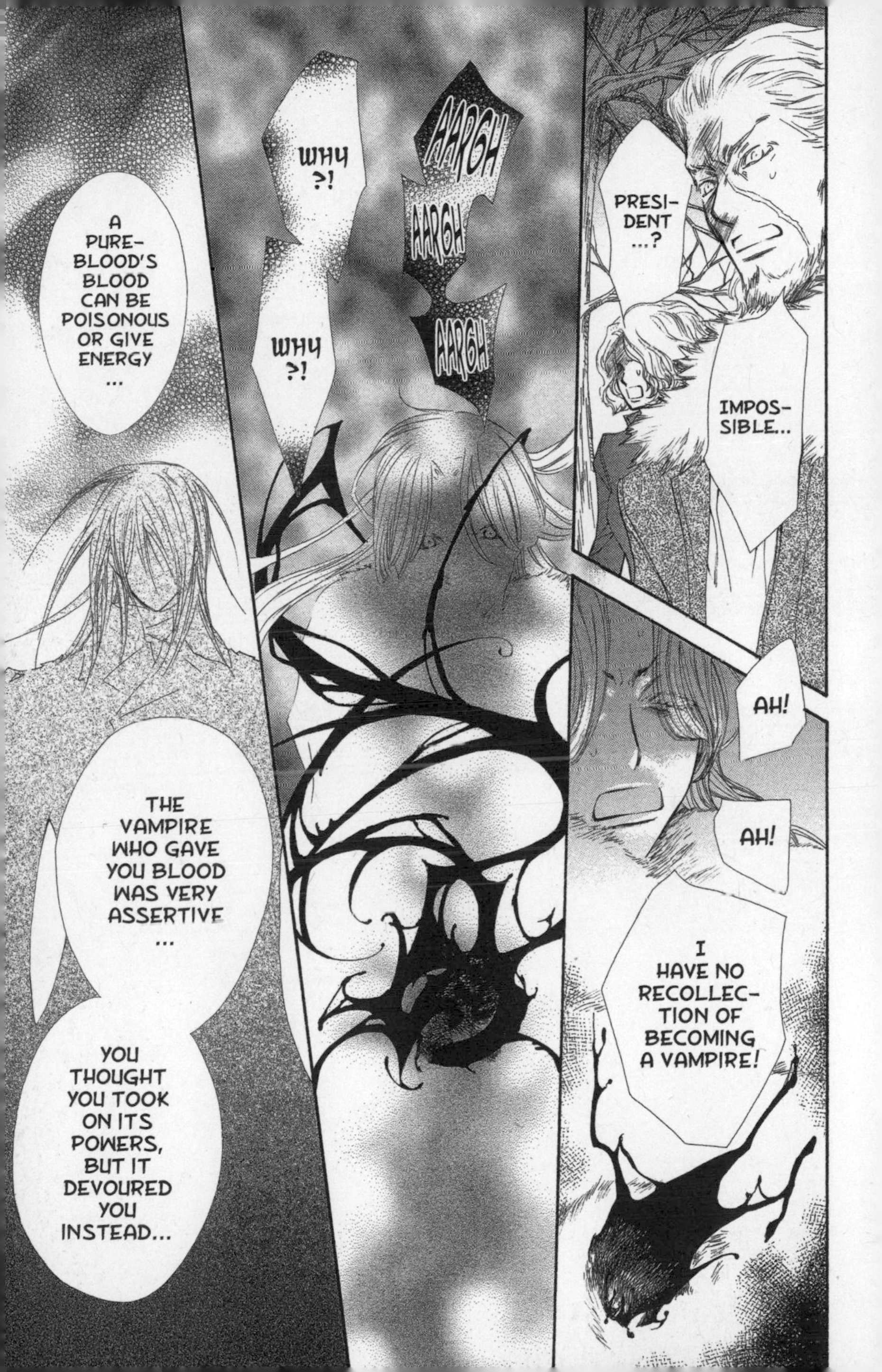
PRESI-DENT ...?
IMPOS-SIBLE...
AH!
AH!
I HAVE NO RECOLLEC-TION OF BECOMING A VAMPIRE!
AARGH
AARGH
AARGH
WHY ?!
WHY ?!
A PURE-BLOOD'S BLOOD CAN BE POISONOUS OR GIVE ENERGY ...
THE VAMPIRE WHO GAVE YOU BLOOD WAS VERY ASSERTIVE ...
YOU THOUGHT YOU TOOK ON ITS POWERS, BUT IT DEVOURED YOU INSTEAD...

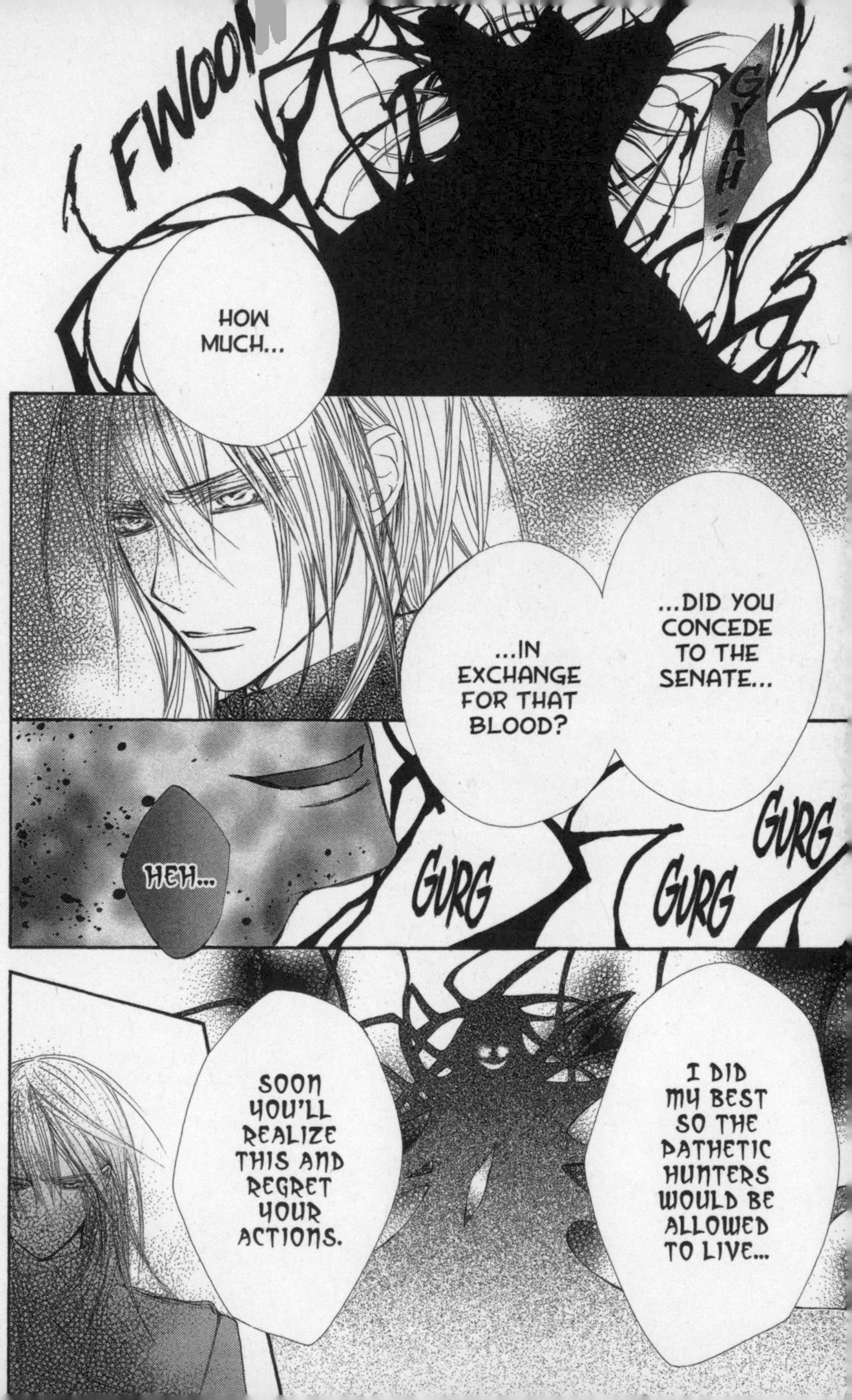
GYAH...
FWOOM
HOW MUCH...
...DID YOU CONCEDE TO THE SENATE...
...IN EXCHANGE FOR THAT BLOOD?
GURG
GURG
GURG
HEH...
I DID MY BEST SO THE PATHETIC HUNTERS WOULD BE ALLOWED TO LIVE...
SOON YOU'LL REALIZE THIS AND REGRET YOUR ACTIONS.

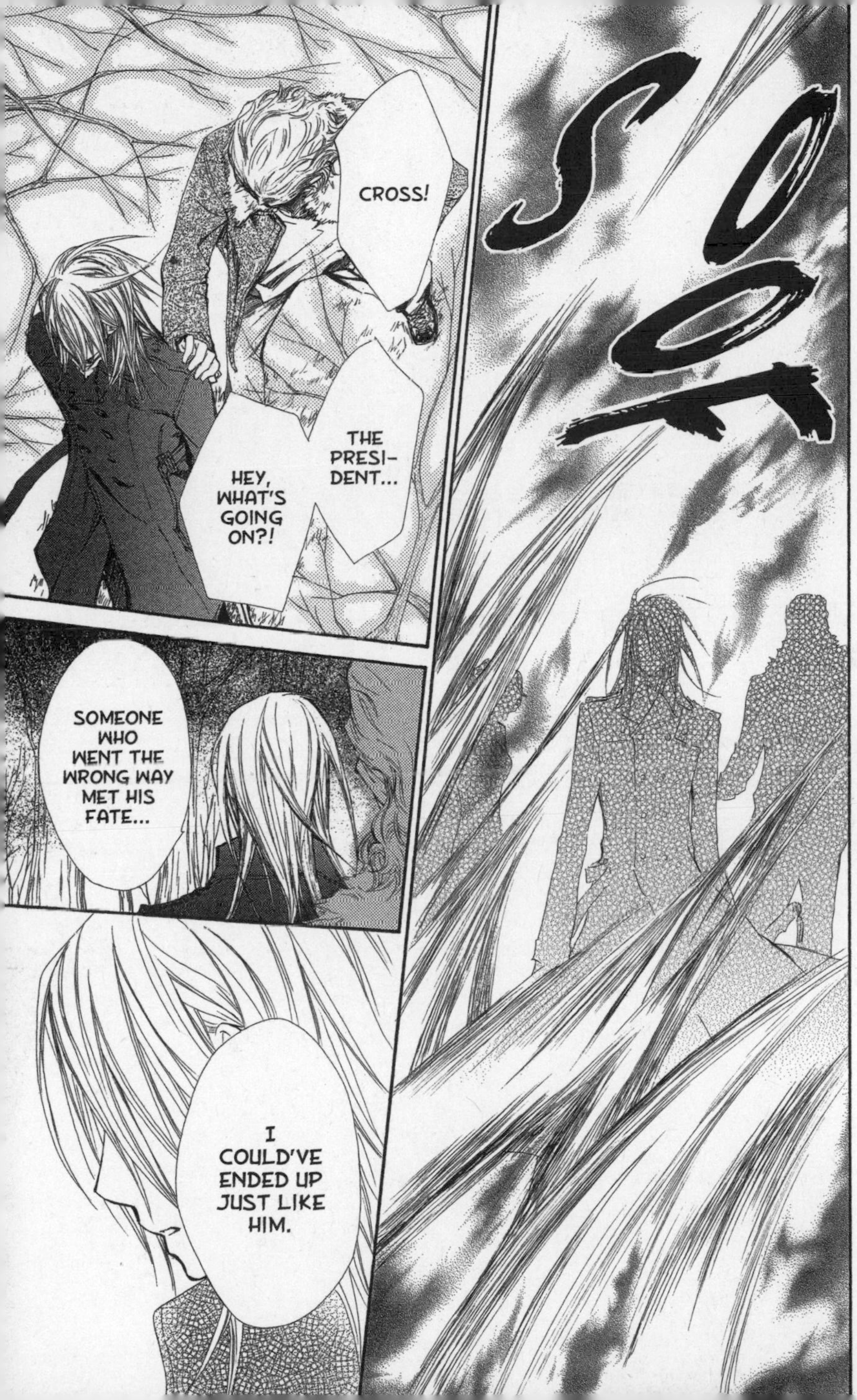
SOOK
CROSS!
THE PRESI-DENT...
HEY, WHAT'S GOING ON?!
SOMEONE WHO WENT THE WRONG WAY MET HIS FATE...
I COULD'VE ENDED UP JUST LIKE HIM.

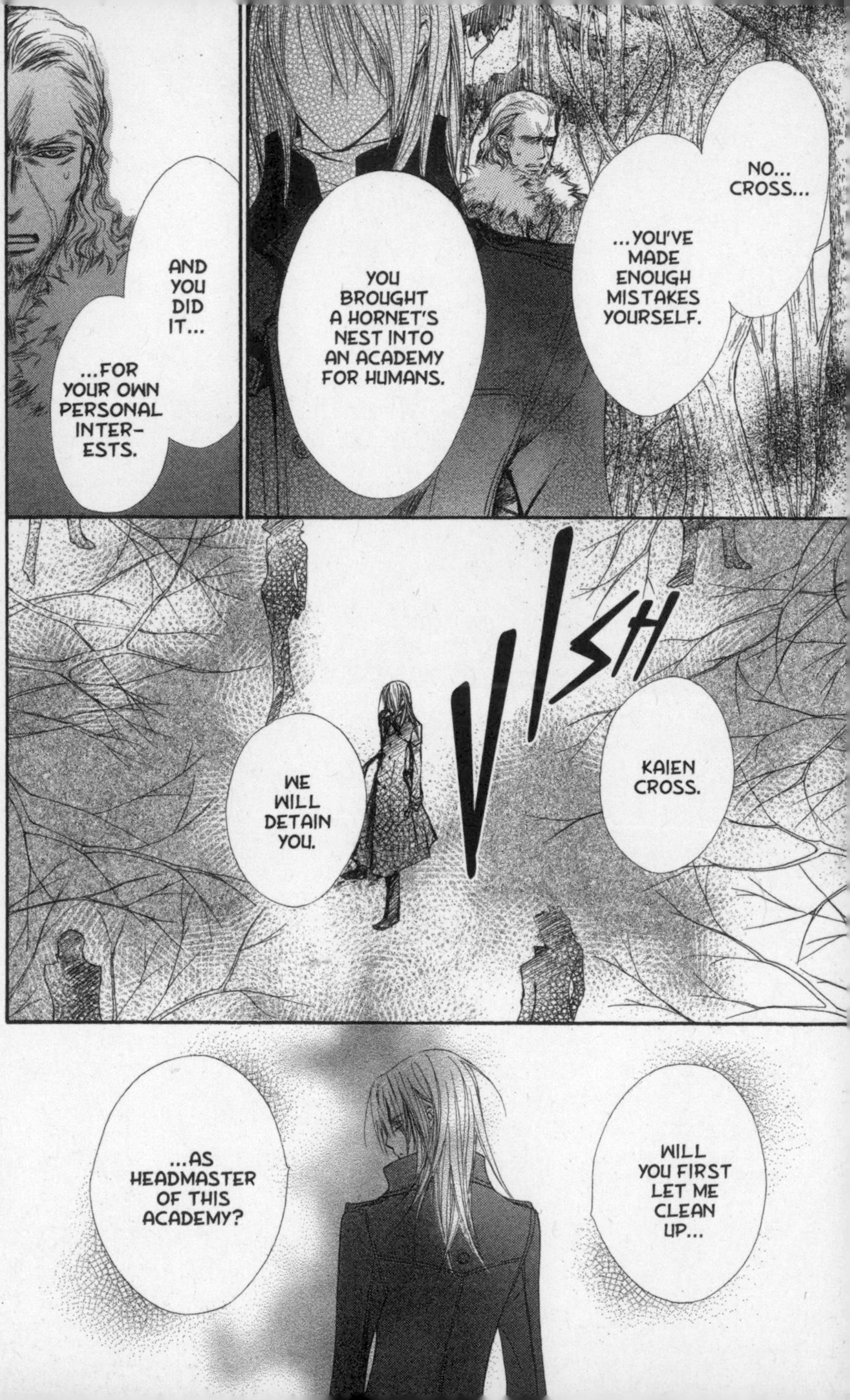
NO... CROSS...
...YOU'VE MADE ENOUGH MISTAKES YOURSELF.
YOU BROUGHT A HORNET'S NEST INTO AN ACADEMY FOR HUMANS.
AND YOU DID IT...
...FOR YOUR OWN PERSONAL INTER-ESTS.
KAIEN CROSS.
VISH
WE WILL DETAIN YOU.
WILL YOU FIRST LET ME CLEAN UP...
...AS HEADMASTER OF THIS ACADEMY?

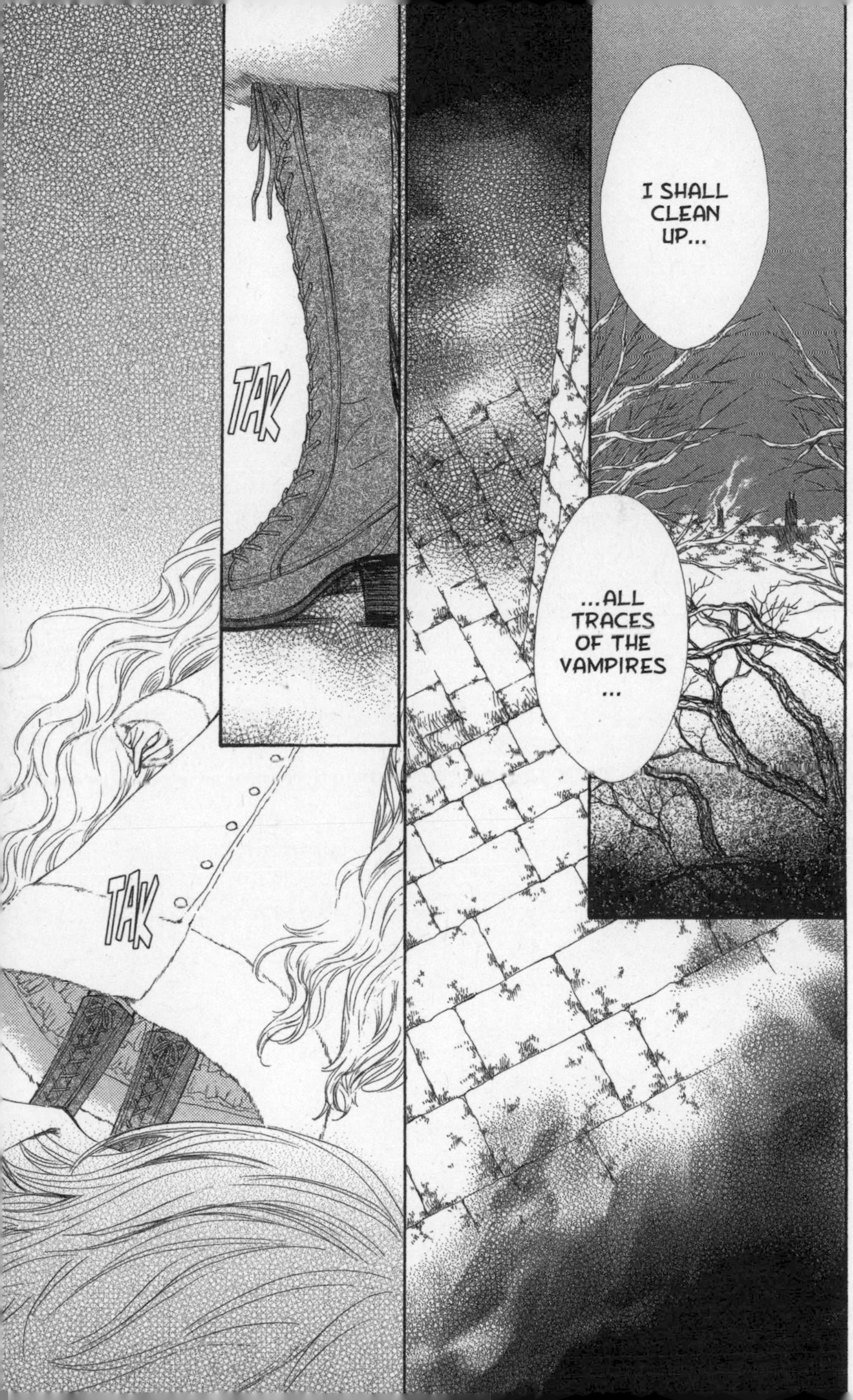
I SHALL CLEAN UP...
...ALL TRACES OF THE VAMPIRES ...
TAK
TAK

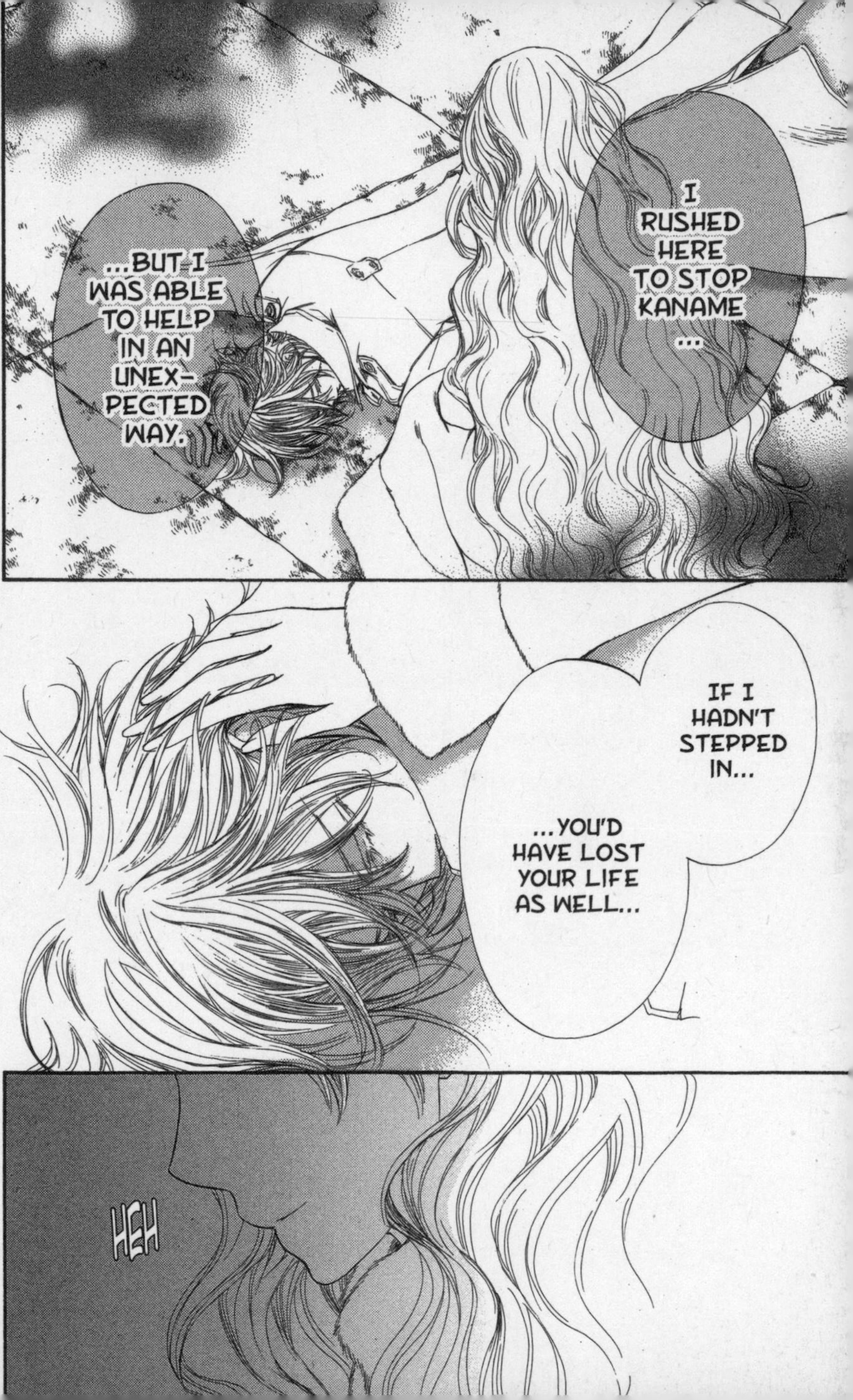
I RUSHED HERE TO STOP KANAME ...
...BUT I WAS ABLE TO HELP IN AN UNEX-PECTED WAY.
IF I HADN'T STEPPED IN...
...YOU'D HAVE LOST YOUR LIFE AS WELL...
HEH

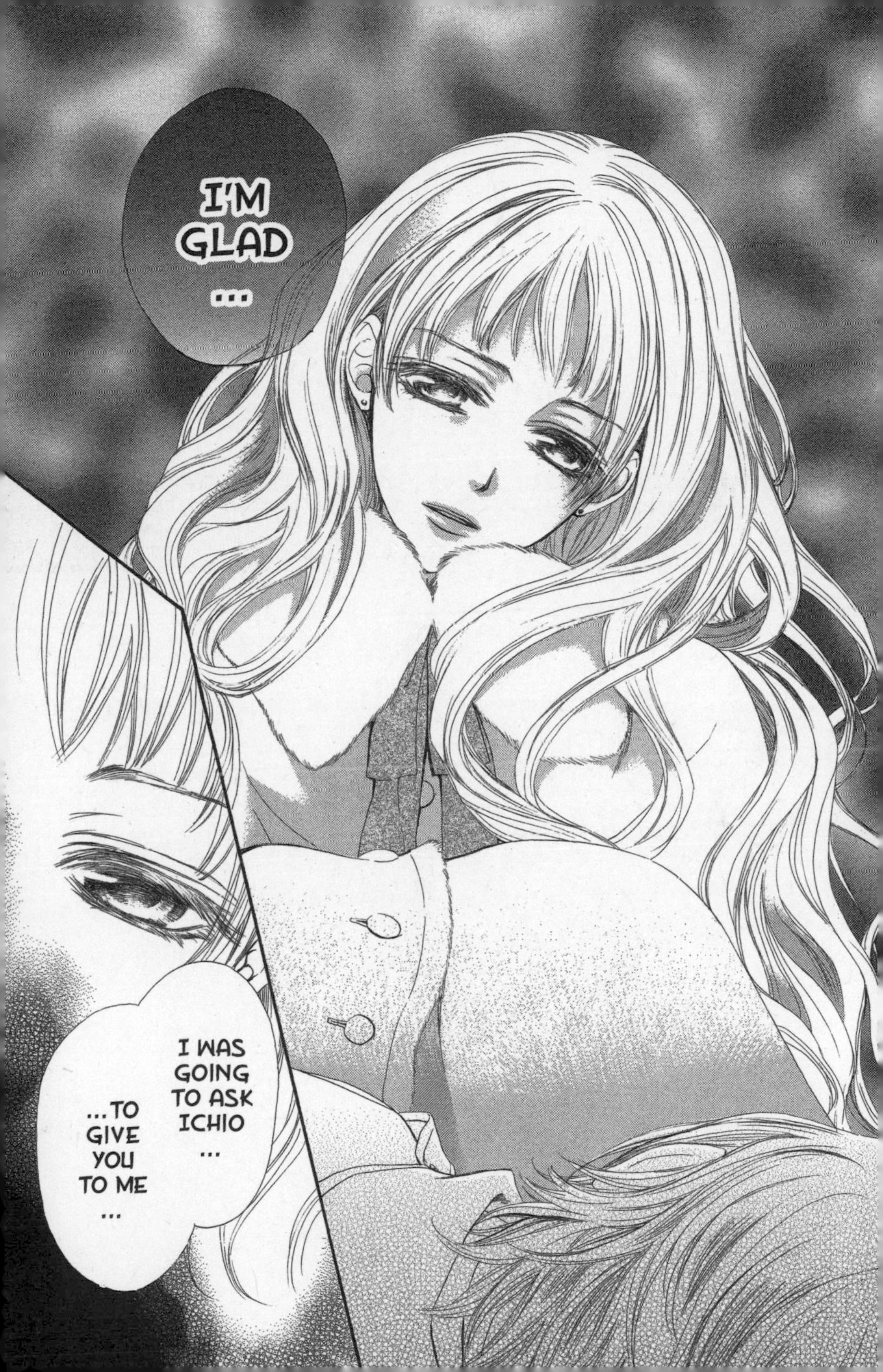
I'M GLAD ...
I WAS GOING TO ASK ICHIO ...
...TO GIVE YOU TO ME ...

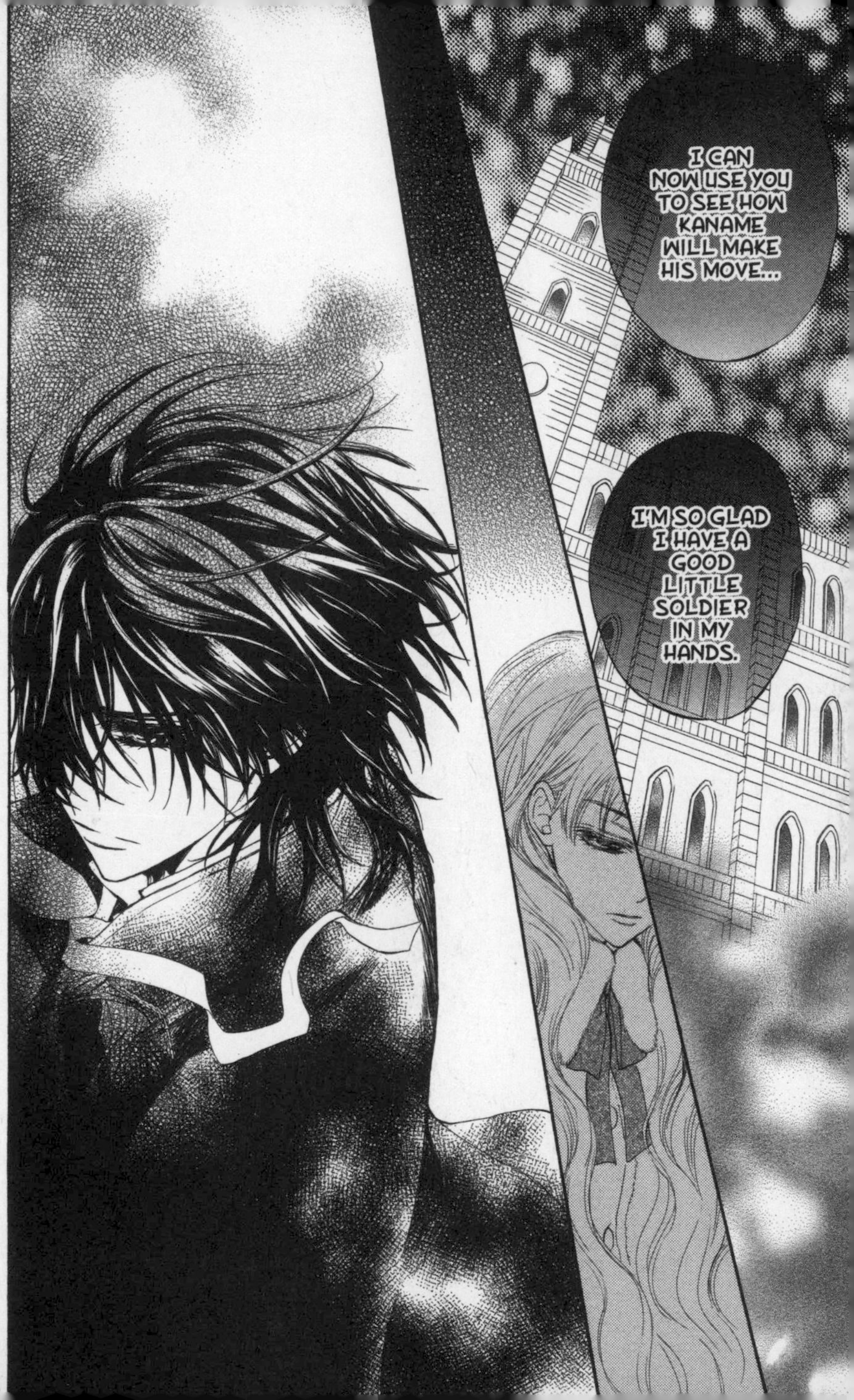
I CAN NOW USE YOU TO SEE HOW KANAME WILL MAKE HIS MOVE...
I'M SO GLAD I HAVE A GOOD LITTLE SOLDIER IN MY HANDS.

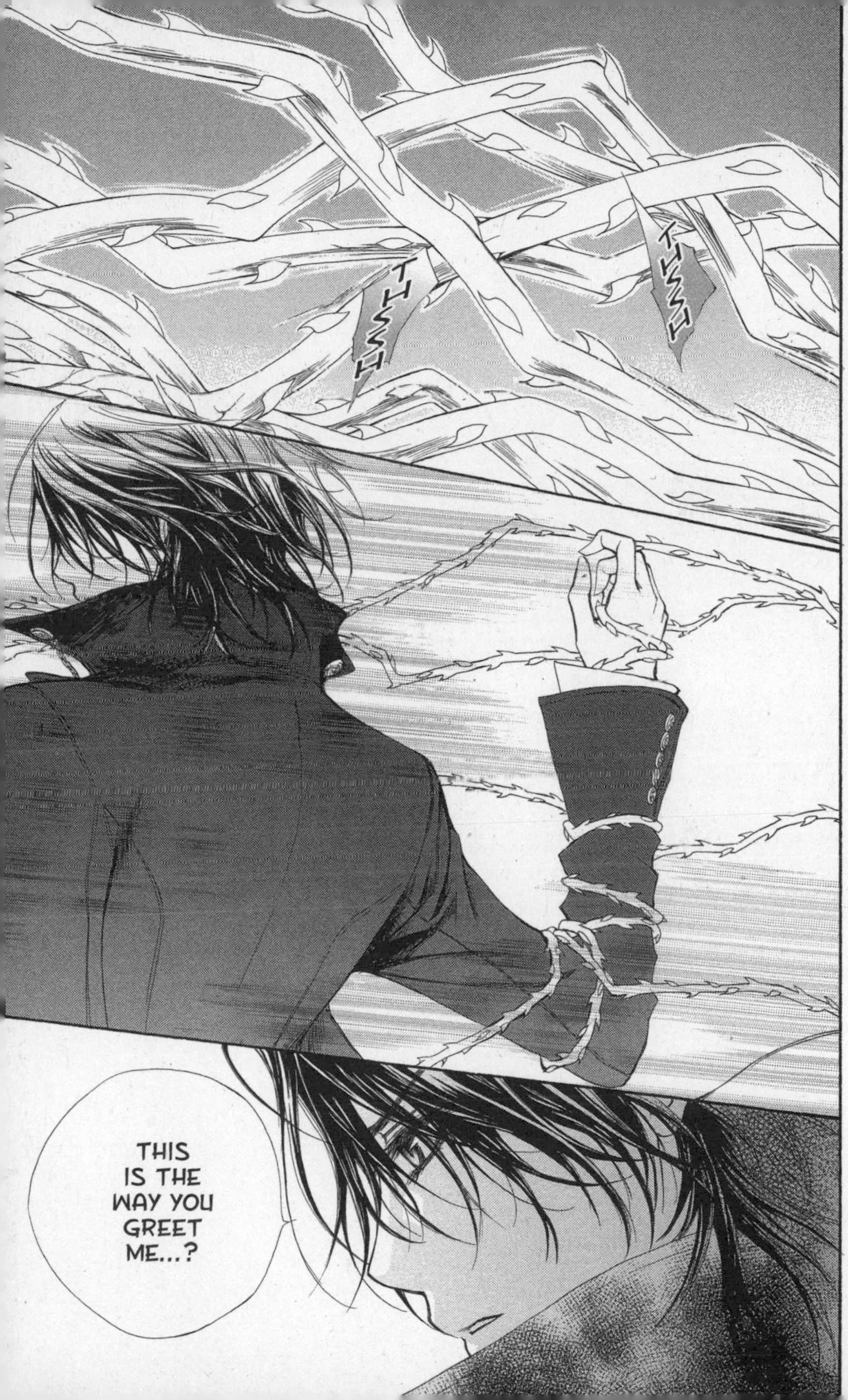
THWSH
THWSH
THIS IS THE WAY YOU GREET ME...?

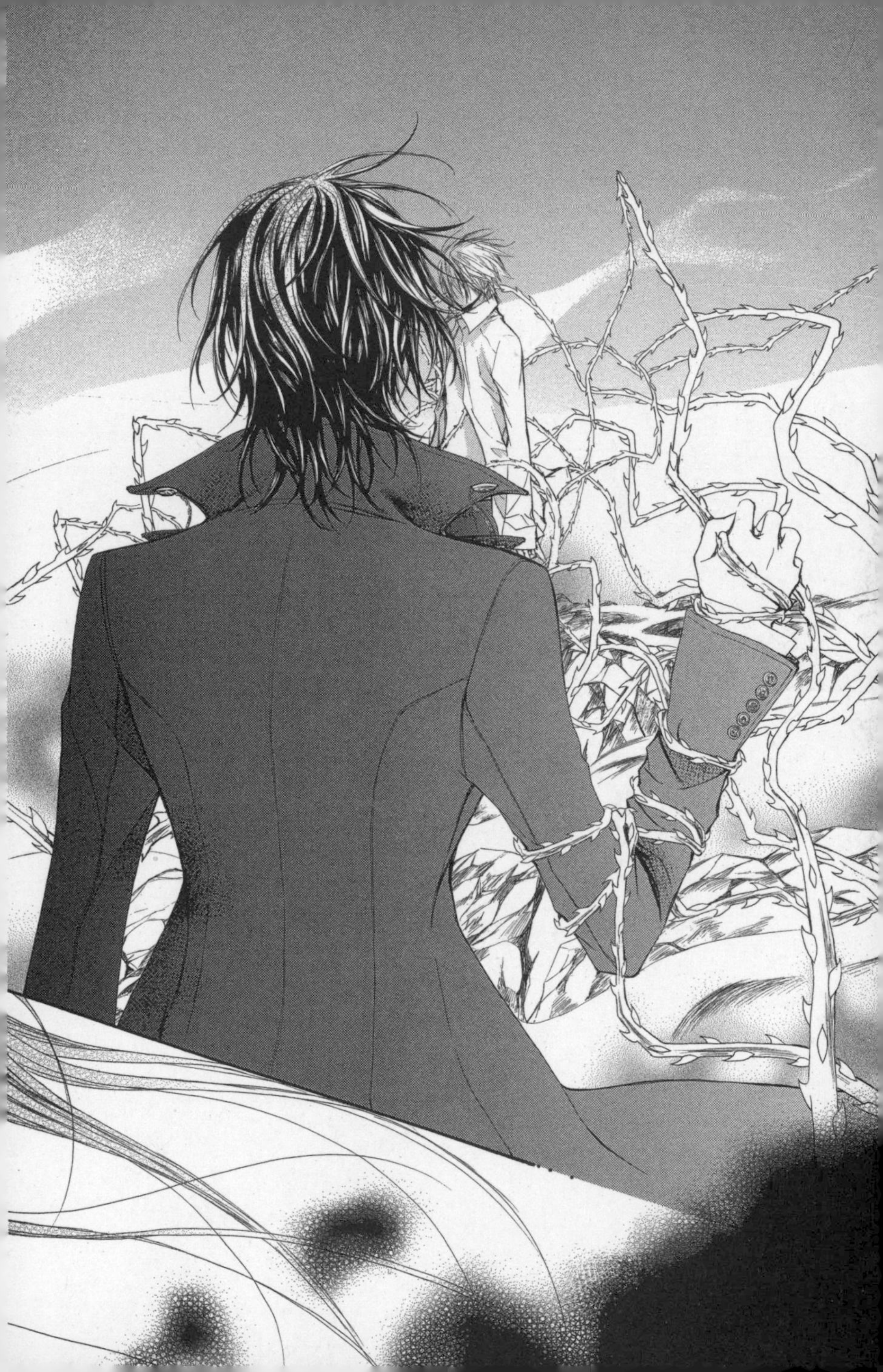

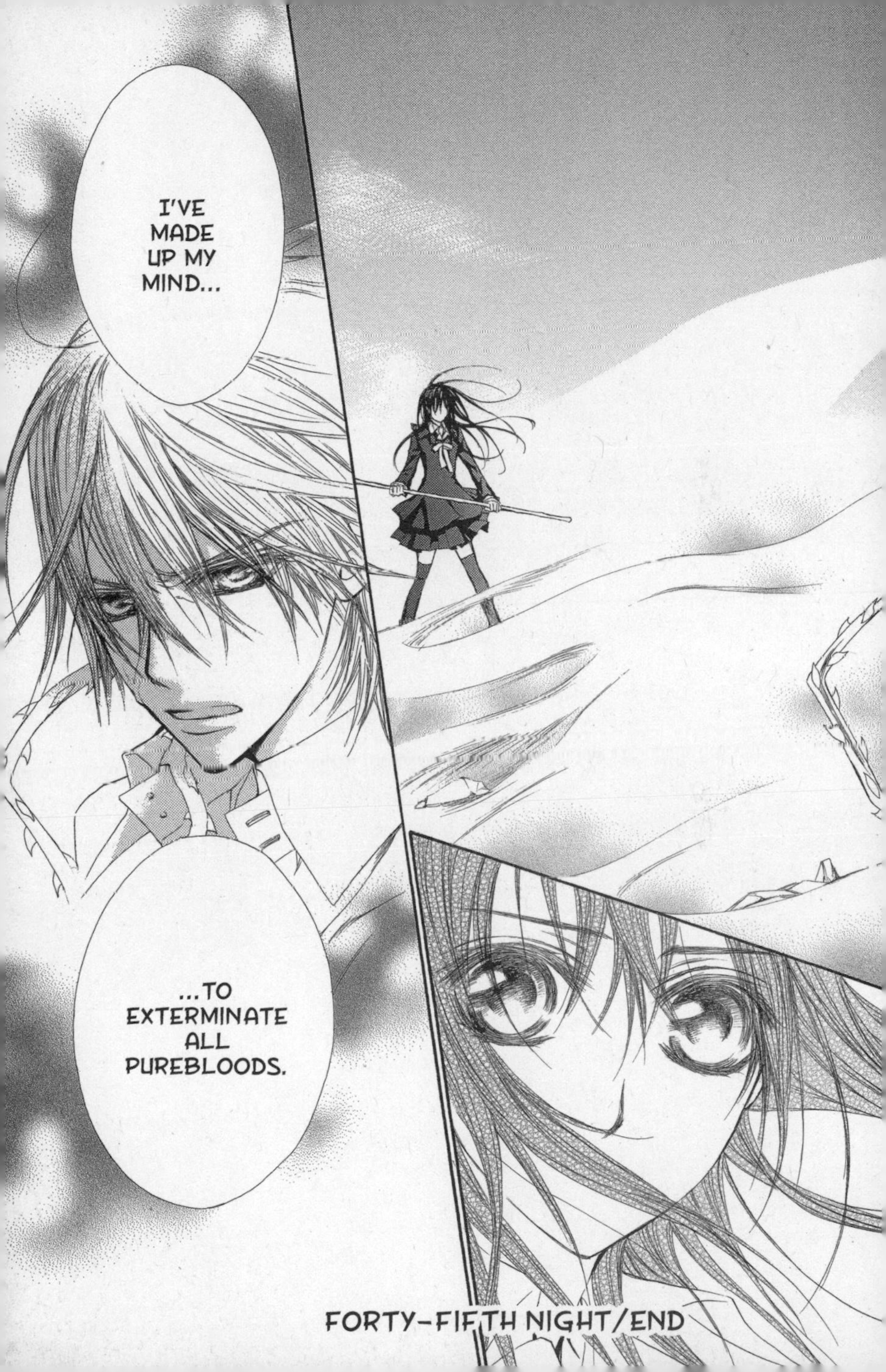
I'VE MADE UP MY MIND...
...TO EXTERMINATE ALL PUREBLOODS.
FORTY-FIFTH NIGHT/END

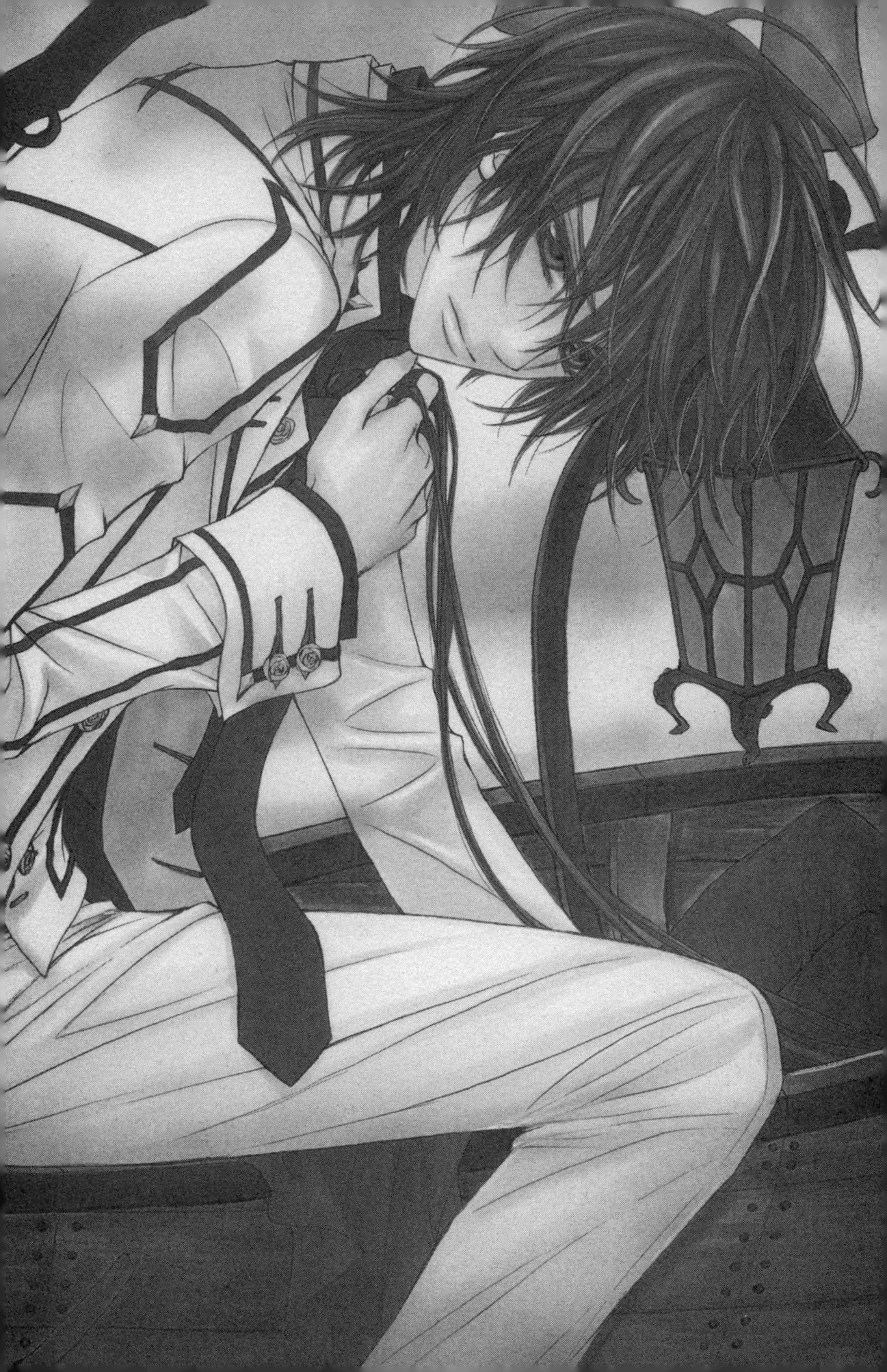

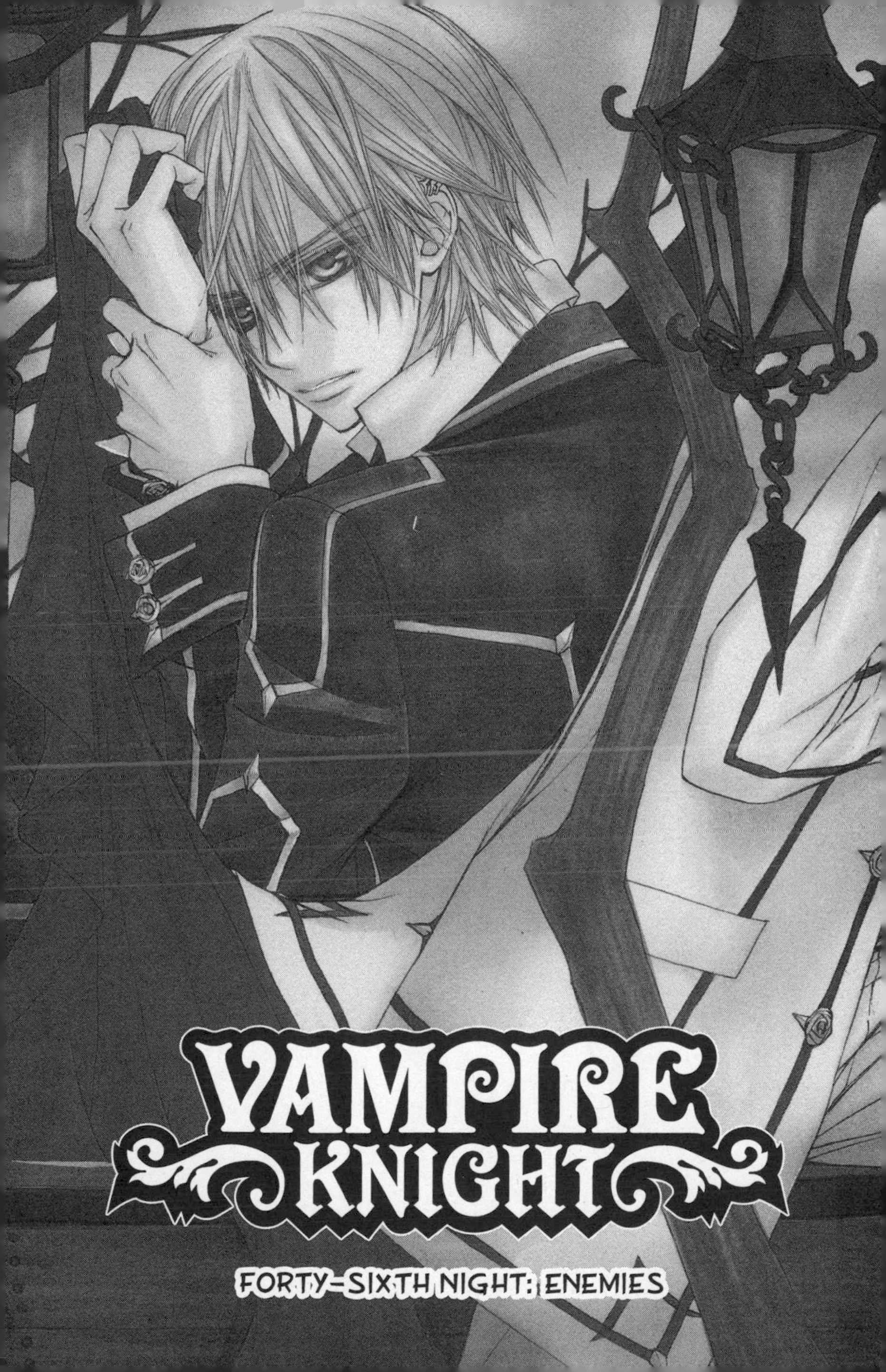
VAMPIRE KNIGHT
FORTY-SIXTH NIGHT: ENEMIES

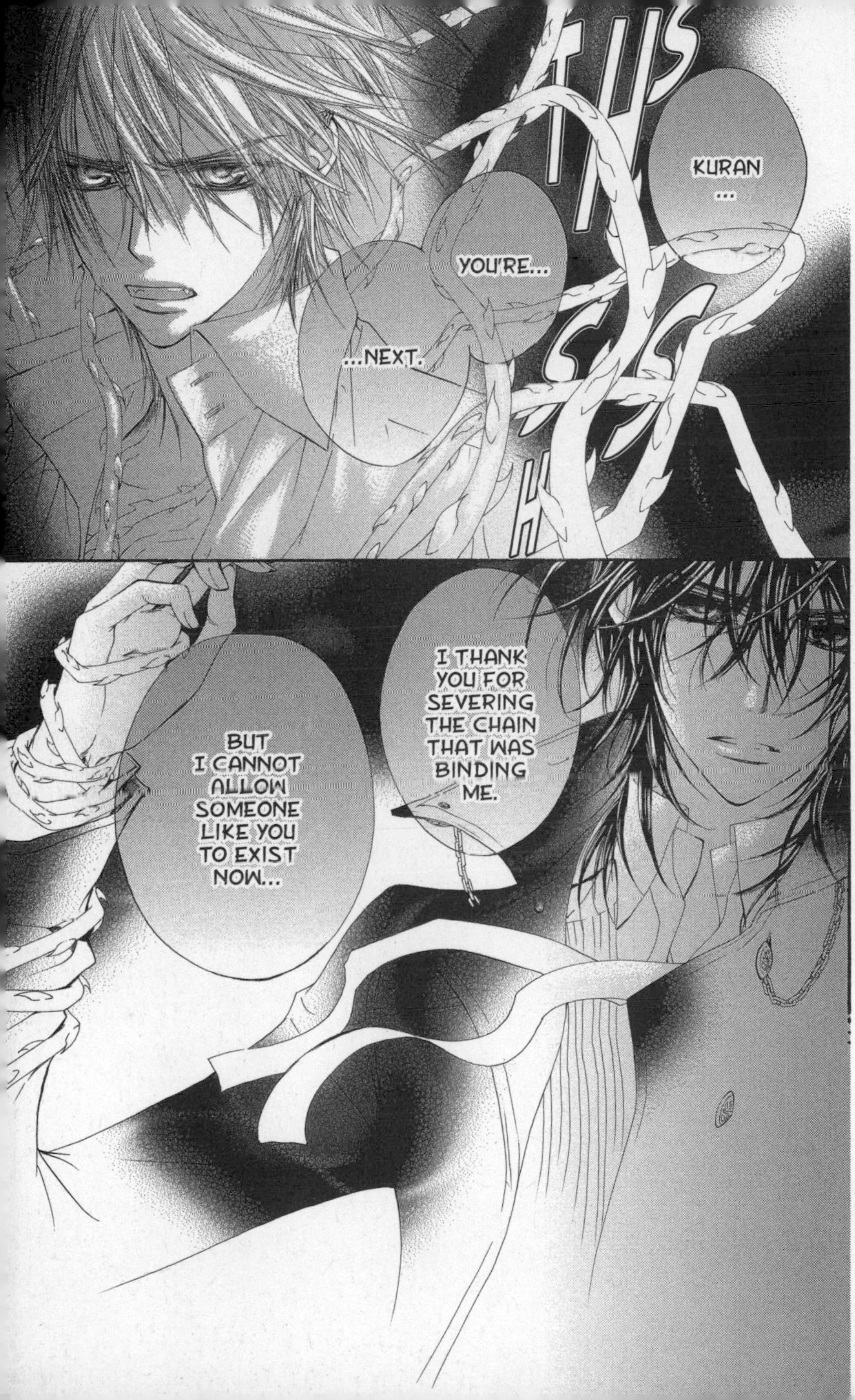
KURAN ...
YOU'RE...
...NEXT.
I THANK YOU FOR SEVERING THE CHAIN THAT WAS BINDING ME.
BUT I CANNOT ALLOW SOMEONE LIKE YOU TO EXIST NOW...

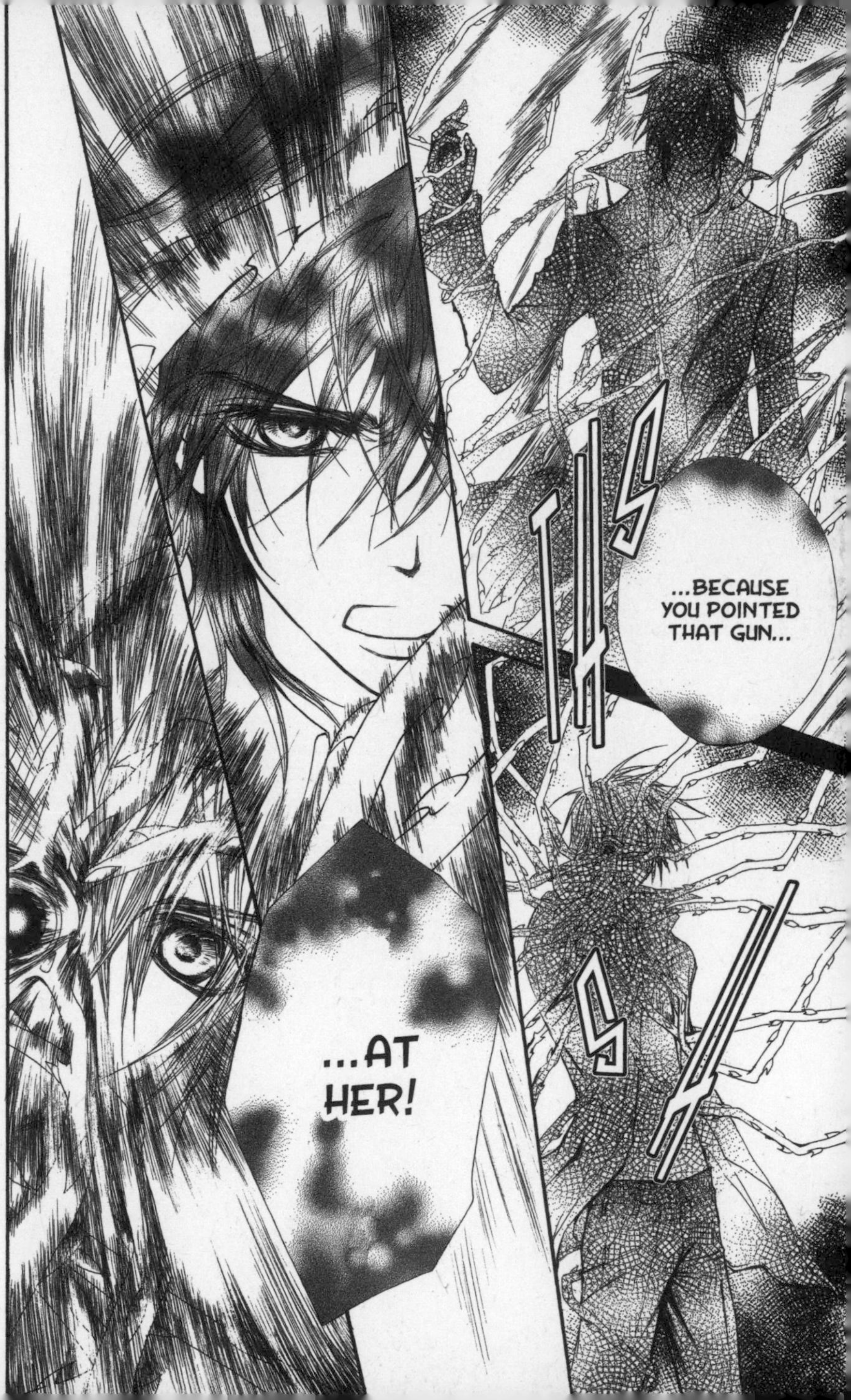
...BECAUSE YOU POINTED THAT GUN...
...AT HER!

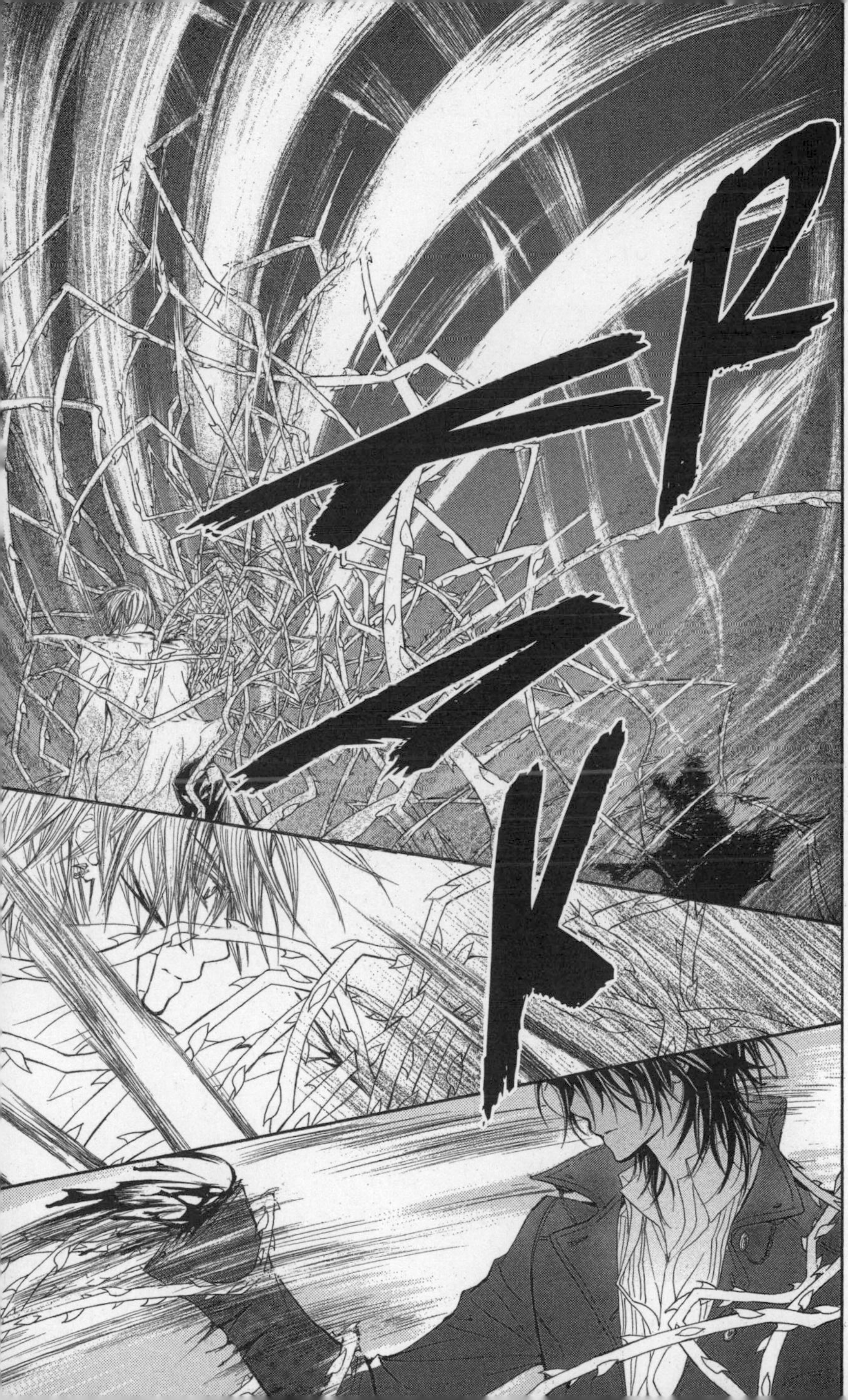

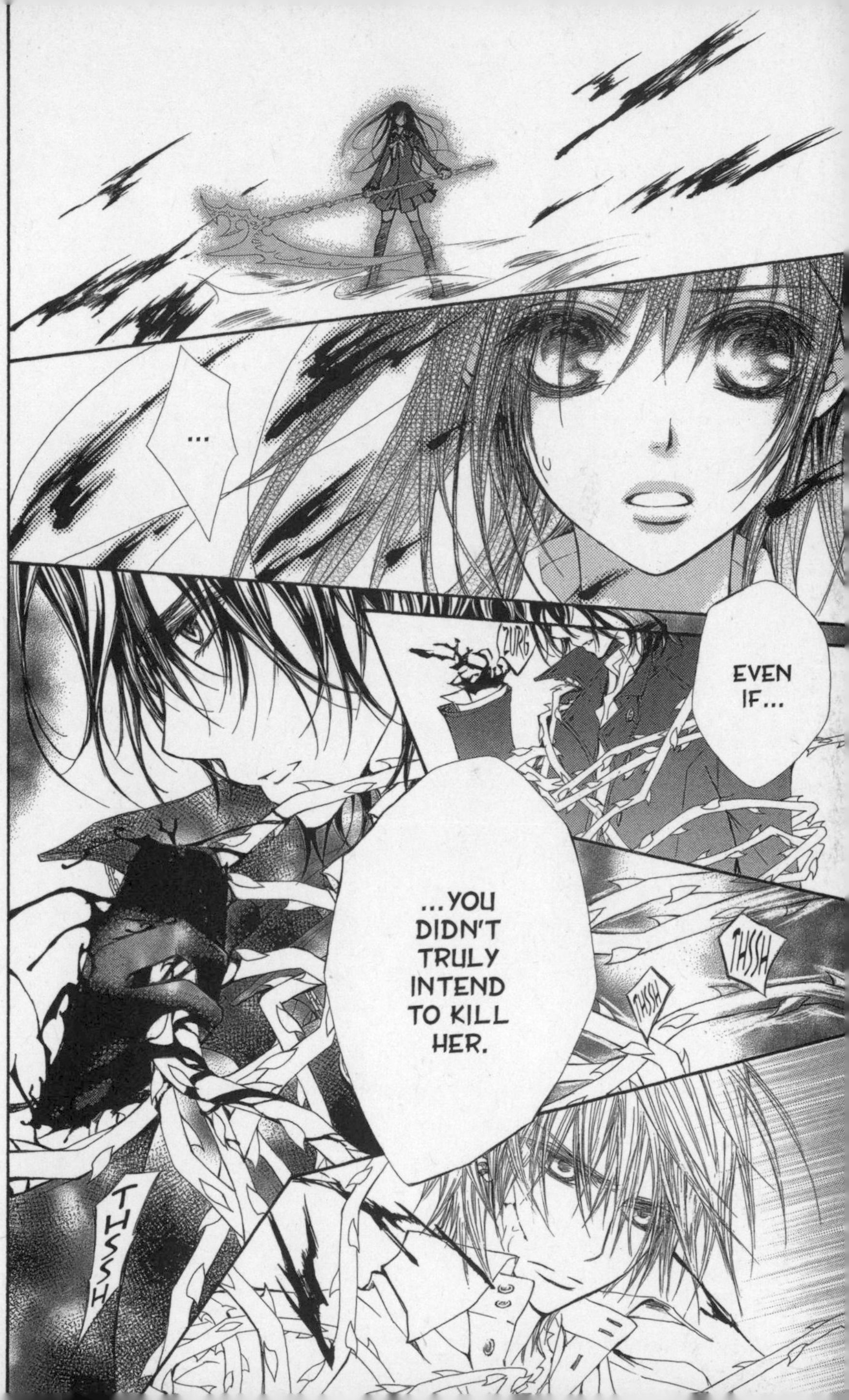
...
ZURG
EVEN IF...
...YOU DIDN'T TRULY INTEND TO KILL HER.
THSSH
THSSH
THSSH

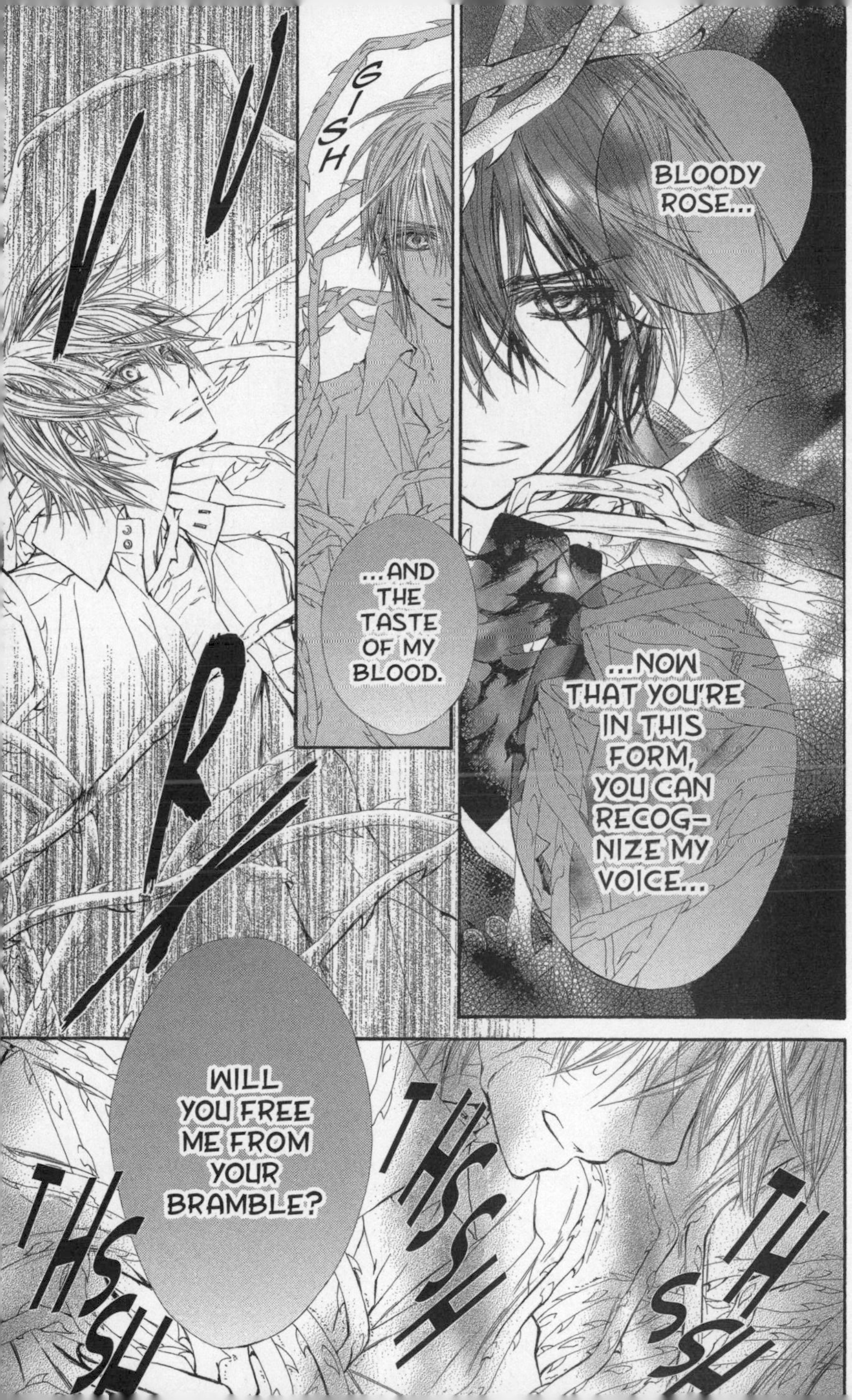
BLOODY ROSE...
...NOW THAT YOU'RE IN THIS FORM, YOU CAN RECOG- NIZE MY VOICE...
GISH
...AND THE TASTE OF MY BLOOD.
WILL YOU FREE ME FROM YOUR BRAMBLE?

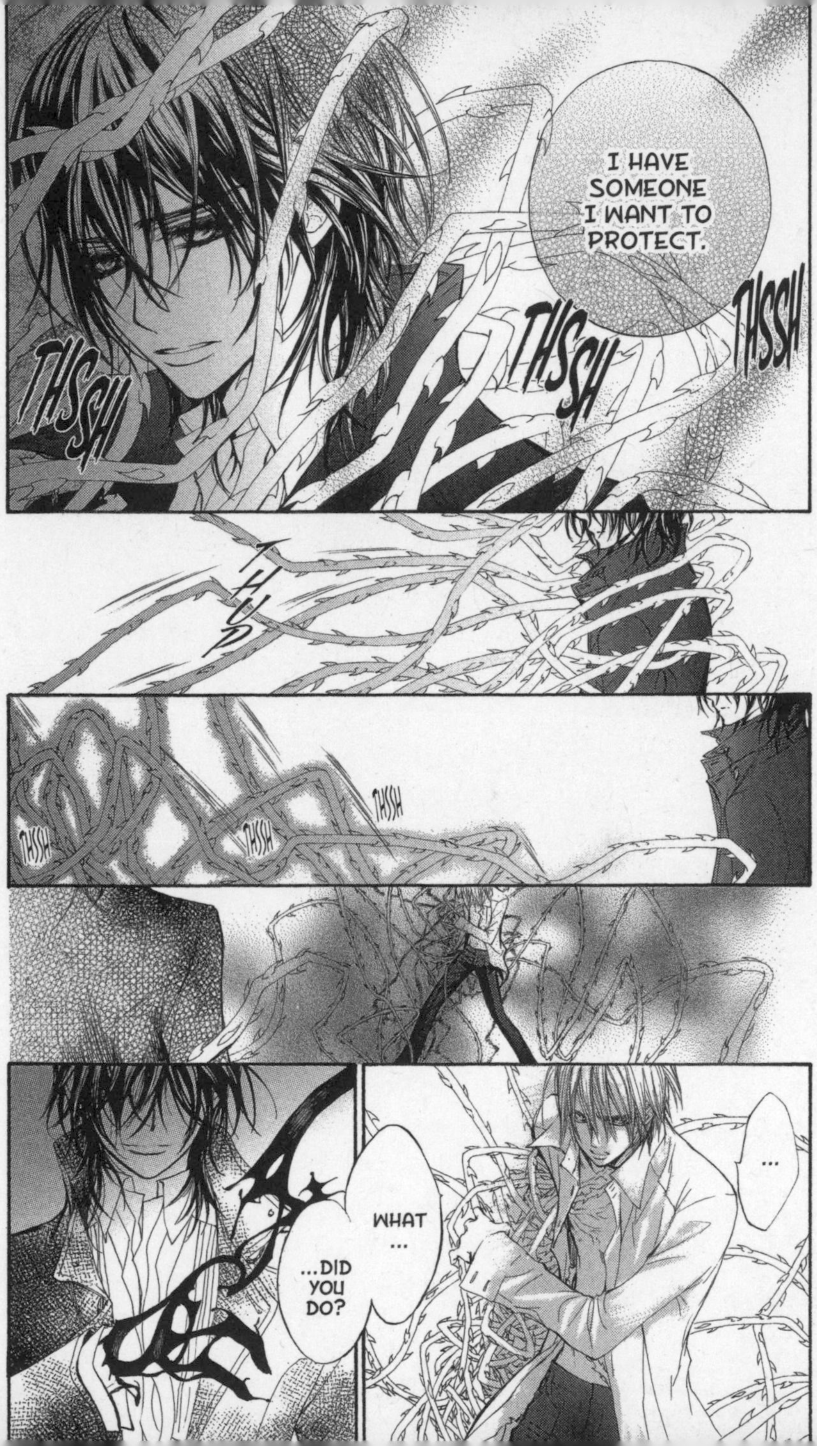
I HAVE SOMEONE I WANT TO PROTECT.
THSSH
THSSH
THSSH
THUD
THSSH
THSSH
THSSH
...
WHAT ...
...DID YOU DO?

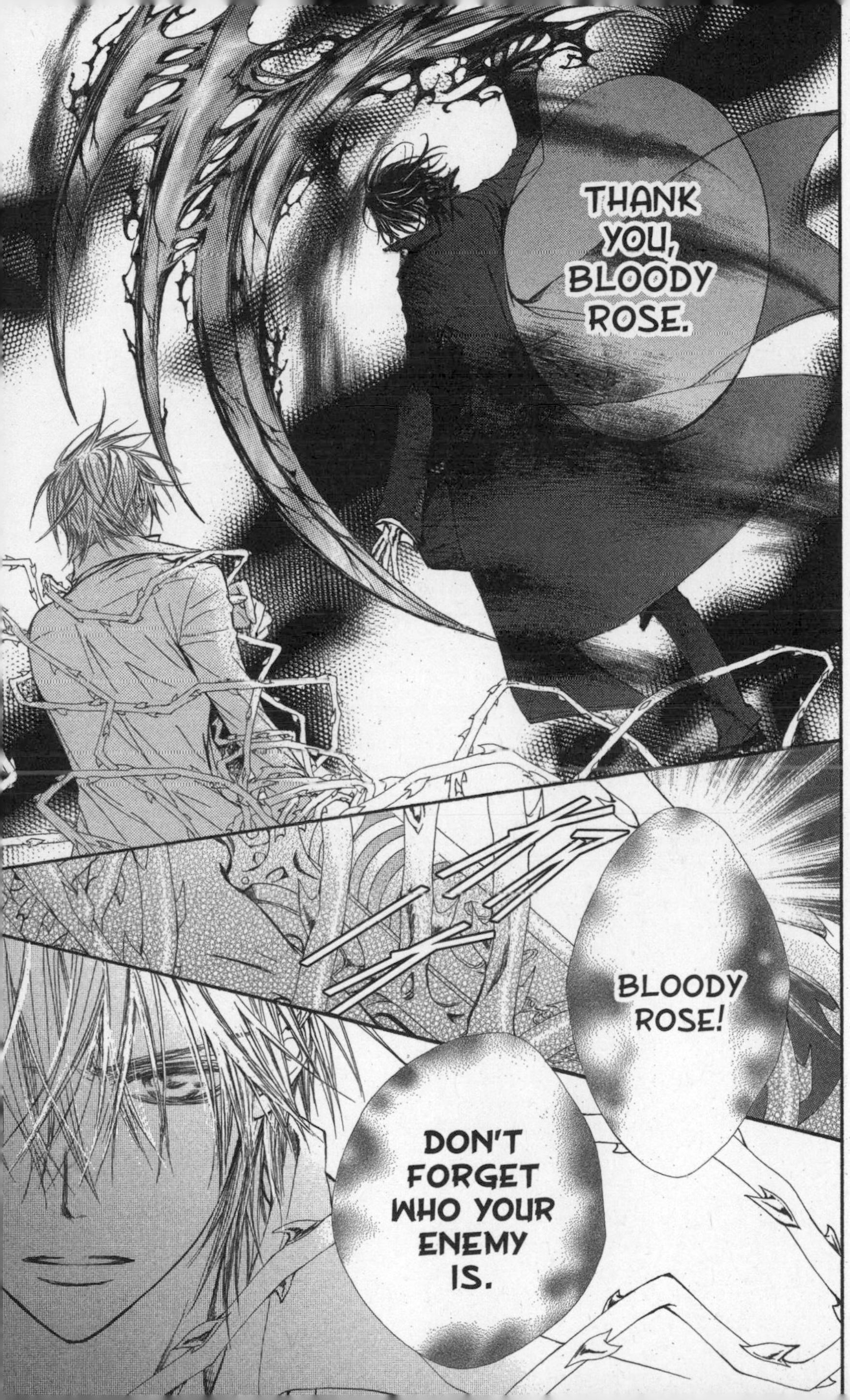
THANK YOU, BLOODY ROSE.
BLOODY ROSE!
DON'T FORGET WHO YOUR ENEMY IS.

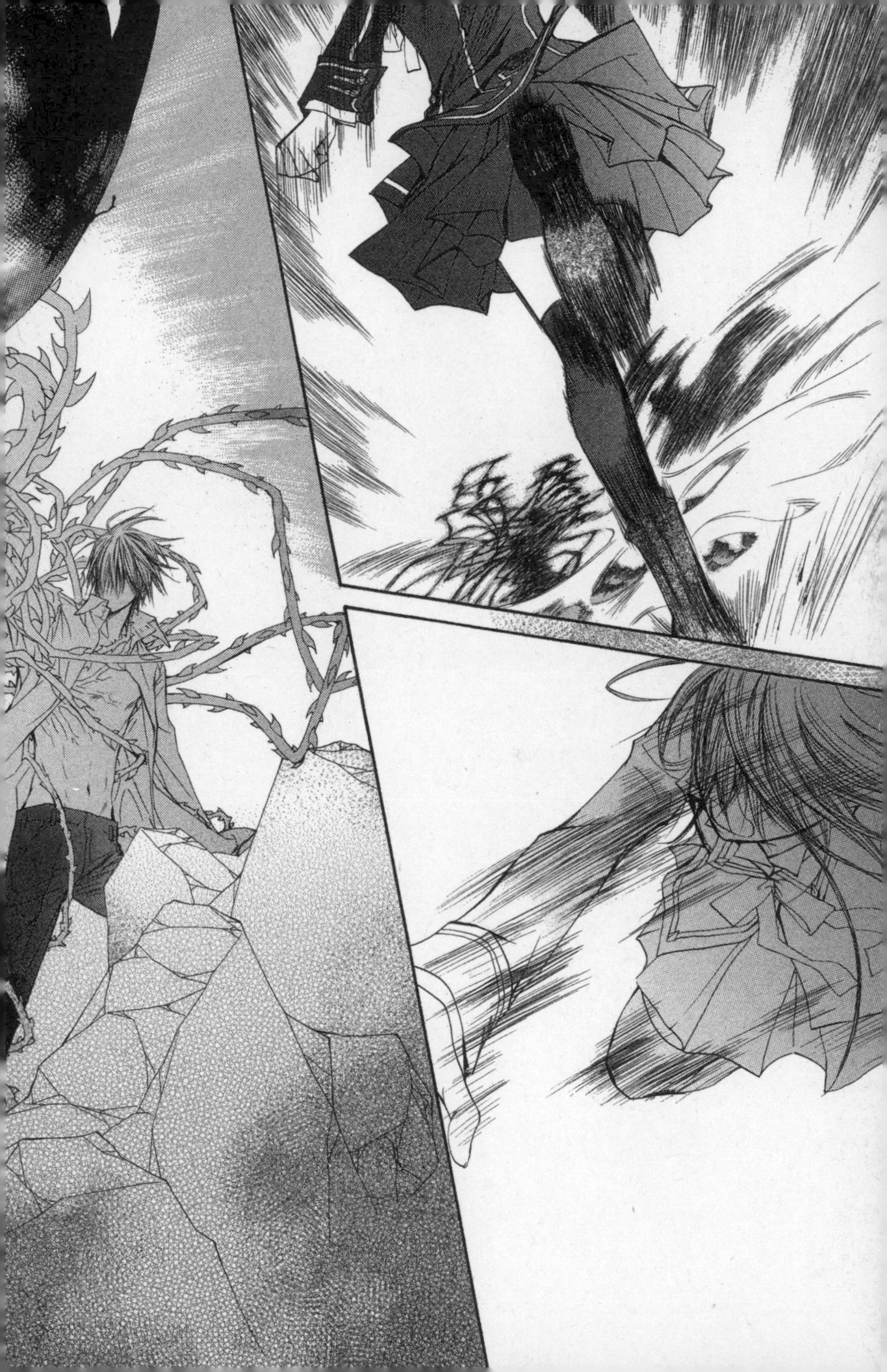

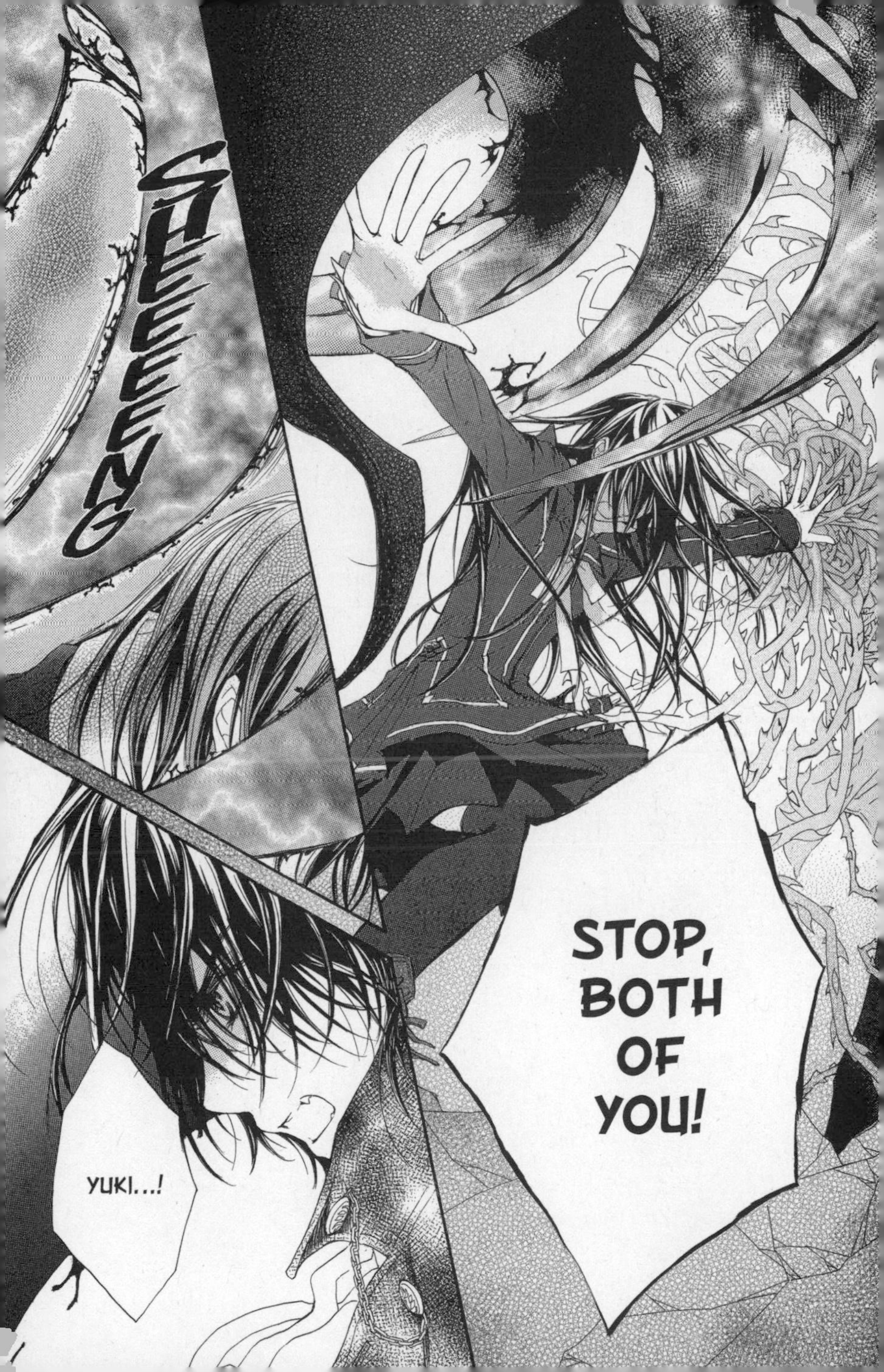
SHEEEENG
STOP, BOTH OF YOU!
YUKI...!

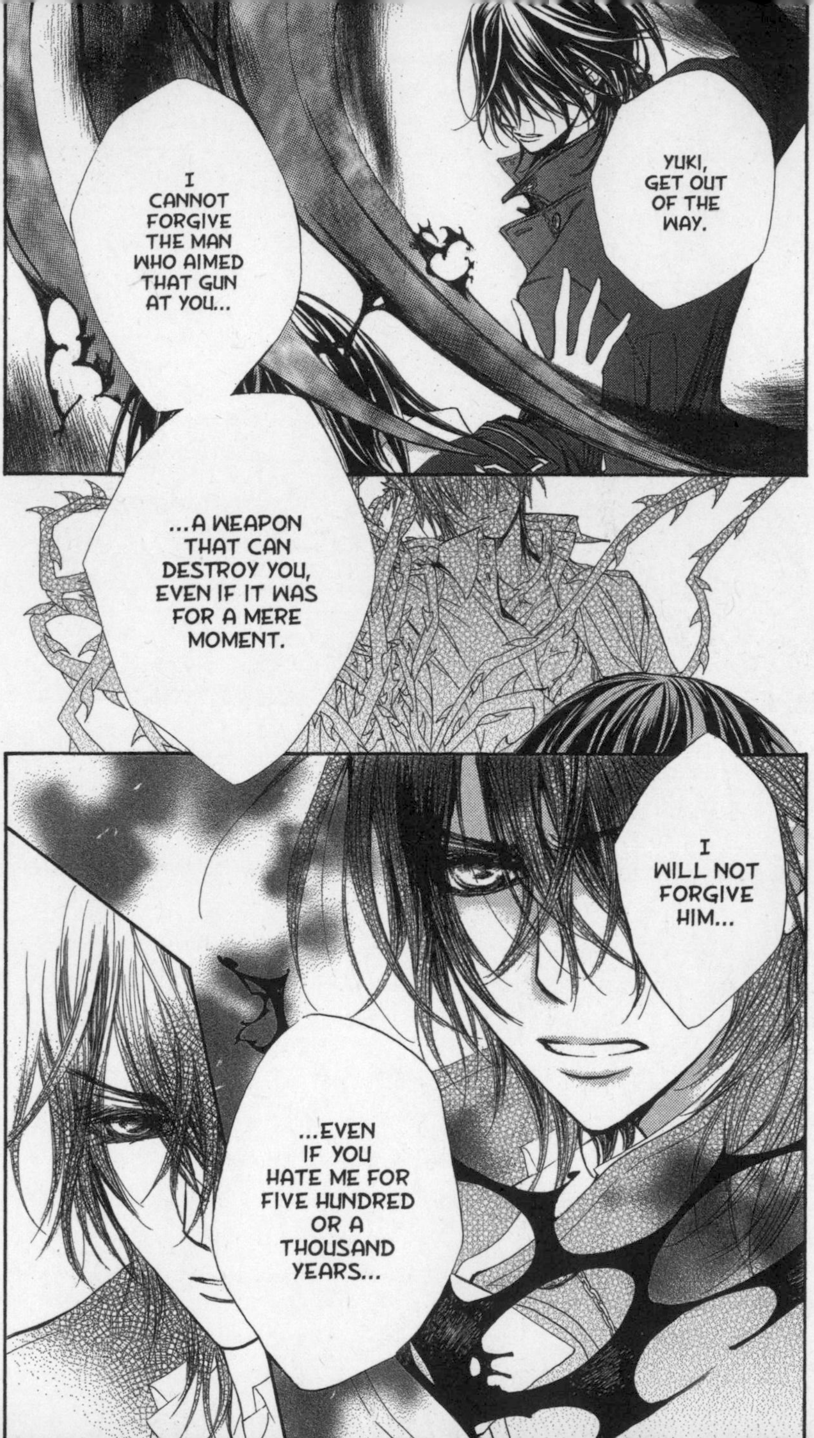
YUKI, GET OUT OF THE WAY.
I CANNOT FORGIVE THE MAN WHO AIMED THAT GUN AT YOU...
...A WEAPON THAT CAN DESTROY YOU, EVEN IF IT WAS FOR A MERE MOMENT.
I WILL NOT FORGIVE HIM...
...EVEN IF YOU HATE ME FOR FIVE HUNDRED OR A THOUSAND YEARS...

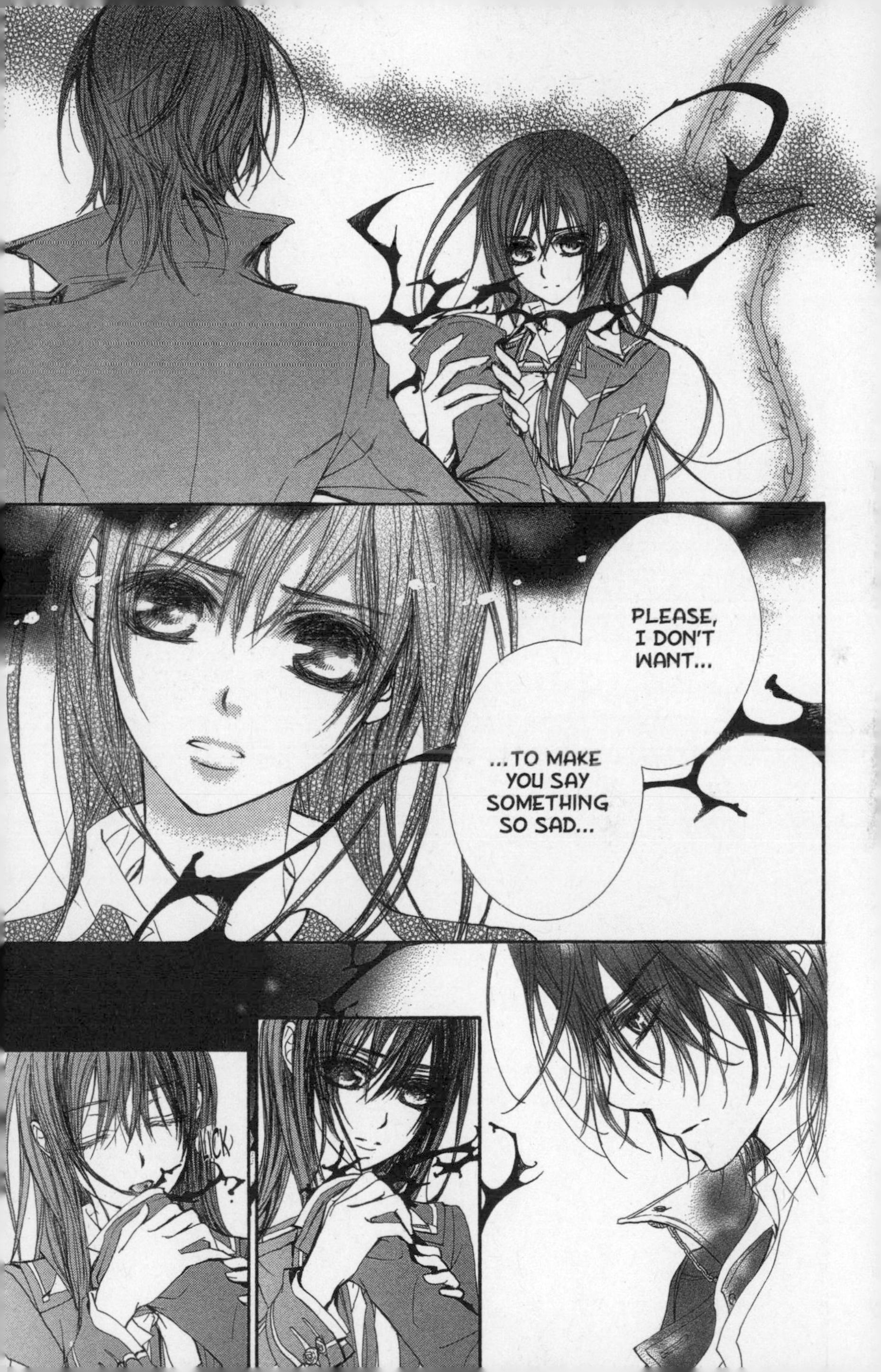
PLEASE, I DON'T WANT...
...TO MAKE YOU SAY SOMETHING SO SAD...
LICK
?

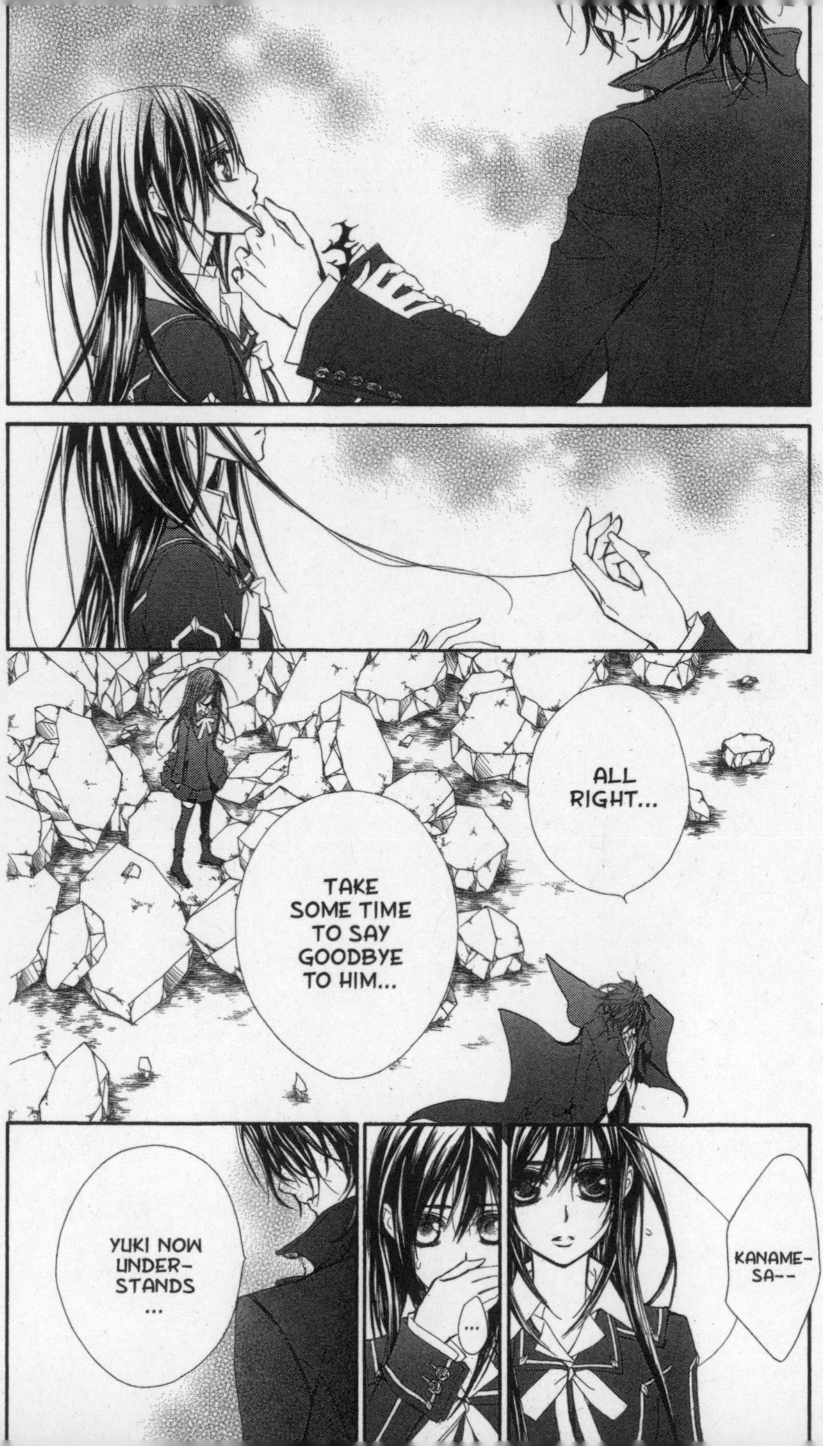
ALL RIGHT...
TAKE SOME TIME TO SAY GOODBYE TO HIM...
KANAME-SA--
...
YUKI NOW UNDER-STANDS ...

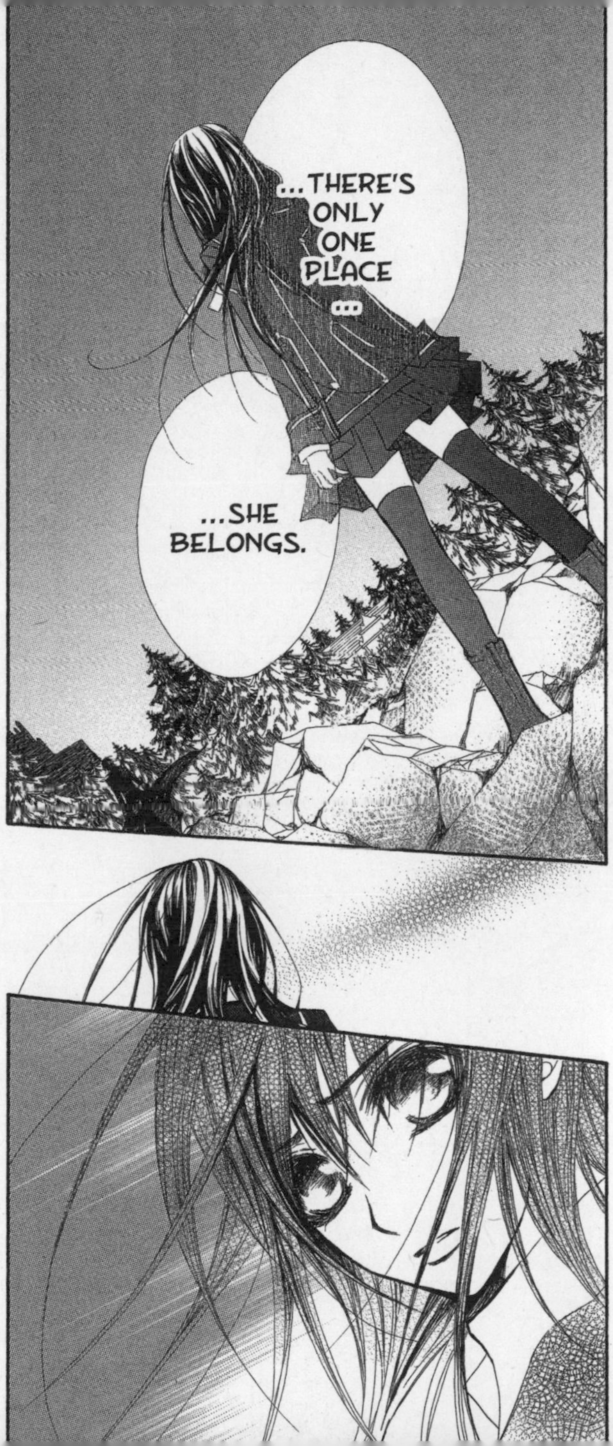
...THERE'S ONLY ONE PLACE ...
...SHE BELONGS.

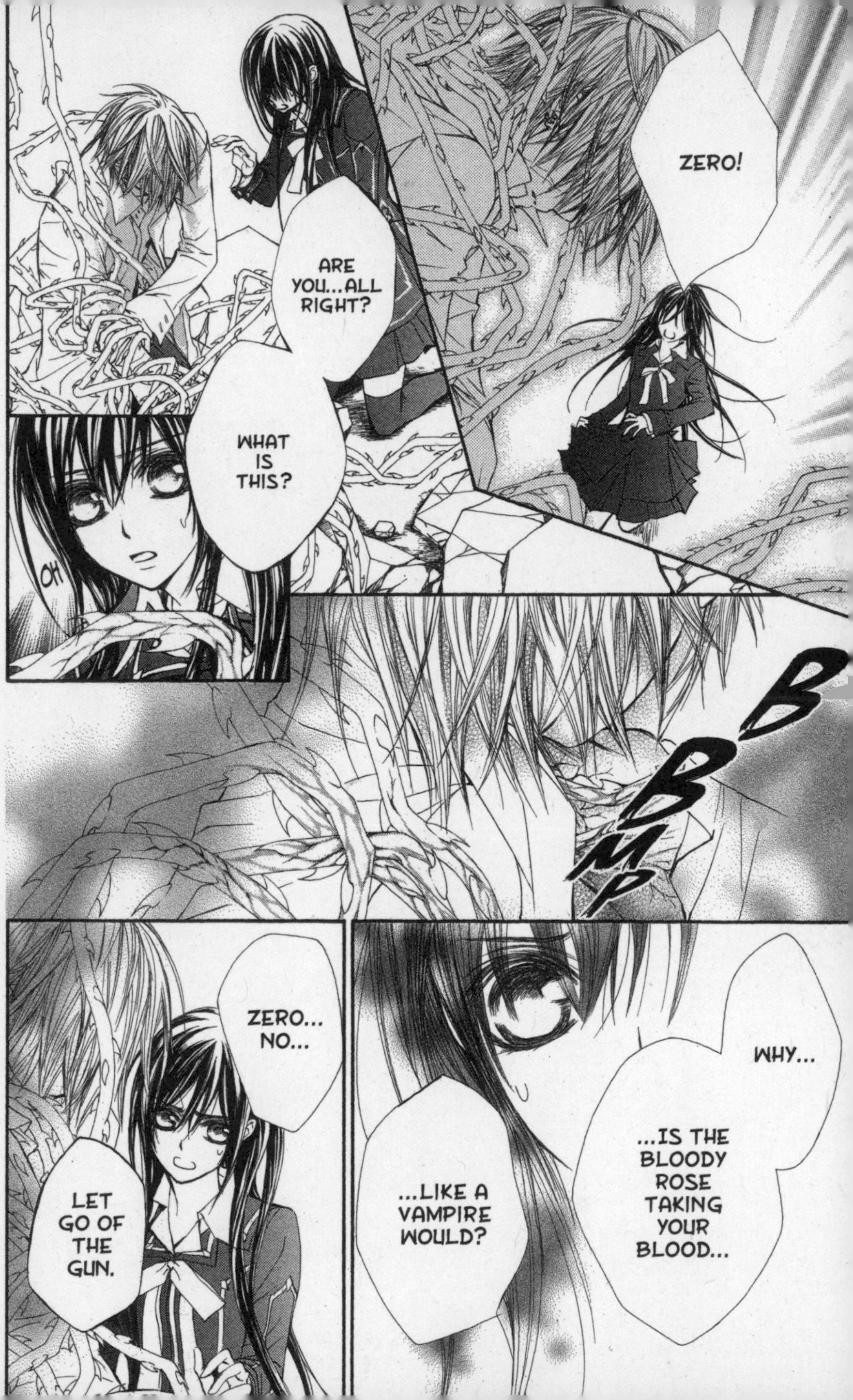
ZERO!
ARE YOU...ALL RIGHT?
WHAT IS THIS?
OH
BBMP
WHY...
...IS THE BLOODY ROSE TAKING YOUR BLOOD...
...LIKE A VAMPIRE WOULD?
ZERO... NO...
LET GO OF THE GUN.

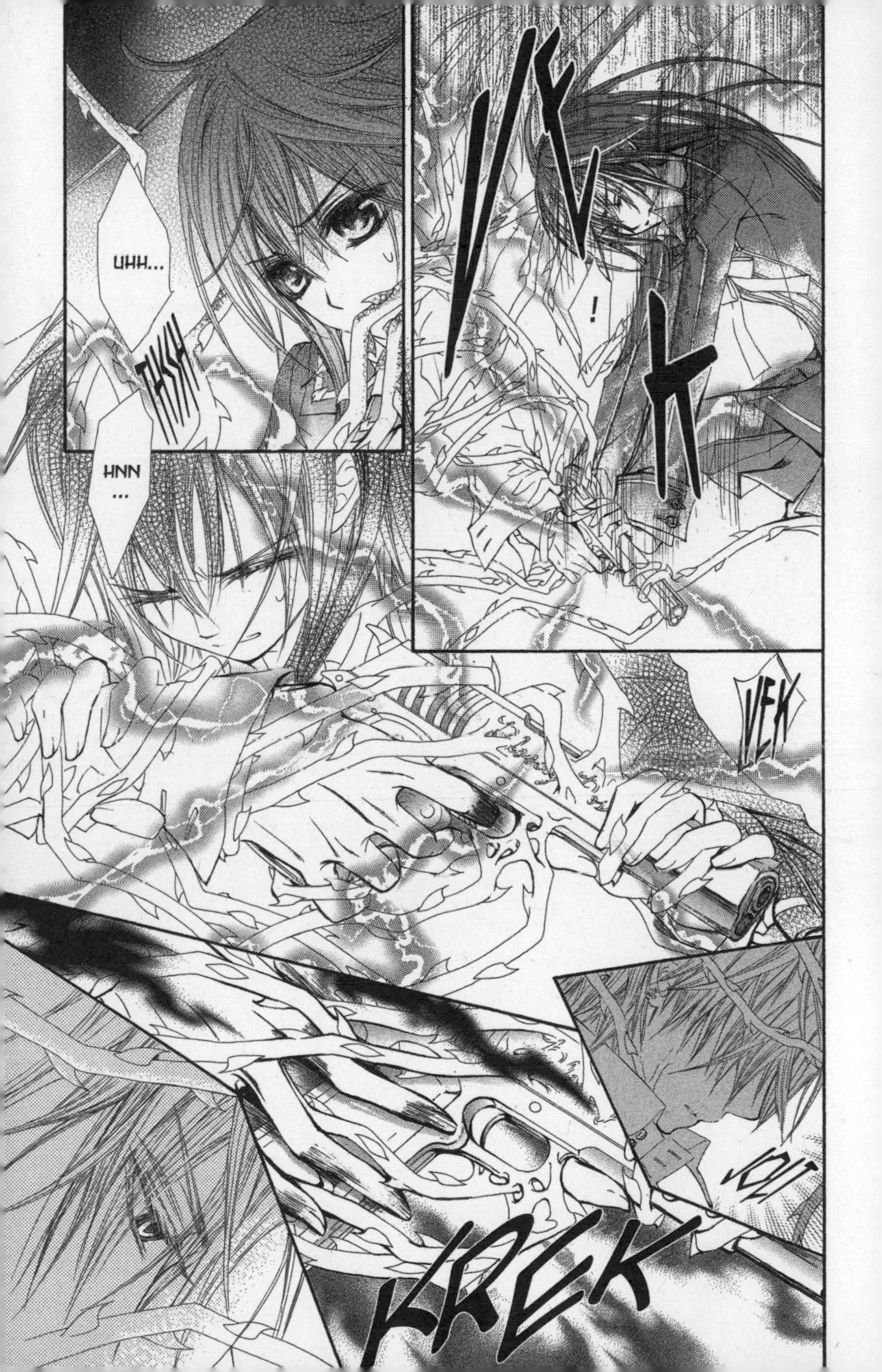
!
UHH...
THSH
HNN ...
VEK
JOLT
KRCK

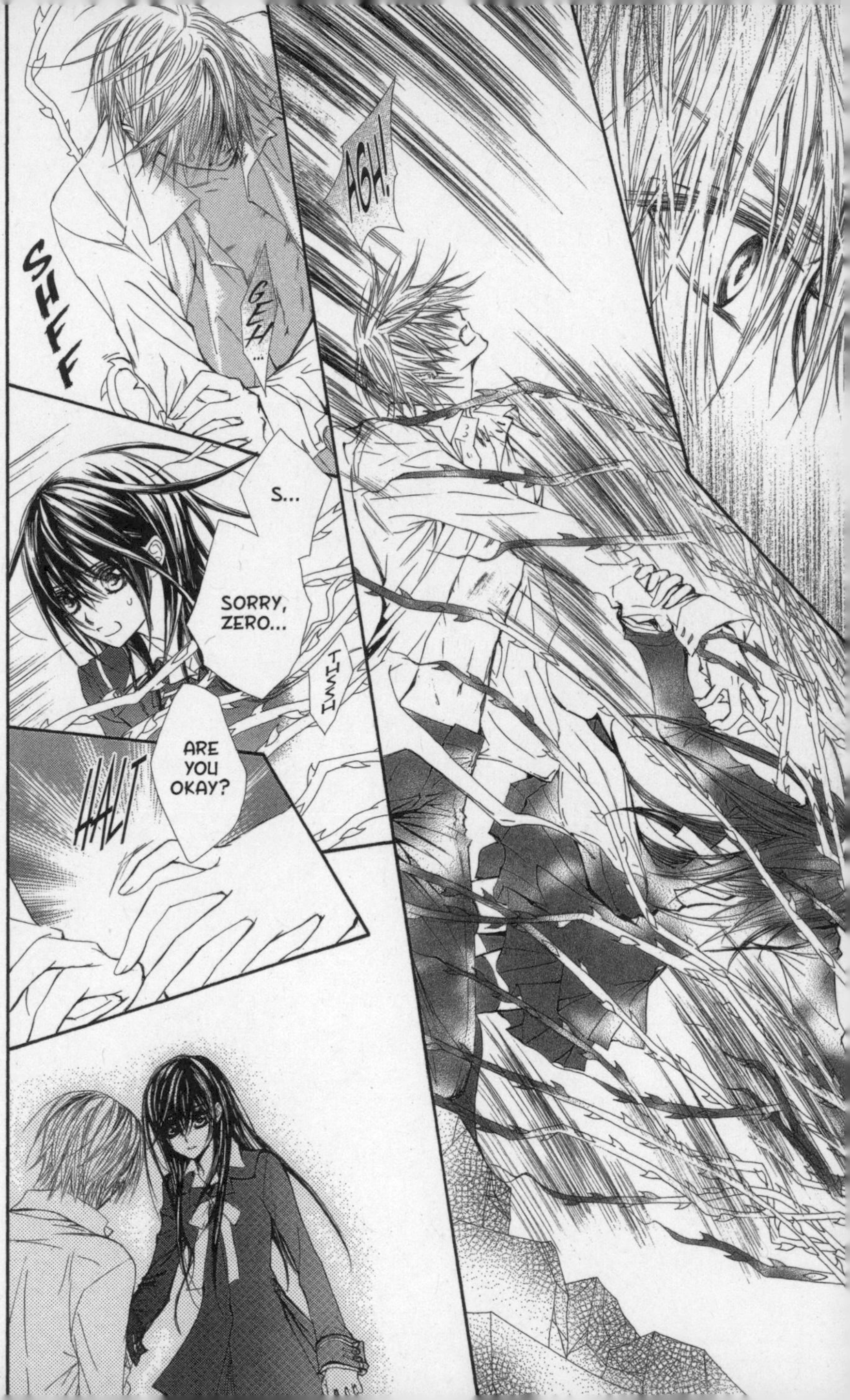
AGH!
SHFF
GEH...
S...
SORRY, ZERO...
TWIST
ARE YOU OKAY?
HALT

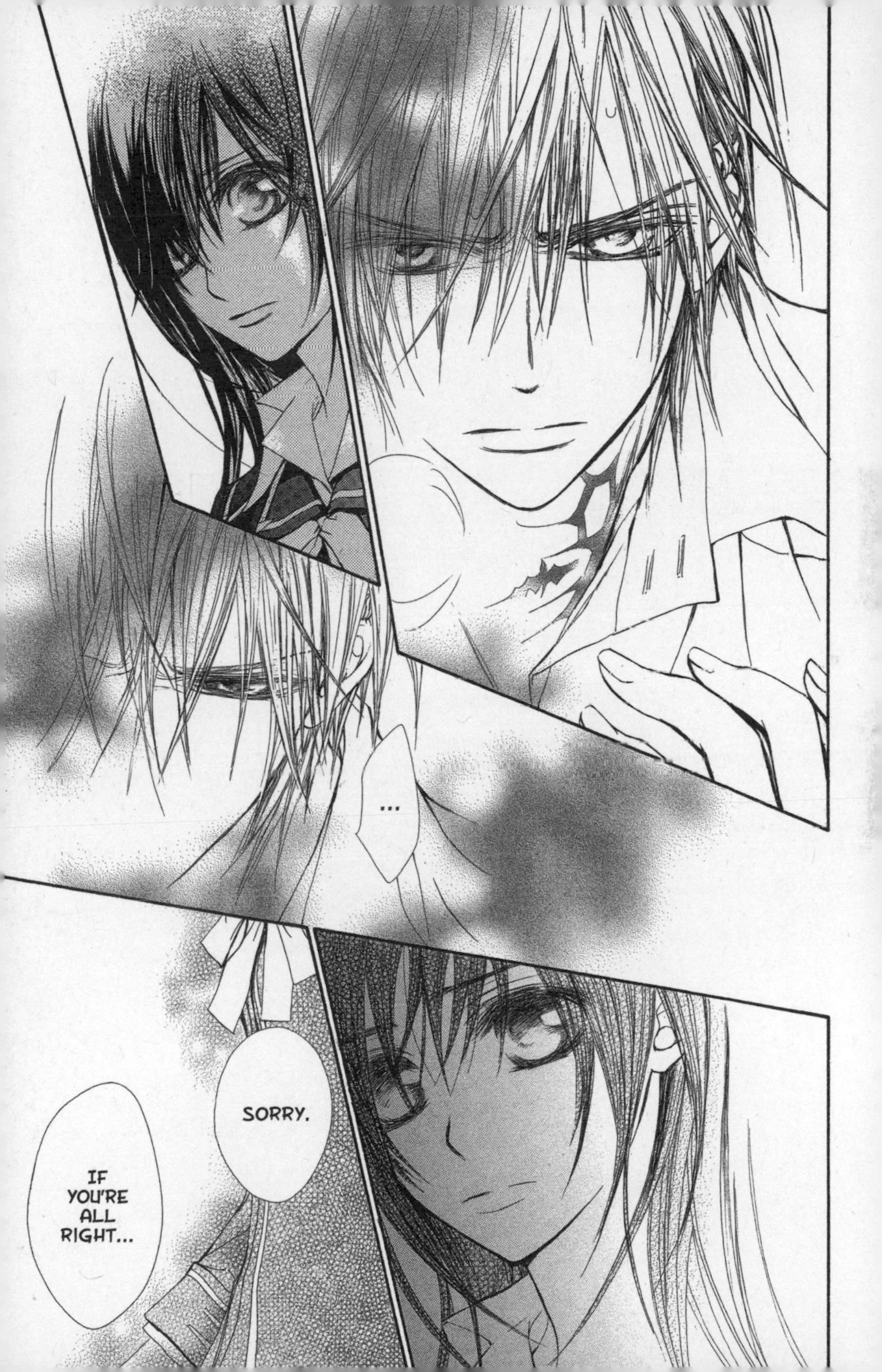
...
SORRY.
IF YOU'RE ALL RIGHT...

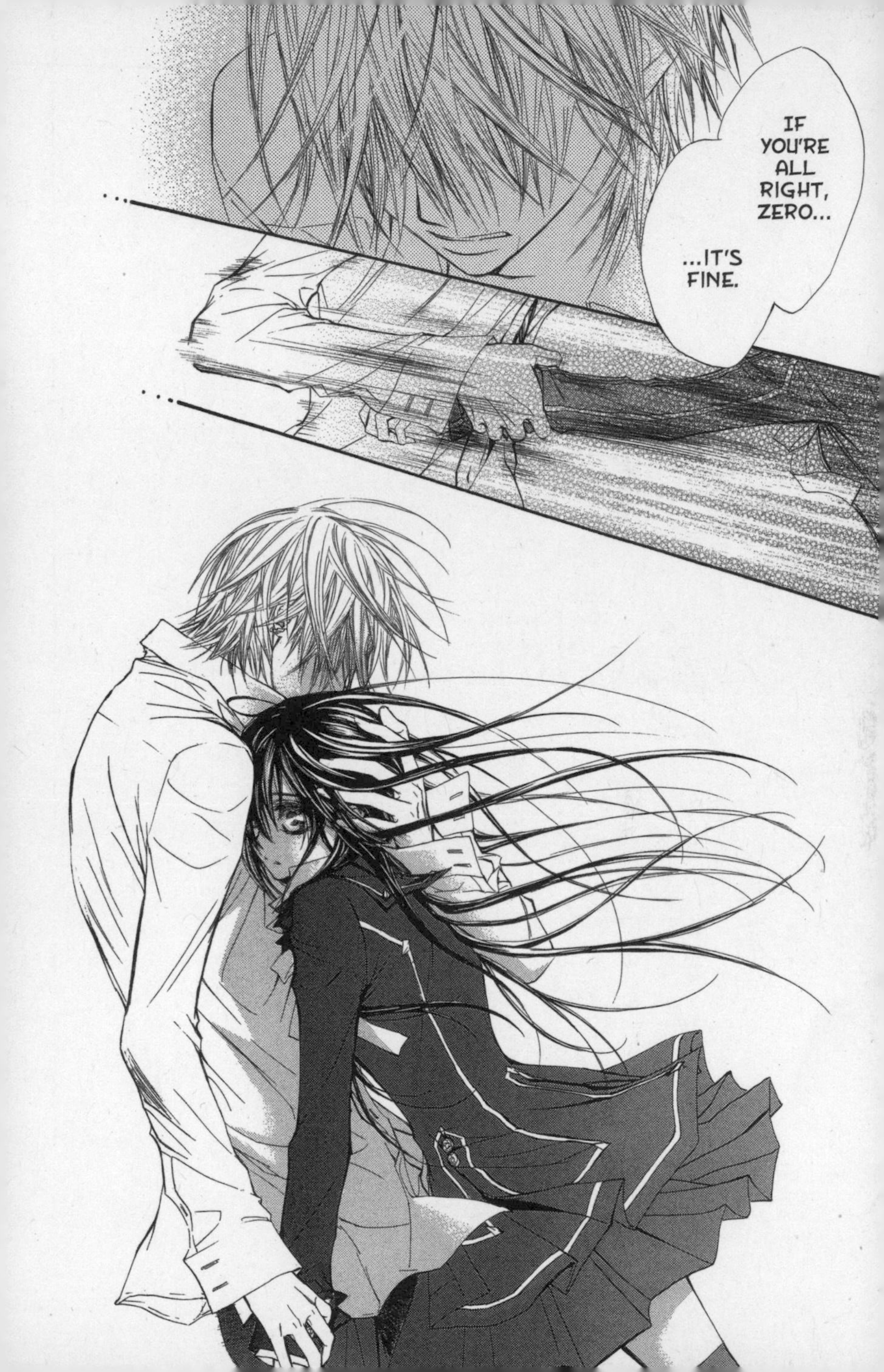
IF YOU'RE ALL RIGHT, ZERO...
...IT'S FINE.
...
...

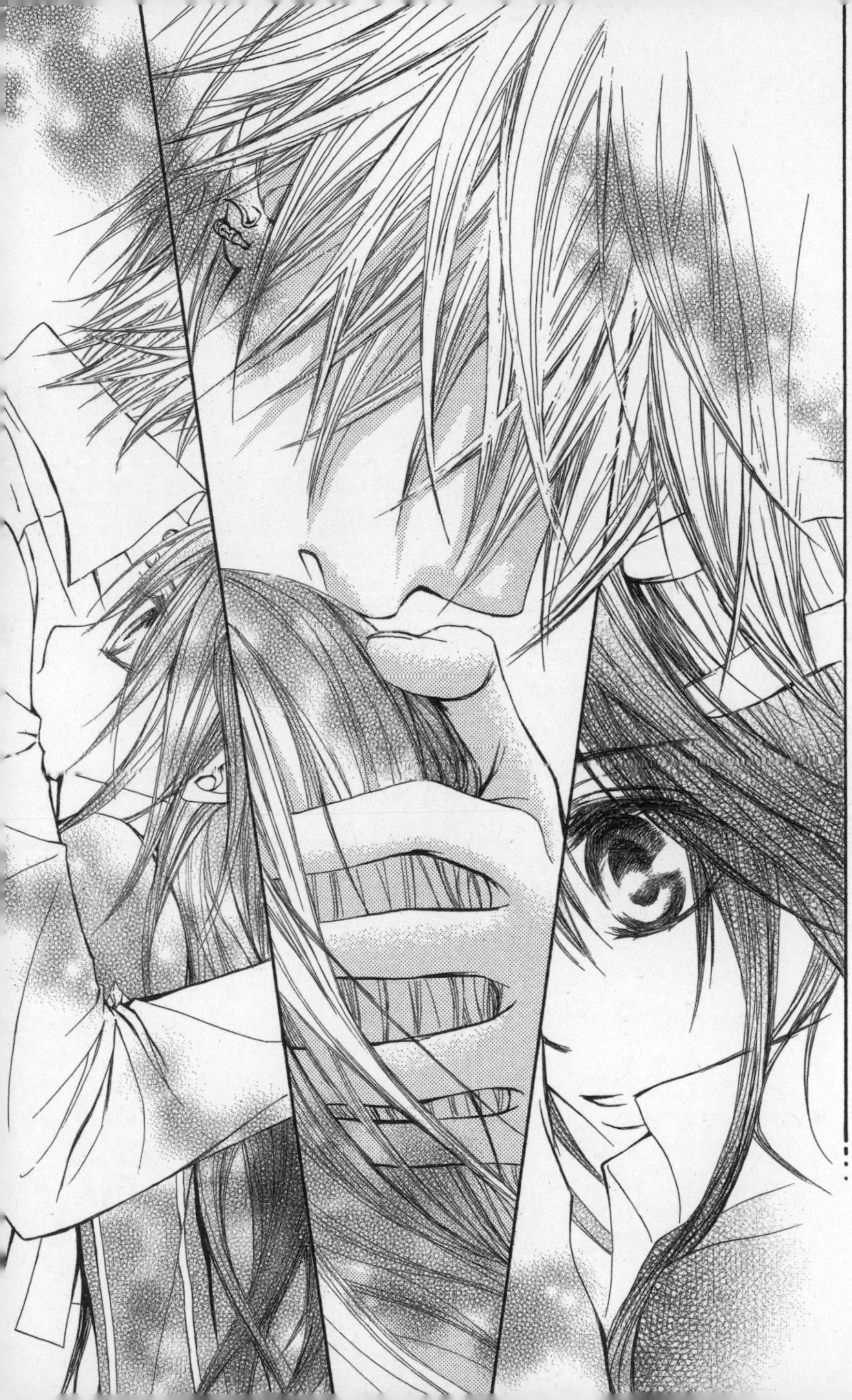

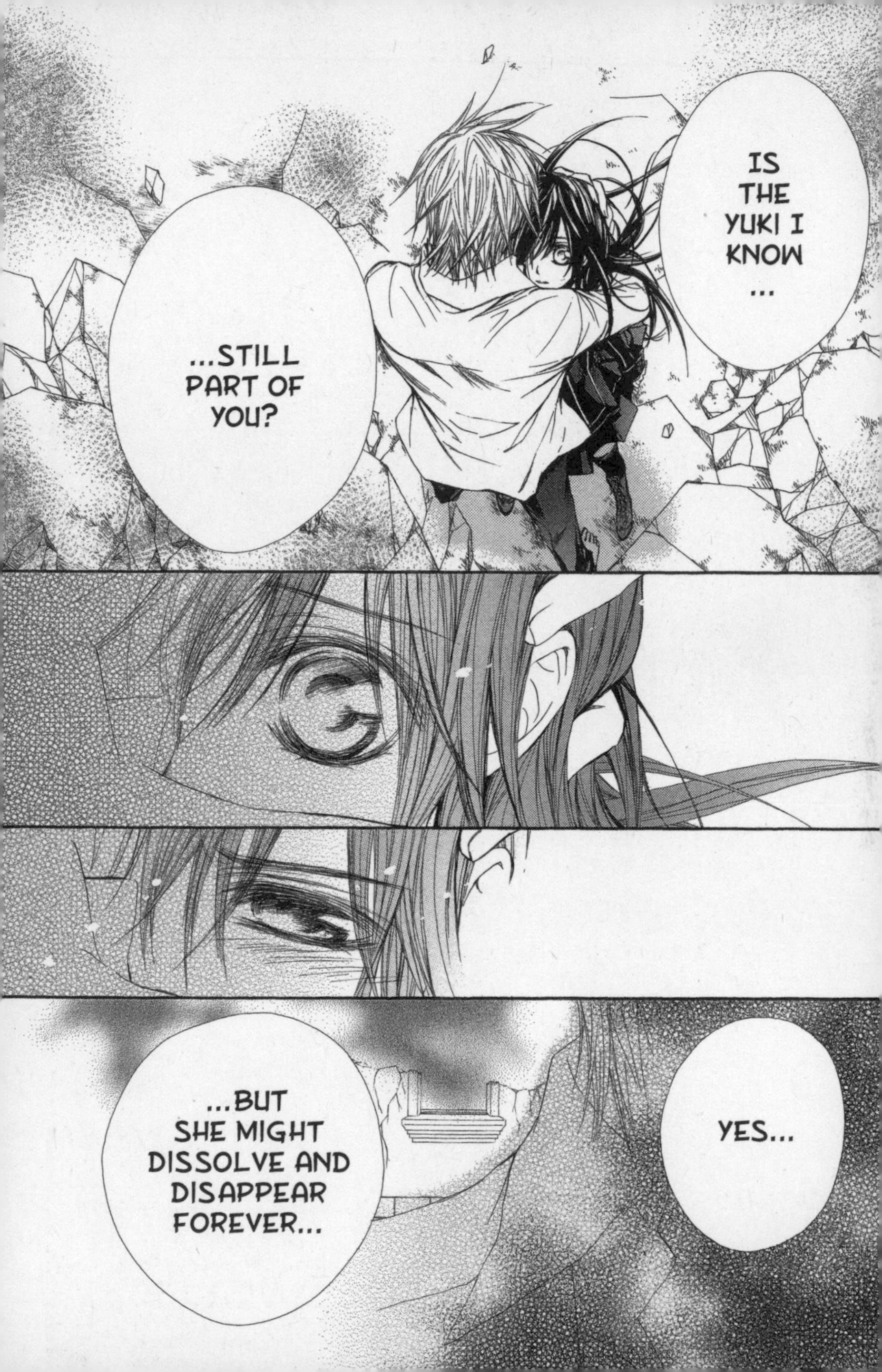
IS THE YUKI I KNOW ...
...STILL PART OF YOU?
YES...
...BUT SHE MIGHT DISSOLVE AND DISAPPEAR FOREVER...

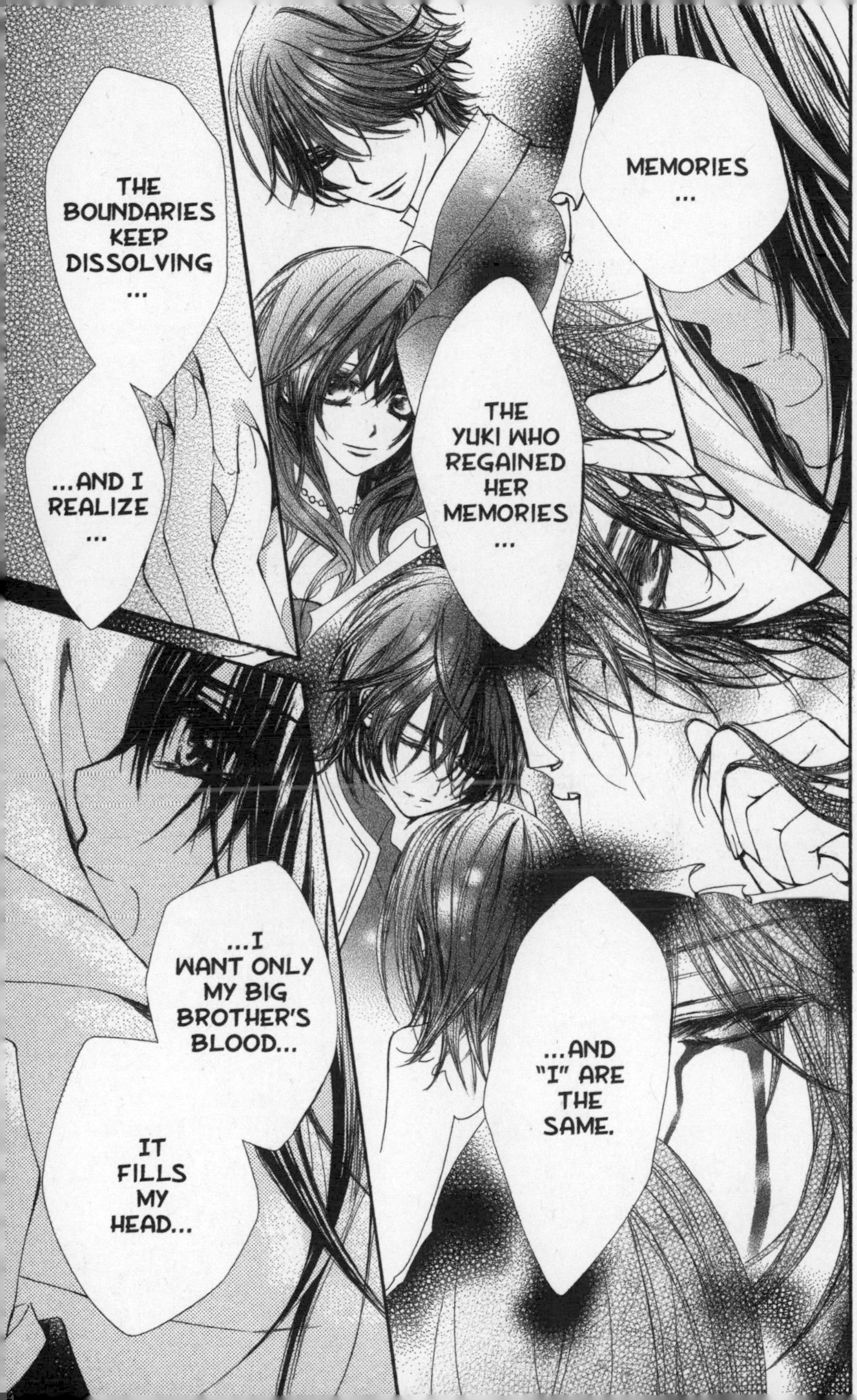
MEMORIES ...
THE YUKI WHO REGAINED HER MEMORIES ...
THE BOUNDARIES KEEP DISSOLVING ...
...AND I REALIZE ...
...AND "I" ARE THE SAME.
...I WANT ONLY MY BIG BROTHER'S BLOOD...
IT FILLS MY HEAD...

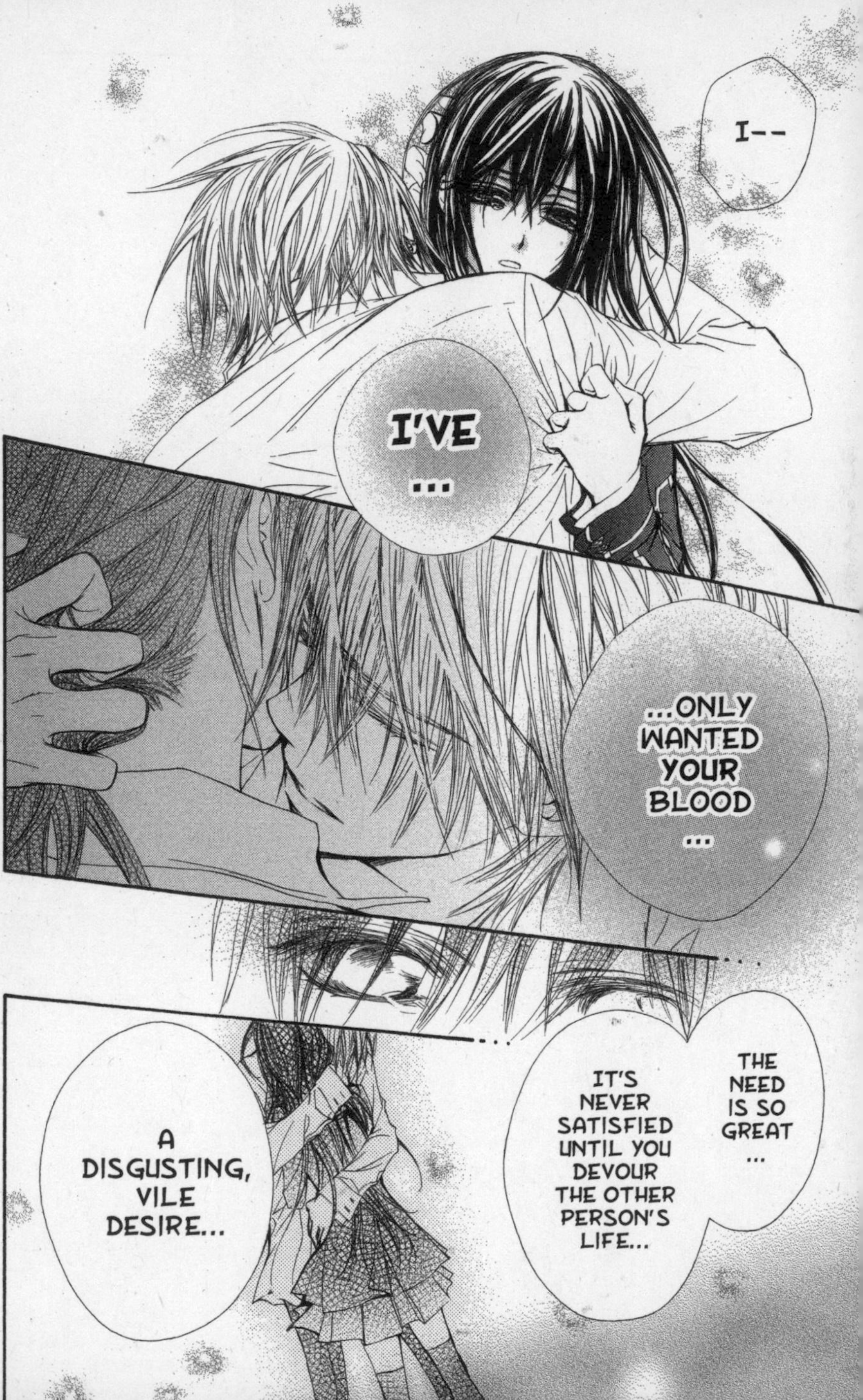
I--
I'VE ...
...ONLY WANTED YOUR BLOOD ...
THE NEED IS SO GREAT ...
IT'S NEVER SATISFIED UNTIL YOU DEVOUR THE OTHER PERSON'S LIFE...
A DISGUSTING, VILE DESIRE...

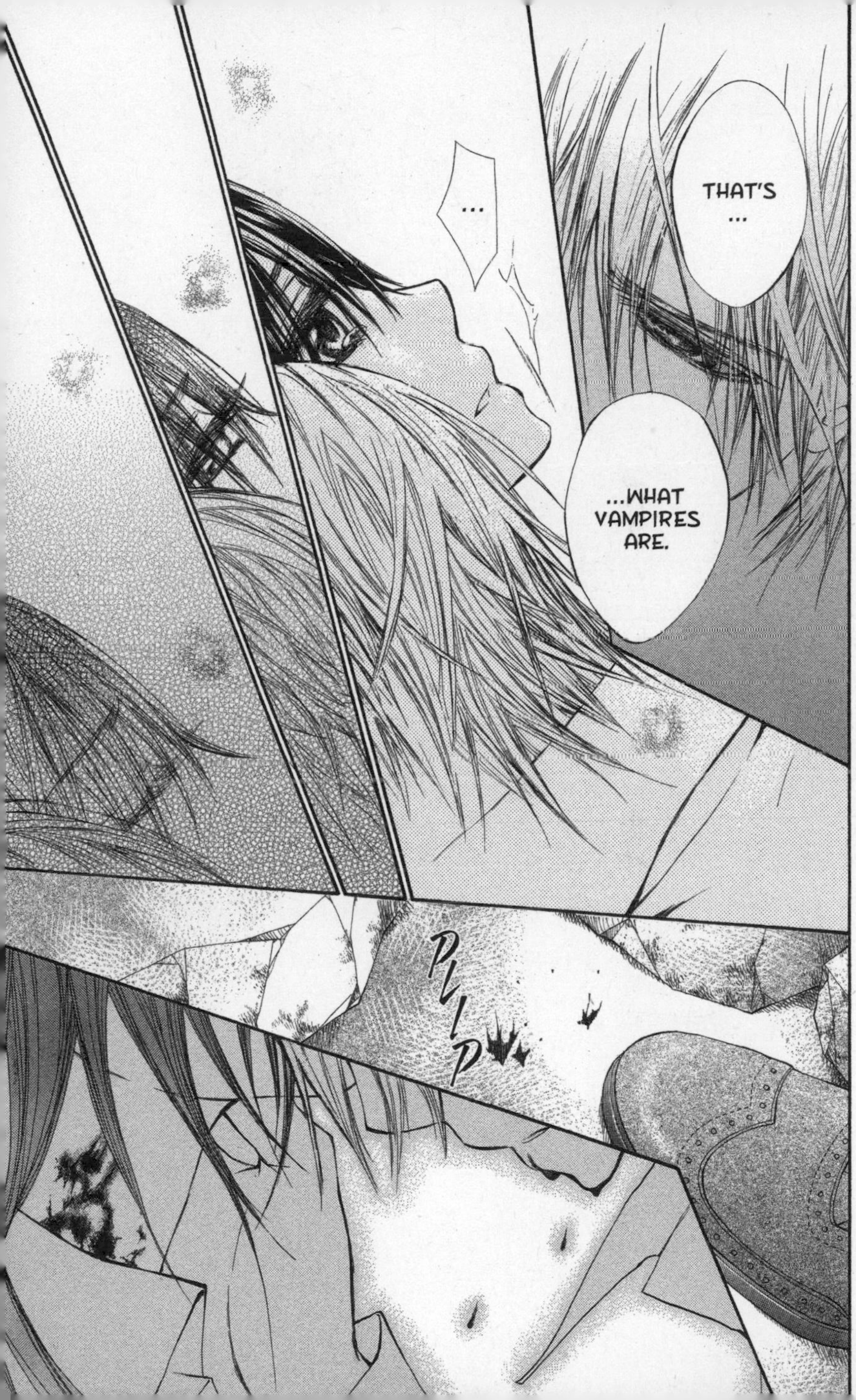
THAT'S ...
...WHAT VAMPIRES ARE.
...
PLIP

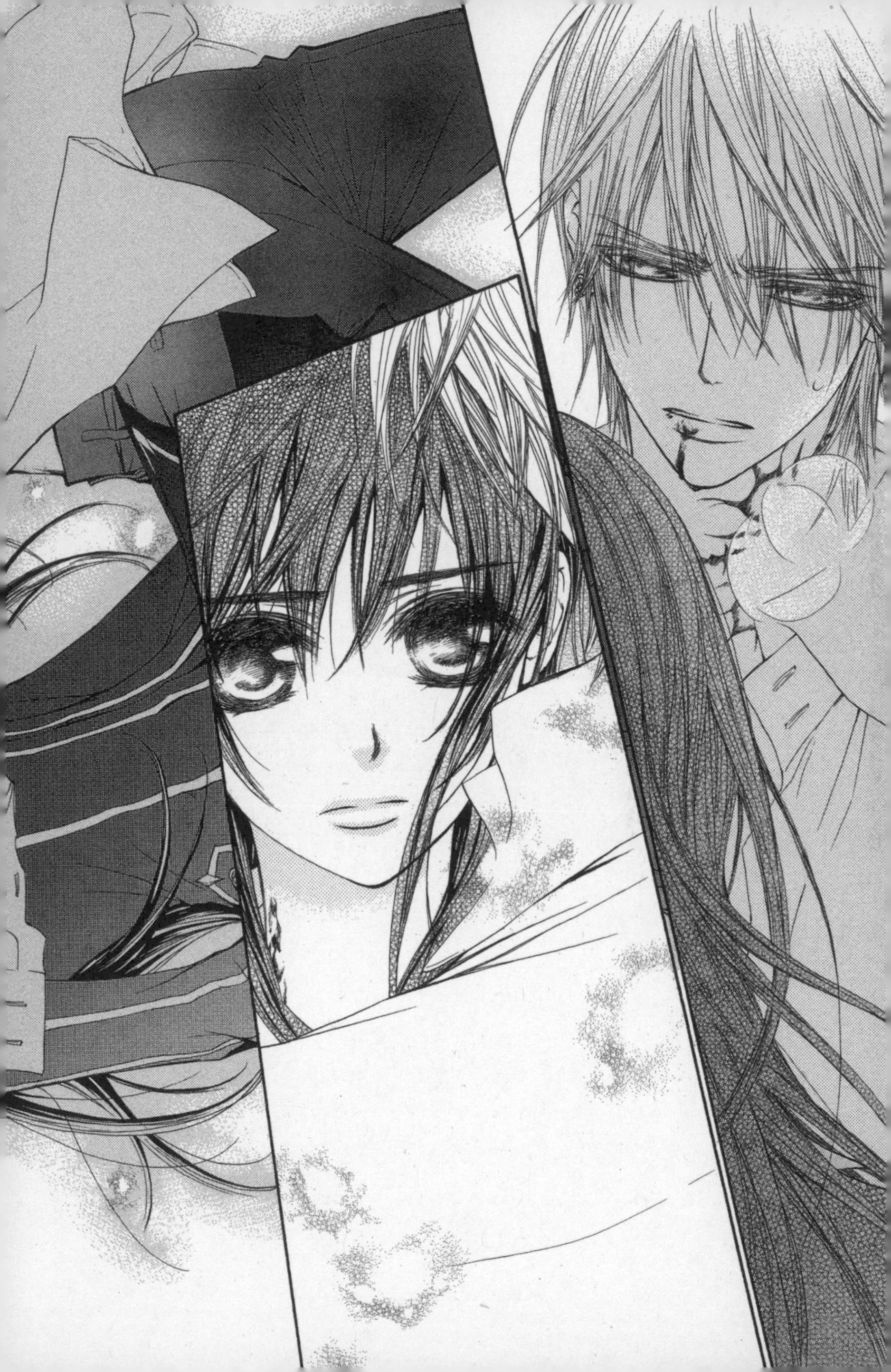

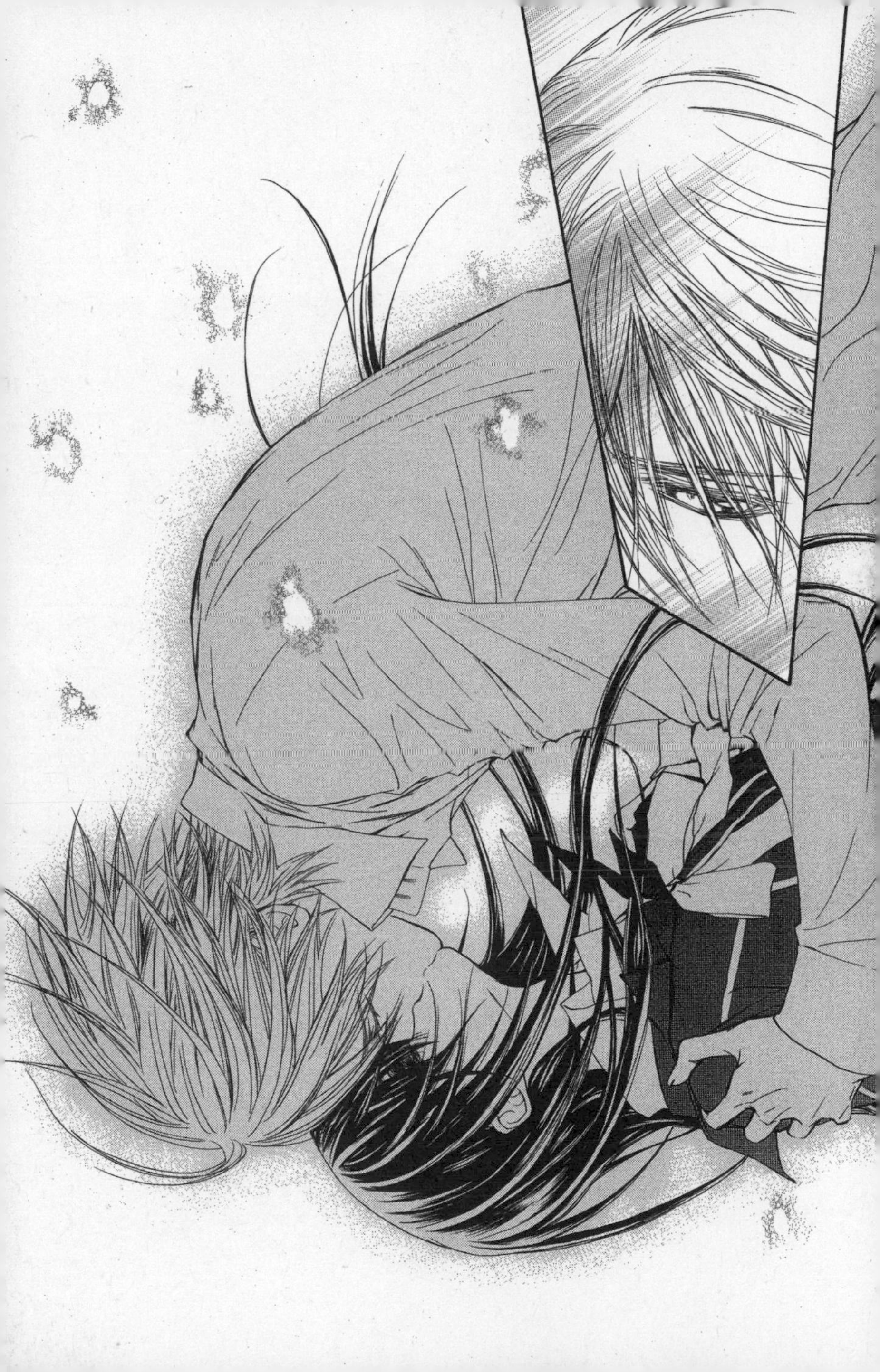

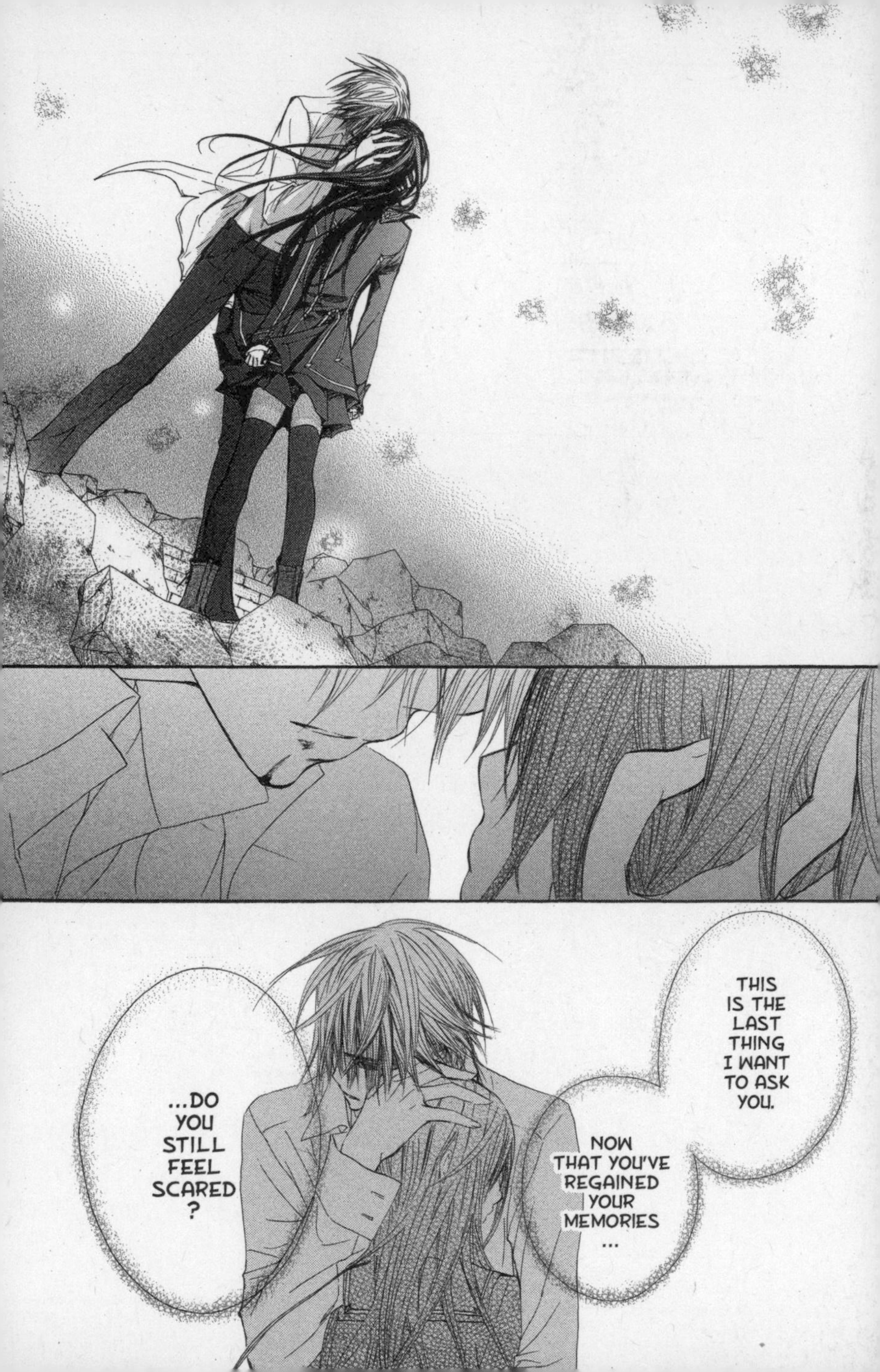
THIS IS THE LAST THING I WANT TO ASK YOU.
NOW THAT YOU'VE REGAINED YOUR MEMORIES...
...DO YOU STILL FEEL SCARED?

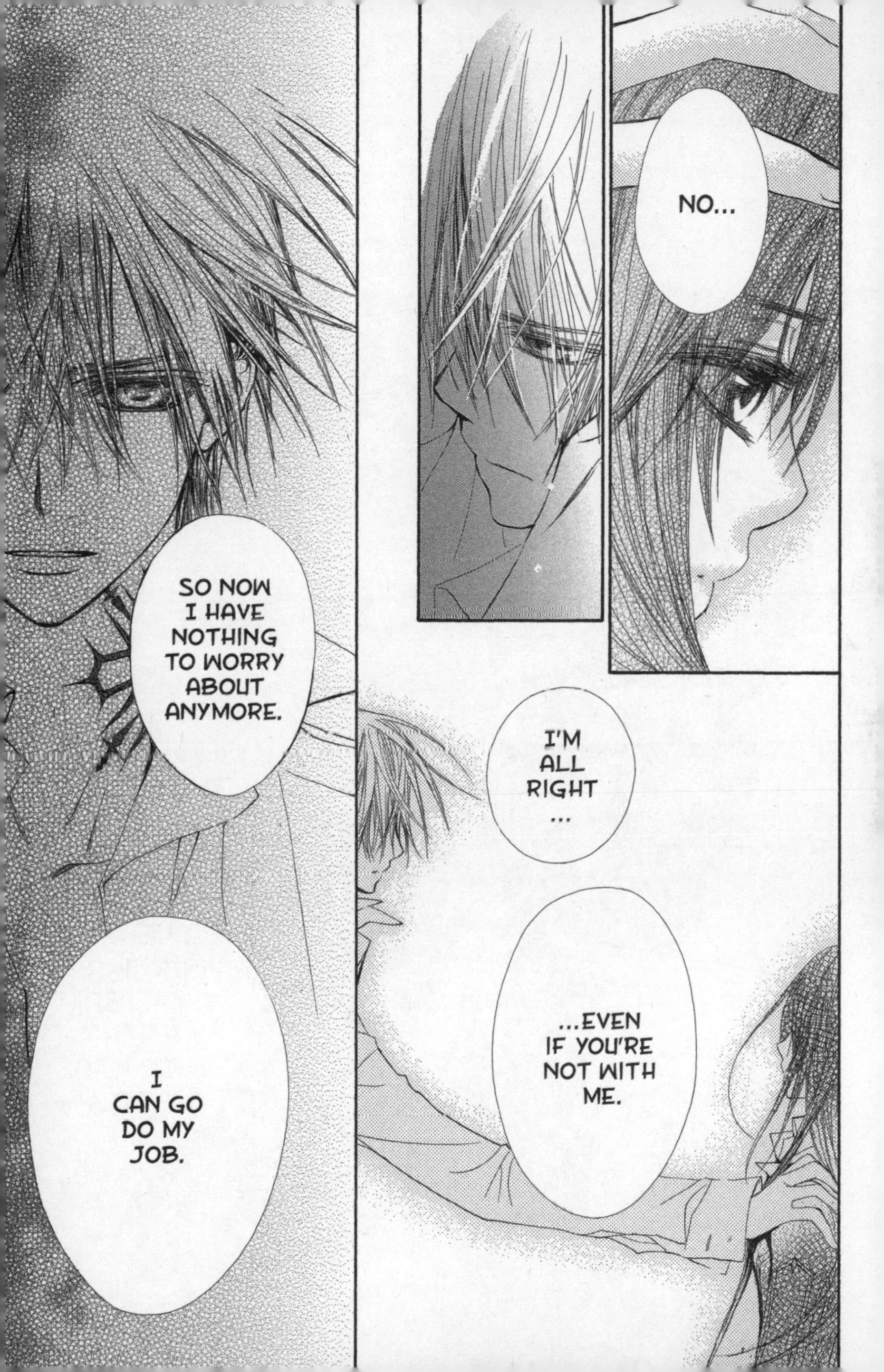
NO...
I'M ALL RIGHT ...
...EVEN IF YOU'RE NOT WITH ME.
SO NOW I HAVE NOTHING TO WORRY ABOUT ANYMORE.
I CAN GO DO MY JOB.

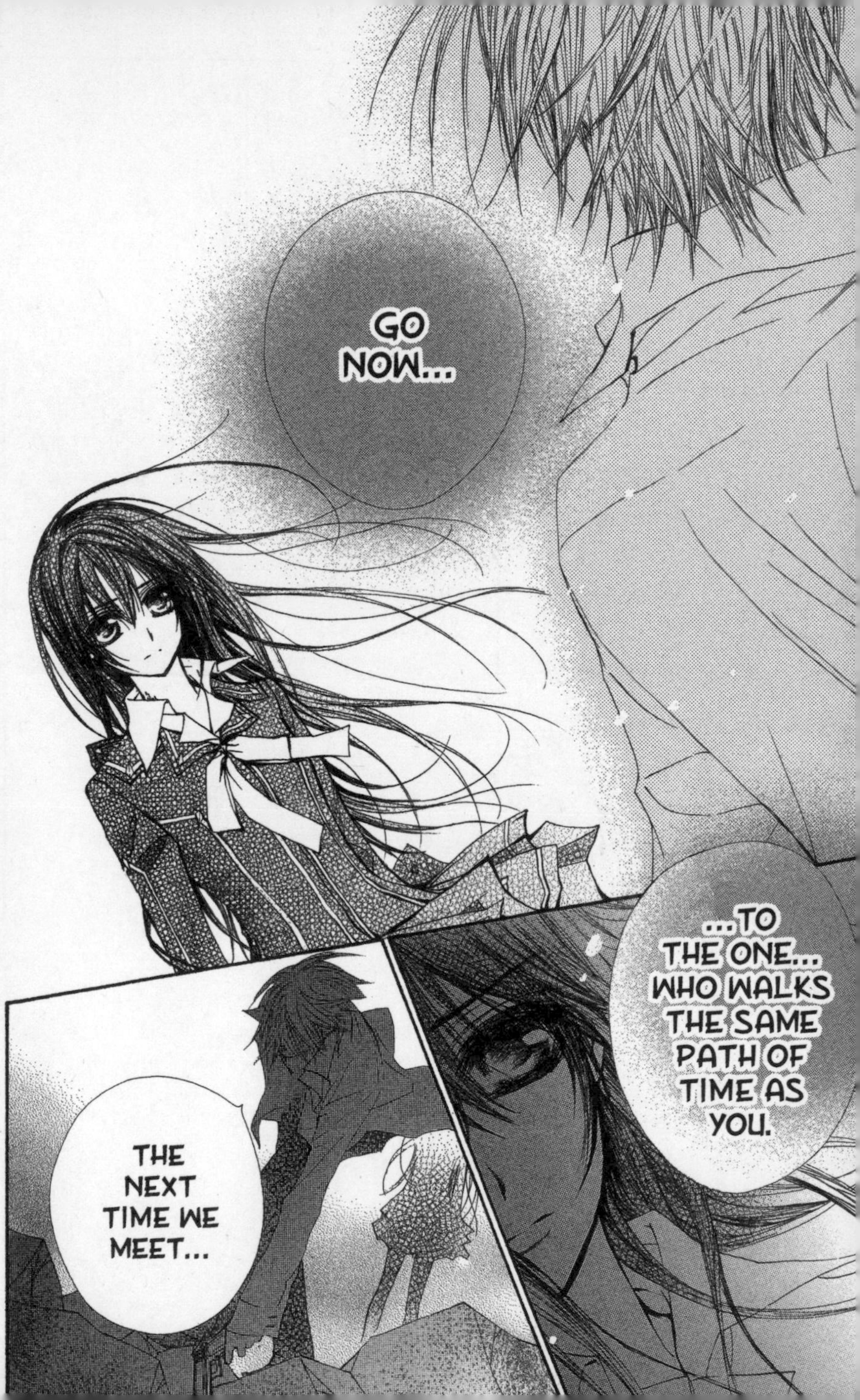
GO NOW...
...TO THE ONE... WHO WALKS THE SAME PATH OF TIME AS YOU.
THE NEXT TIME WE MEET...

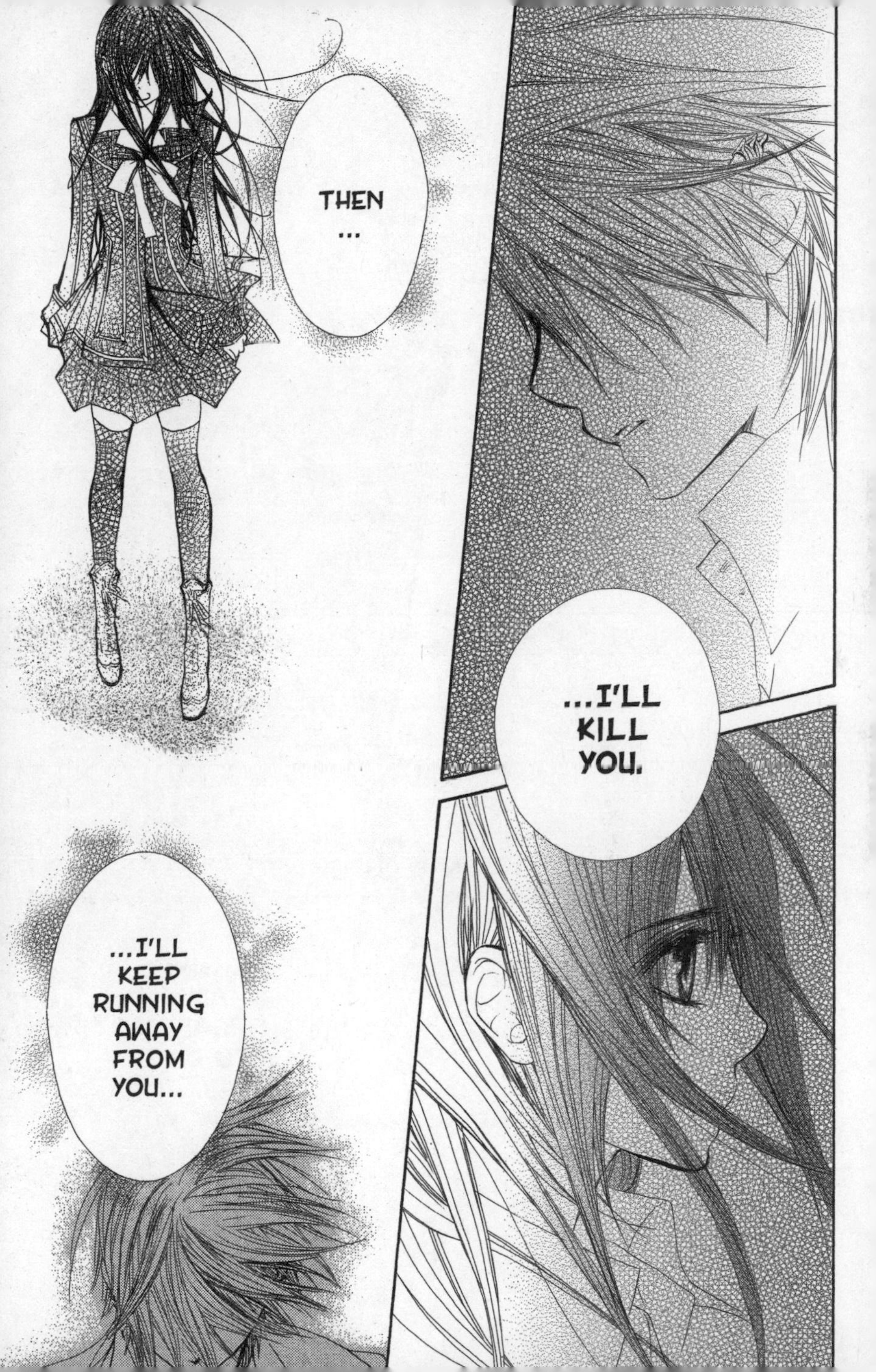
...I'LL KILL YOU.
THEN ...
...I'LL KEEP RUNNING AWAY FROM YOU...

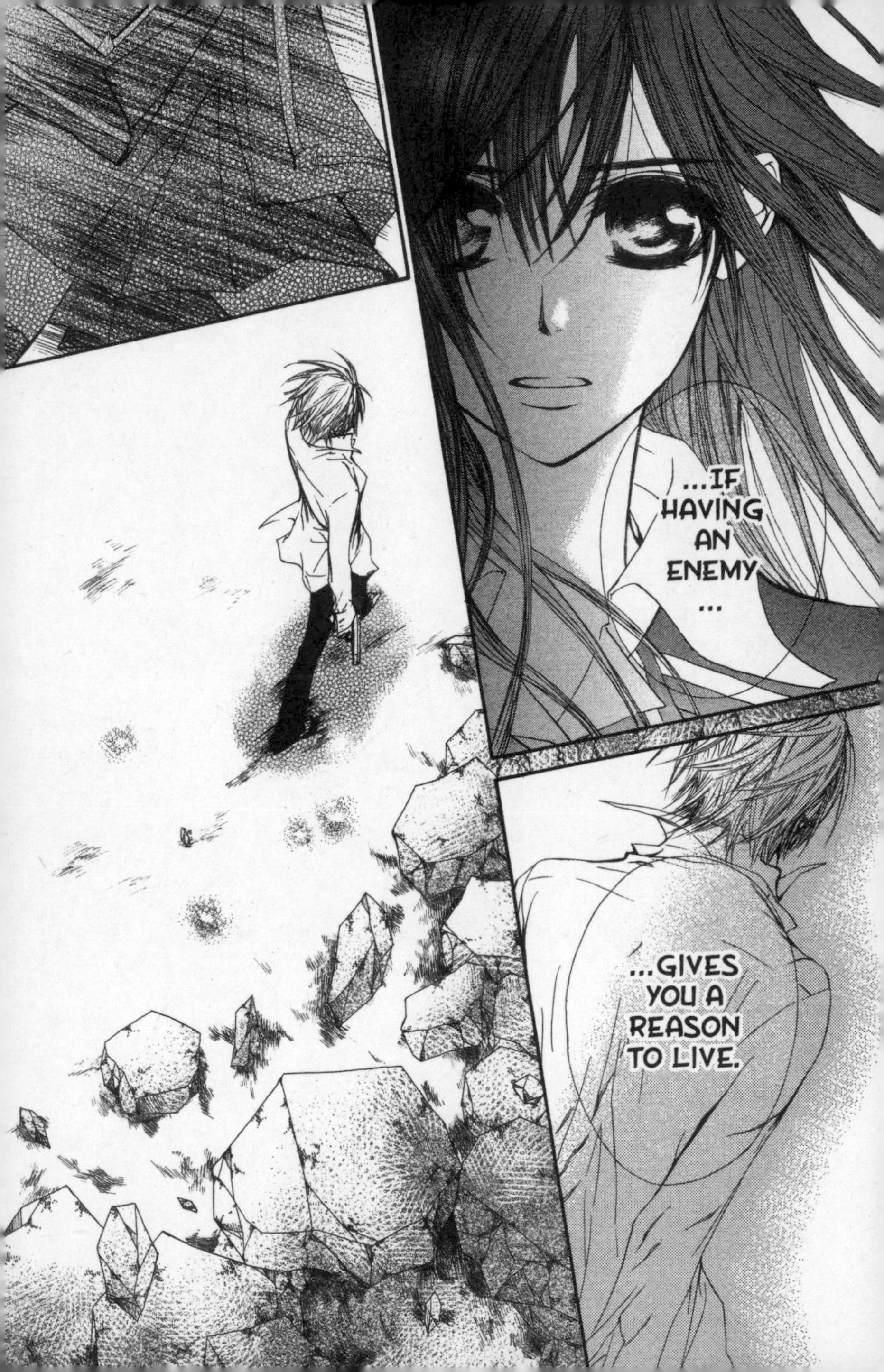
...IF HAVING AN ENEMY ...
...GIVES YOU A REASON TO LIVE.

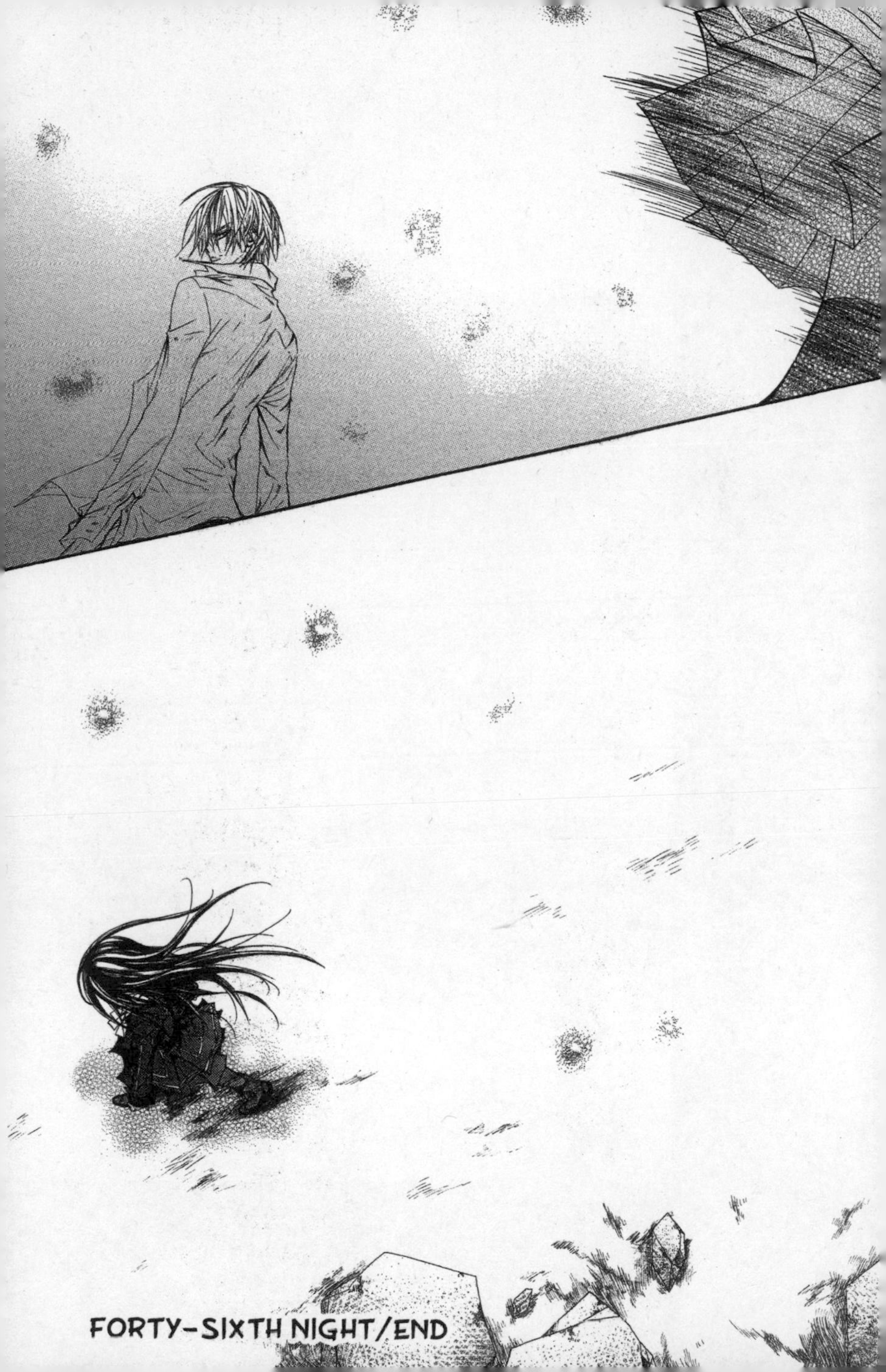
FORTY-SIXTH NIGHT/END

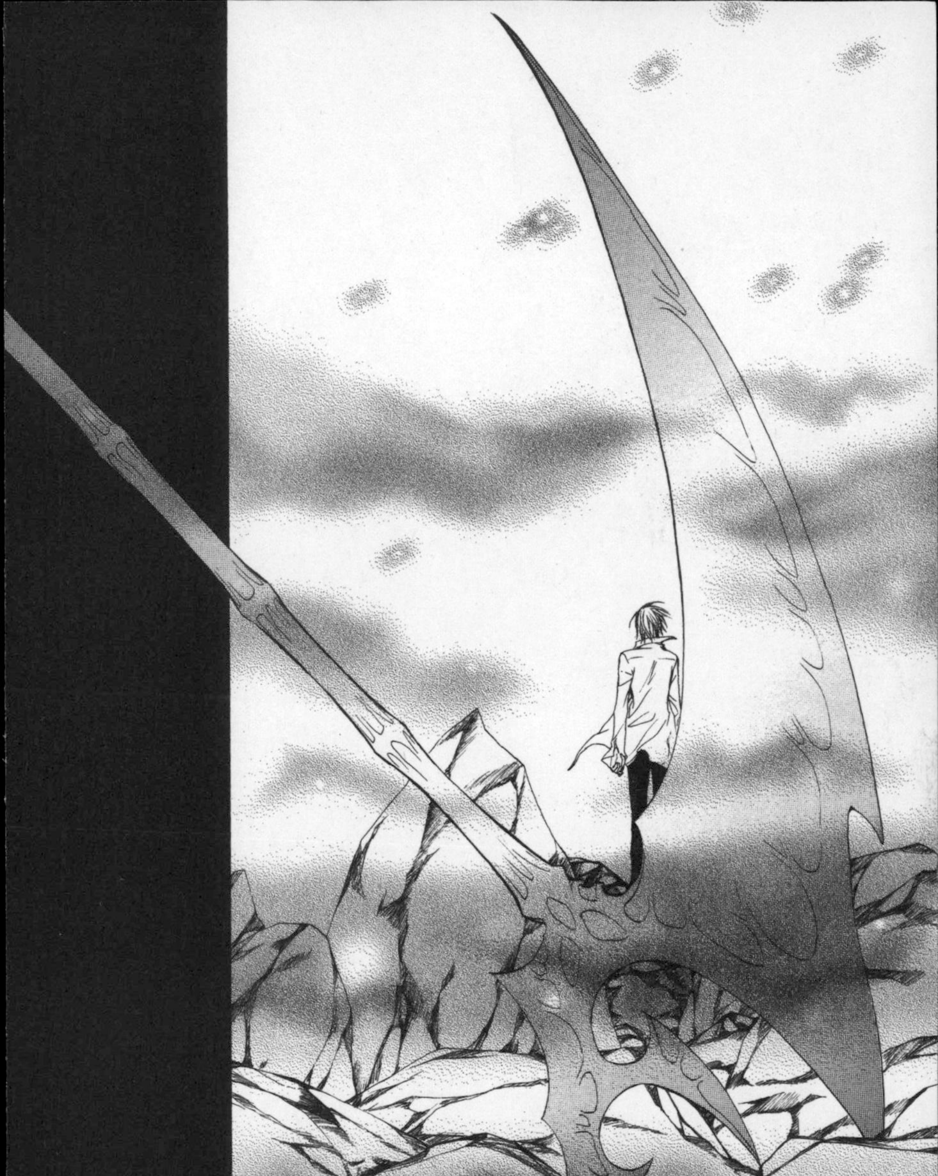

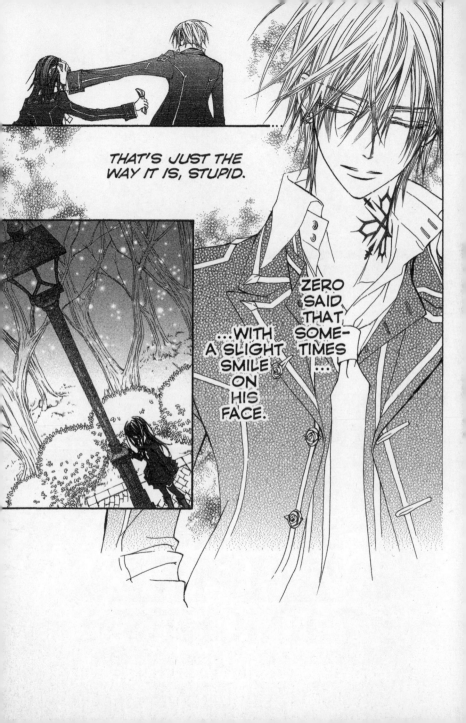

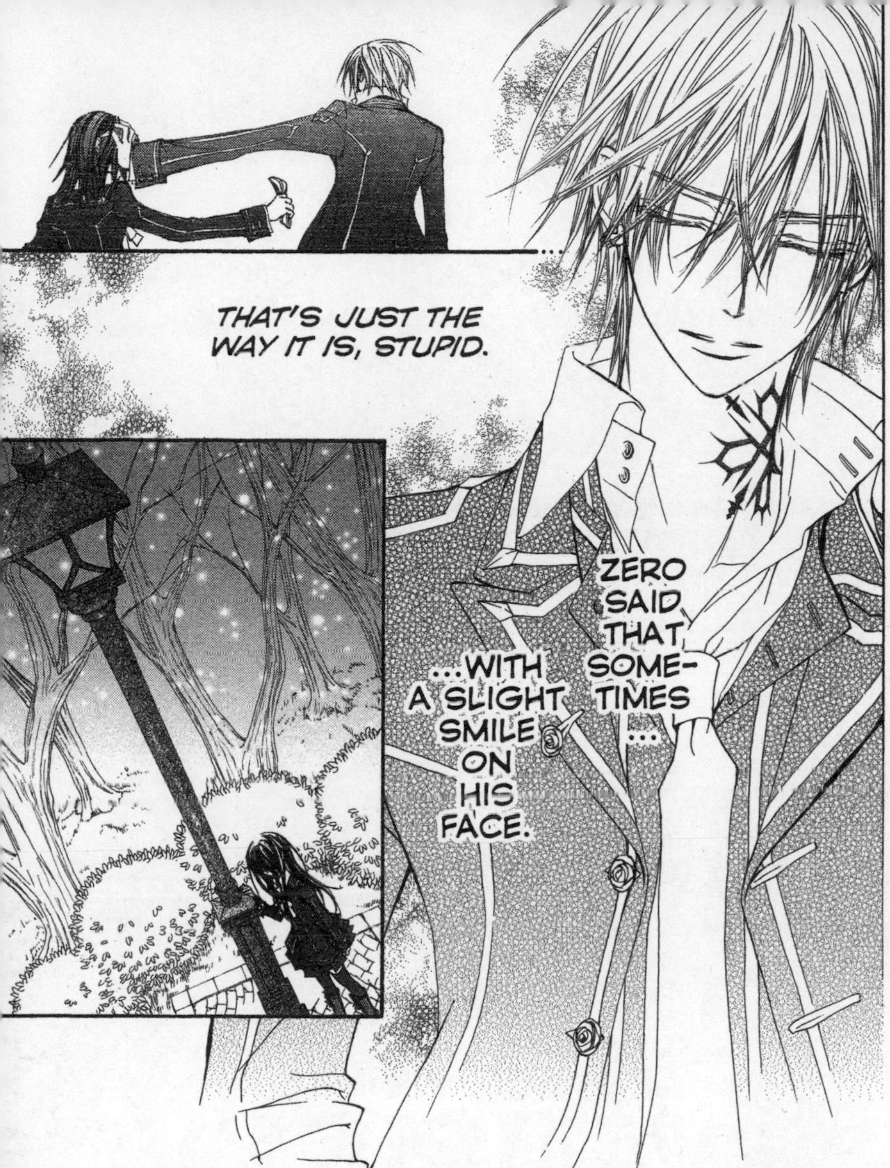
THAT'S JUST THE WAY IT IS, STUPID.
ZERO SAID THAT SOMETIMES...
...WITH A SLIGHT SMILE ON HIS FACE.

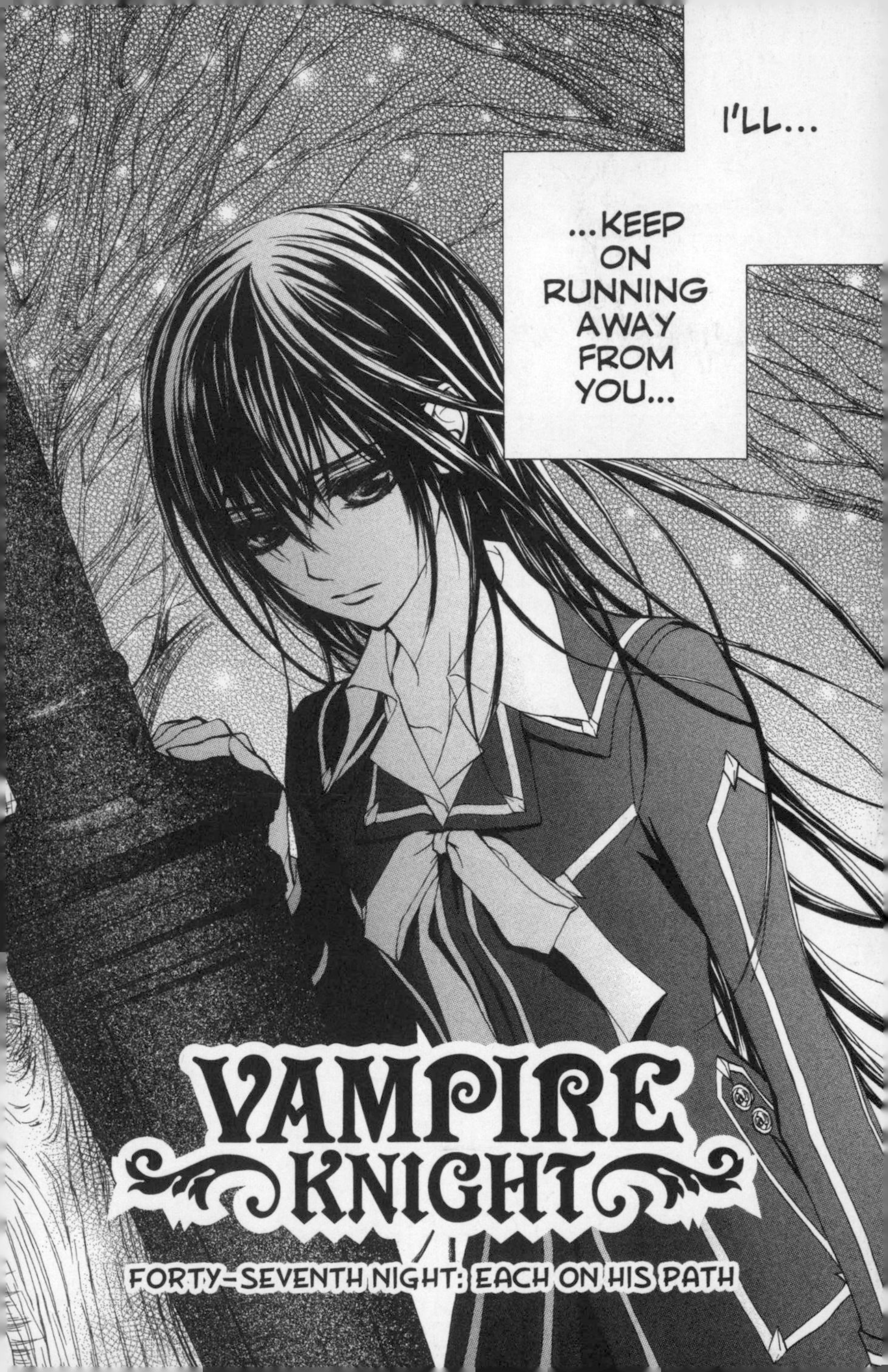
I'LL...
...KEEP ON RUNNING AWAY FROM YOU...
VAMPIRE KNIGHT
FORTY-SEVENTH NIGHT: EACH ON HIS PATH

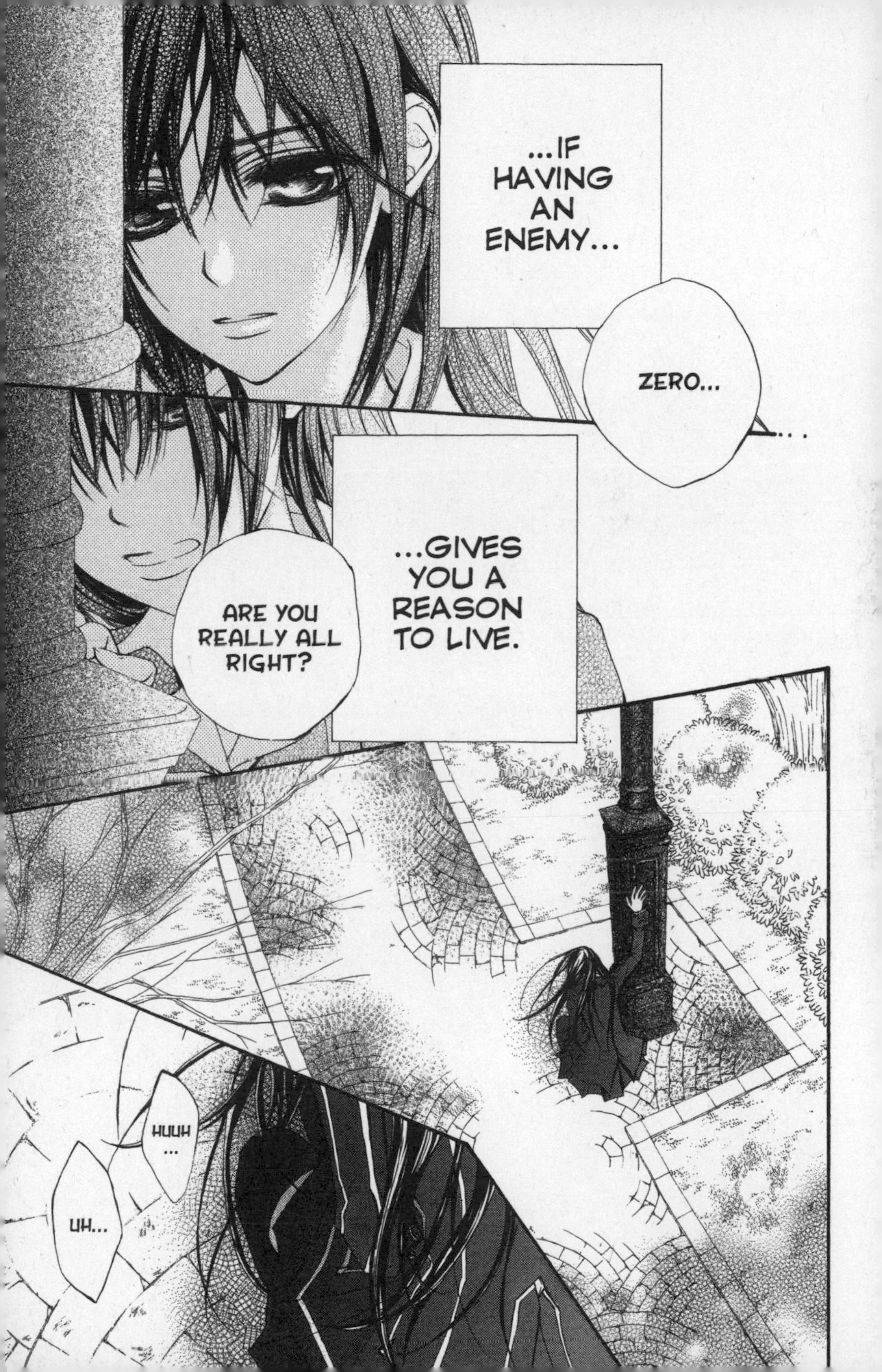
...IF HAVING AN ENEMY...
ZERO...
...GIVES YOU A REASON TO LIVE.
ARE YOU REALLY ALL RIGHT?
HUUH ...
UH...

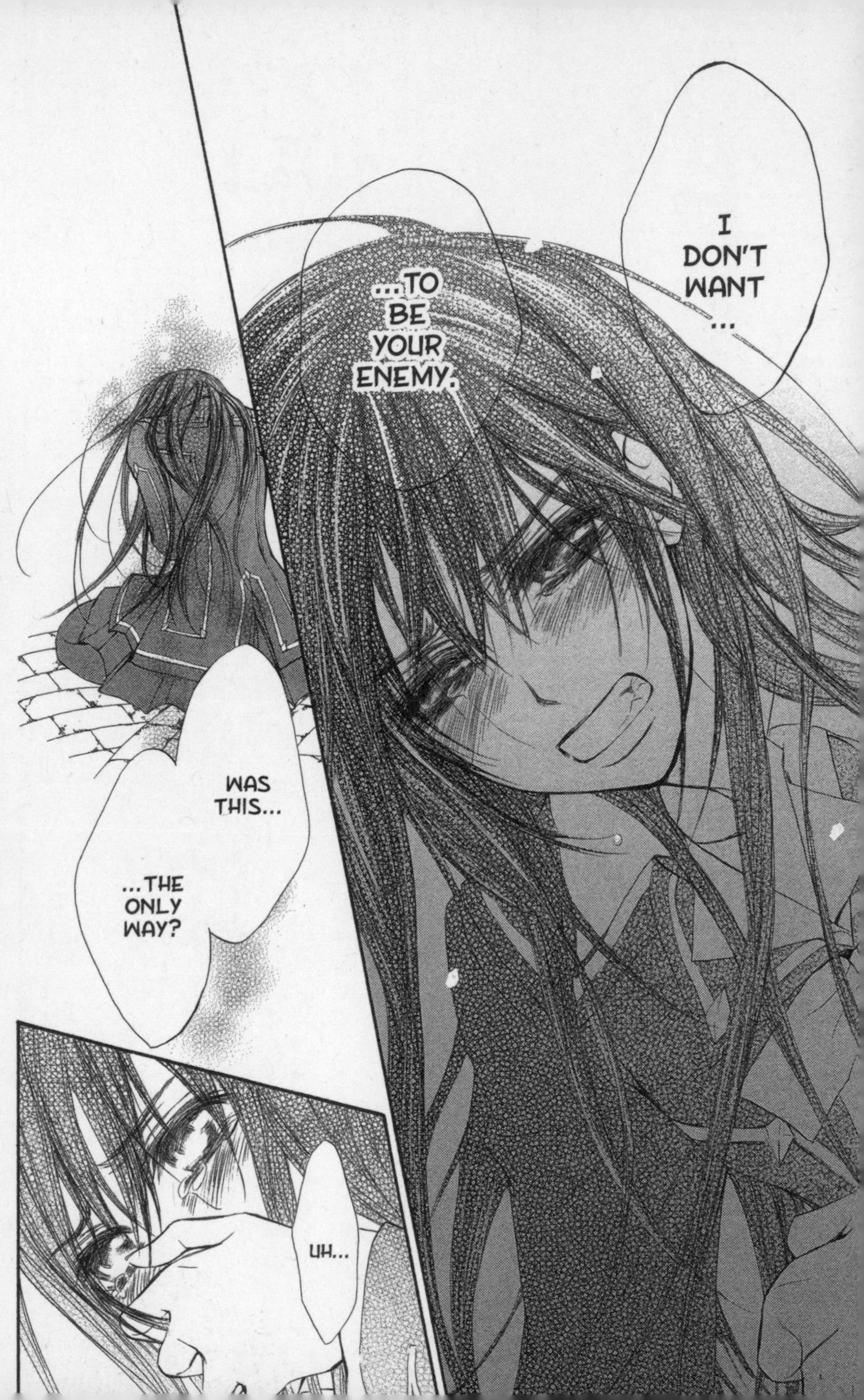
I DON'T WANT ...
...TO BE YOUR ENEMY.
WAS THIS...
...THE ONLY WAY?
UH...

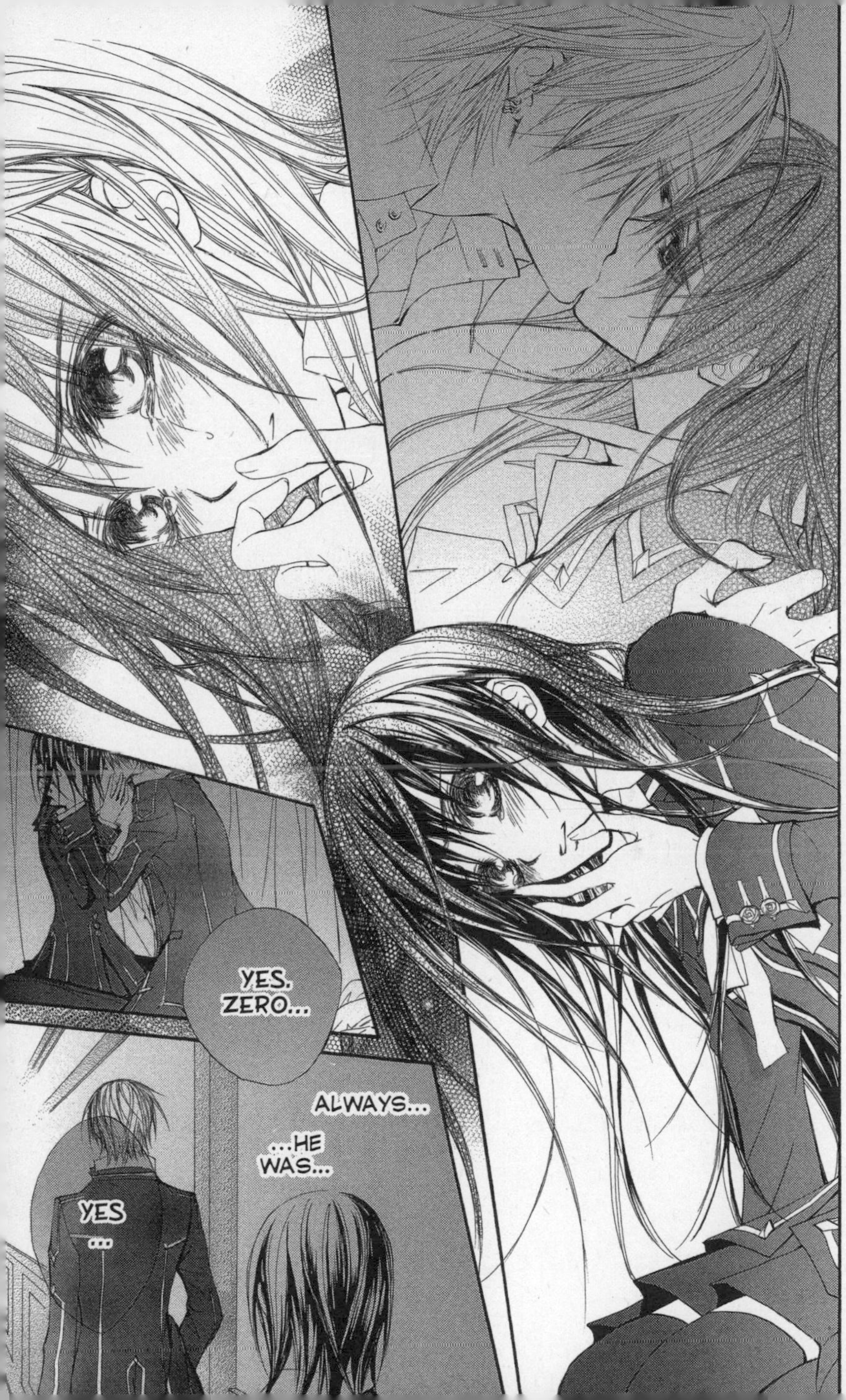
YES. ZERO...
ALWAYS...
...HE WAS...
YES ...

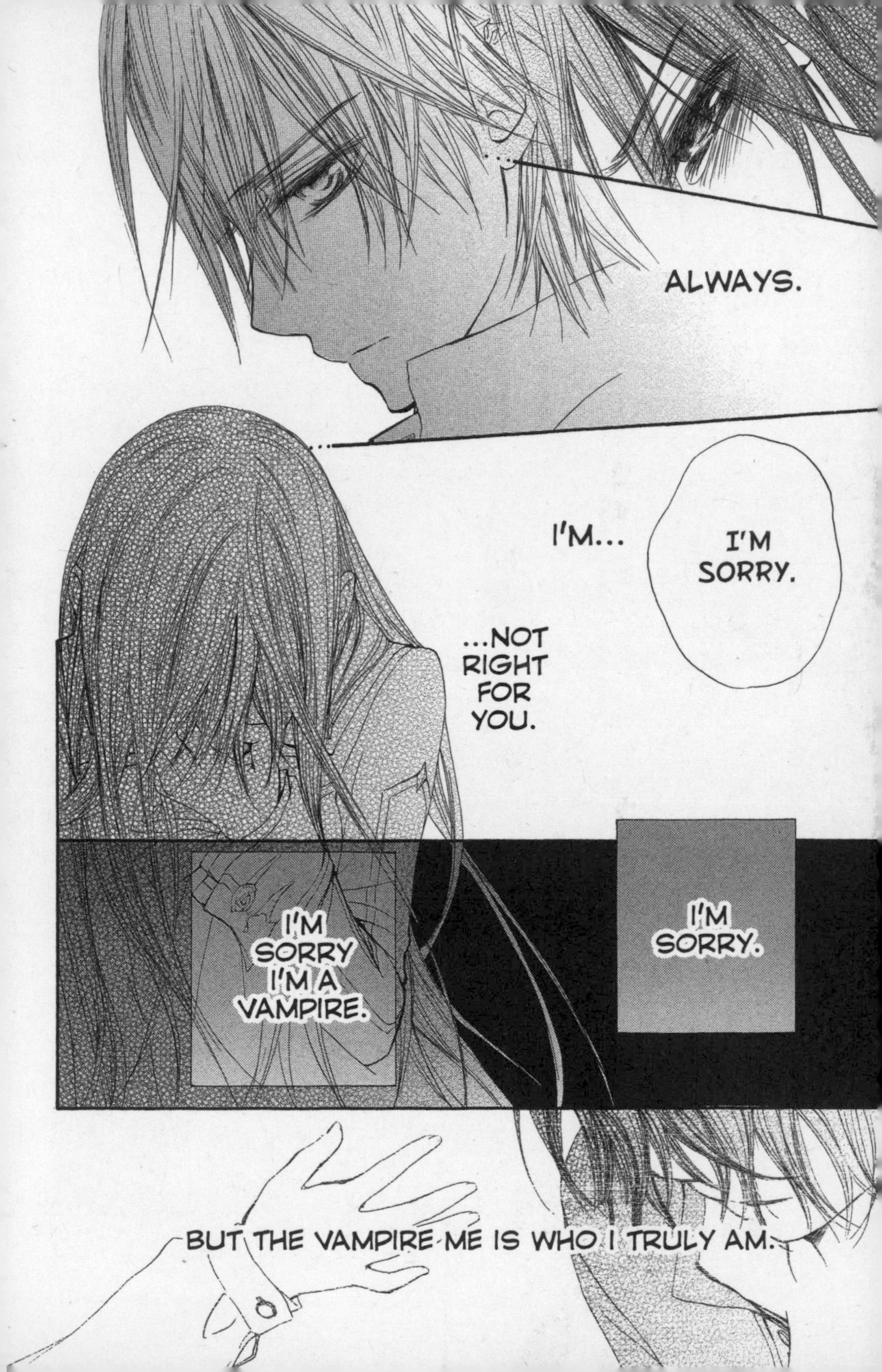
ALWAYS.
I'M SORRY.
I'M...
...NOT RIGHT FOR YOU.
I'M SORRY.
I'M SORRY I'M A VAMPIRE.
BUT THE VAMPIRE ME IS WHO I TRULY AM.

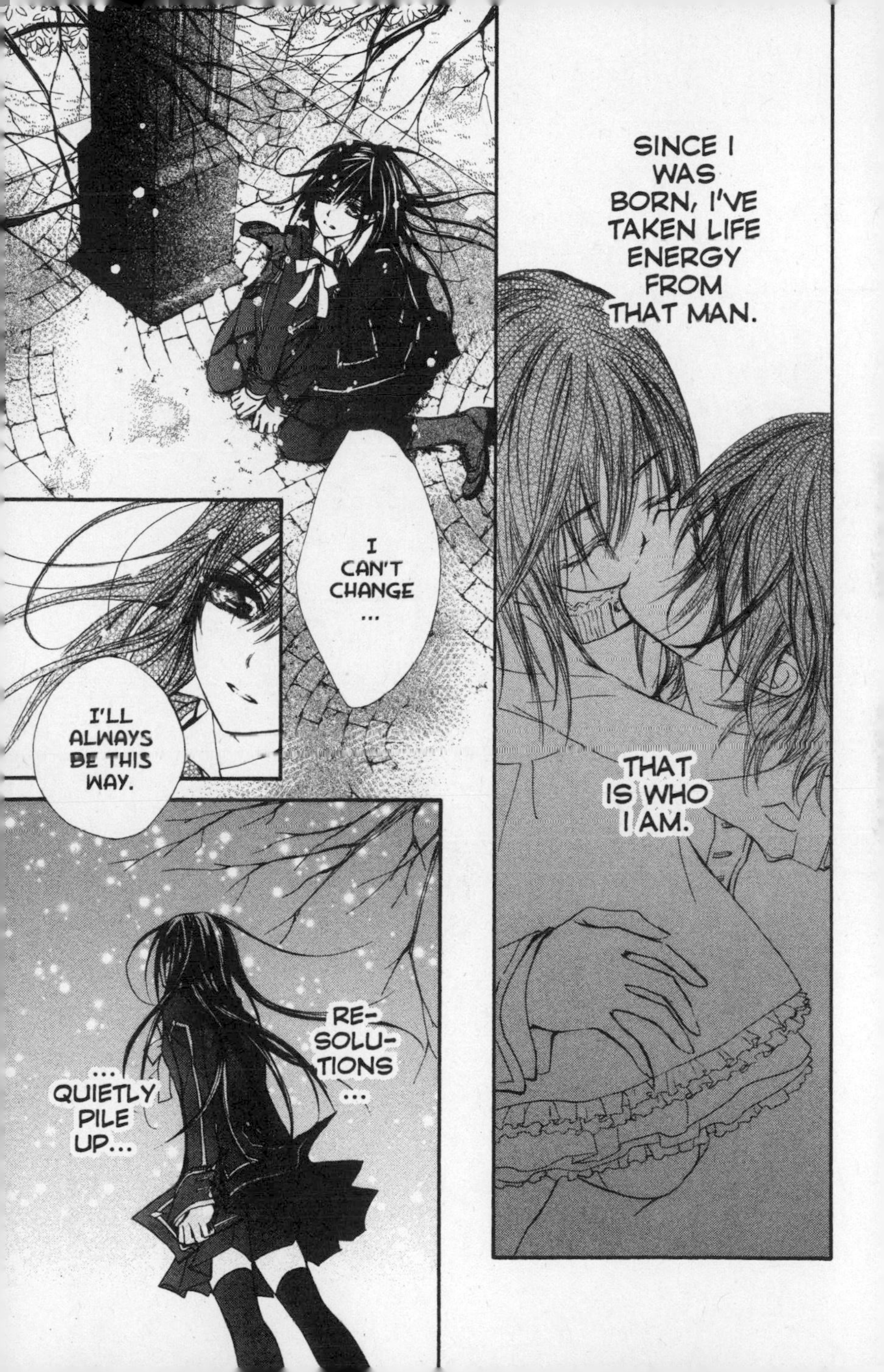
SINCE I WAS BORN, I'VE TAKEN LIFE ENERGY FROM THAT MAN.
THAT IS WHO I AM.
I CAN'T CHANGE ...
I'LL ALWAYS BE THIS WAY.
RE-SOLUTIONS ...
... QUIETLY PILE UP...

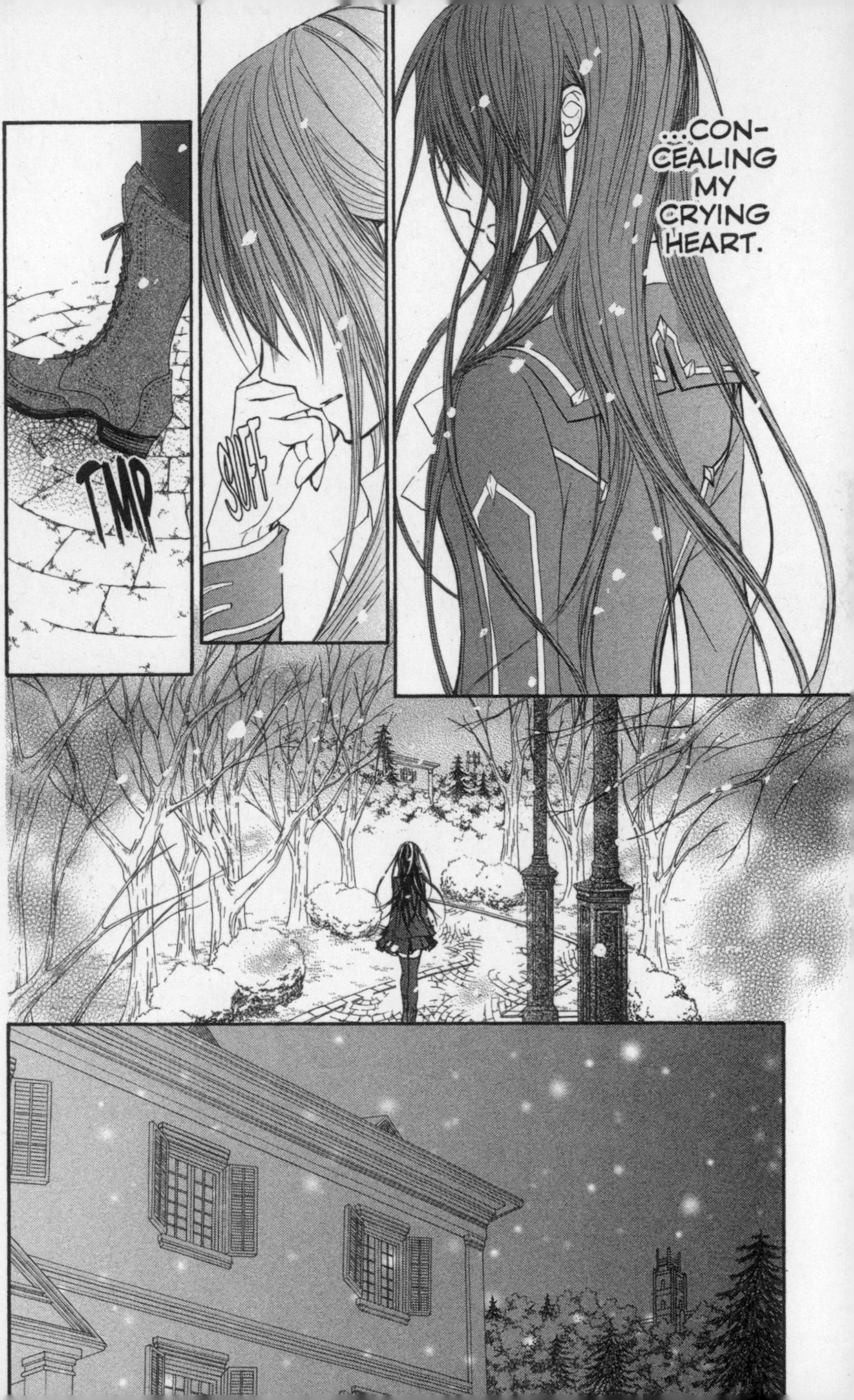
...CON-CEALING MY CRYING HEART.
SNIFF
TMP

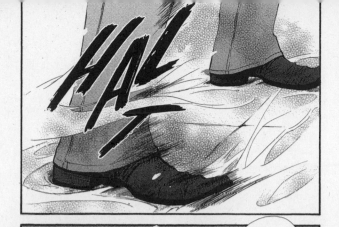

HA!

YOU DISPOSED OF EVERY SINGLE ONE.

NOW I'VE GOT LESS WORK...

PUOOO

...

VAMPIRES WHO REBEL AGAINST THE SENATE...

...ARE SHUNNED BY THEIR FAMILIES AT BEST. AT WORST, THEY'RE KILLED.

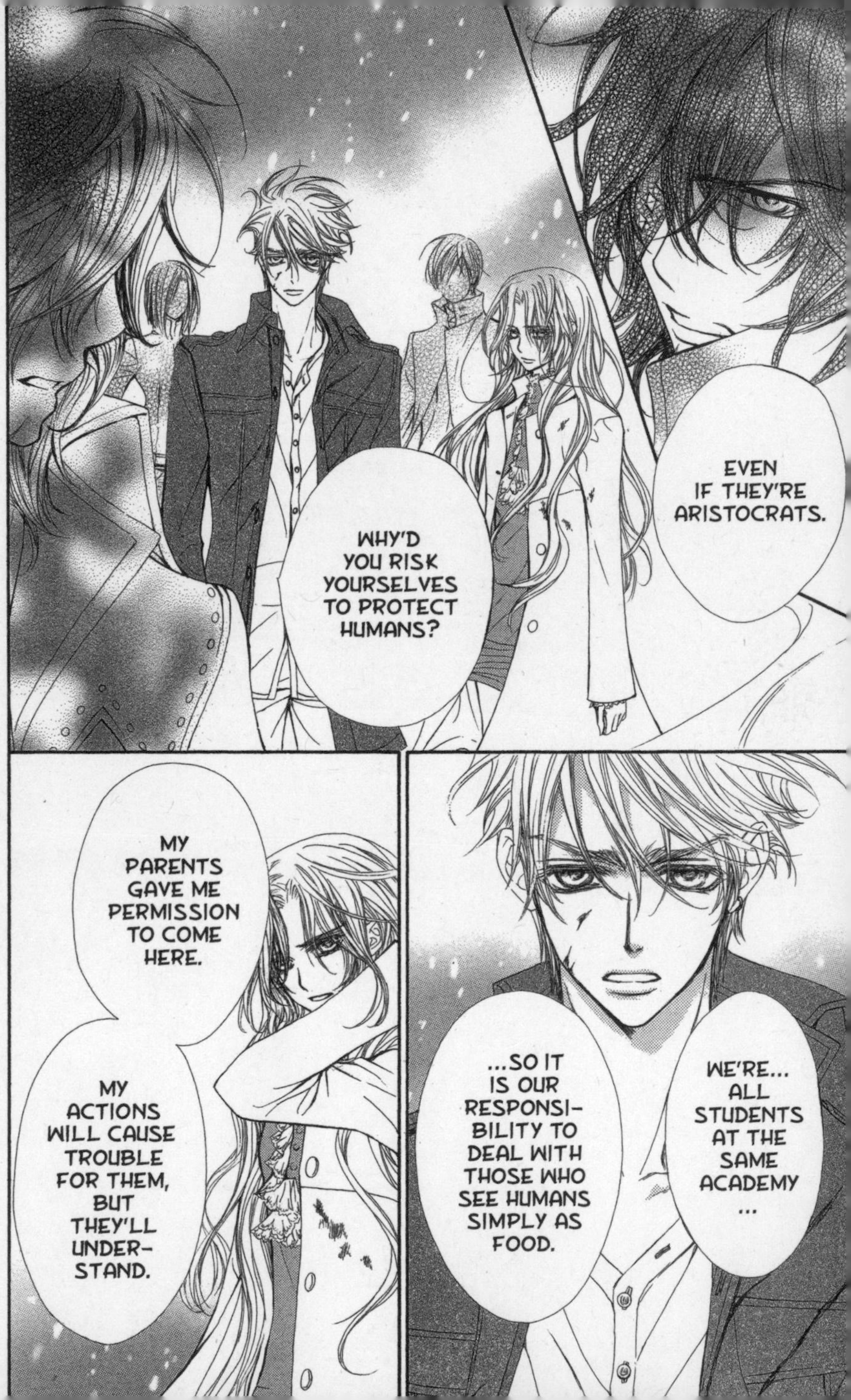
EVEN IF THEY'RE ARISTOCRATS.
WHY'D YOU RISK YOURSELVES TO PROTECT HUMANS?
WE'RE... ALL STUDENTS AT THE SAME ACADEMY ...
...SO IT IS OUR RESPONSI-BILITY TO DEAL WITH THOSE WHO SEE HUMANS SIMPLY AS FOOD.
MY PARENTS GAVE ME PERMISSION TO COME HERE.
MY ACTIONS WILL CAUSE TROUBLE FOR THEM, BUT THEY'LL UNDER-STAND.

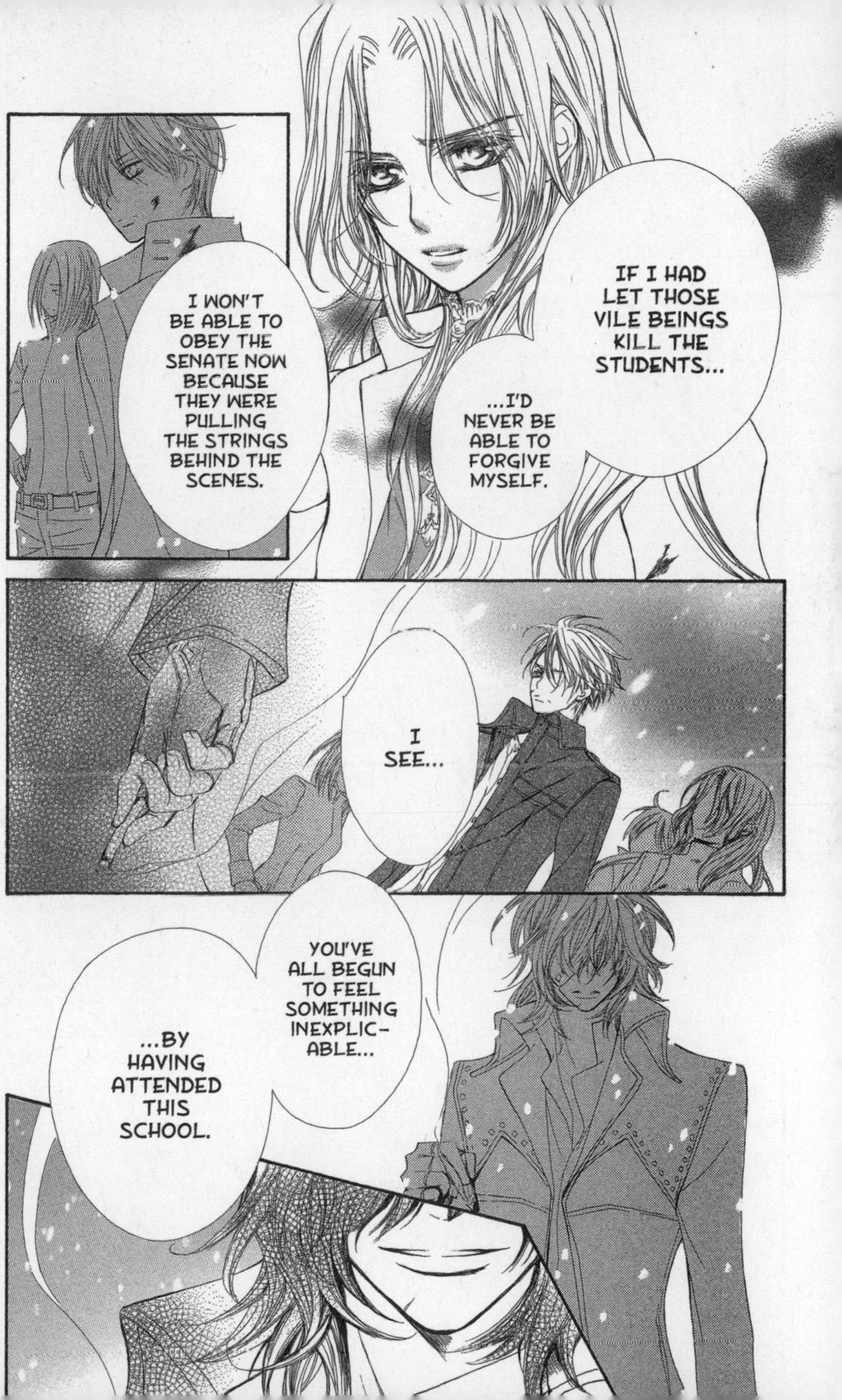
IF I HAD LET THOSE VILE BEINGS KILL THE STUDENTS...
...I'D NEVER BE ABLE TO FORGIVE MYSELF.
I WON'T BE ABLE TO OBEY THE SENATE NOW BECAUSE THEY WERE PULLING THE STRINGS BEHIND THE SCENES.
I SEE...
YOU'VE ALL BEGUN TO FEEL SOMETHING INEXPLIC-ABLE...
...BY HAVING ATTENDED THIS SCHOOL.

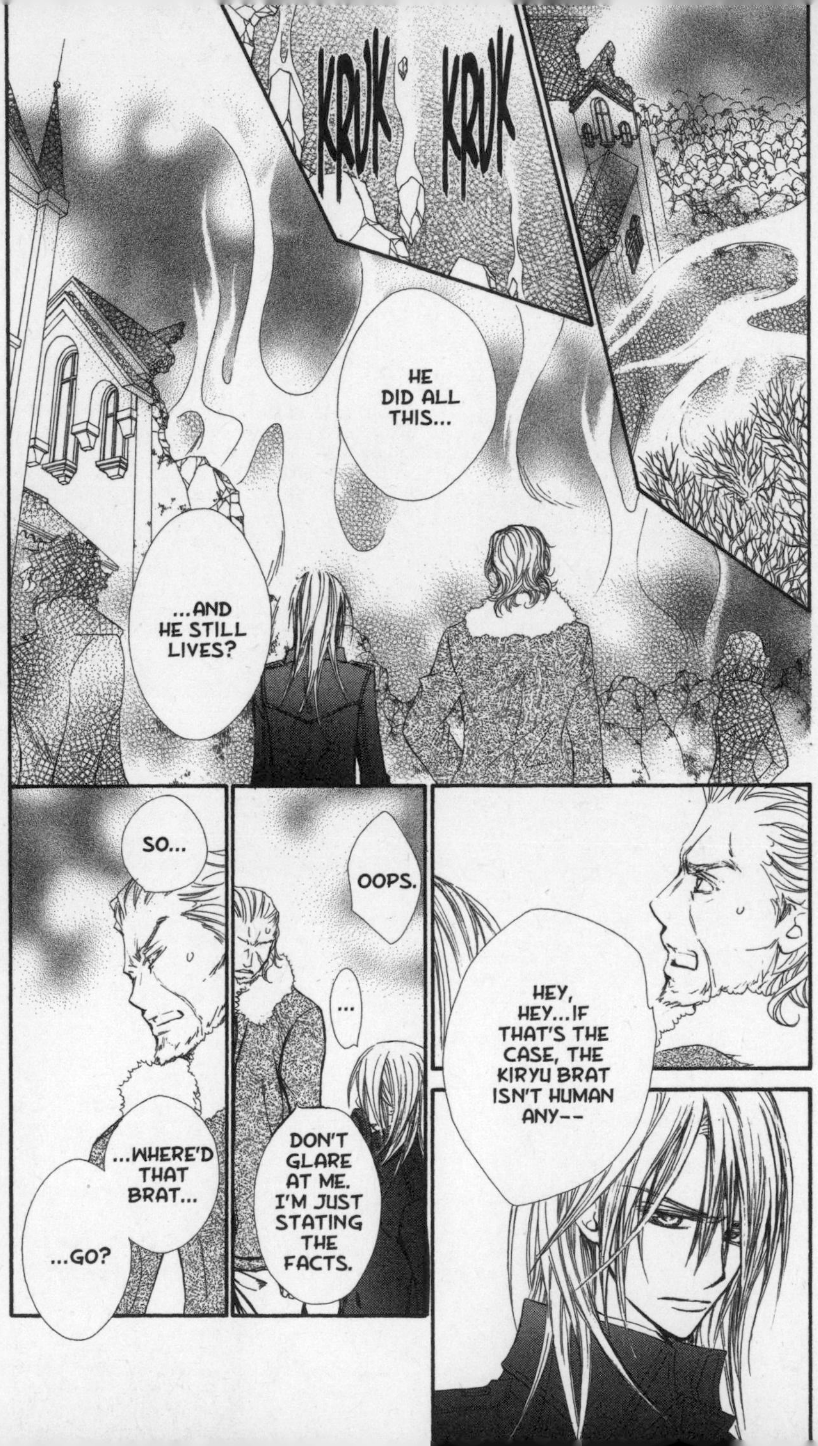
KRUK KRUK
HE DID ALL THIS...
...AND HE STILL LIVES?
HEY, HEY...IF THAT'S THE CASE, THE KIRYU BRAT ISN'T HUMAN ANY--
OOPS.
...
DON'T GLARE AT ME. I'M JUST STATING THE FACTS.
SO...
...WHERE'D THAT BRAT...
...GO?

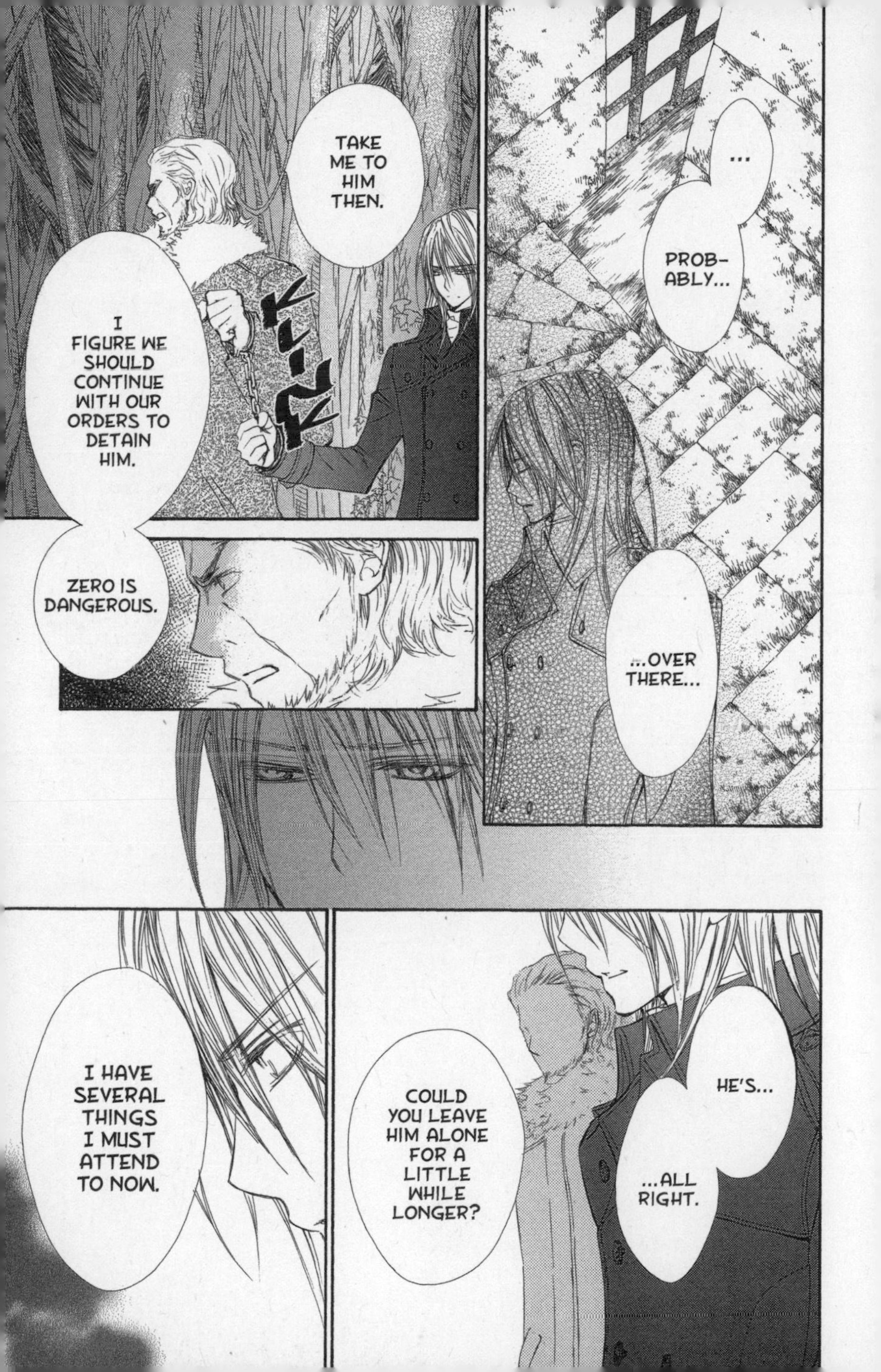
...
PROBABLY...
...OVER THERE...
TAKE ME TO HIM THEN.
I FIGURE WE SHOULD CONTINUE WITH OUR ORDERS TO DETAIN HIM.
ZERO IS DANGEROUS.
HE'S...
...ALL RIGHT.
COULD YOU LEAVE HIM ALONE FOR A LITTLE WHILE LONGER?
I HAVE SEVERAL THINGS I MUST ATTEND TO NOW.

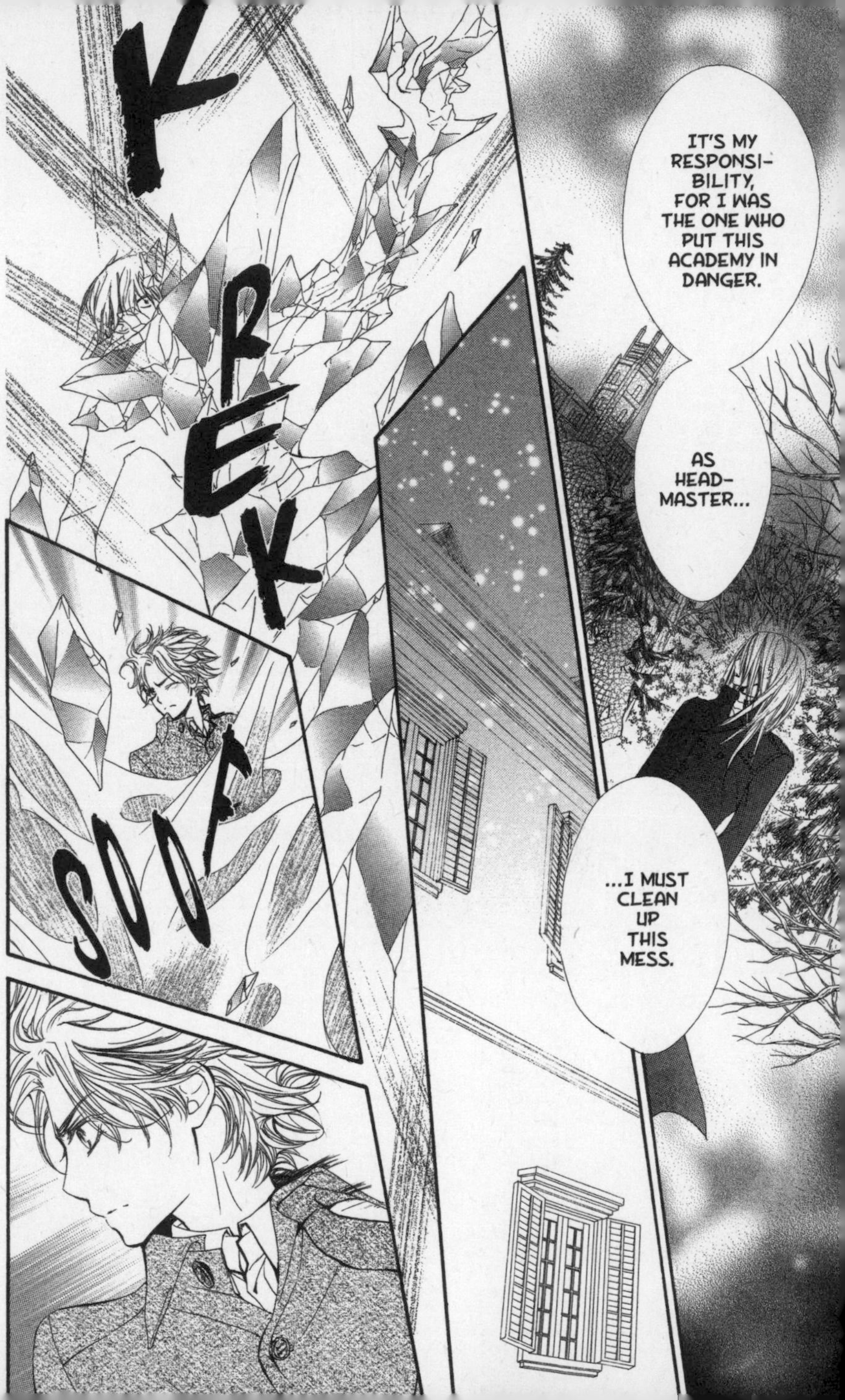
IT'S MY RESPONSI-BILITY, FOR I WAS THE ONE WHO PUT THIS ACADEMY IN DANGER.
AS HEAD-MASTER...
...I MUST CLEAN UP THIS MESS.
KREK
SOOF

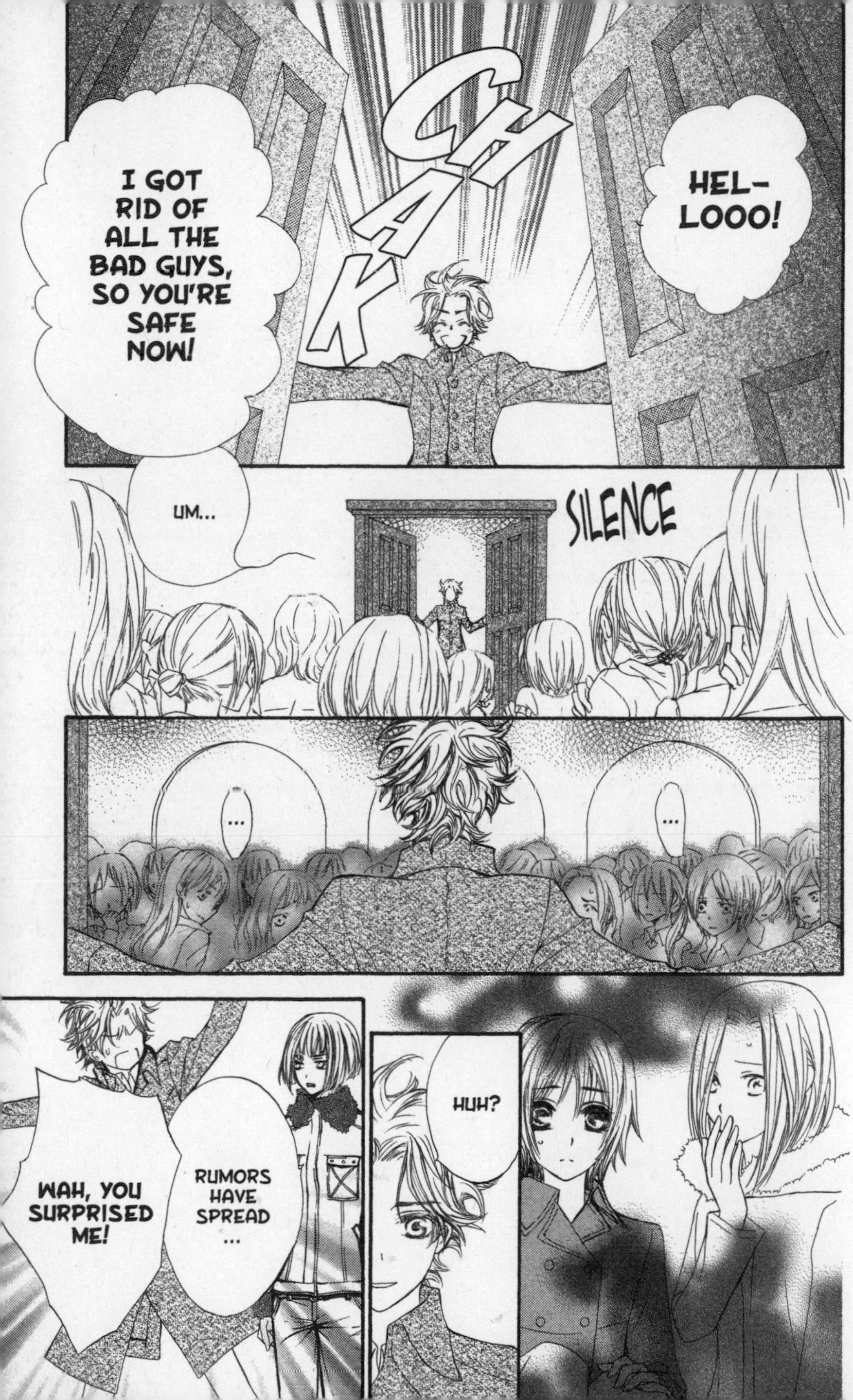
HEL-LOOO!
CHAK
I GOT RID OF ALL THE BAD GUYS, SO YOU'RE SAFE NOW!
SILENCE
UM...
...
...
HUH?
RUMORS HAVE SPREAD ...
WAH, YOU SURPRISED ME!

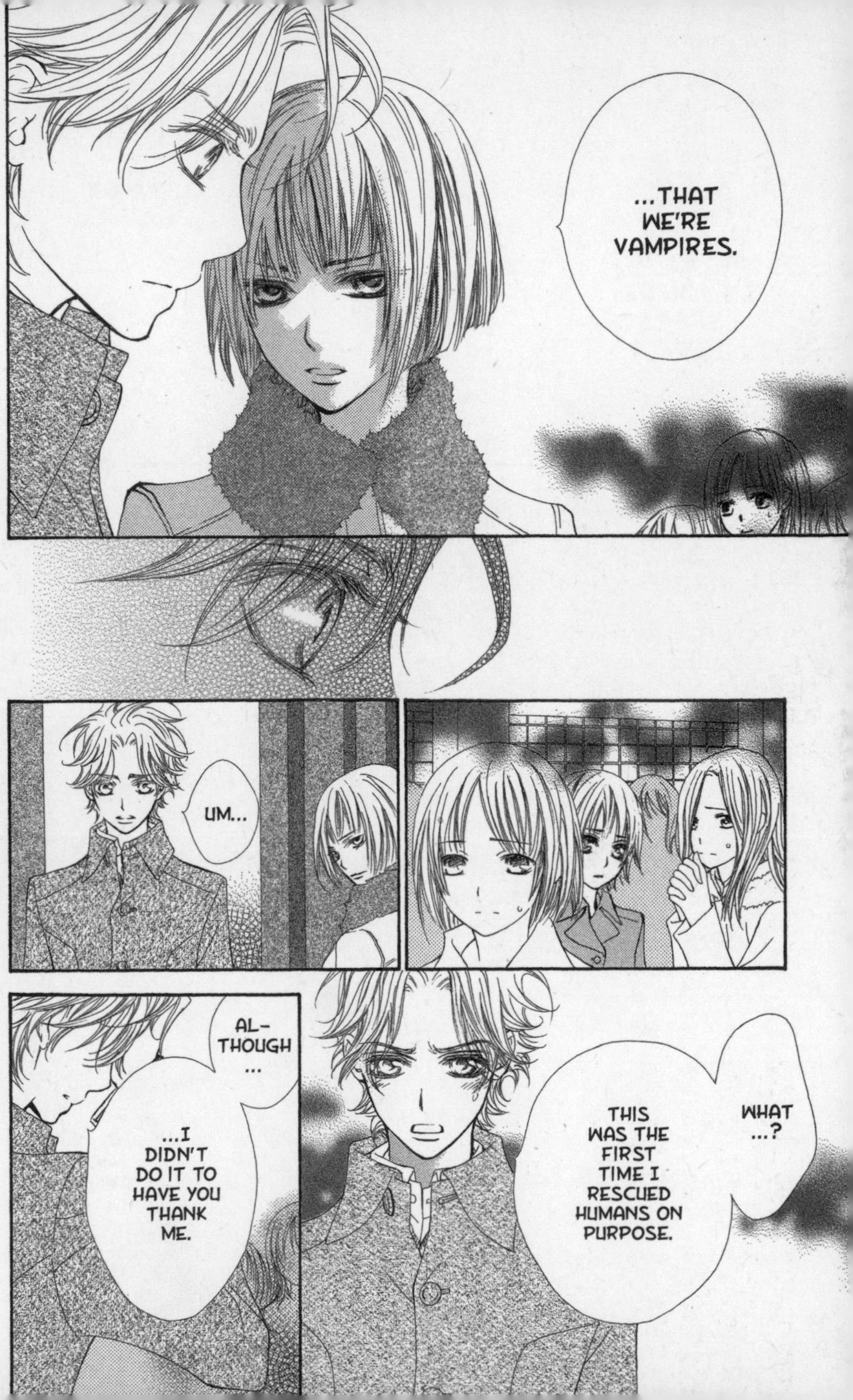
...THAT WE'RE VAMPIRES.
UM...
WHAT ...?
THIS WAS THE FIRST TIME I RESCUED HUMANS ON PURPOSE.
AL-THOUGH ...
...I DIDN'T DO IT TO HAVE YOU THANK ME.

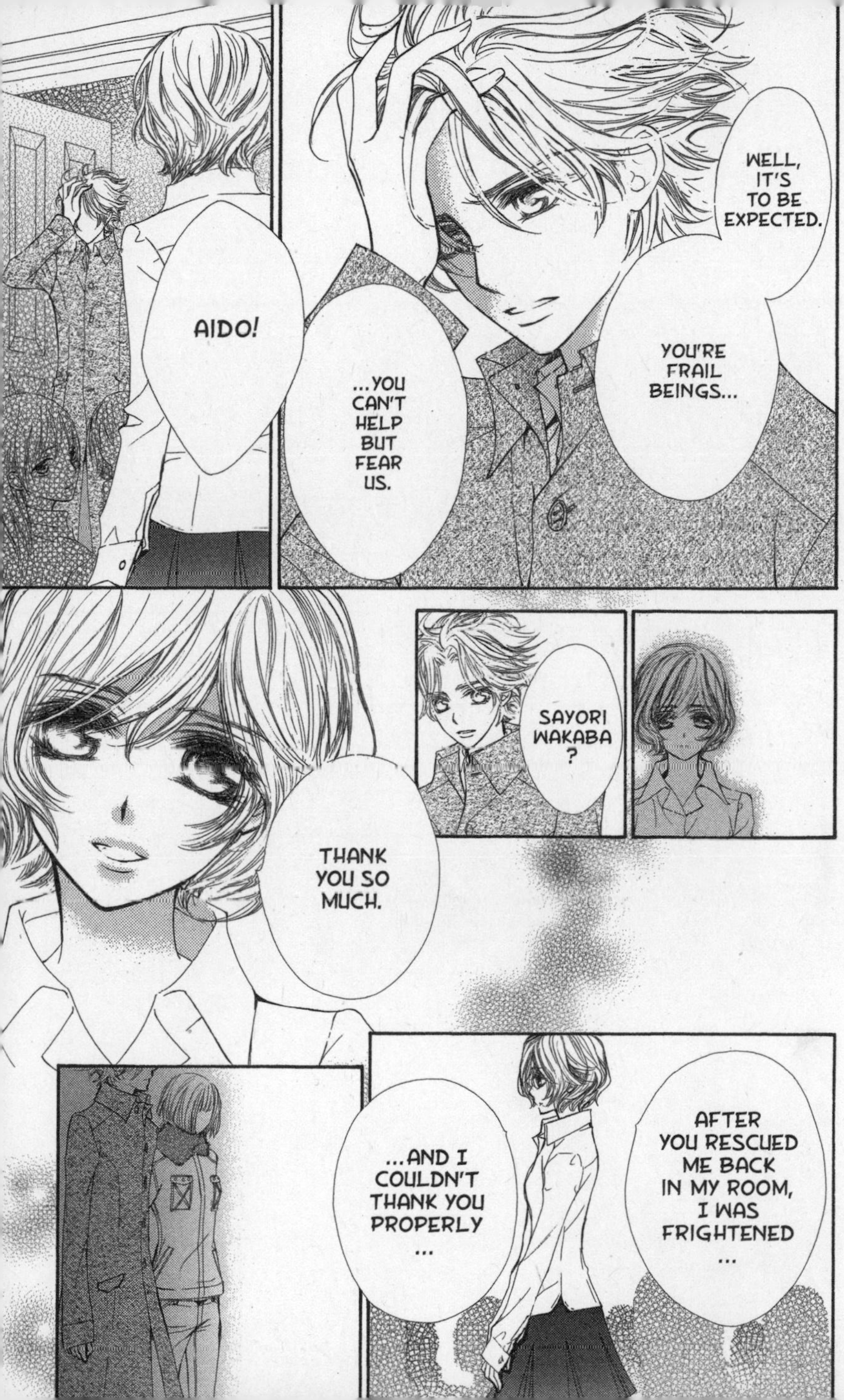
WELL, IT'S TO BE EXPECTED.
YOU'RE FRAIL BEINGS...
...YOU CAN'T HELP BUT FEAR US.
AIDO!
SAYORI WAKABA?
THANK YOU SO MUCH.
AFTER YOU RESCUED ME BACK IN MY ROOM, I WAS FRIGHTENED ...
...AND I COULDN'T THANK YOU PROPERLY ...

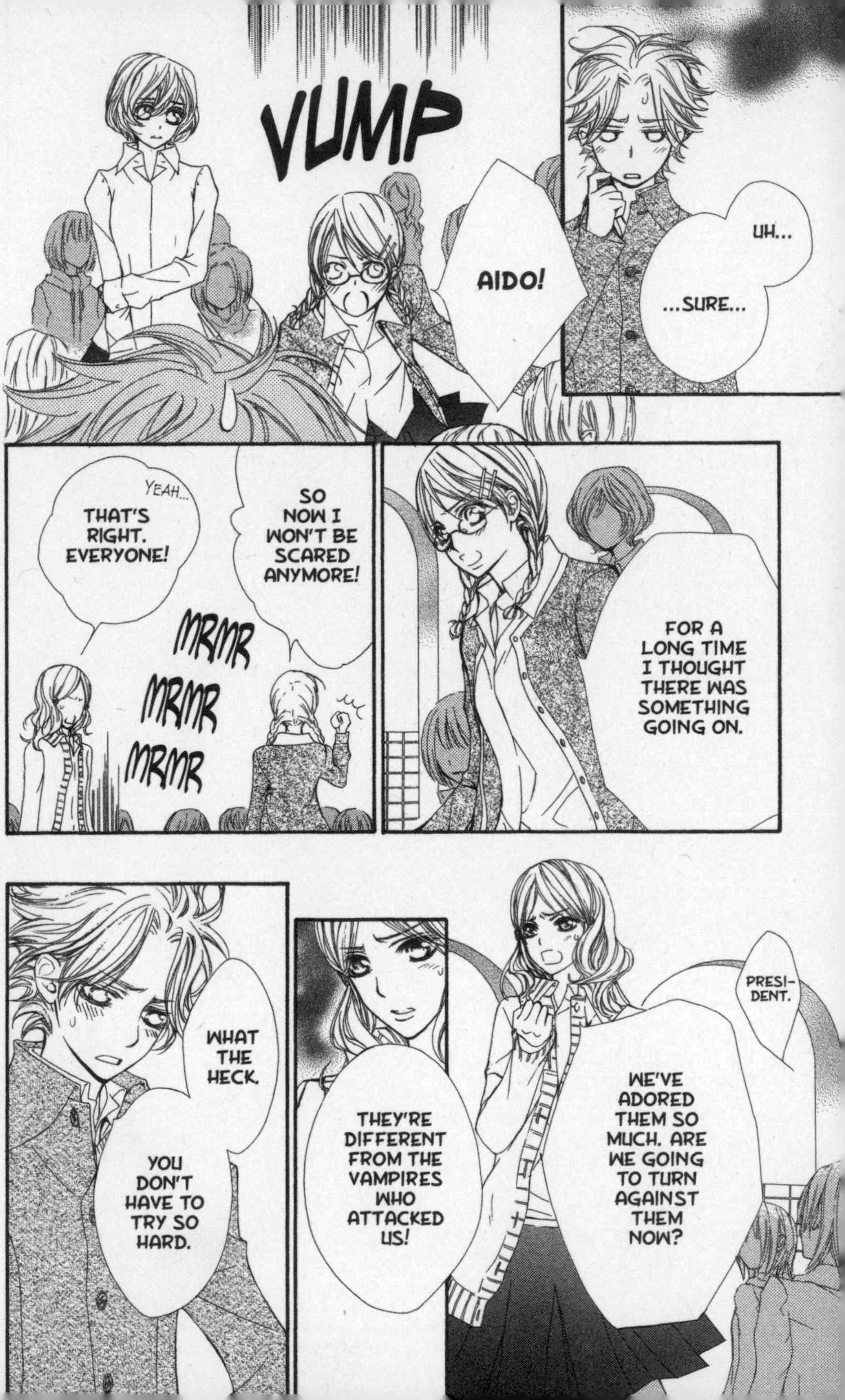
VUMP
AIDO!
UH...
...SURE...
FOR A LONG TIME I THOUGHT THERE WAS SOMETHING GOING ON.
SO NOW I WON'T BE SCARED ANYMORE!
YEAH... THAT'S RIGHT. EVERYONE!
MRMR
MRMR
MRMR
PRESI-DENT.
WE'VE ADORED THEM SO MUCH. ARE WE GOING TO TURN AGAINST THEM NOW?
THEY'RE DIFFERENT FROM THE VAMPIRES WHO ATTACKED US!
WHAT THE HECK.
YOU DON'T HAVE TO TRY SO HARD.

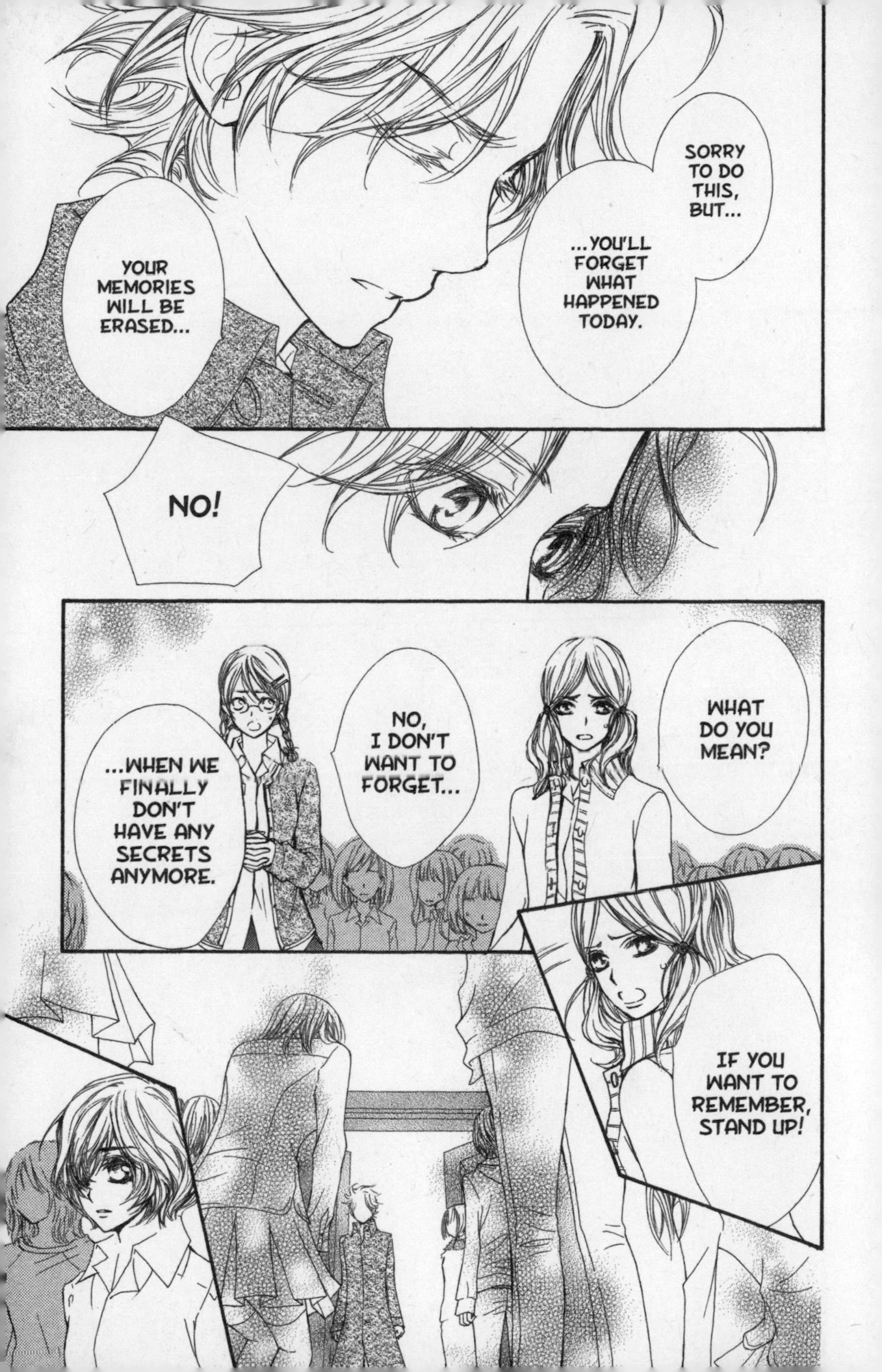
SORRY TO DO THIS, BUT...
...YOU'LL FORGET WHAT HAPPENED TODAY.
YOUR MEMORIES WILL BE ERASED...
NO!
WHAT DO YOU MEAN?
NO, I DON'T WANT TO FORGET...
...WHEN WE FINALLY DON'T HAVE ANY SECRETS ANYMORE.
IF YOU WANT TO REMEMBER, STAND UP!

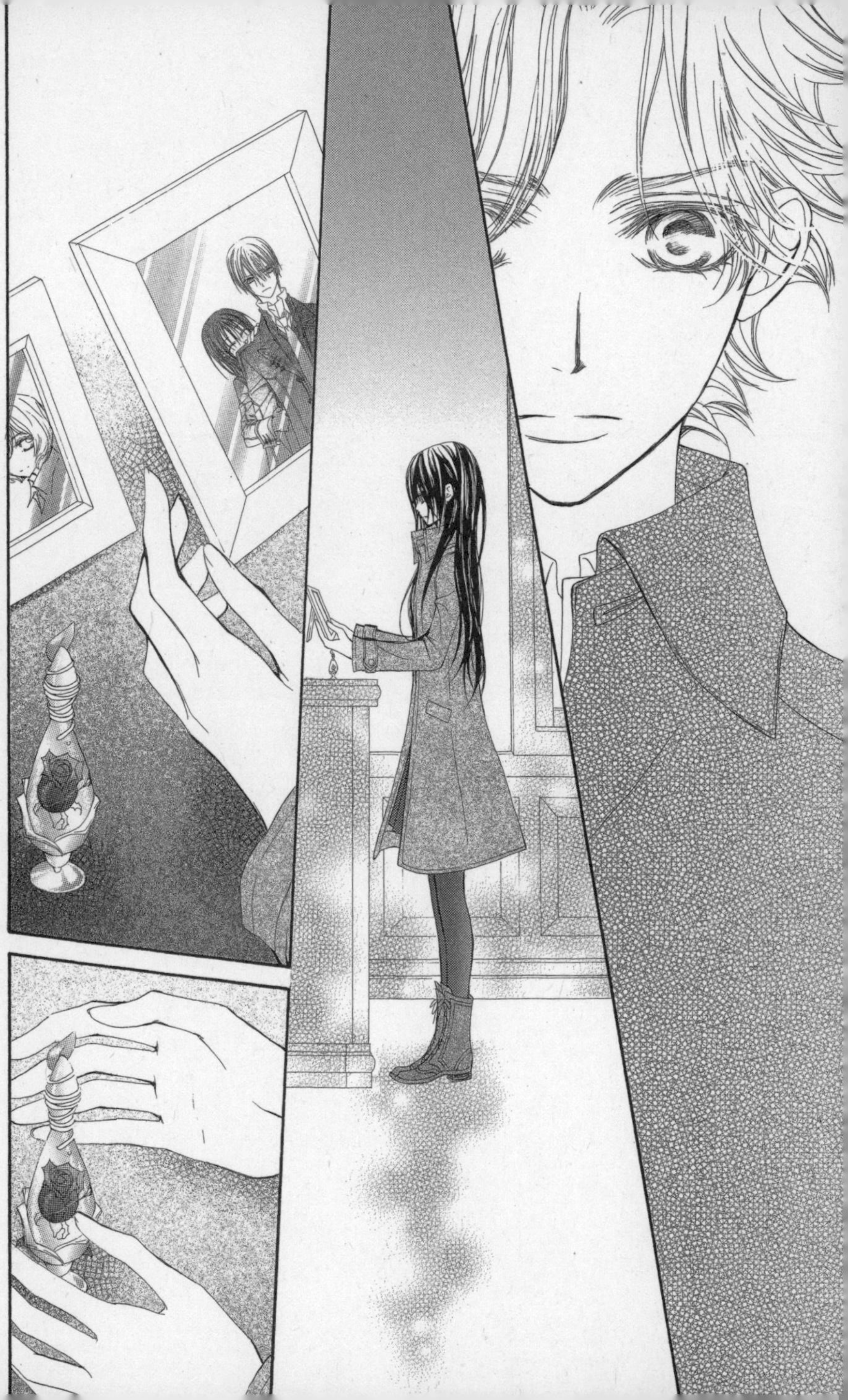

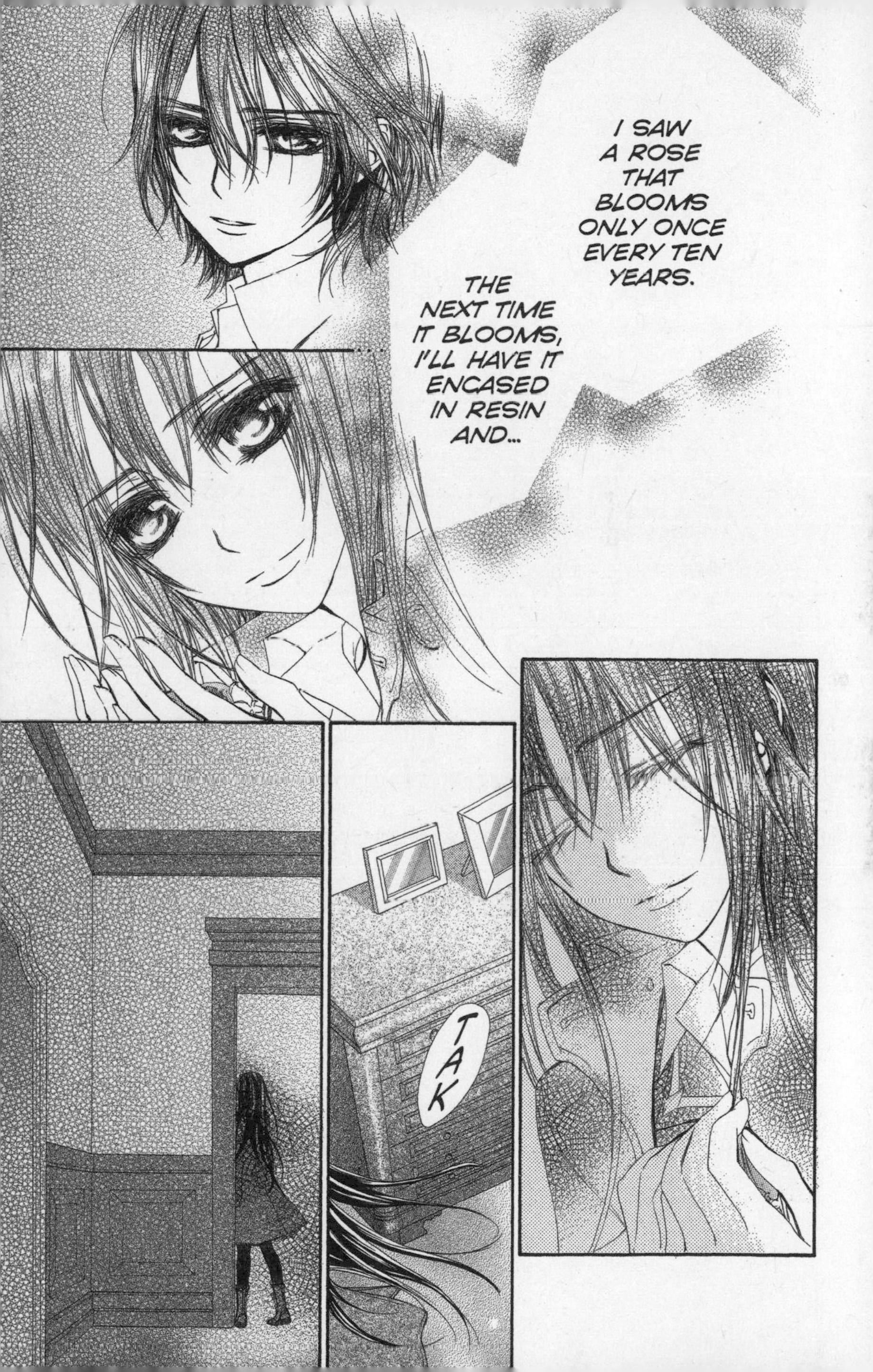
I SAW A ROSE THAT BLOOMS ONLY ONCE EVERY TEN YEARS.
THE NEXT TIME IT BLOOMS, I'LL HAVE IT ENCASED IN RESIN AND...
TAK

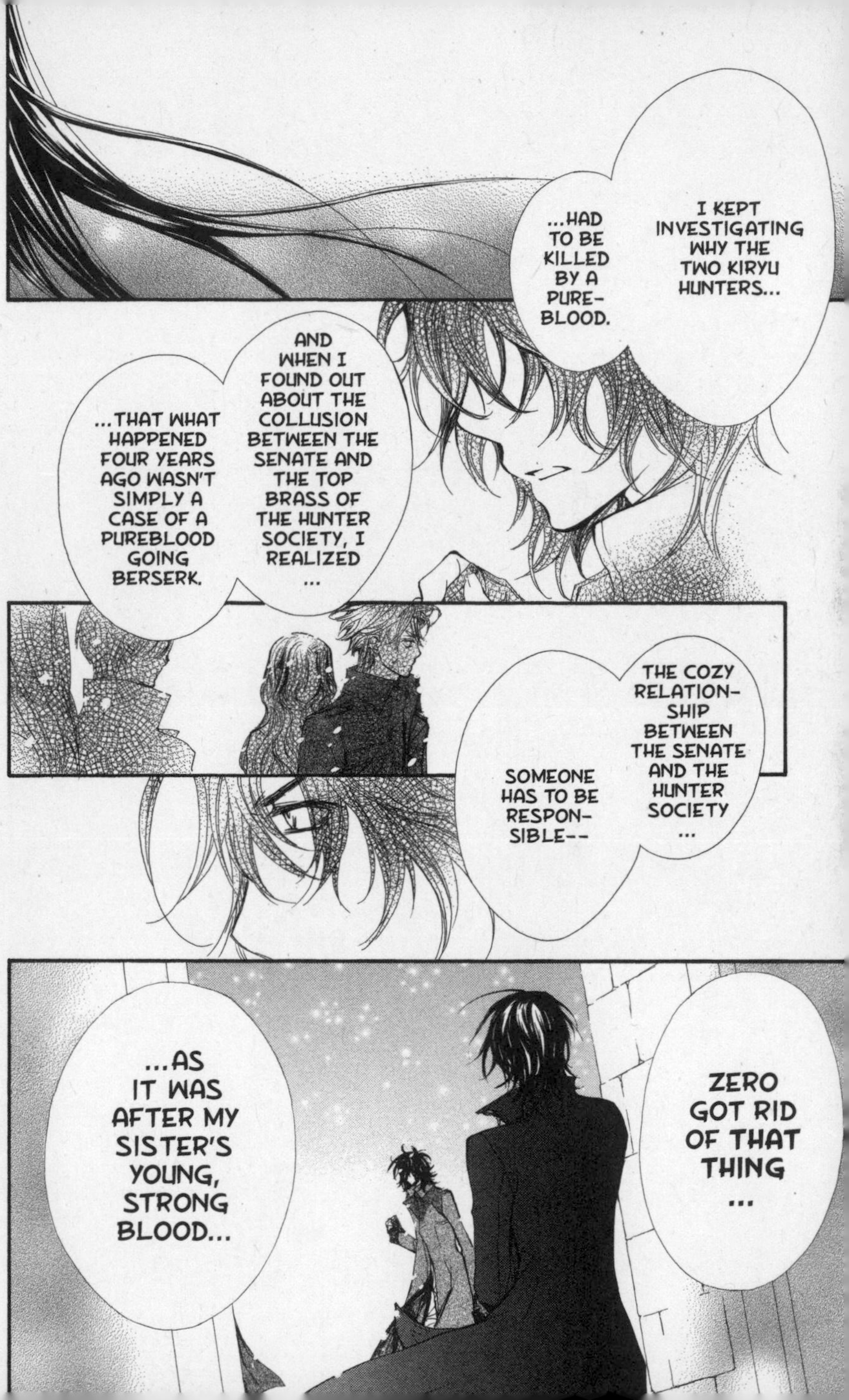
I KEPT INVESTIGATING WHY THE TWO KIRYU HUNTERS...
...HAD TO BE KILLED BY A PURE-BLOOD.
AND WHEN I FOUND OUT ABOUT THE COLLUSION BETWEEN THE SENATE AND THE TOP BRASS OF THE HUNTER SOCIETY, I REALIZED ...
...THAT WHAT HAPPENED FOUR YEARS AGO WASN'T SIMPLY A CASE OF A PUREBLOOD GOING BERSERK.
THE COZY RELATION-SHIP BETWEEN THE SENATE AND THE HUNTER SOCIETY ...
SOMEONE HAS TO BE RESPON-SIBLE--
ZERO GOT RID OF THAT THING ...
...AS IT WAS AFTER MY SISTER'S YOUNG, STRONG BLOOD...

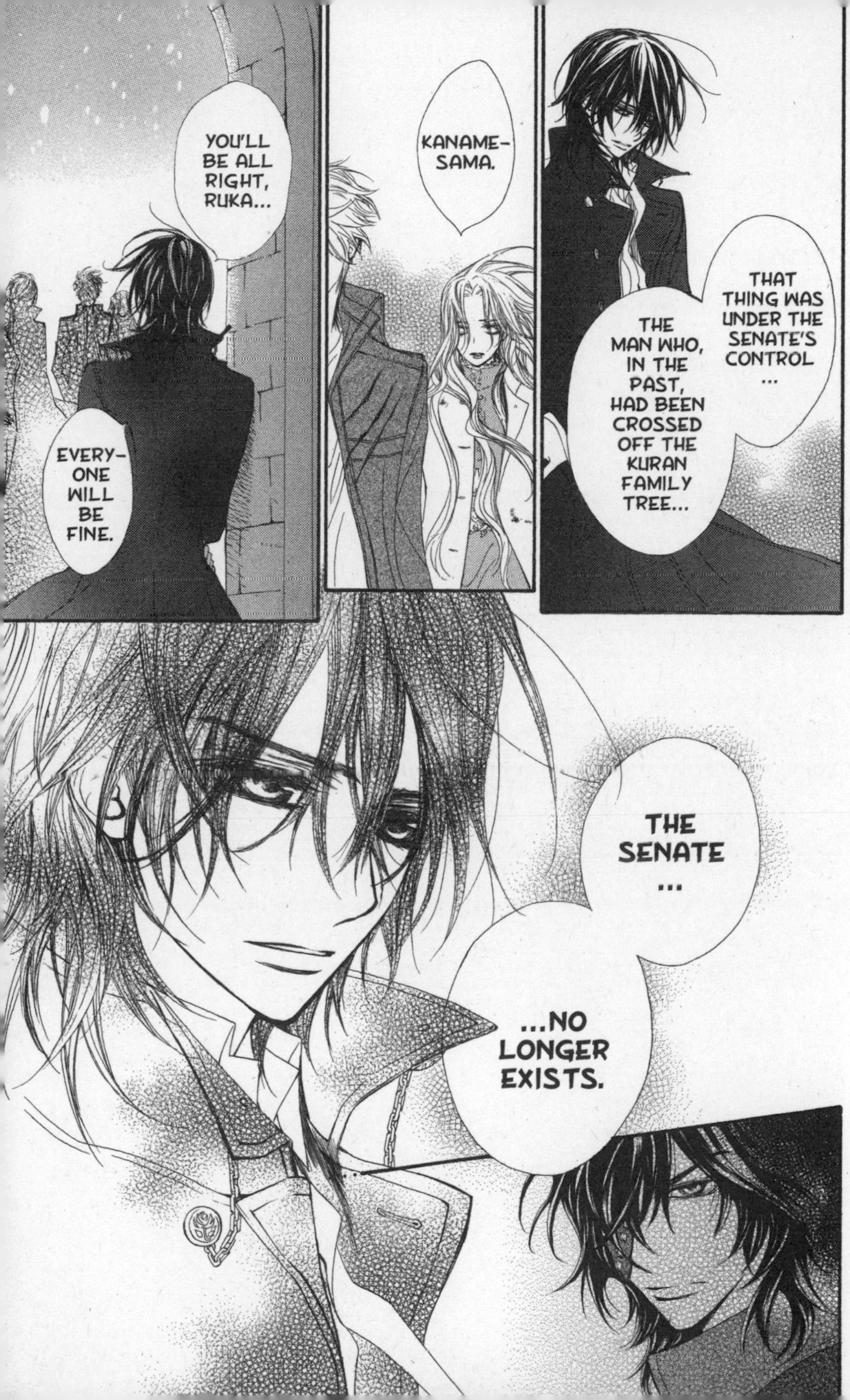
THAT THING WAS UNDER THE SENATE'S CONTROL ...
THE MAN WHO, IN THE PAST, HAD BEEN CROSSED OFF THE KURAN FAMILY TREE...
KANAME-SAMA.
YOU'LL BE ALL RIGHT, RUKA...
EVERY-ONE WILL BE FINE.
THE SENATE ...
...NO LONGER EXISTS.

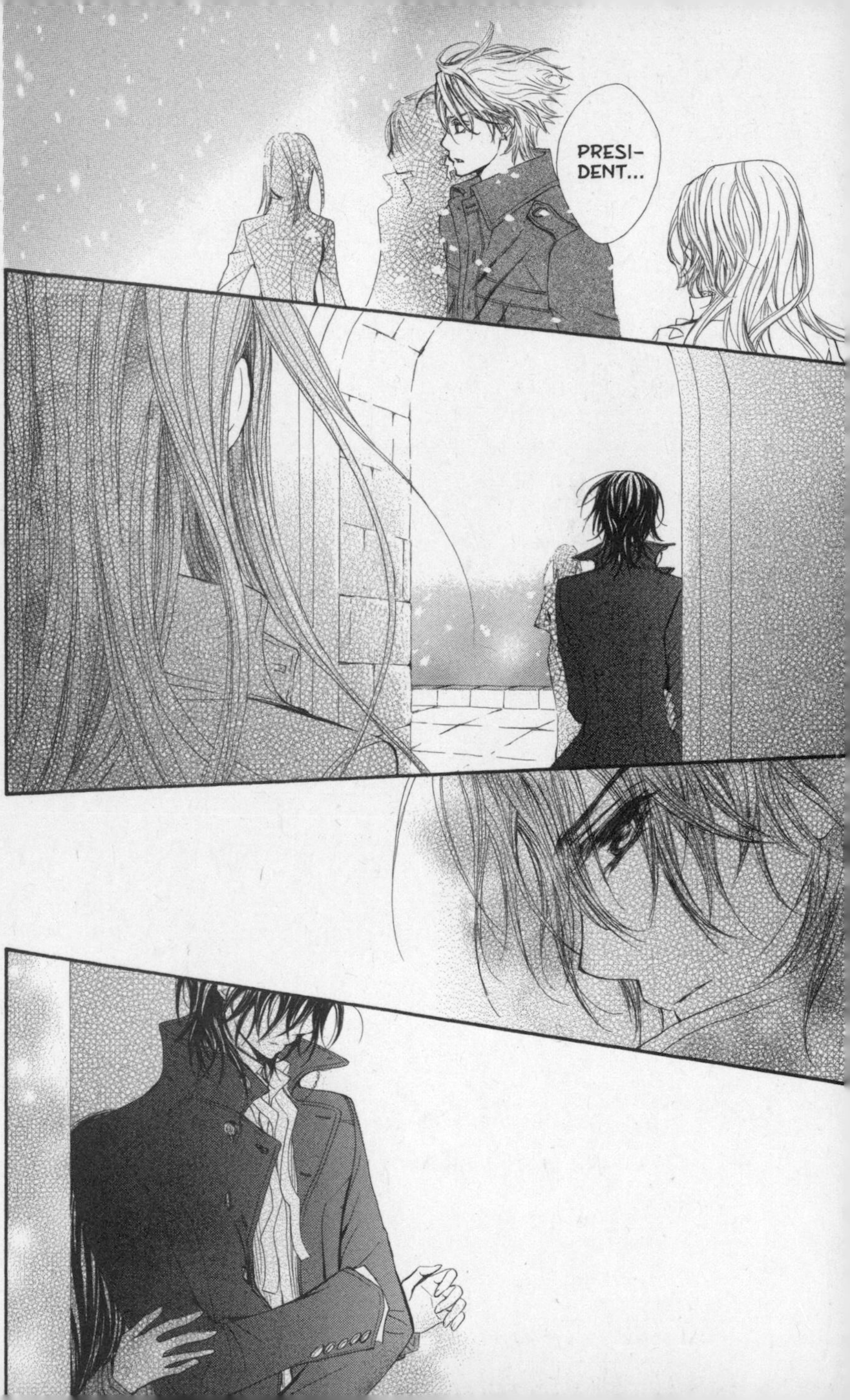
PRESI-
DENT...

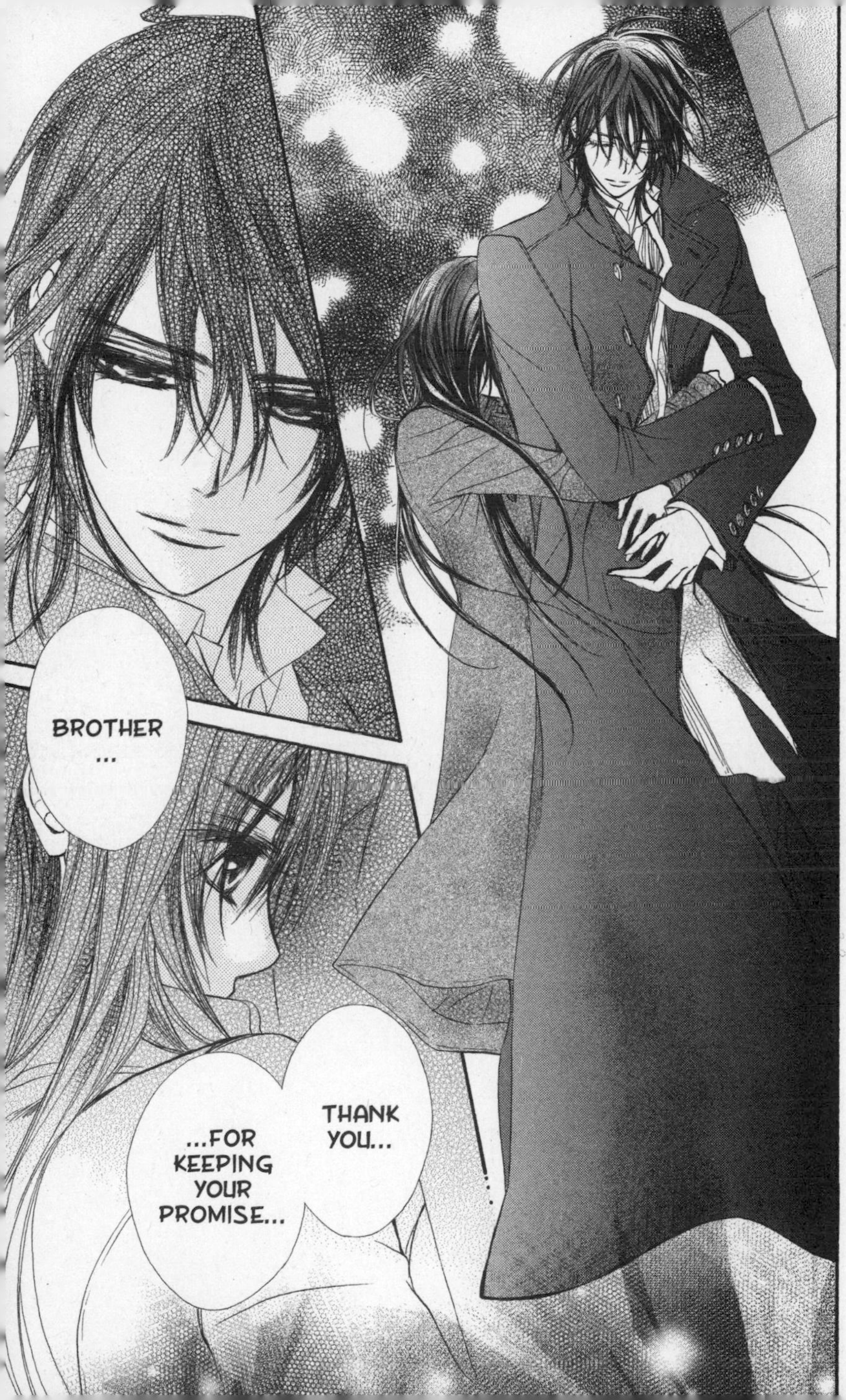
BROTHER ...
THANK YOU...
...FOR KEEPING YOUR PROMISE...

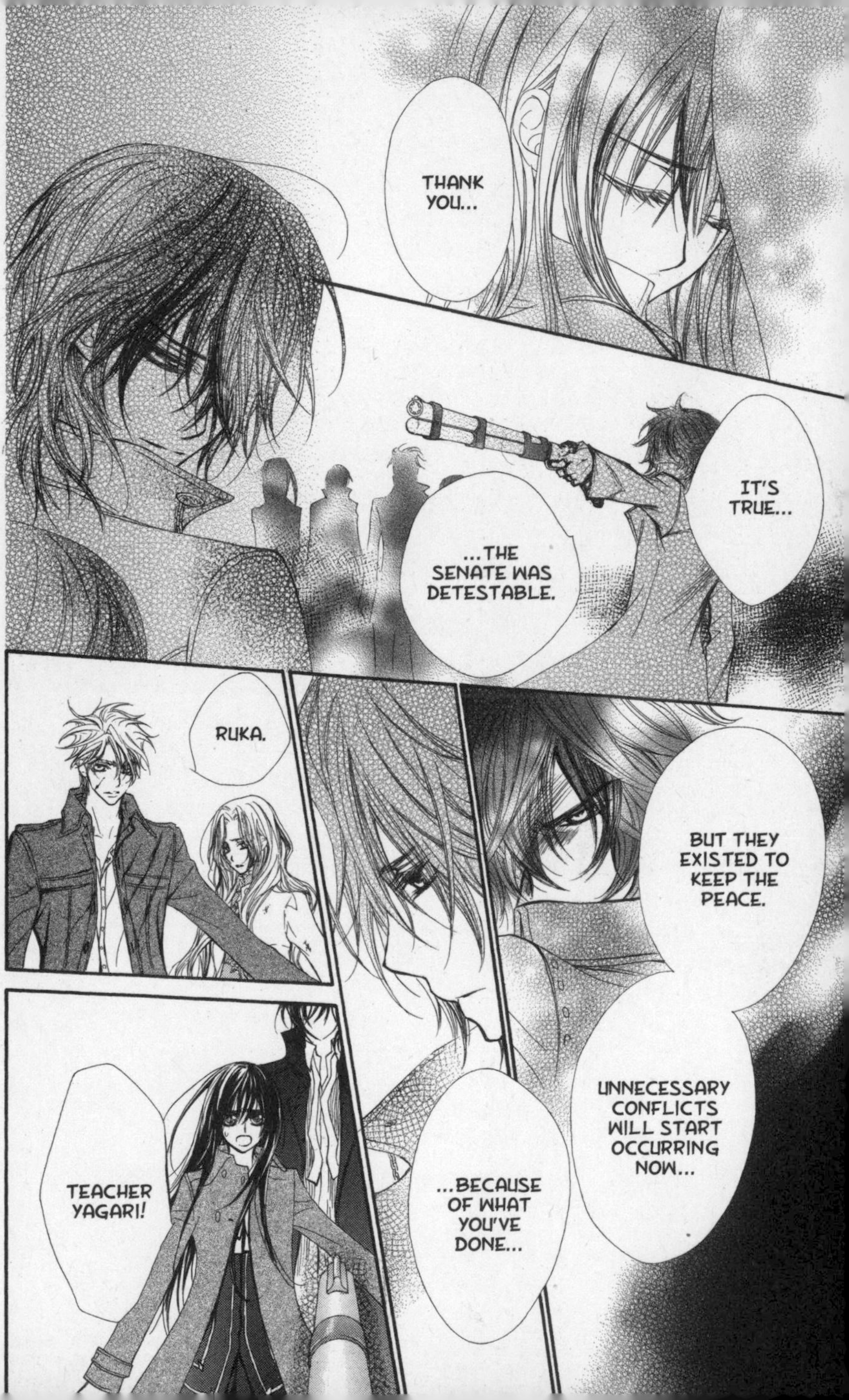
THANK YOU...
IT'S TRUE...
...THE SENATE WAS DETESTABLE.
BUT THEY EXISTED TO KEEP THE PEACE.
UNNECESSARY CONFLICTS WILL START OCCURRING NOW...
...BECAUSE OF WHAT YOU'VE DONE...
RUKA.
TEACHER YAGARI!

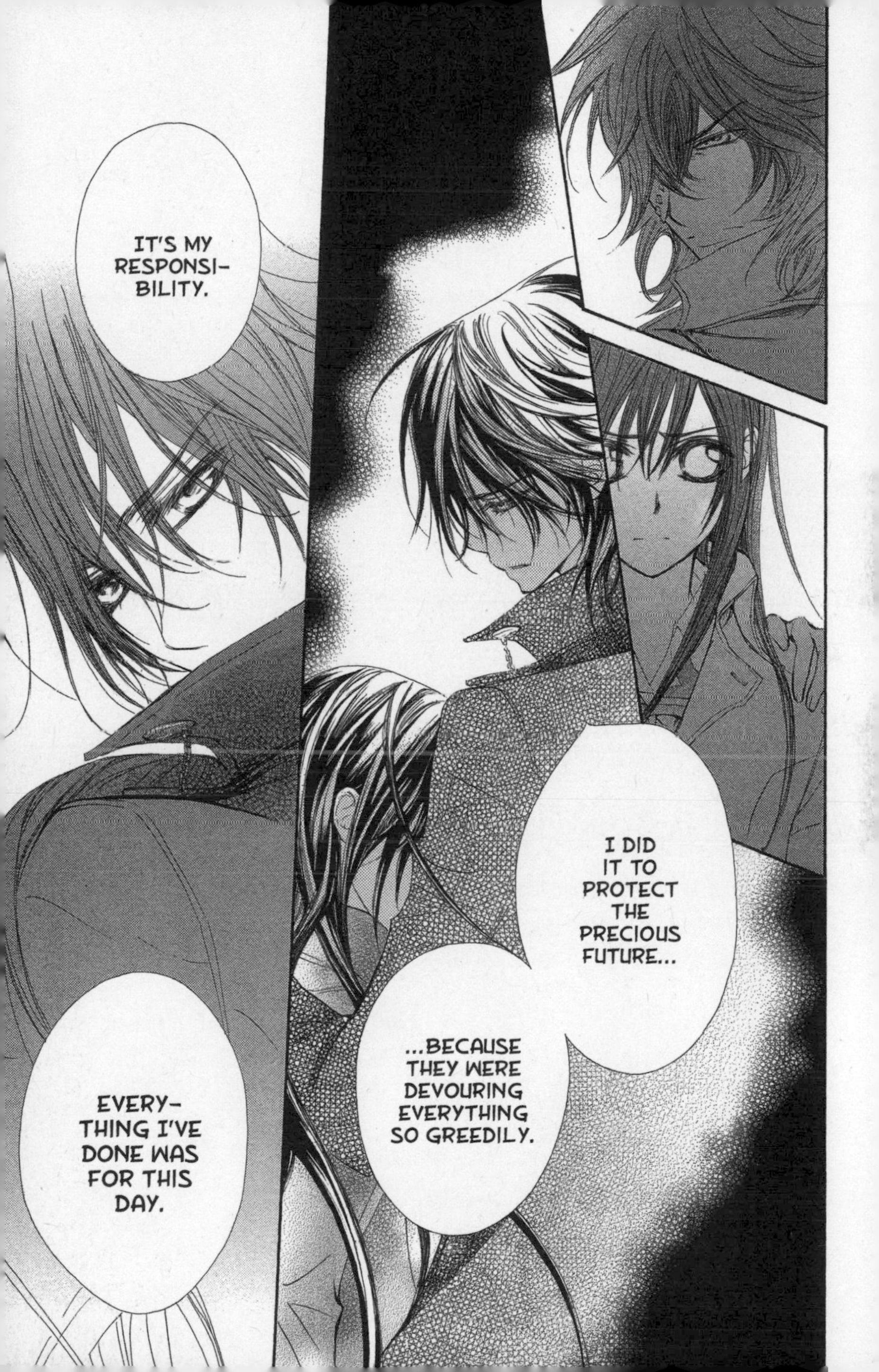
I DID IT TO PROTECT THE PRECIOUS FUTURE...
...BECAUSE THEY WERE DEVOURING EVERYTHING SO GREEDILY.
IT'S MY RESPONSIBILITY.
EVERYTHING I'VE DONE WAS FOR THIS DAY.

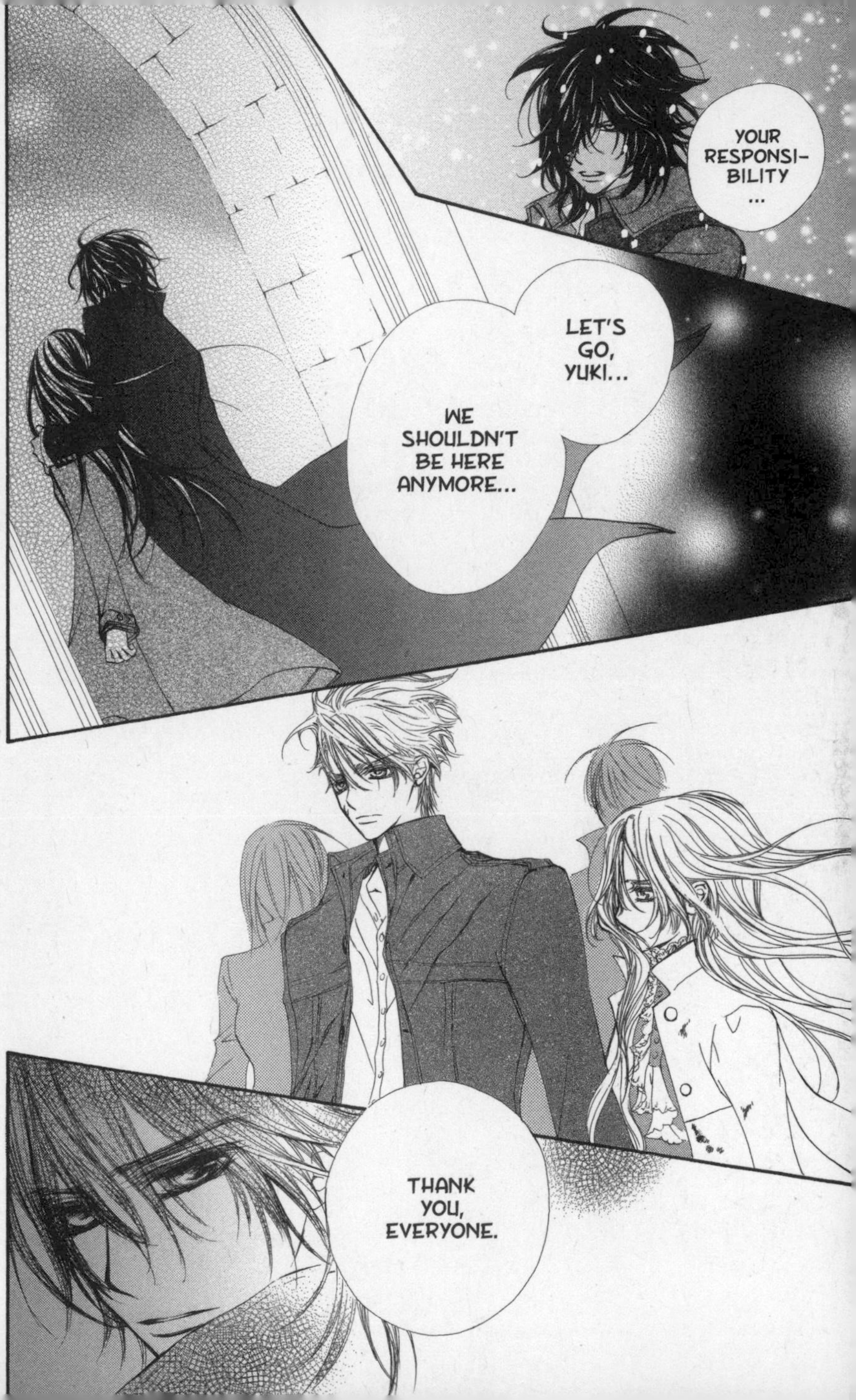
YOUR RESPONSI-BILITY ...
LET'S GO, YUKI...
WE SHOULDN'T BE HERE ANYMORE...
THANK YOU, EVERYONE.

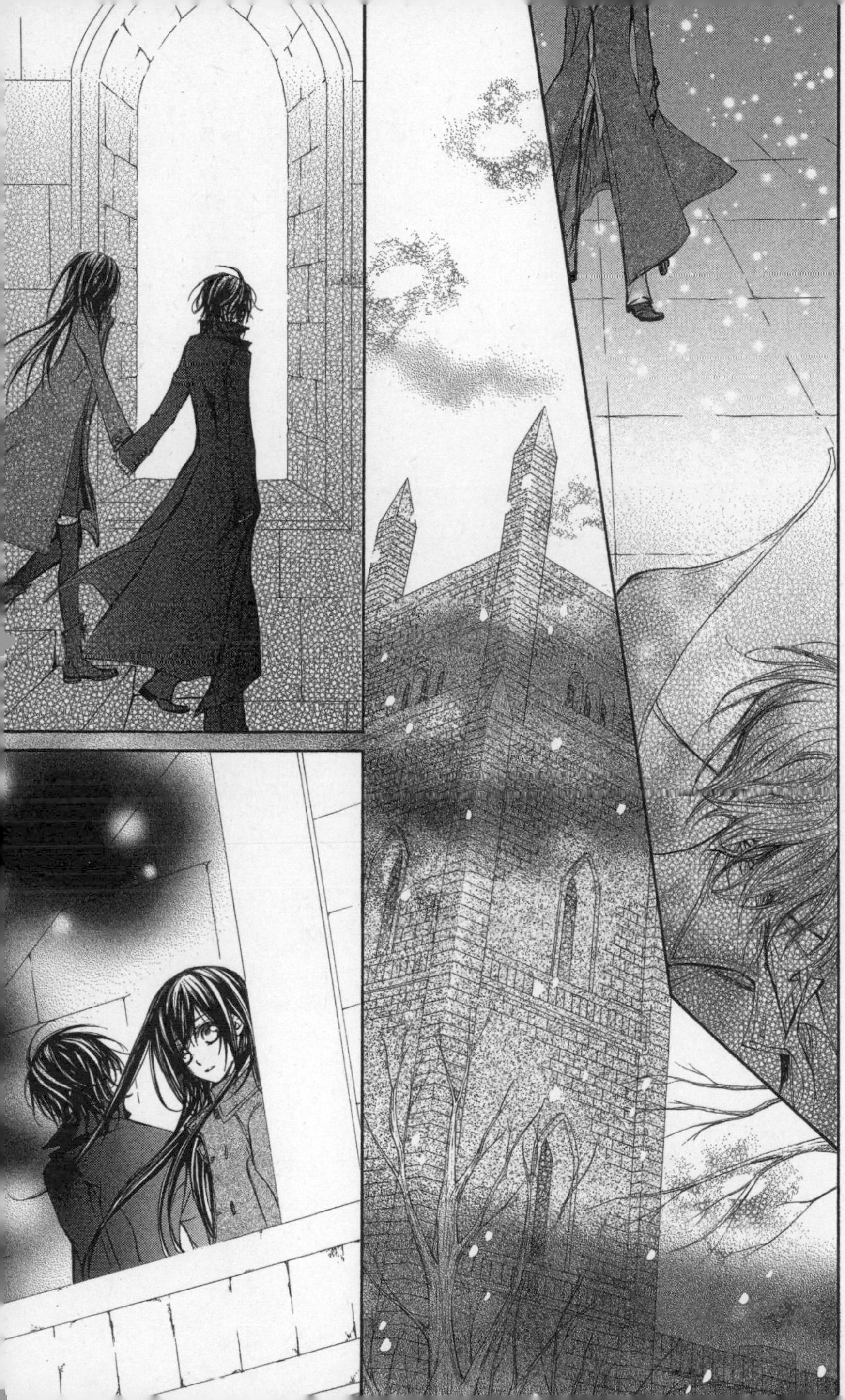

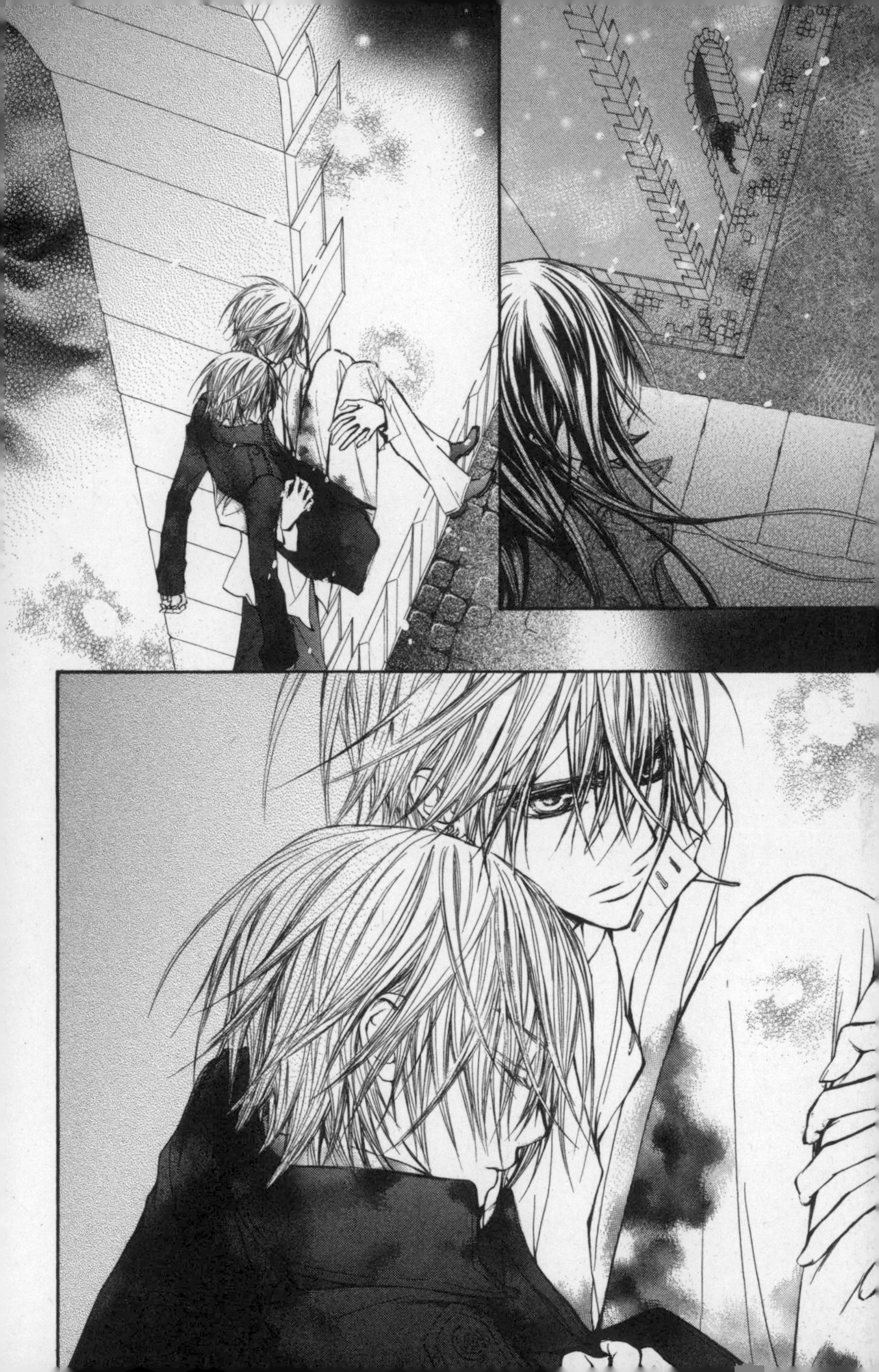

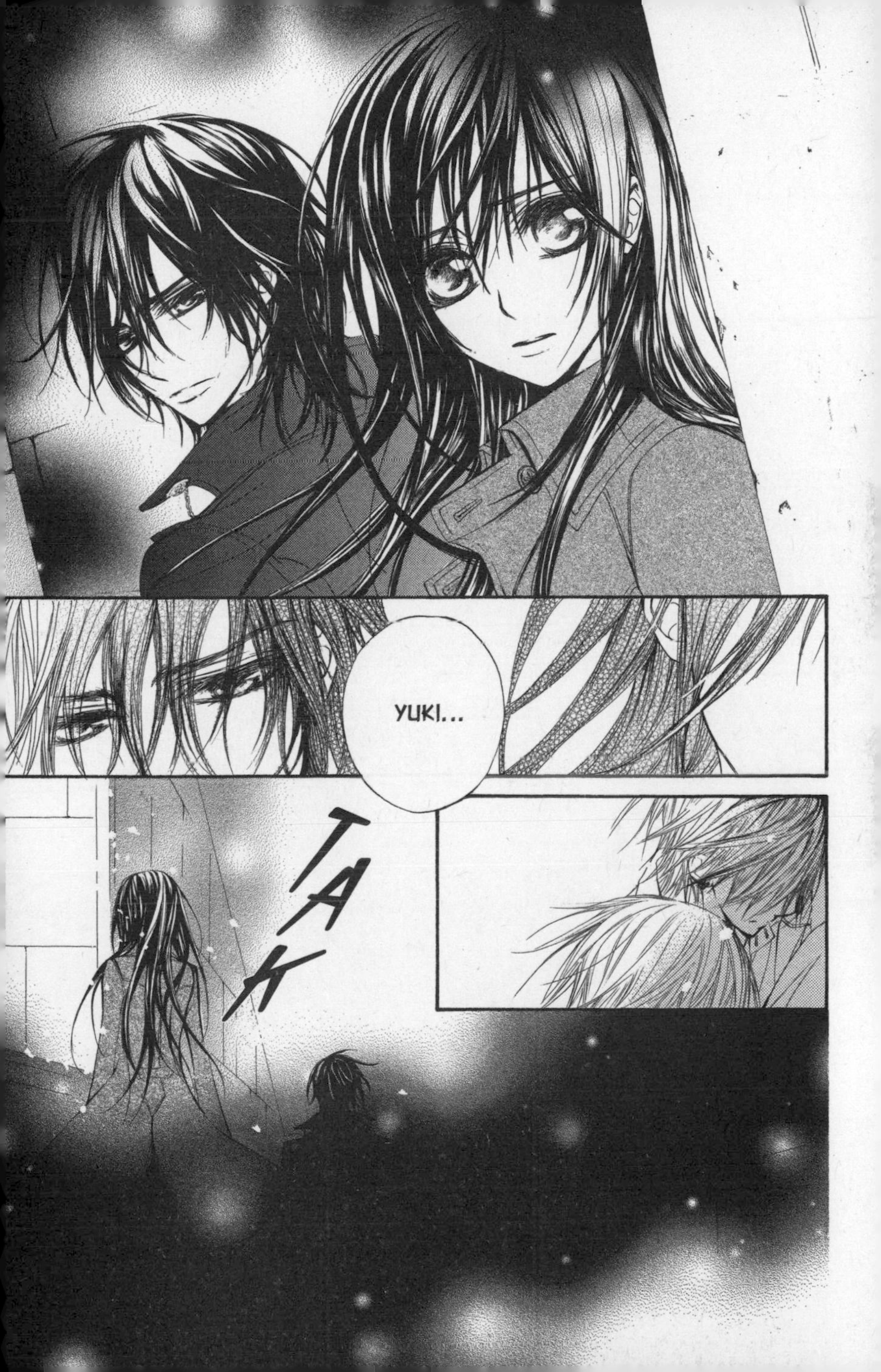
YUKI...
TAK

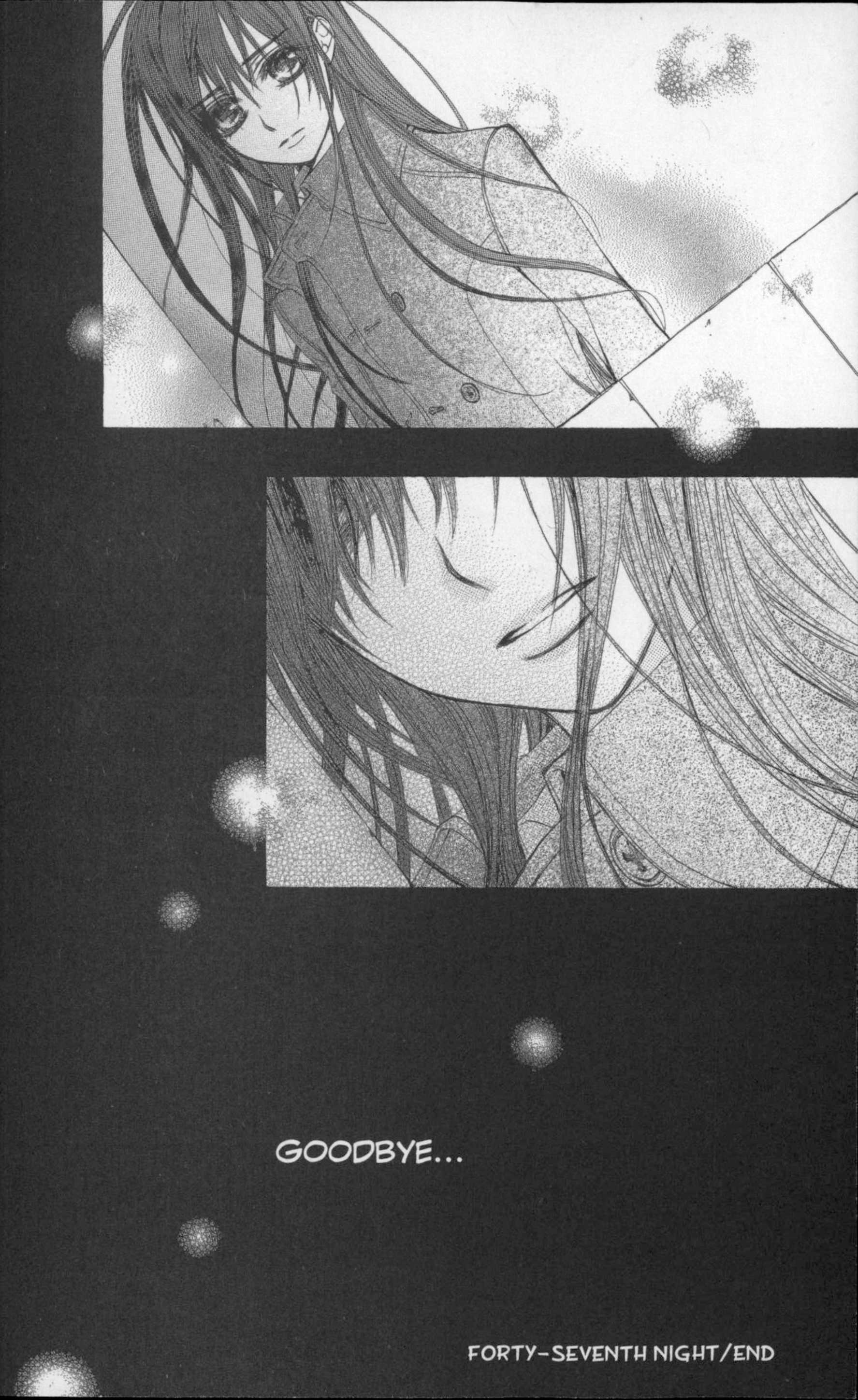
GOODBYE...
FORTY-SEVENTH NIGHT/END

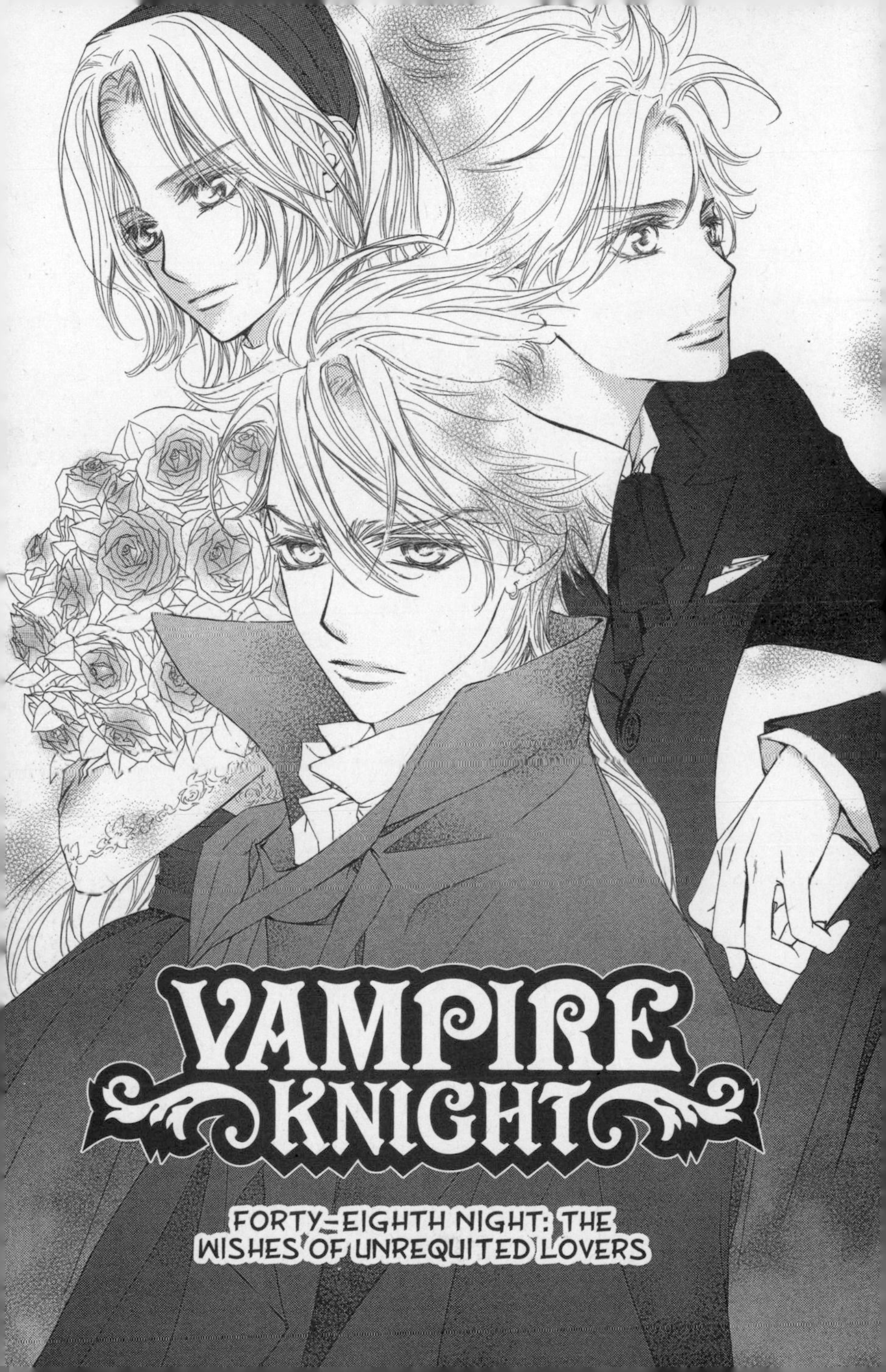
VAMPIRE KNIGHT
FORTY-EIGHTH NIGHT: THE WISHES OF UNREQUITED LOVERS

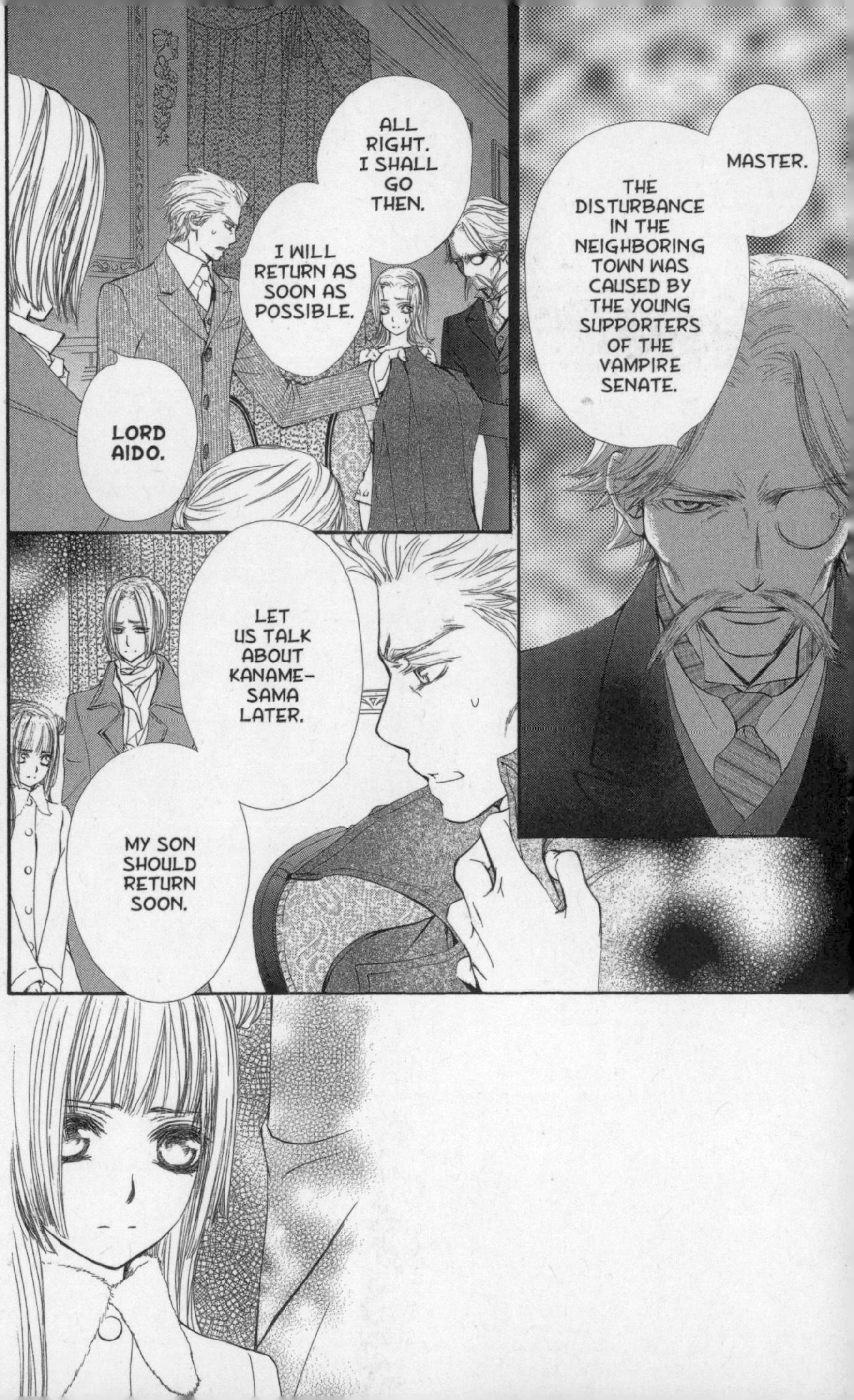
MASTER.
THE DISTURBANCE IN THE NEIGHBORING TOWN WAS CAUSED BY THE YOUNG SUPPORTERS OF THE VAMPIRE SENATE.
ALL RIGHT. I SHALL GO THEN.
I WILL RETURN AS SOON AS POSSIBLE.
LORD AIDO.
LET US TALK ABOUT KANAME-SAMA LATER.
MY SON SHOULD RETURN SOON.

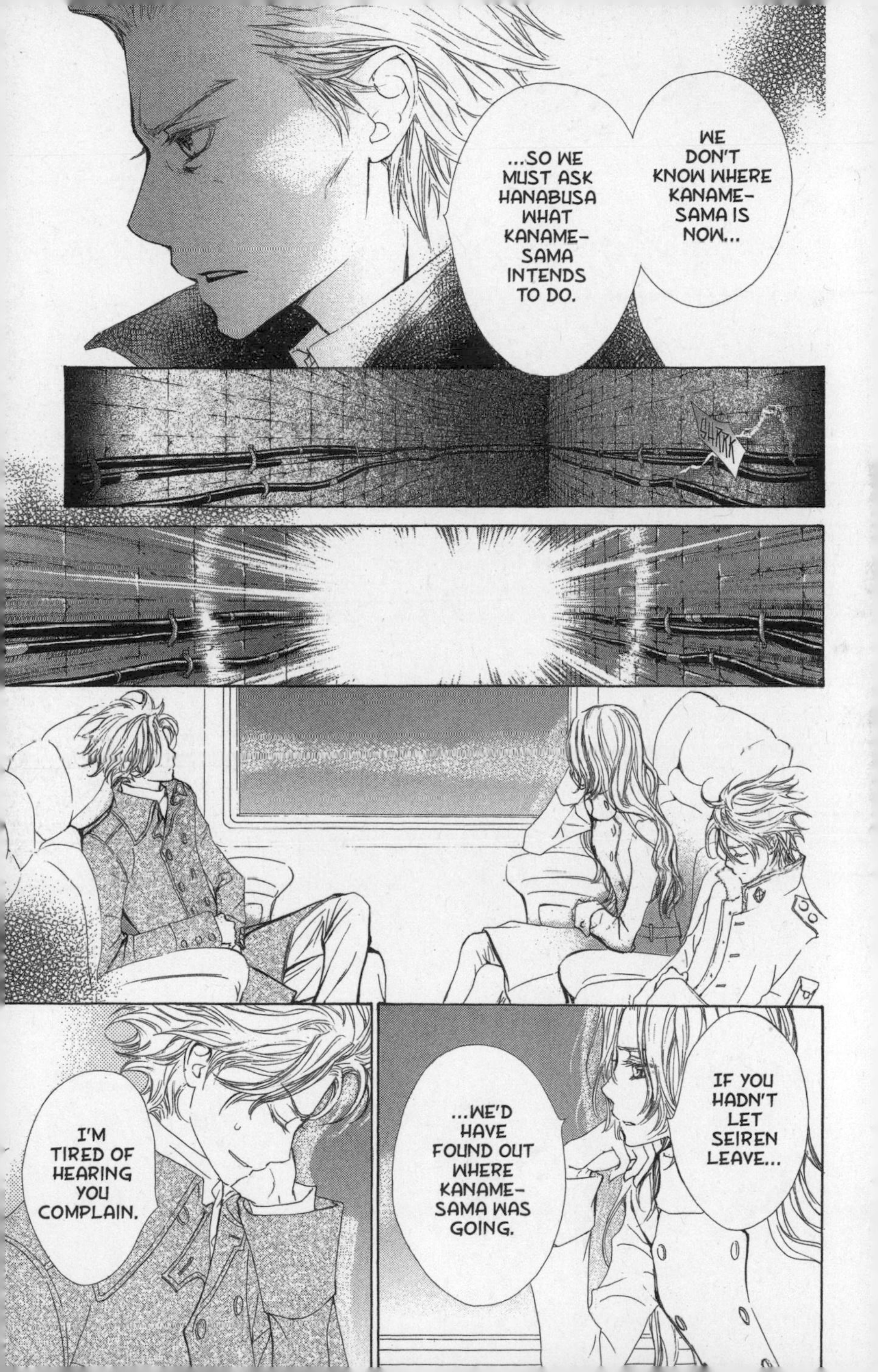
WE DON'T KNOW WHERE KANAME-SAMA IS NOW...
...SO WE MUST ASK HANABUSA WHAT KANAME-SAMA INTENDS TO DO.
SHRKK
IF YOU HADN'T LET SEIREN LEAVE...
...WE'D HAVE FOUND OUT WHERE KANAME-SAMA WAS GOING.
I'M TIRED OF HEARING YOU COMPLAIN.

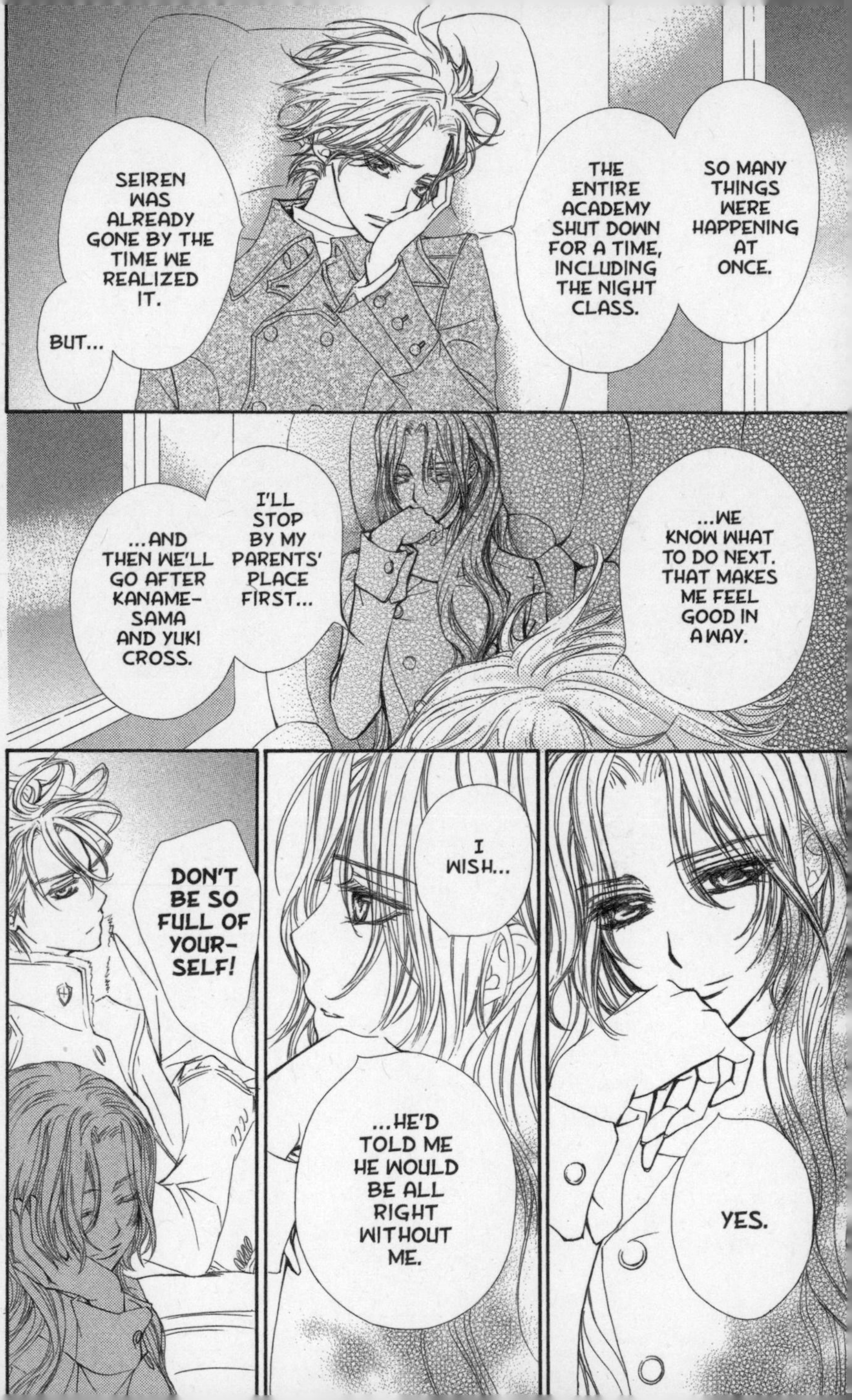
SO MANY THINGS WERE HAPPENING AT ONCE.
THE ENTIRE ACADEMY SHUT DOWN FOR A TIME, INCLUDING THE NIGHT CLASS.
SEIREN WAS ALREADY GONE BY THE TIME WE REALIZED IT.
BUT...
...WE KNOW WHAT TO DO NEXT. THAT MAKES ME FEEL GOOD IN A WAY.
I'LL STOP BY MY PARENTS' PLACE FIRST...
...AND THEN WE'LL GO AFTER KANAME-SAMA AND YUKI CROSS.
YES.
I WISH...
...HE'D TOLD ME HE WOULD BE ALL RIGHT WITHOUT ME.
DON'T BE SO FULL OF YOUR-SELF!

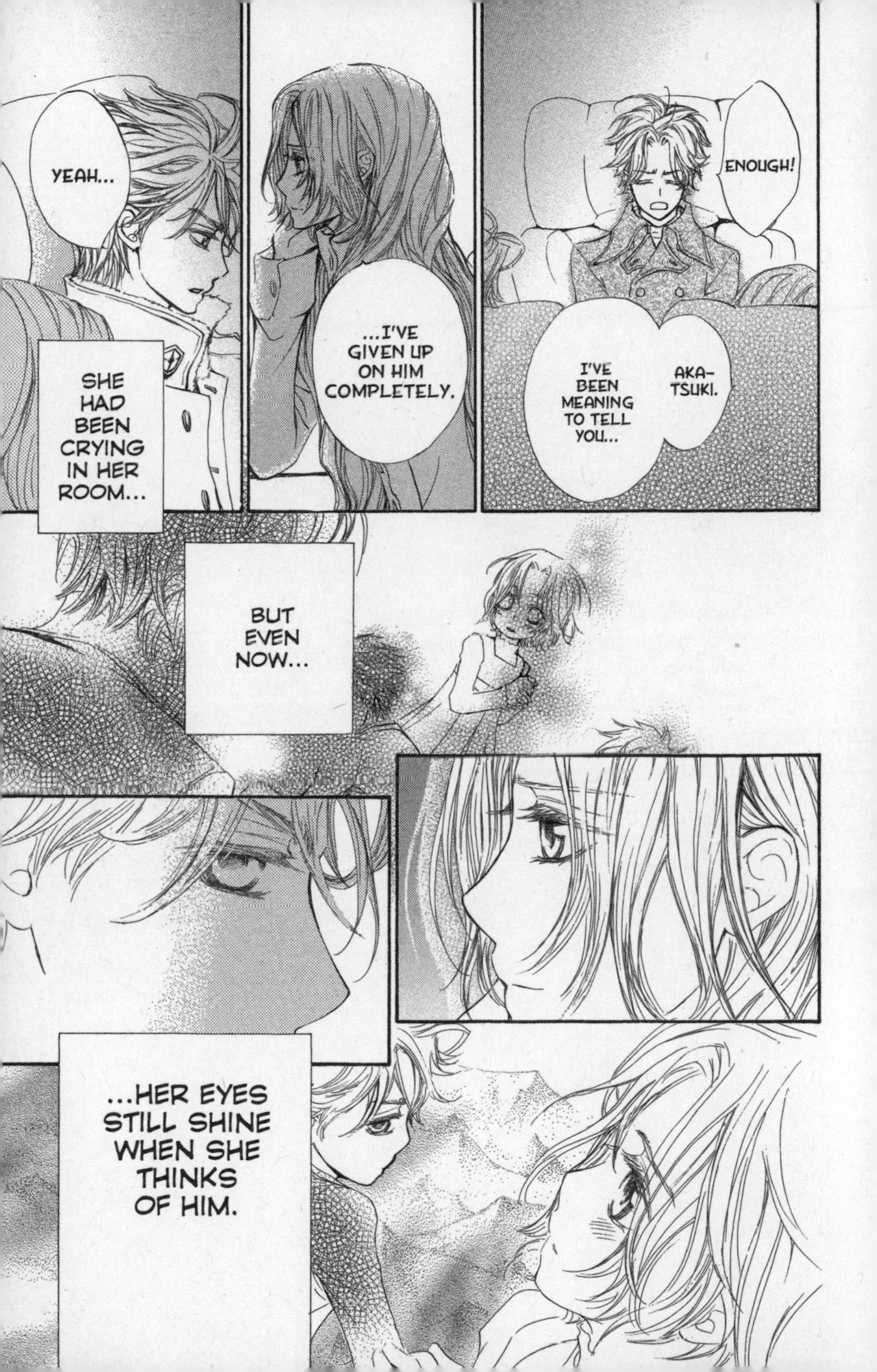
ENOUGH!
AKA-TSUKI. I'VE BEEN MEANING TO TELL YOU...
...I'VE GIVEN UP ON HIM COMPLETELY.
YEAH...
SHE HAD BEEN CRYING IN HER ROOM...
BUT EVEN NOW...
...HER EYES STILL SHINE WHEN SHE THINKS OF HIM.

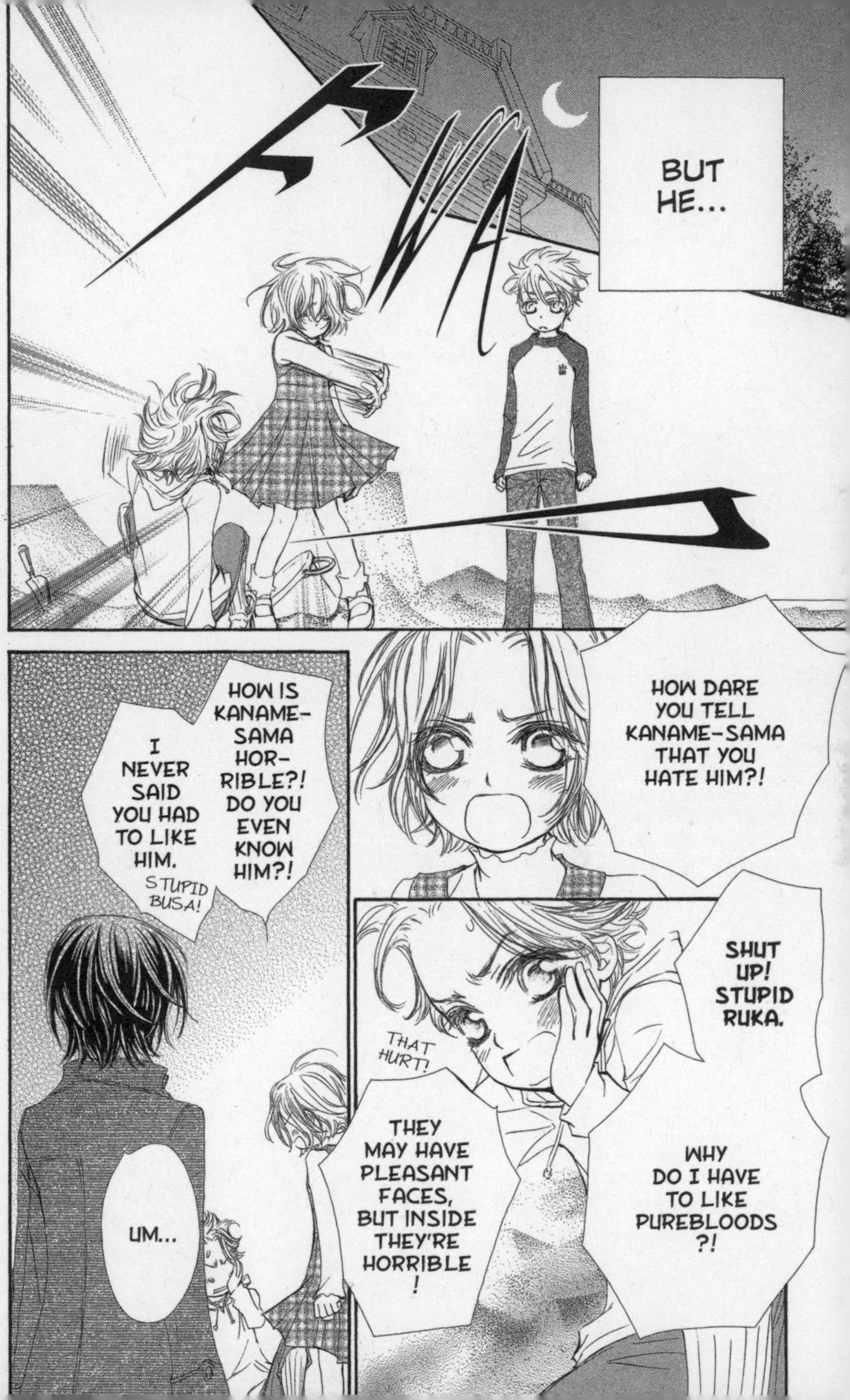
BUT HE...
HOW DARE YOU TELL KANAME-SAMA THAT YOU HATE HIM?!
SHUT UP! STUPID RUKA.
THAT HURT!
WHY DO I HAVE TO LIKE PUREBLOODS ?!
THEY MAY HAVE PLEASANT FACES, BUT INSIDE THEY'RE HORRIBLE !
HOW IS KANAME-SAMA HOR-RIBLE?! DO YOU EVEN KNOW HIM?!
I NEVER SAID YOU HAD TO LIKE HIM.
STUPID BUSA!
UM...

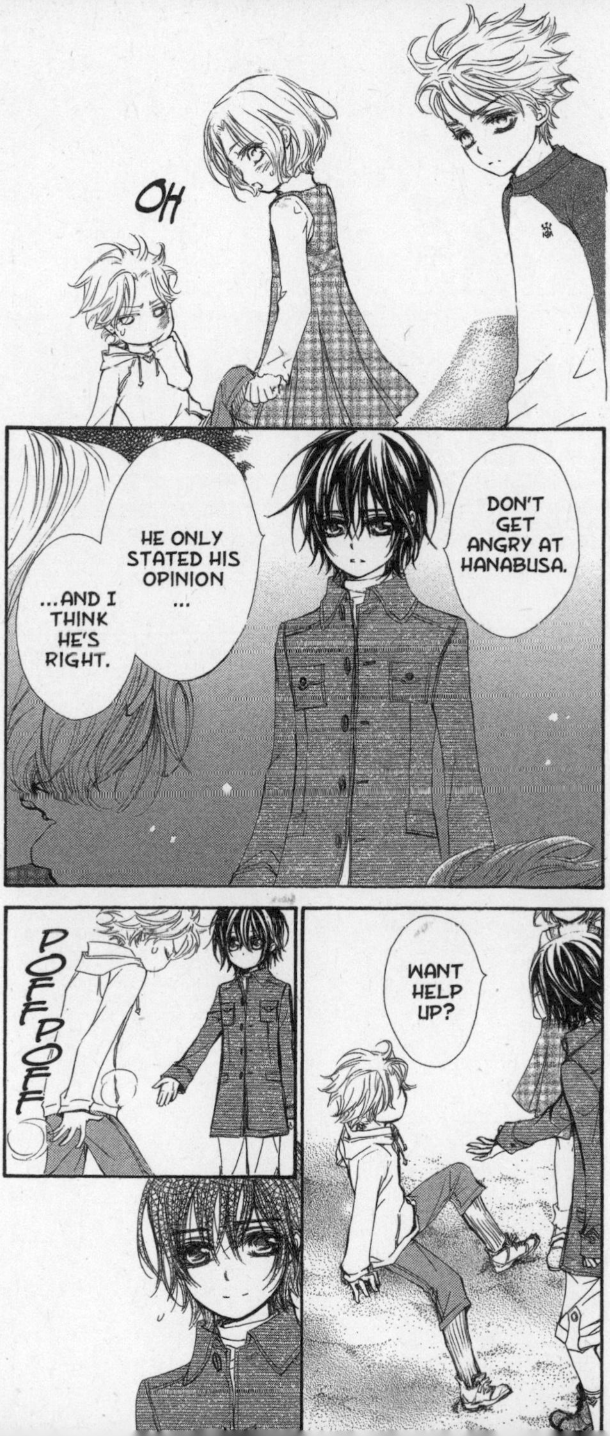
OH
DON'T GET ANGRY AT HANABUSA.
HE ONLY STATED HIS OPINION ...
...AND I THINK HE'S RIGHT.
WANT HELP UP?
POFF POFF

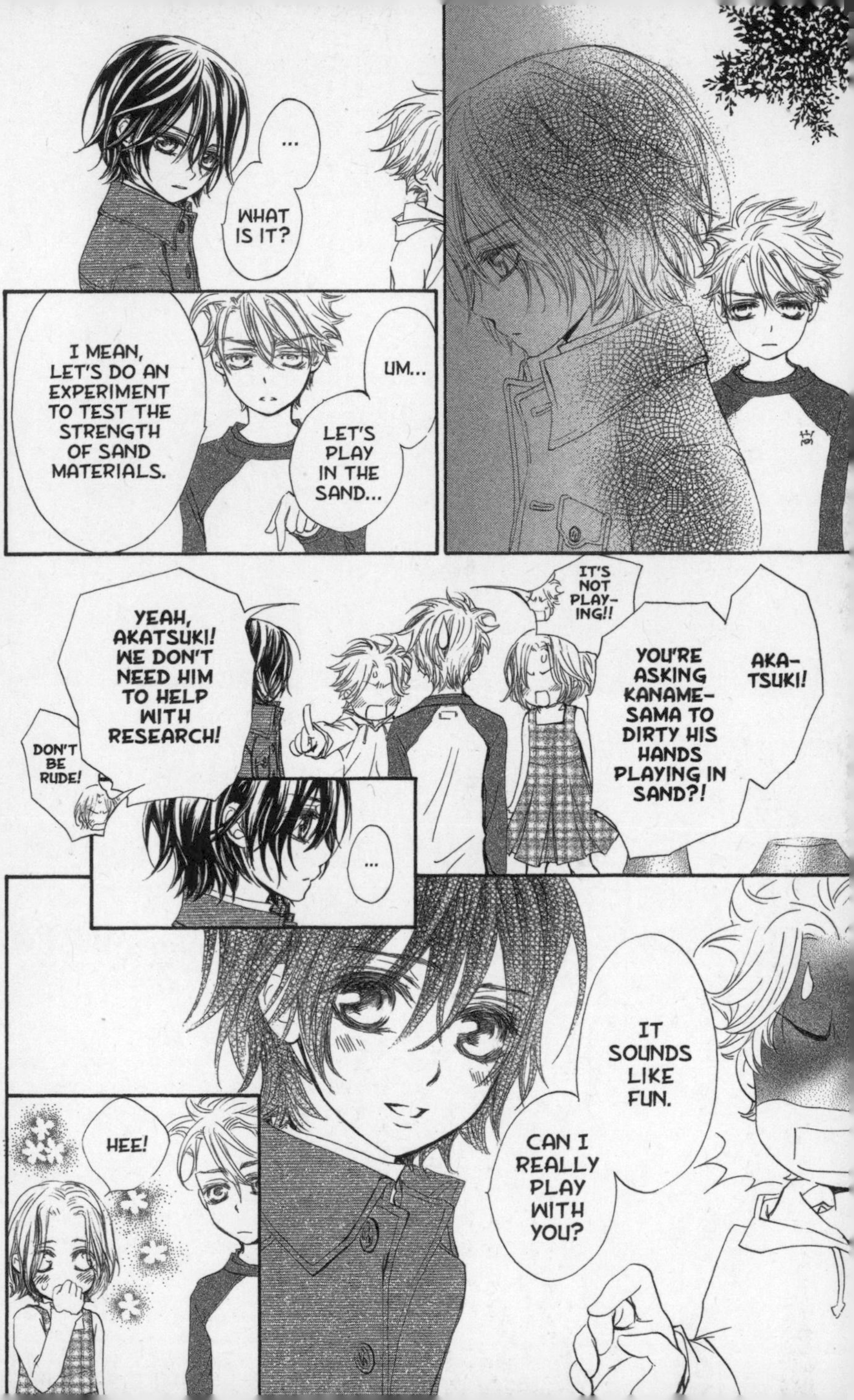
...
WHAT IS IT?
UM...
LET'S PLAY IN THE SAND...
I MEAN, LET'S DO AN EXPERIMENT TO TEST THE STRENGTH OF SAND MATERIALS.
AKA-TSUKI!
YOU'RE ASKING KANAME-SAMA TO DIRTY HIS HANDS PLAYING IN SAND?!
IT'S NOT PLAY-ING!!
YEAH, AKATSUKI! WE DON'T NEED HIM TO HELP WITH RESEARCH!
DON'T BE RUDE!
...
IT SOUNDS LIKE FUN.
CAN I REALLY PLAY WITH YOU?
HEE!

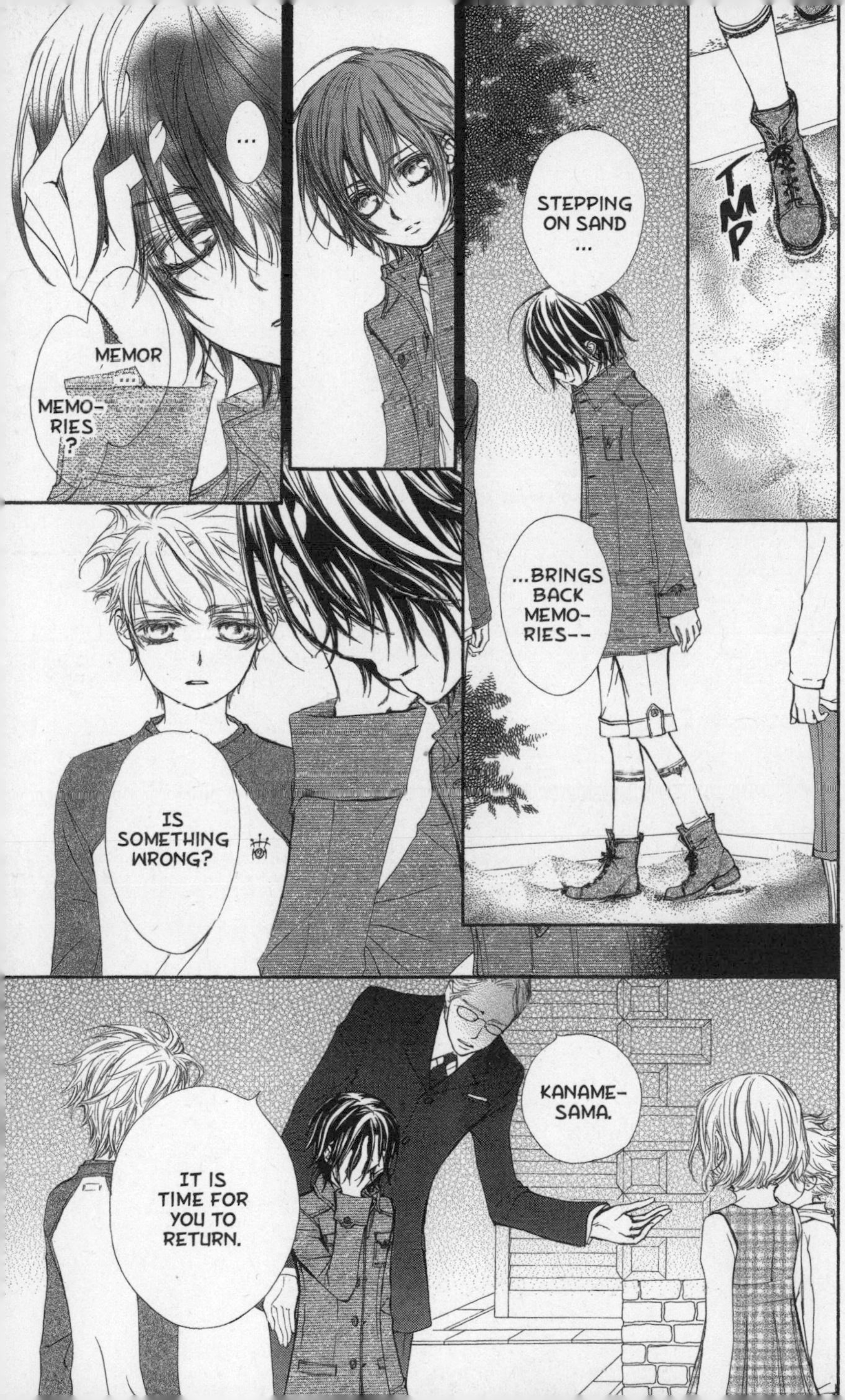
TMP
STEPPING ON SAND ...
...BRINGS BACK MEMORIES--
...
MEMOR ... MEMORIES?
IS SOMETHING WRONG?
KANAME-SAMA.
IT IS TIME FOR YOU TO RETURN.

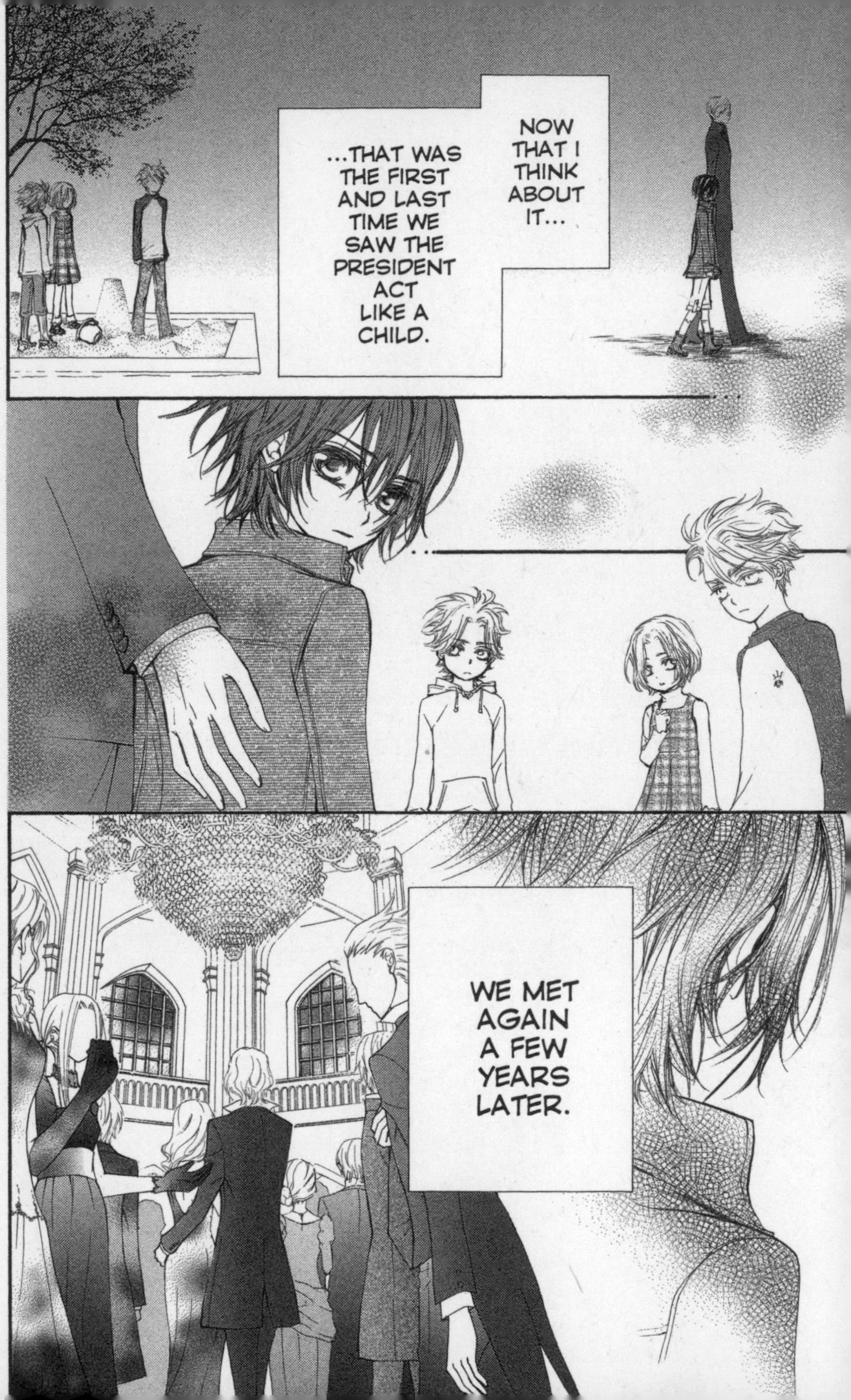
NOW THAT I THINK ABOUT IT...
...THAT WAS THE FIRST AND LAST TIME WE SAW THE PRESIDENT ACT LIKE A CHILD.
WE MET AGAIN A FEW YEARS LATER.

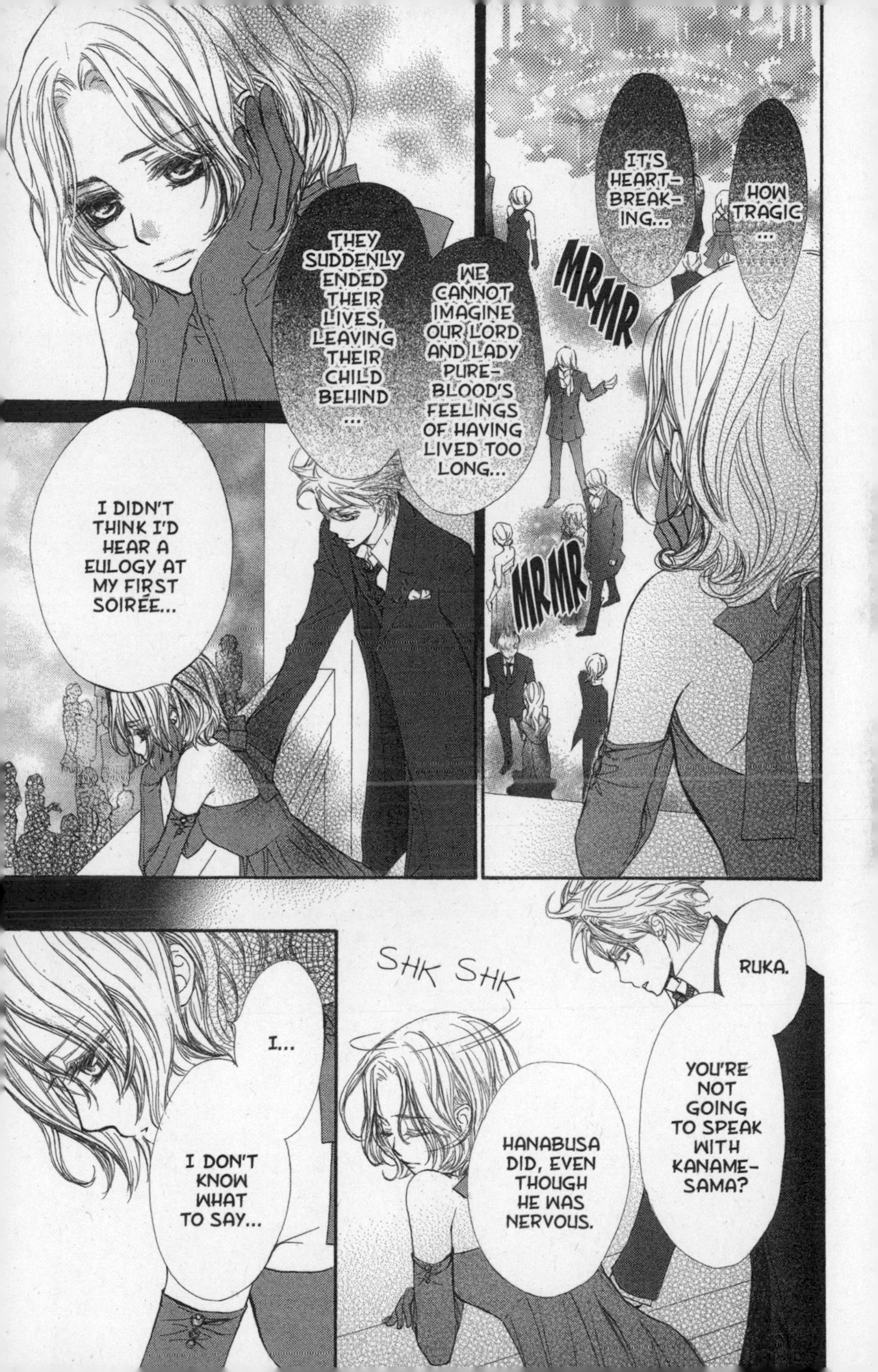
HOW TRAGIC...
IT'S HEART-BREAKING...
MRMR
MRMR
WE CANNOT IMAGINE OUR LORD AND LADY PUREBLOOD'S FEELINGS OF HAVING LIVED TOO LONG...
THEY SUDDENLY ENDED THEIR LIVES, LEAVING THEIR CHILD BEHIND...
I DIDN'T THINK I'D HEAR A EULOGY AT MY FIRST SOIRÉE...
RUKA.
YOU'RE NOT GOING TO SPEAK WITH KANAME-SAMA?
SHK SHK
HANABUSA DID, EVEN THOUGH HE WAS NERVOUS.
I...
I DON'T KNOW WHAT TO SAY...

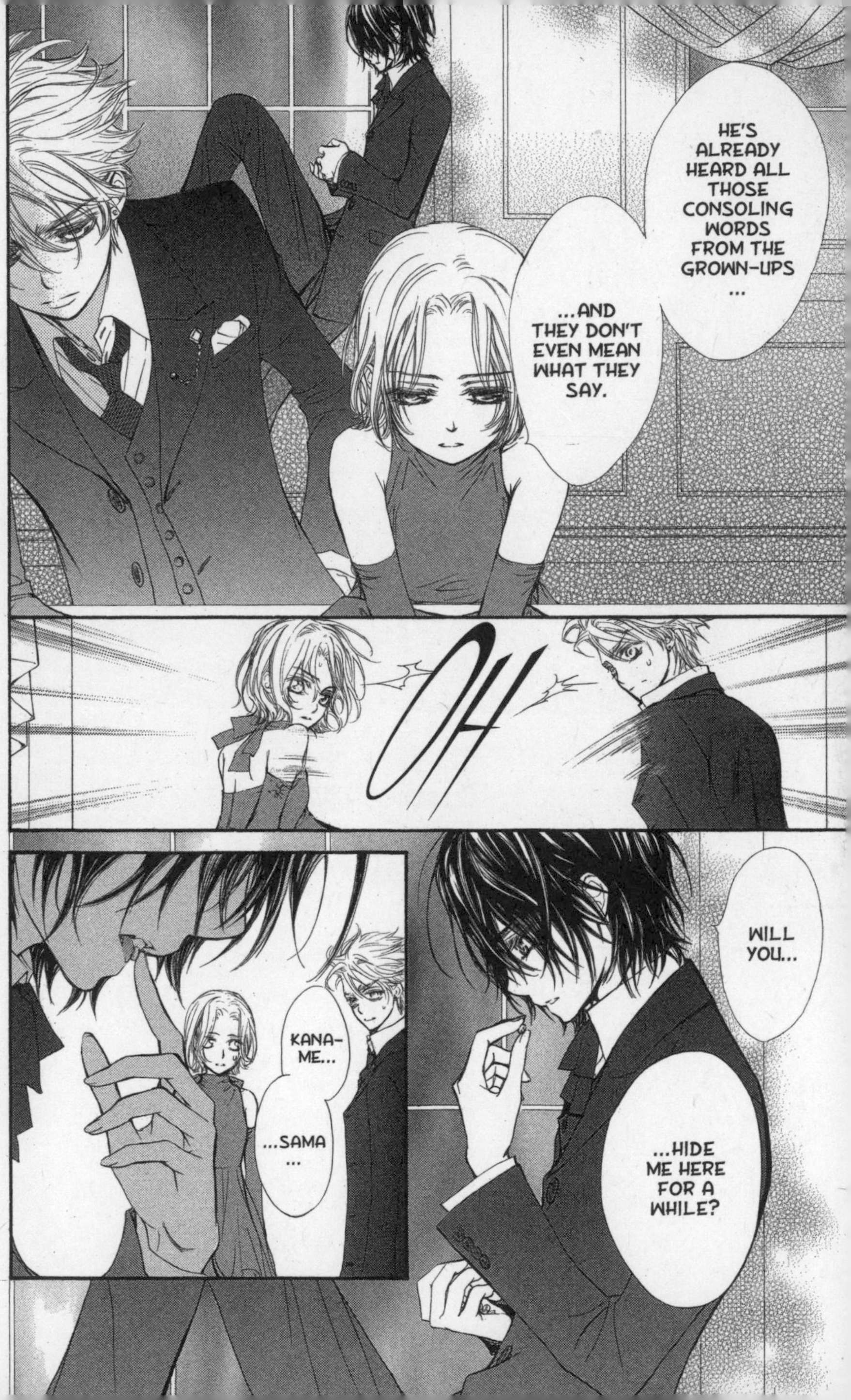
HE'S ALREADY HEARD ALL THOSE CONSOLING WORDS FROM THE GROWN-UPS...
...AND THEY DON'T EVEN MEAN WHAT THEY SAY.
OH
WILL YOU...
...HIDE ME HERE FOR A WHILE?
KANA-ME...
...SAMA...

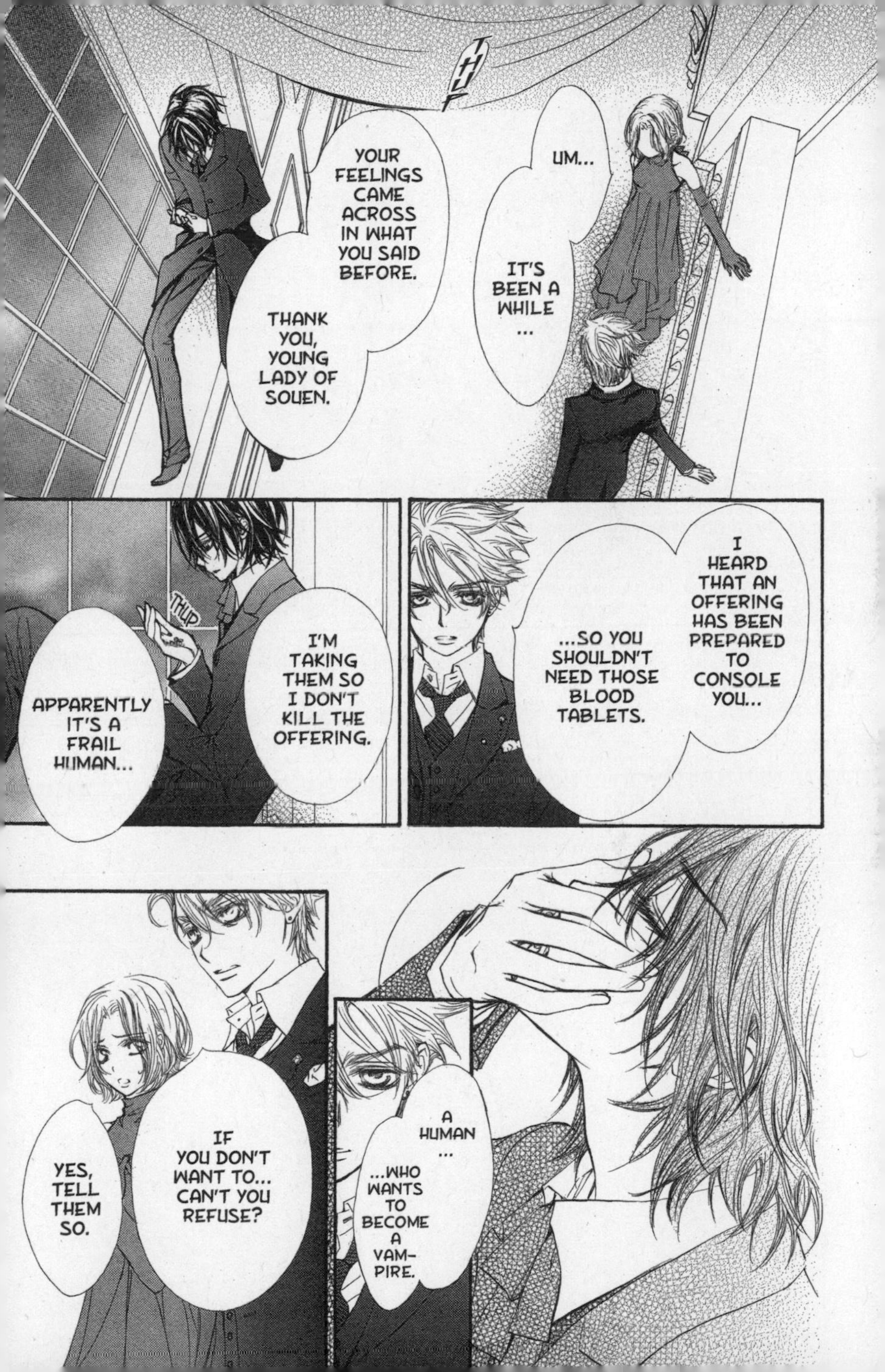
UM...
IT'S BEEN A WHILE ...
THUP
YOUR FEELINGS CAME ACROSS IN WHAT YOU SAID BEFORE.
THANK YOU, YOUNG LADY OF SOUEN.
I HEARD THAT AN OFFERING HAS BEEN PREPARED TO CONSOLE YOU...
...SO YOU SHOULDN'T NEED THOSE BLOOD TABLETS.
THUP
I'M TAKING THEM SO I DON'T KILL THE OFFERING.
APPARENTLY IT'S A FRAIL HUMAN...
A HUMAN ...
...WHO WANTS TO BECOME A VAMPIRE.
IF YOU DON'T WANT TO... CAN'T YOU REFUSE?
YES, TELL THEM SO.

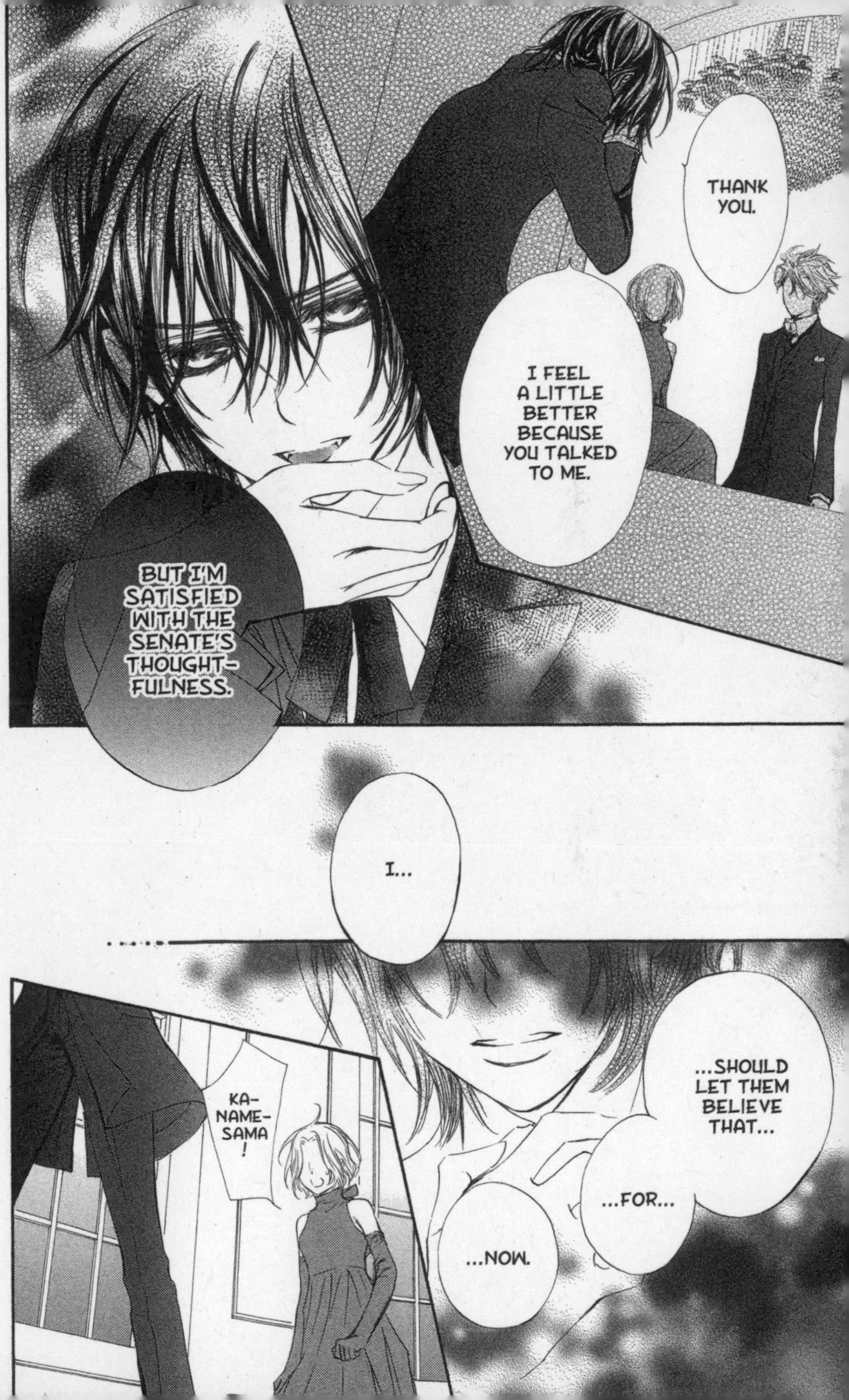
THANK YOU.
I FEEL A LITTLE BETTER BECAUSE YOU TALKED TO ME.
BUT I'M SATISFIED WITH THE SENATE'S THOUGHT-FULNESS.
I...
...SHOULD LET THEM BELIEVE THAT...
...FOR...
...NOW.
KA-NAME-SAMA!

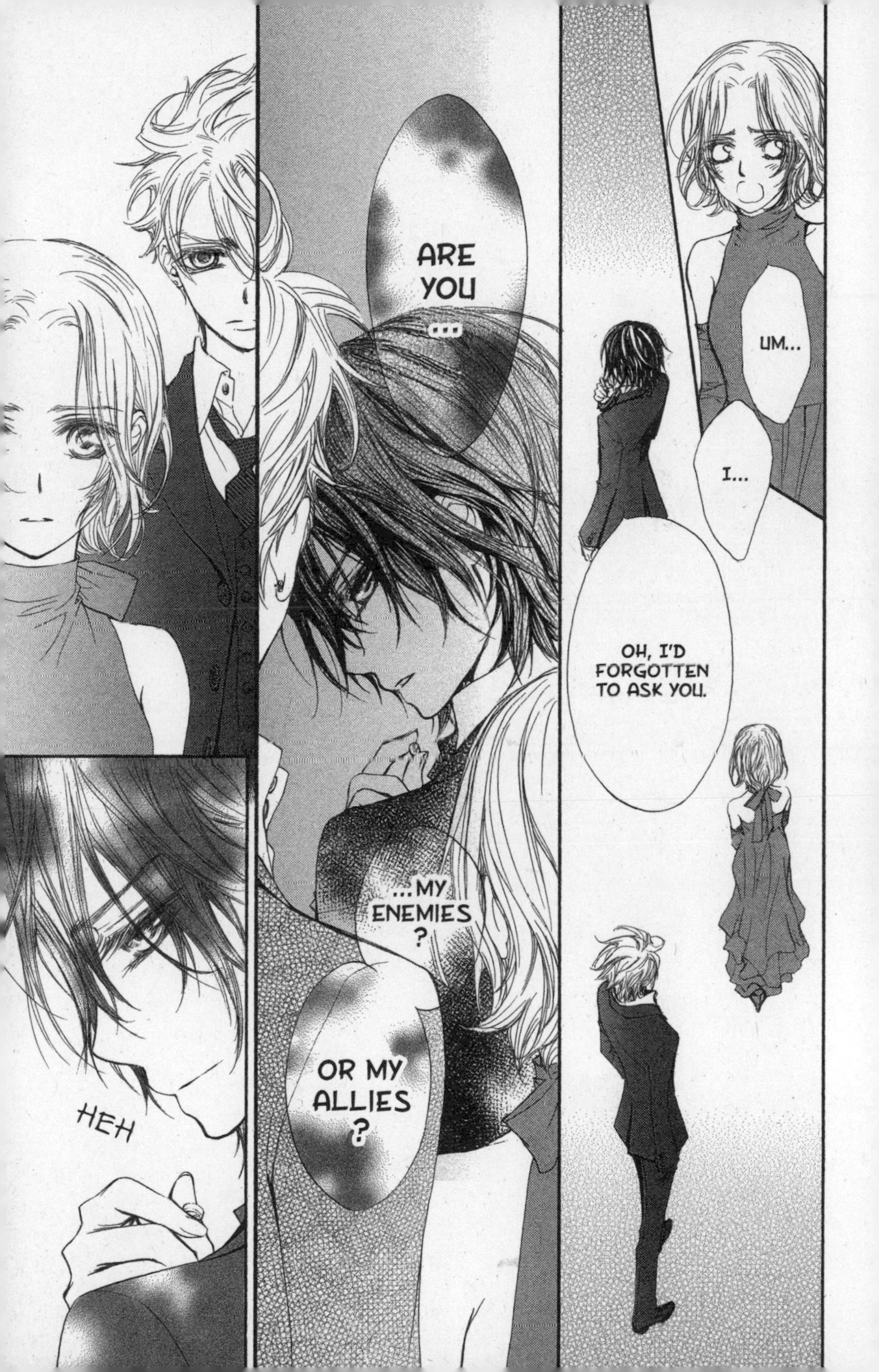
UM...
I...
OH, I'D FORGOTTEN TO ASK YOU.
ARE YOU ...
...MY ENEMIES?
OR MY ALLIES?
HEH

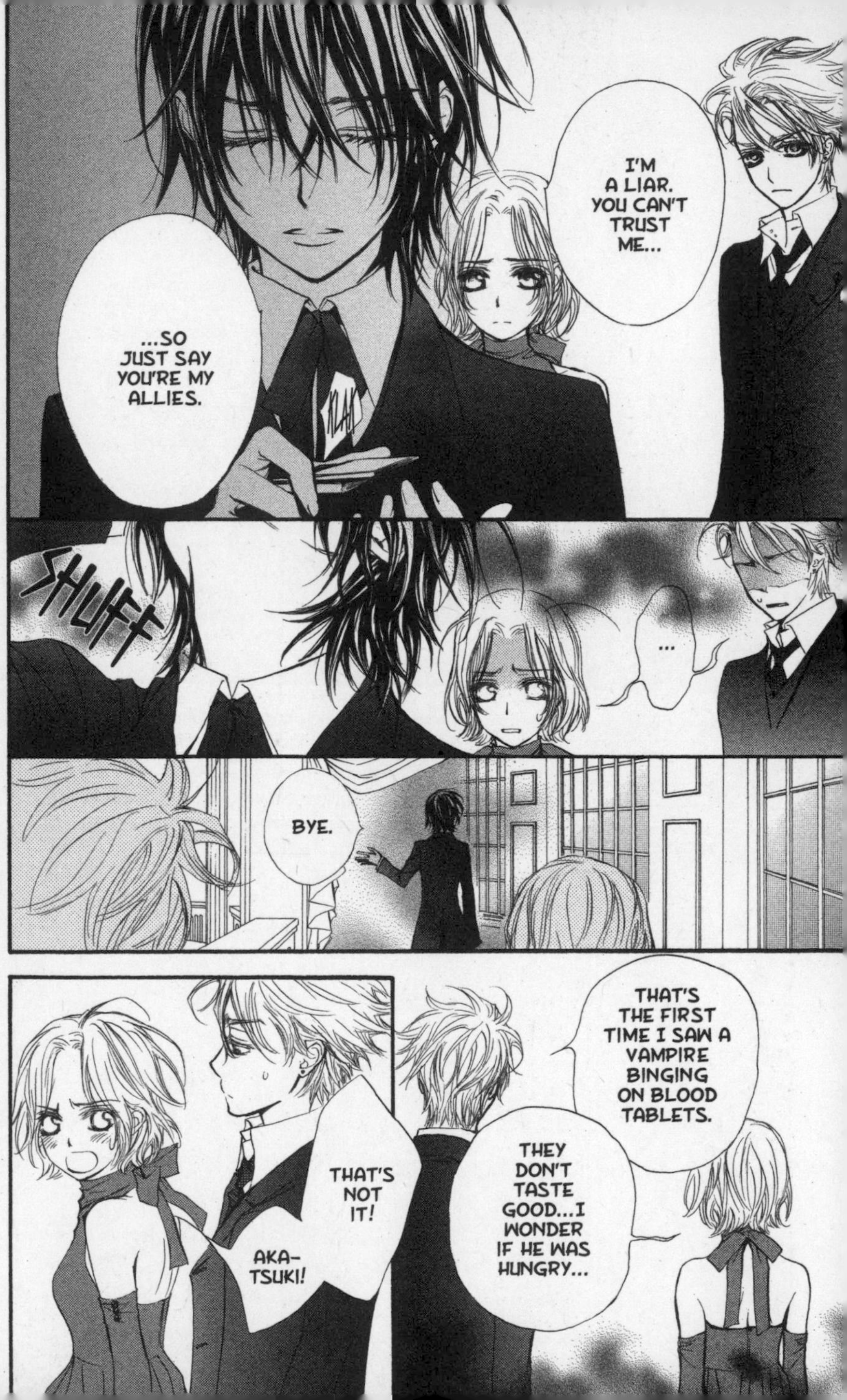
I'M A LIAR. YOU CAN'T TRUST ME...
...SO JUST SAY YOU'RE MY ALLIES.
KLAK
...
SHUFF
BYE.
THAT'S THE FIRST TIME I SAW A VAMPIRE BINGING ON BLOOD TABLETS.
THEY DON'T TASTE GOOD...I WONDER IF HE WAS HUNGRY...
THAT'S NOT IT!
AKA-TSUKI!

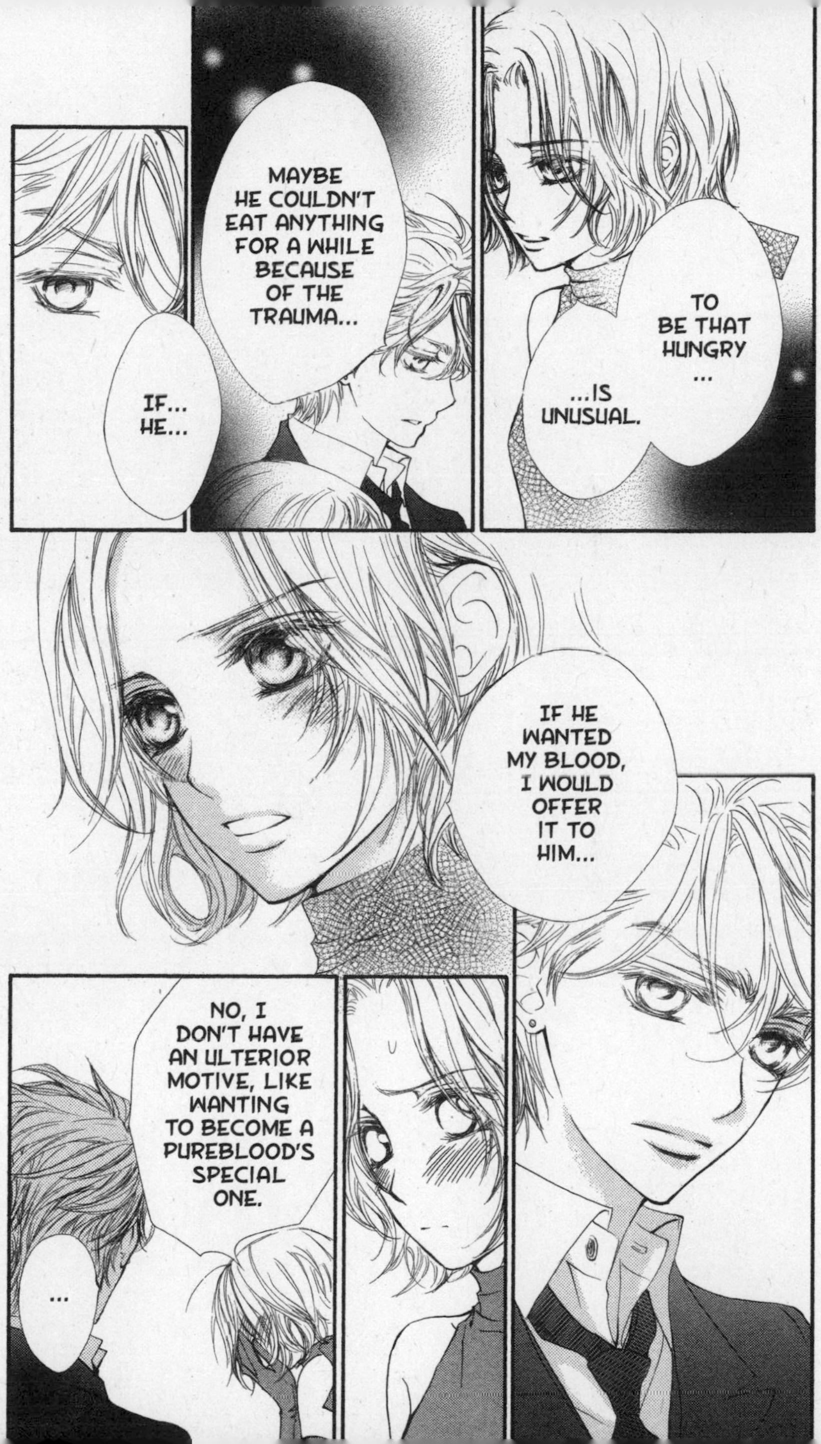
TO BE THAT HUNGRY ...
...IS UNUSUAL.
MAYBE HE COULDN'T EAT ANYTHING FOR A WHILE BECAUSE OF THE TRAUMA...
IF... HE...
IF HE WANTED MY BLOOD, I WOULD OFFER IT TO HIM...
NO, I DON'T HAVE AN ULTERIOR MOTIVE, LIKE WANTING TO BECOME A PUREBLOOD'S SPECIAL ONE.
...

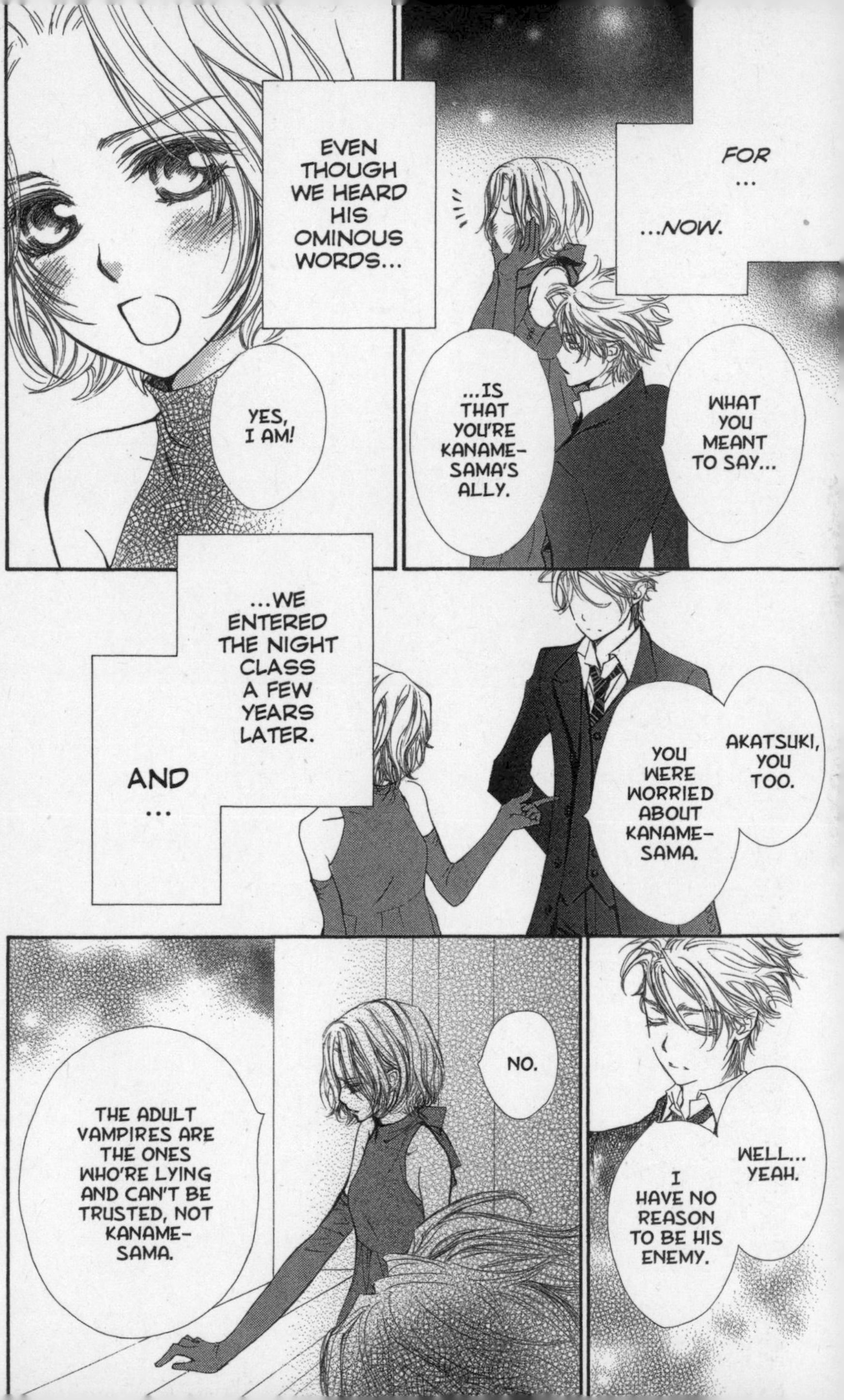
FOR ...
...NOW.
WHAT YOU MEANT TO SAY...
...IS THAT YOU'RE KANAME-SAMA'S ALLY.
EVEN THOUGH WE HEARD HIS OMINOUS WORDS...
YES, I AM!
AKATSUKI, YOU TOO.
YOU WERE WORRIED ABOUT KANAME-SAMA.
...WE ENTERED THE NIGHT CLASS A FEW YEARS LATER.
AND ...
WELL... YEAH.
I HAVE NO REASON TO BE HIS ENEMY.
NO.
THE ADULT VAMPIRES ARE THE ONES WHO'RE LYING AND CAN'T BE TRUSTED, NOT KANAME-SAMA.

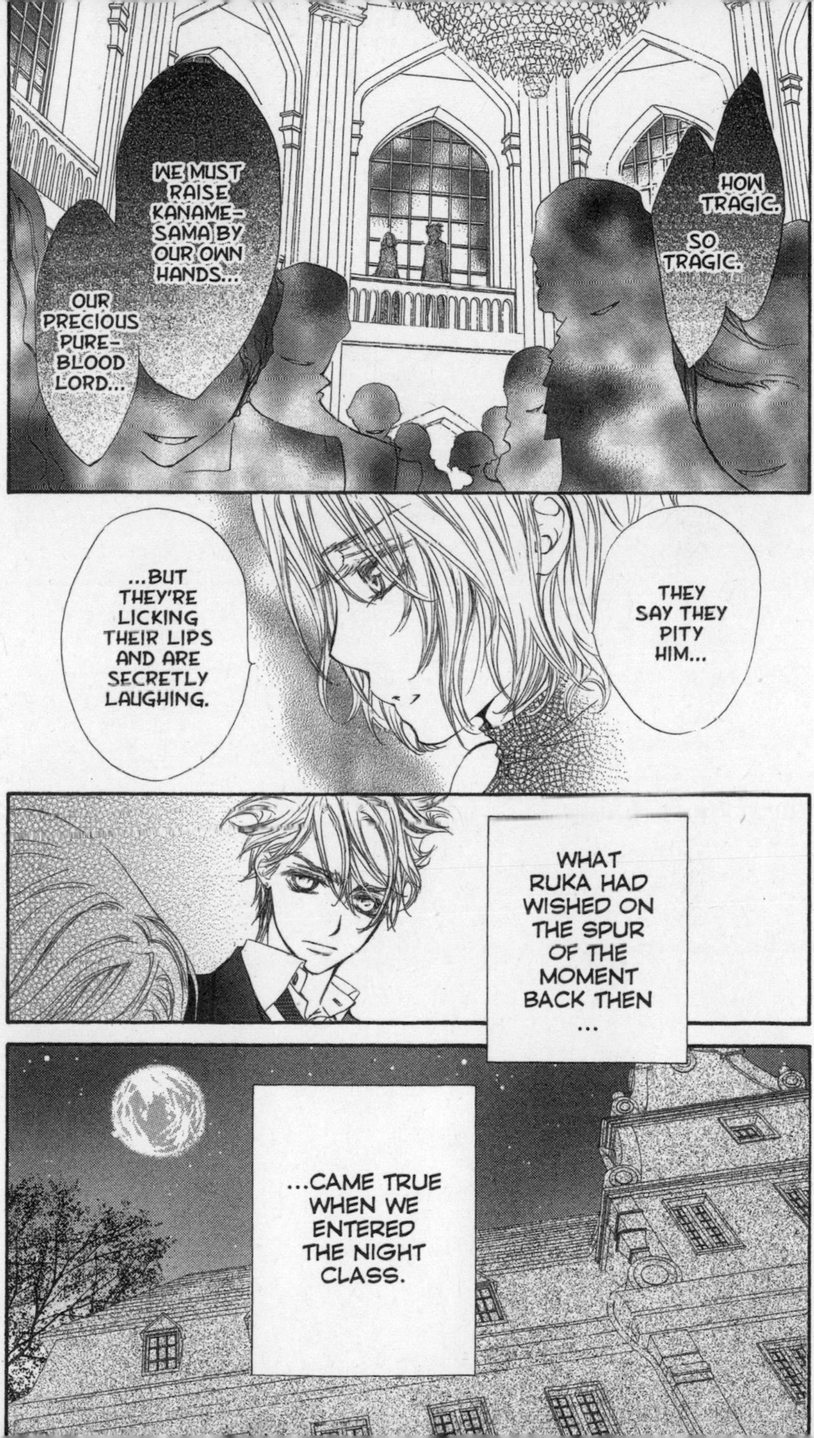
HOW TRAGIC.
SO TRAGIC.
WE MUST RAISE KANAME-SAMA BY OUR OWN HANDS...
OUR PRECIOUS PURE-BLOOD LORD...
THEY SAY THEY PITY HIM...
...BUT THEY'RE LICKING THEIR LIPS AND ARE SECRETLY LAUGHING.
WHAT RUKA HAD WISHED ON THE SPUR OF THE MOMENT BACK THEN ...
...CAME TRUE WHEN WE ENTERED THE NIGHT CLASS.

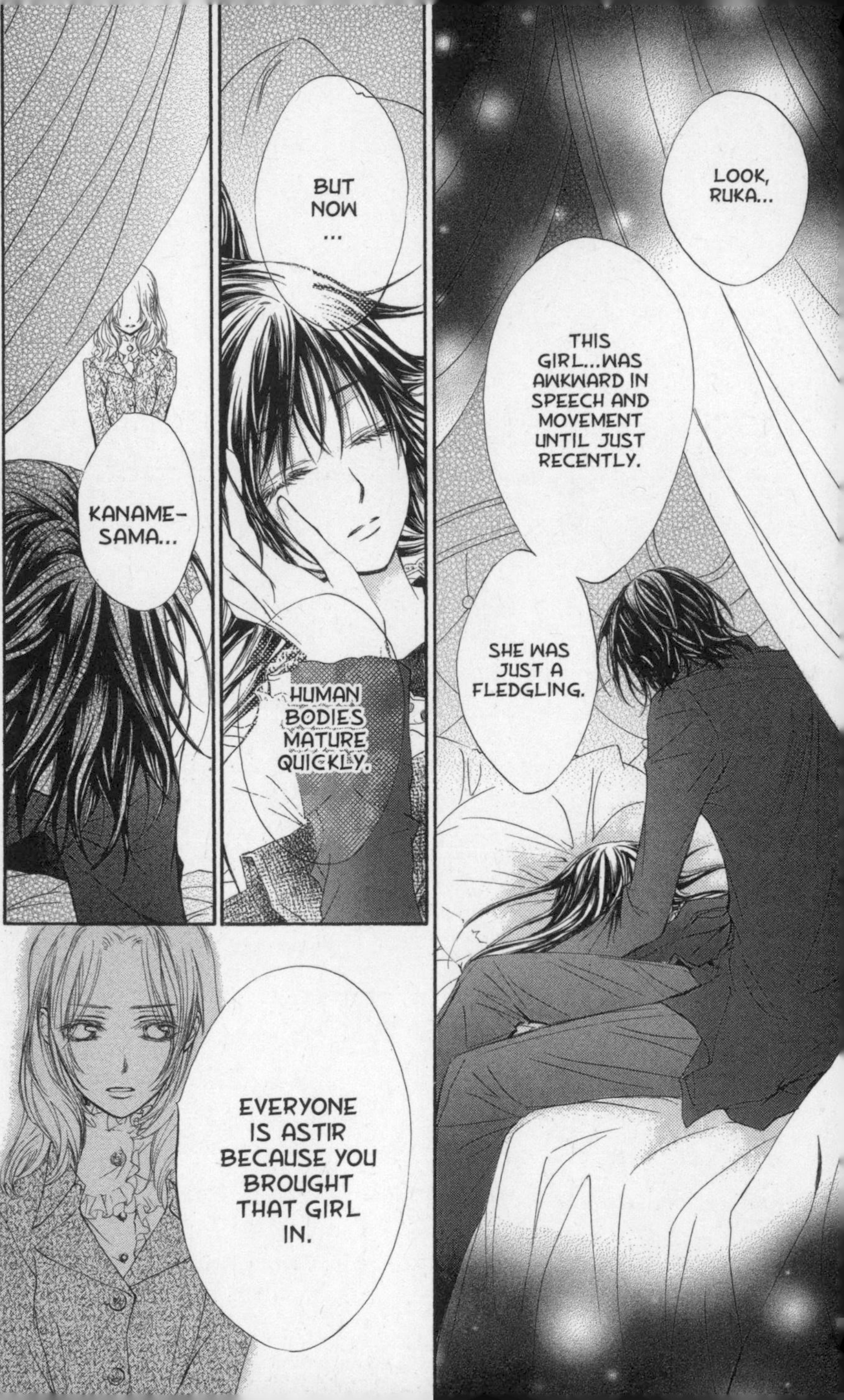
LOOK, RUKA...
THIS GIRL...WAS AWKWARD IN SPEECH AND MOVEMENT UNTIL JUST RECENTLY.
SHE WAS JUST A FLEDGLING.
BUT NOW ...
HUMAN BODIES MATURE QUICKLY.
KANAME-SAMA...
EVERYONE IS ASTIR BECAUSE YOU BROUGHT THAT GIRL IN.

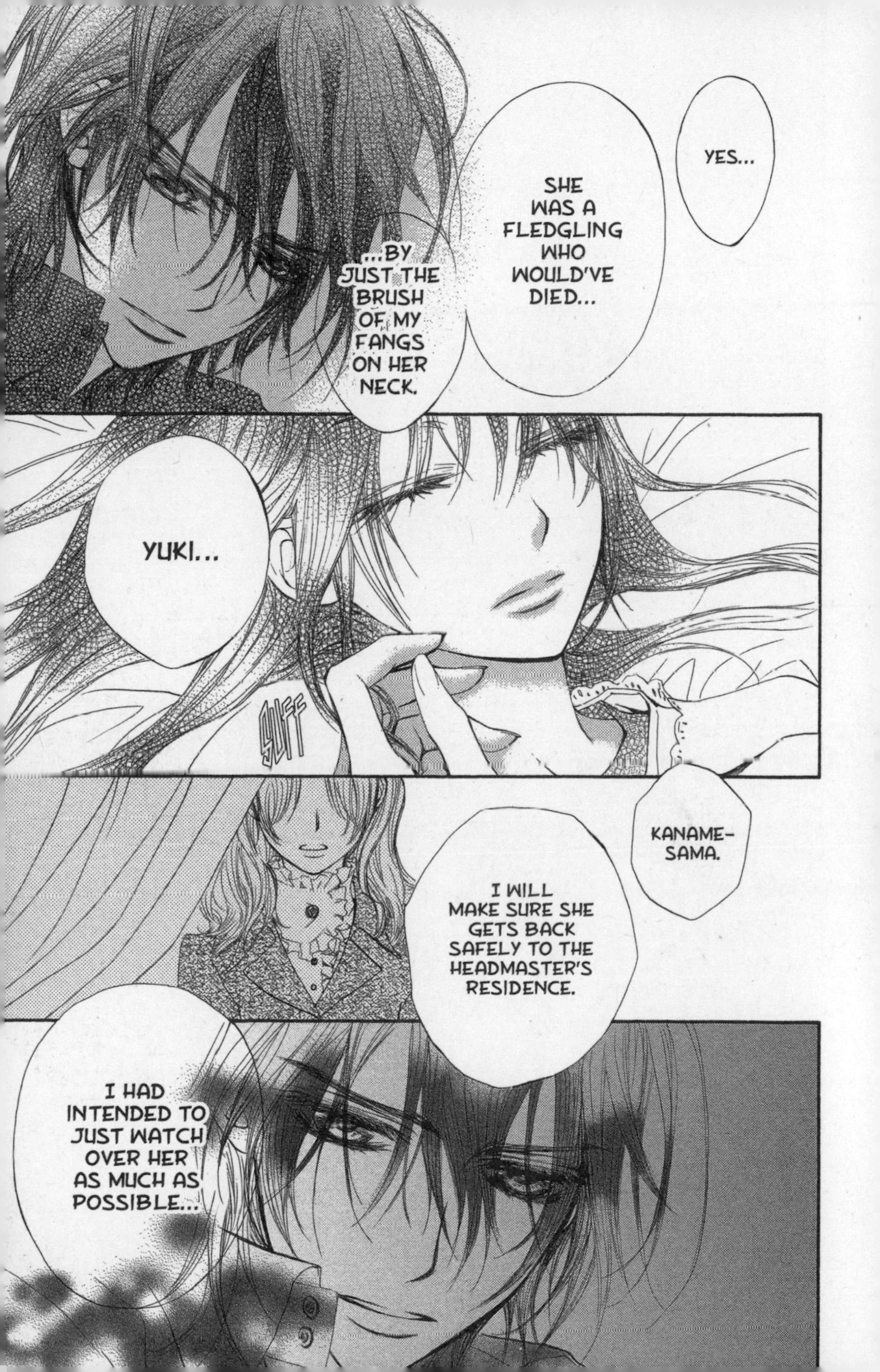
YES...
SHE WAS A FLEDGLING WHO WOULD'VE DIED...
...BY JUST THE BRUSH OF MY FANGS ON HER NECK.
YUKI...
KANAME-SAMA.
I WILL MAKE SURE SHE GETS BACK SAFELY TO THE HEADMASTER'S RESIDENCE.
I HAD INTENDED TO JUST WATCH OVER HER AS MUCH AS POSSIBLE...

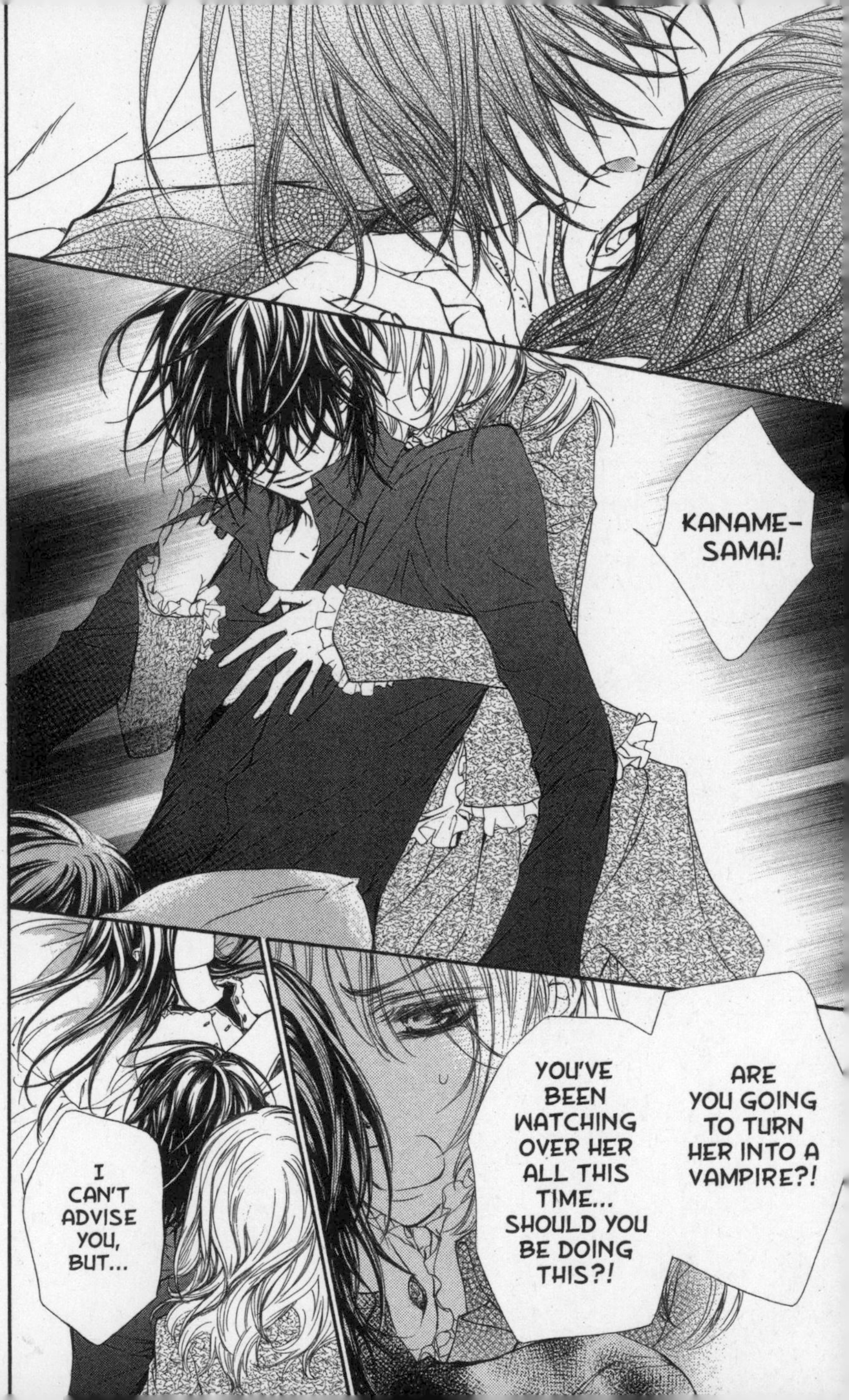
KANAME-SAMA!
ARE YOU GOING TO TURN HER INTO A VAMPIRE?!
YOU'VE BEEN WATCHING OVER HER ALL THIS TIME... SHOULD YOU BE DOING THIS?!
I CAN'T ADVISE YOU, BUT...

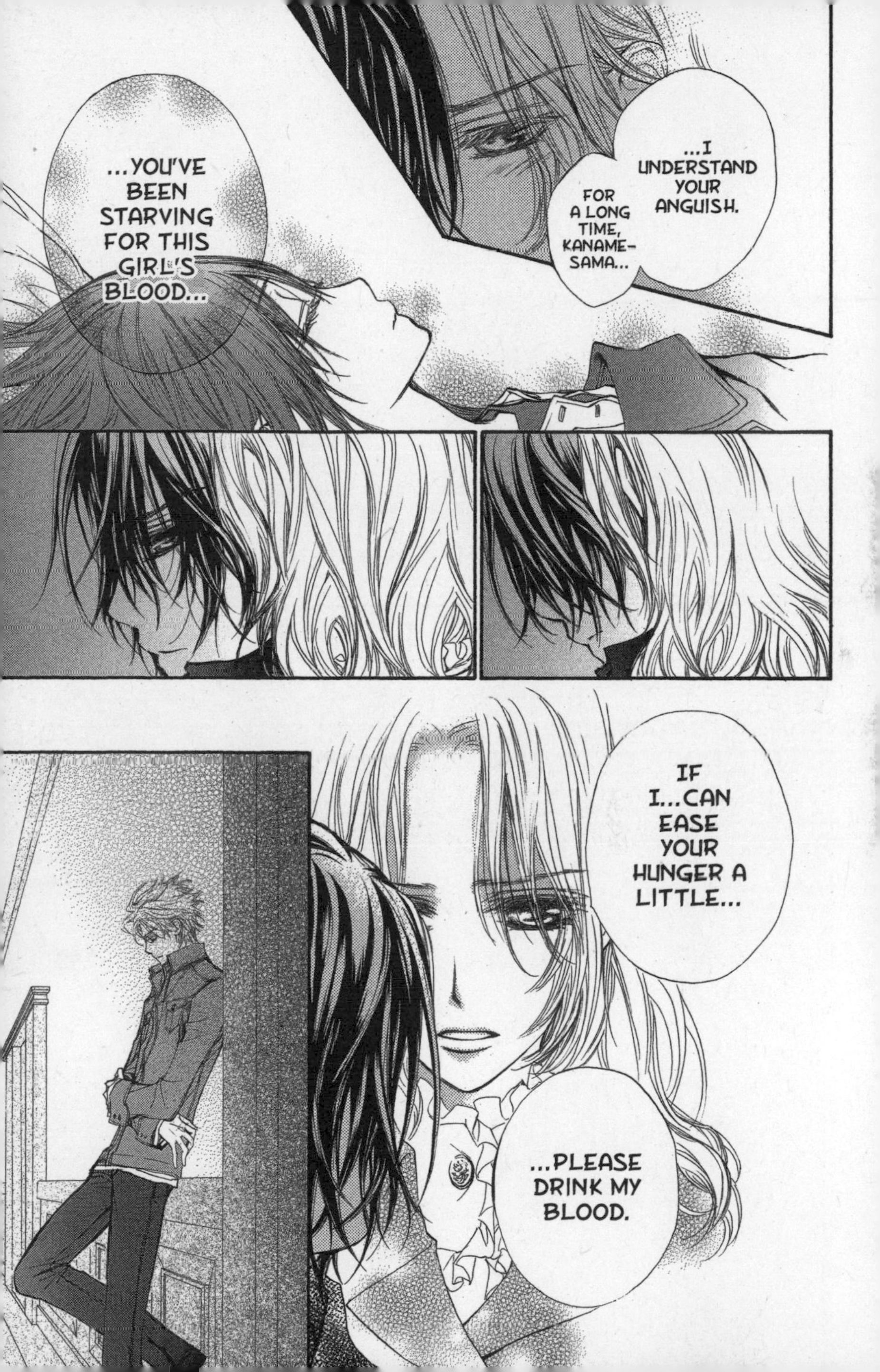
...I UNDERSTAND YOUR ANGUISH.
FOR A LONG TIME, KANAME-SAMA...
...YOU'VE BEEN STARVING FOR THIS GIRL'S BLOOD...
IF I...CAN EASE YOUR HUNGER A LITTLE...
...PLEASE DRINK MY BLOOD.

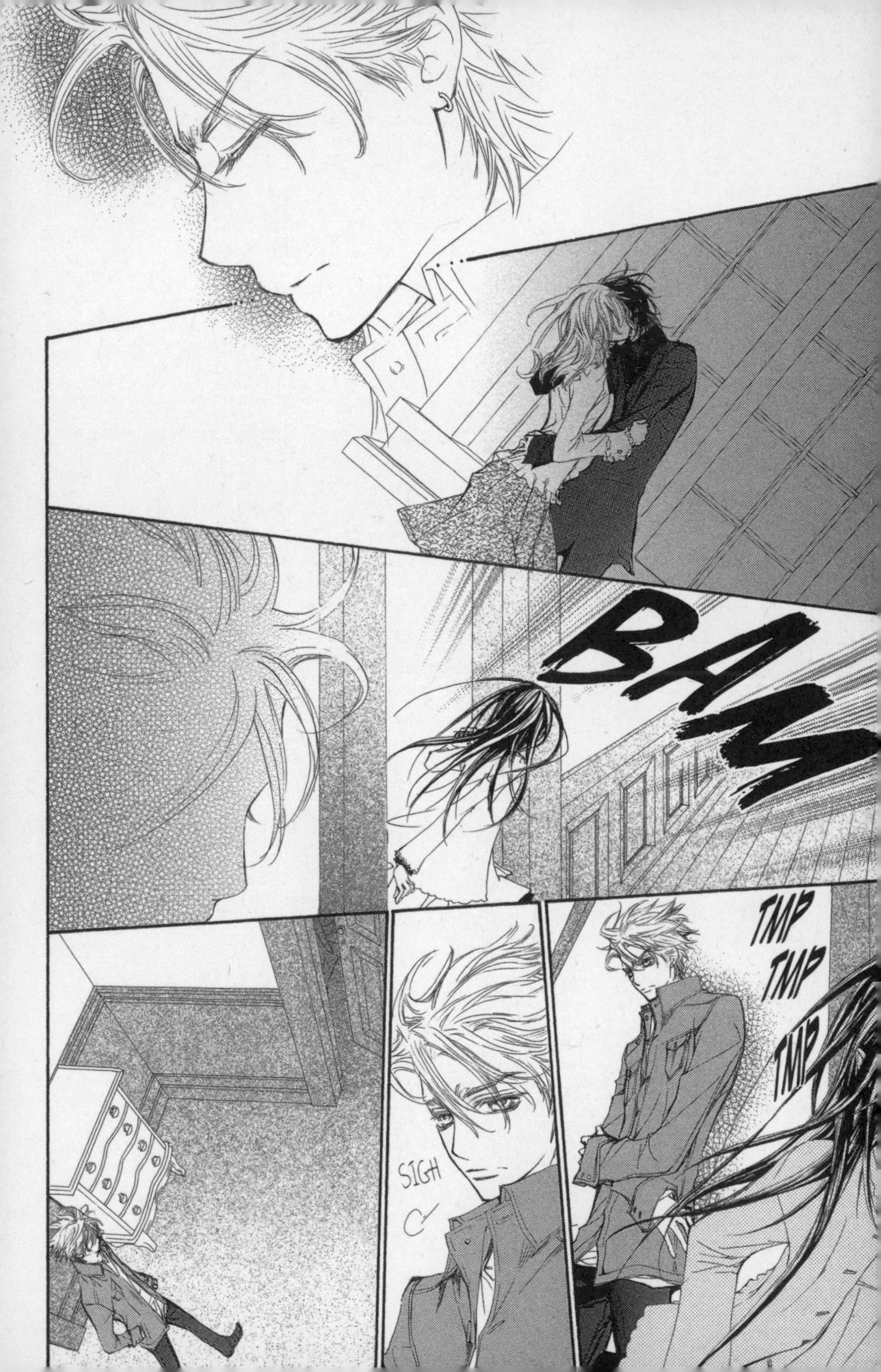

BAM
TMP
TMP
TMP
SIGH

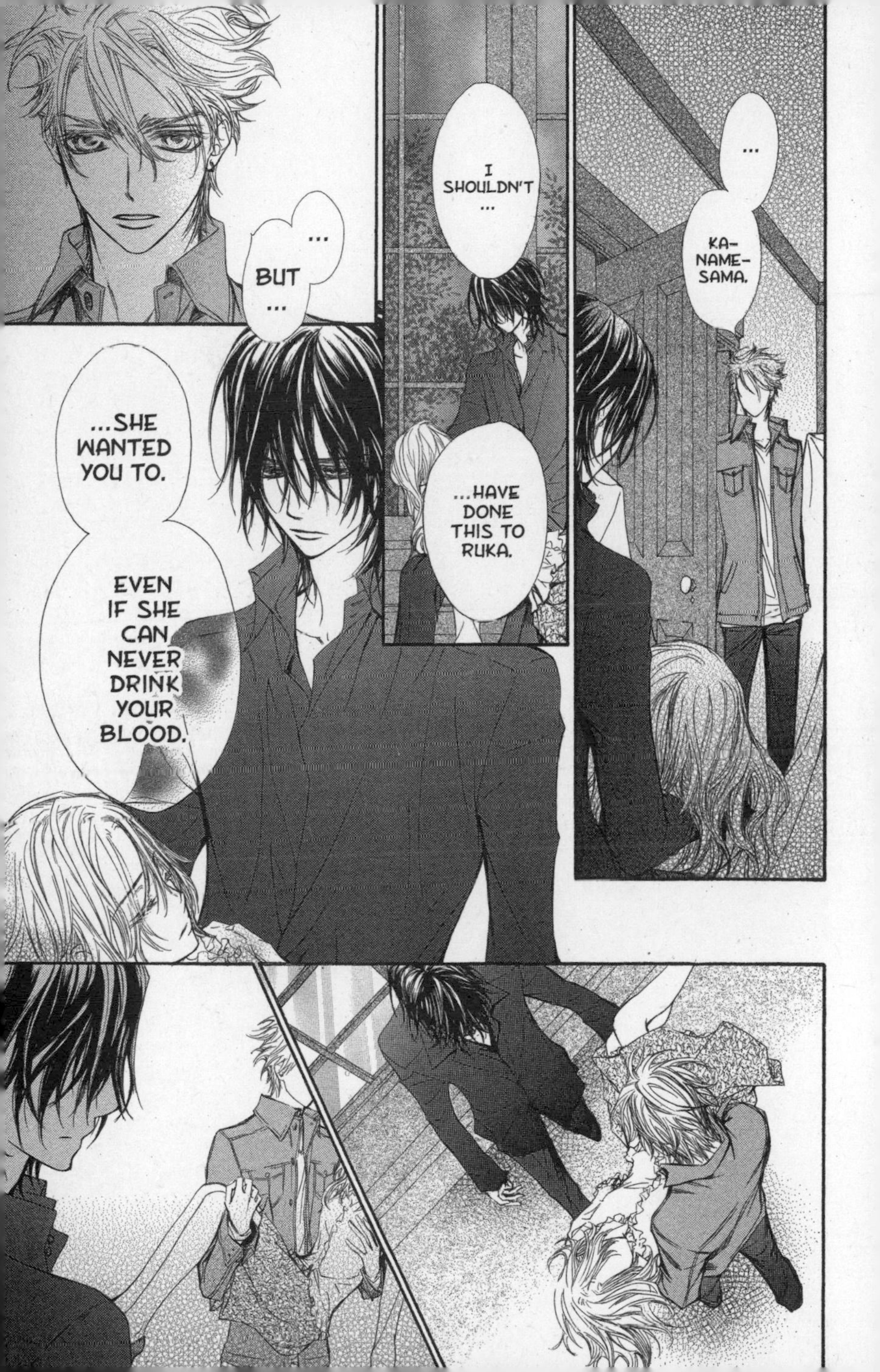
...
KA-NAME-SAMA.
I SHOULDN'T ...
...HAVE DONE THIS TO RUKA.
... BUT ...
...SHE WANTED YOU TO.
EVEN IF SHE CAN NEVER DRINK YOUR BLOOD.

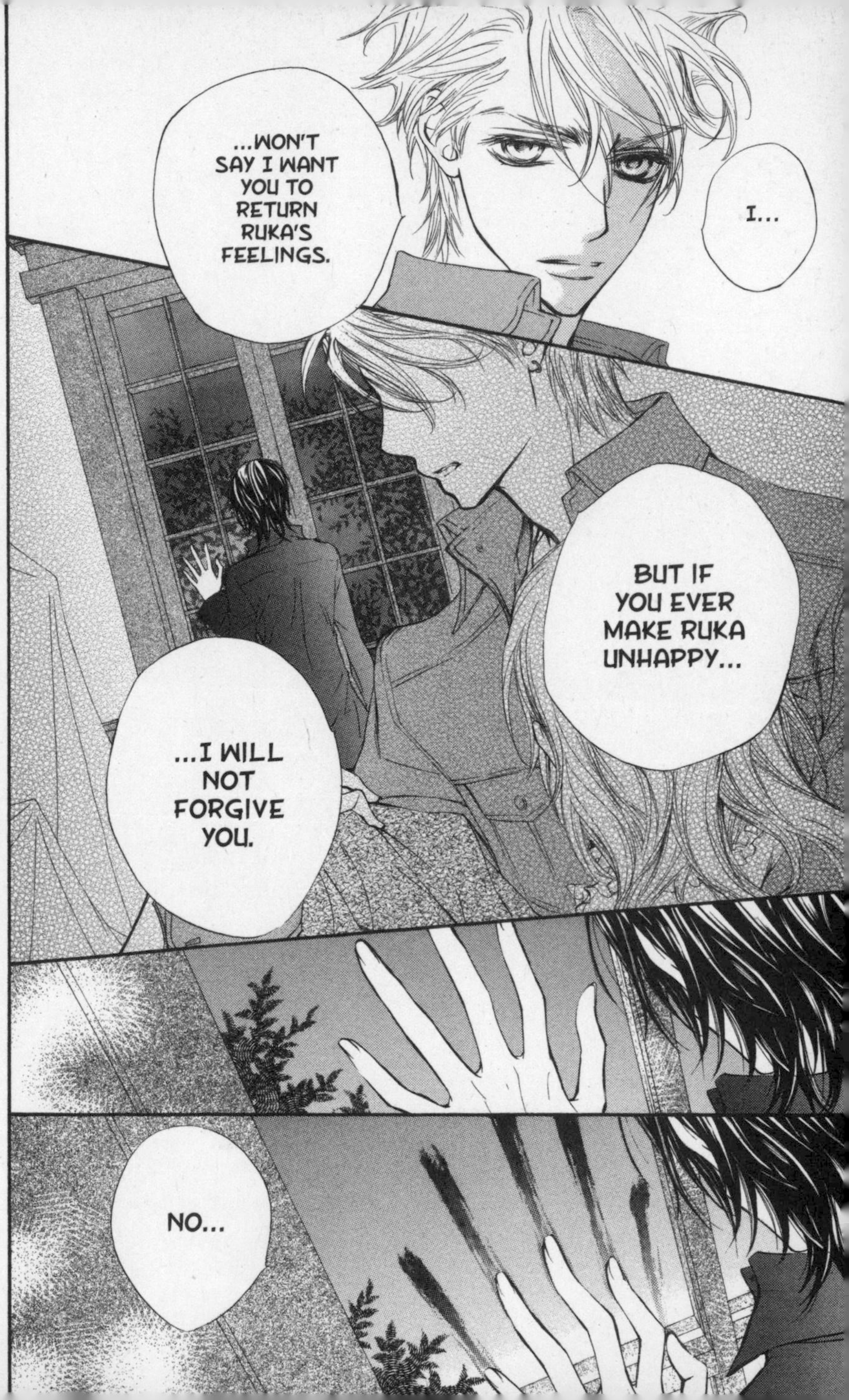
I...
...WON'T SAY I WANT YOU TO RETURN RUKA'S FEELINGS.
BUT IF YOU EVER MAKE RUKA UNHAPPY...
...I WILL NOT FORGIVE YOU.
NO...

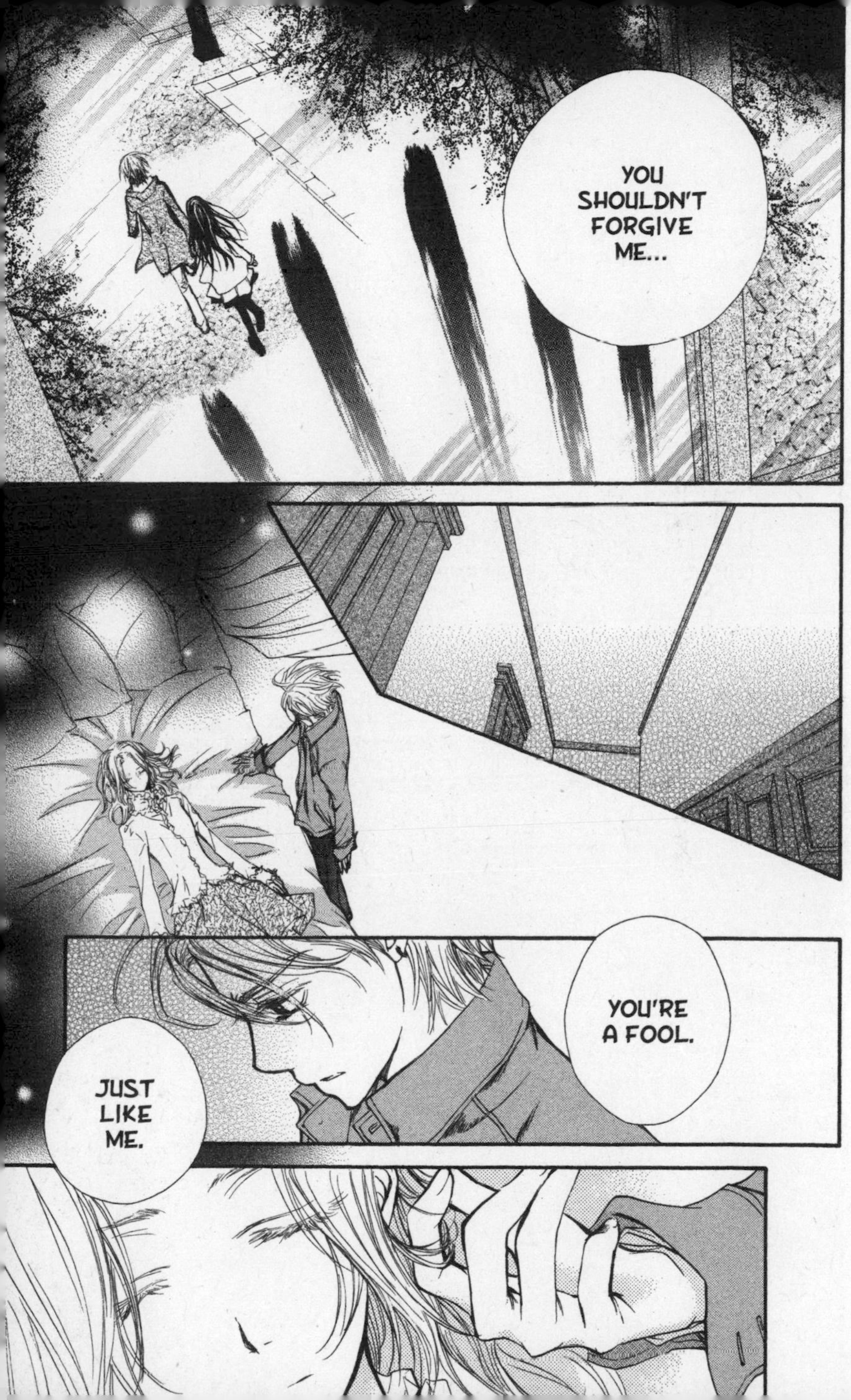
YOU SHOULDN'T FORGIVE ME...
YOU'RE A FOOL.
JUST LIKE ME.

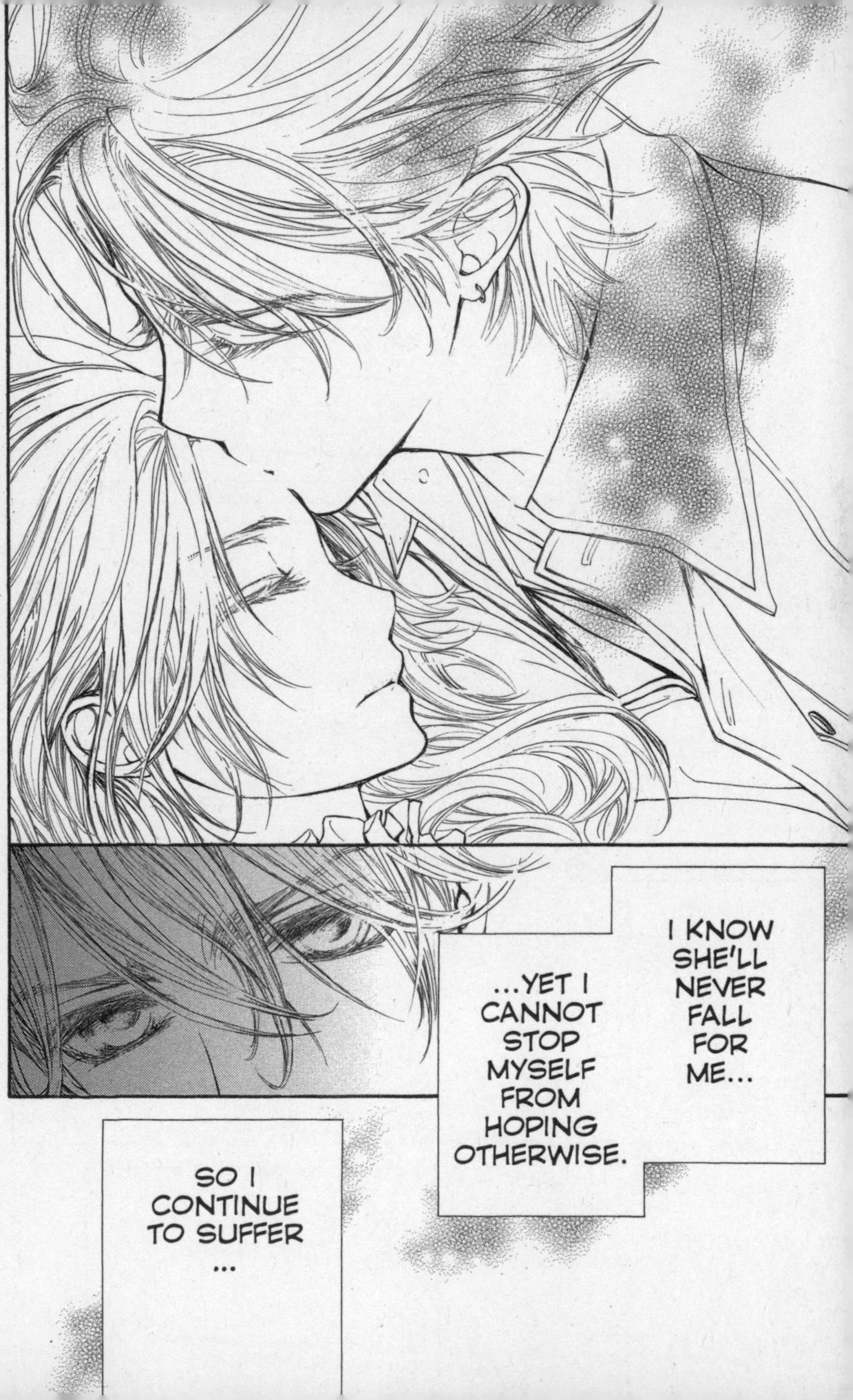
I KNOW SHE'LL NEVER FALL FOR ME...
...YET I CANNOT STOP MYSELF FROM HOPING OTHERWISE.
SO I CONTINUE TO SUFFER ...

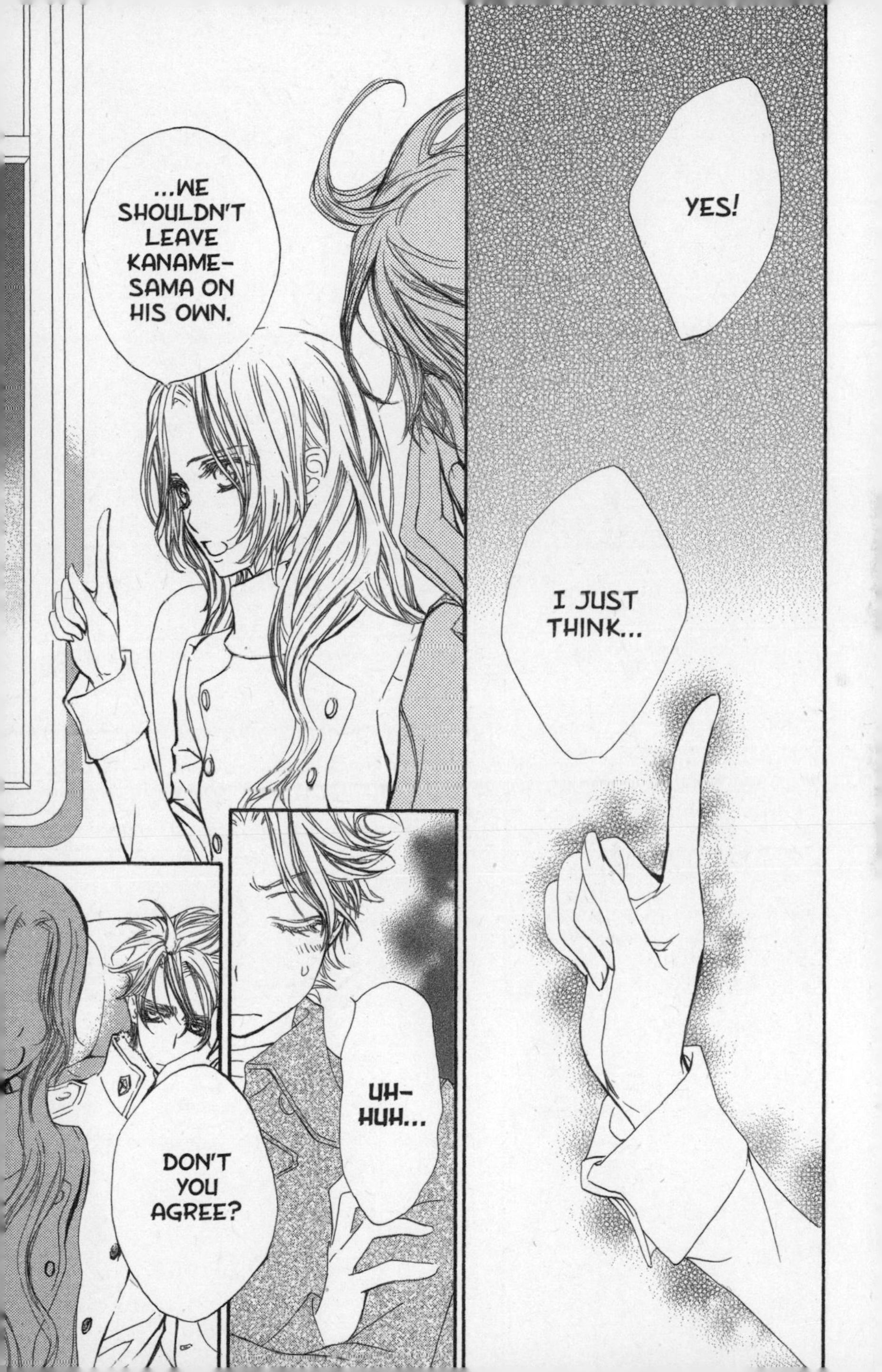
YES!
I JUST THINK...
...WE SHOULDN'T LEAVE KANAME-SAMA ON HIS OWN.
UH-HUH...
DON'T YOU AGREE?

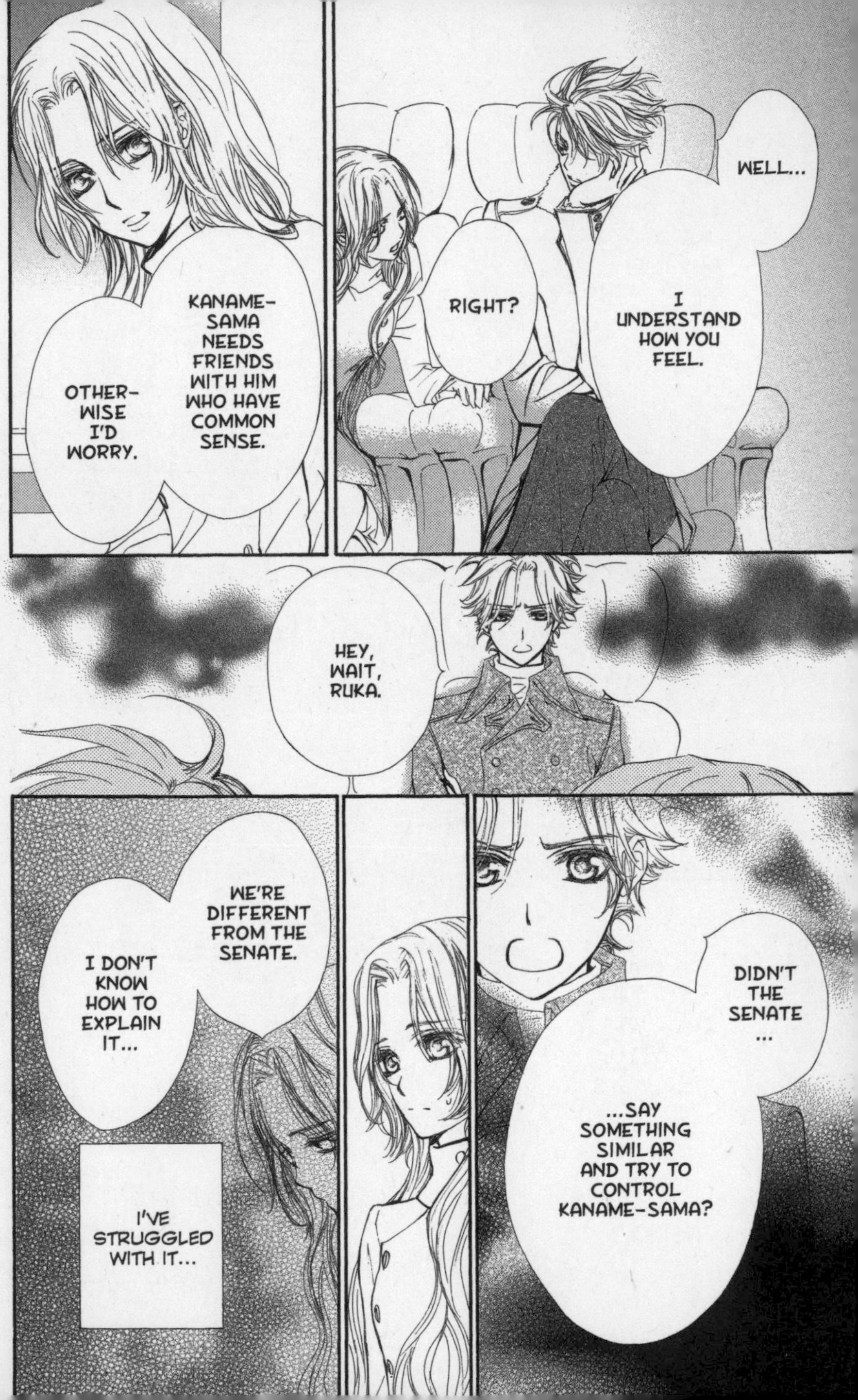
WELL...
I UNDERSTAND HOW YOU FEEL.
RIGHT?
KANAME-SAMA NEEDS FRIENDS WITH HIM WHO HAVE COMMON SENSE.
OTHER-WISE I'D WORRY.
HEY, WAIT, RUKA.
DIDN'T THE SENATE...
...SAY SOMETHING SIMILAR AND TRY TO CONTROL KANAME-SAMA?
WE'RE DIFFERENT FROM THE SENATE.
I DON'T KNOW HOW TO EXPLAIN IT...
I'VE STRUGGLED WITH IT...

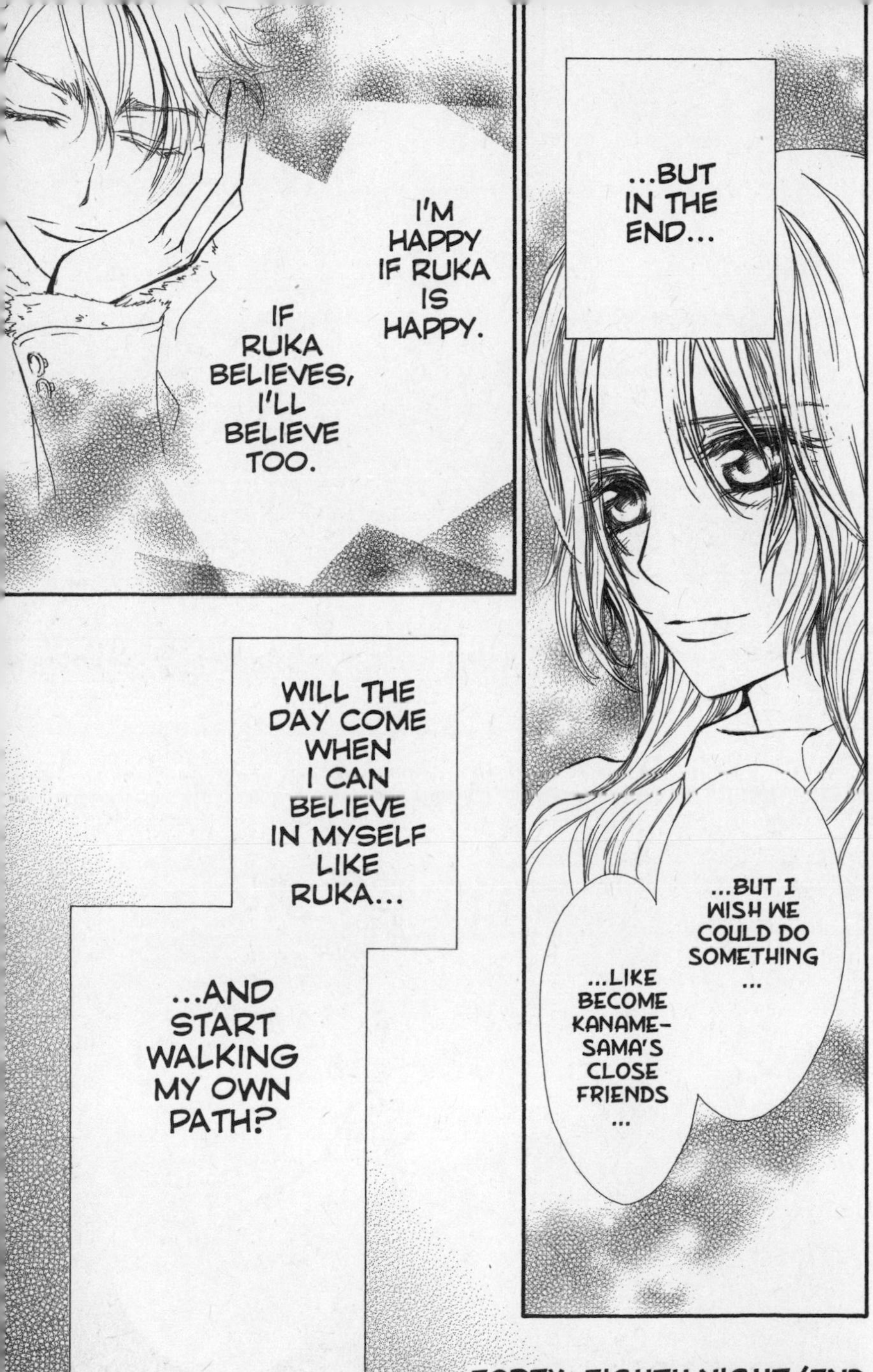
...BUT IN THE END...
...BUT I WISH WE COULD DO SOMETHING...
...LIKE BECOME KANAME-SAMA'S CLOSE FRIENDS...
I'M HAPPY IF RUKA IS HAPPY.
IF RUKA BELIEVES, I'LL BELIEVE TOO.
WILL THE DAY COME WHEN I CAN BELIEVE IN MYSELF LIKE RUKA...
...AND START WALKING MY OWN PATH?

FORTY-EIGHTH NIGHT/END

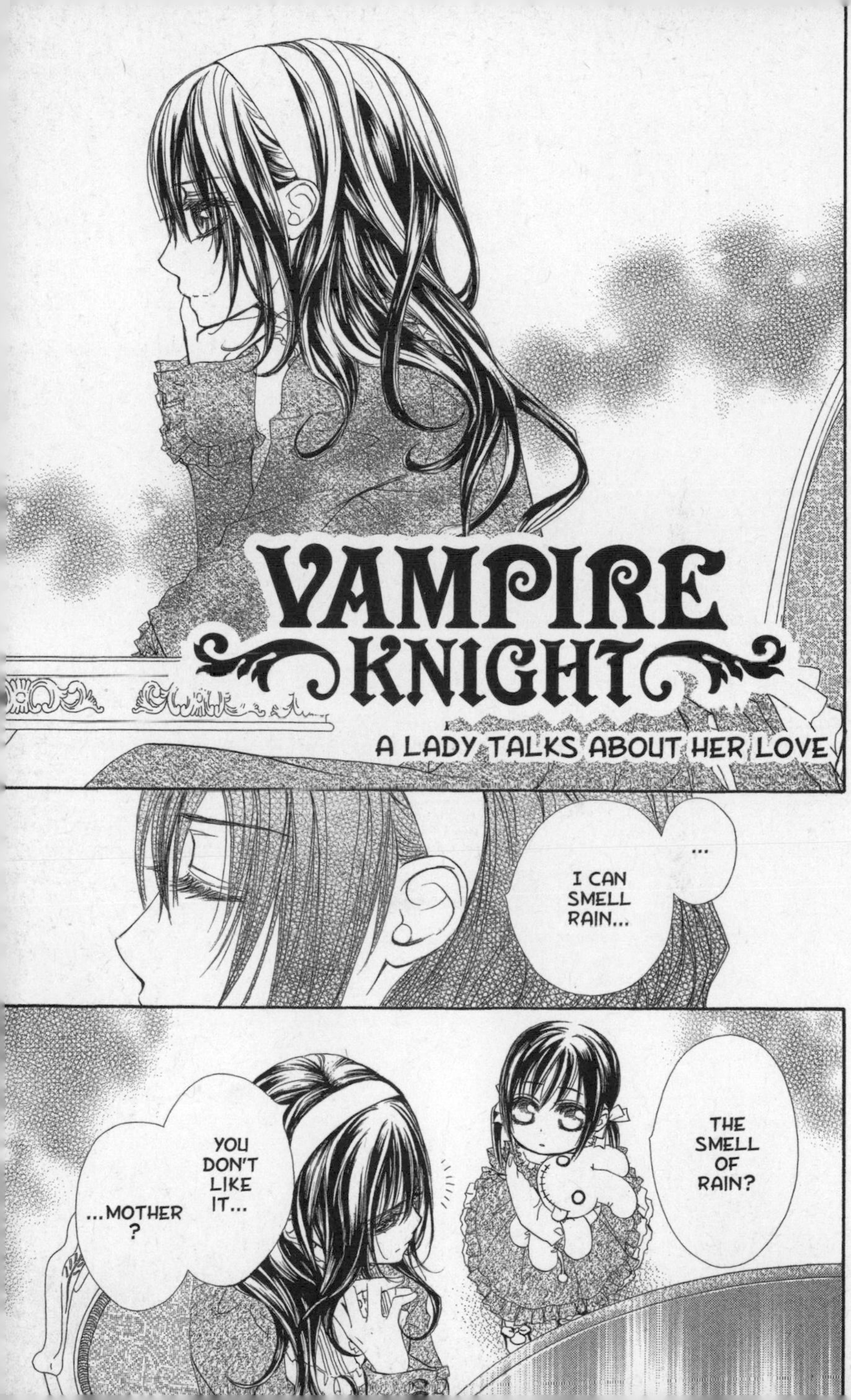
VAMPIRE KNIGHT
A LADY TALKS ABOUT HER LOVE
... I CAN SMELL RAIN...
THE SMELL OF RAIN?
YOU DON'T LIKE IT...
...MOTHER?

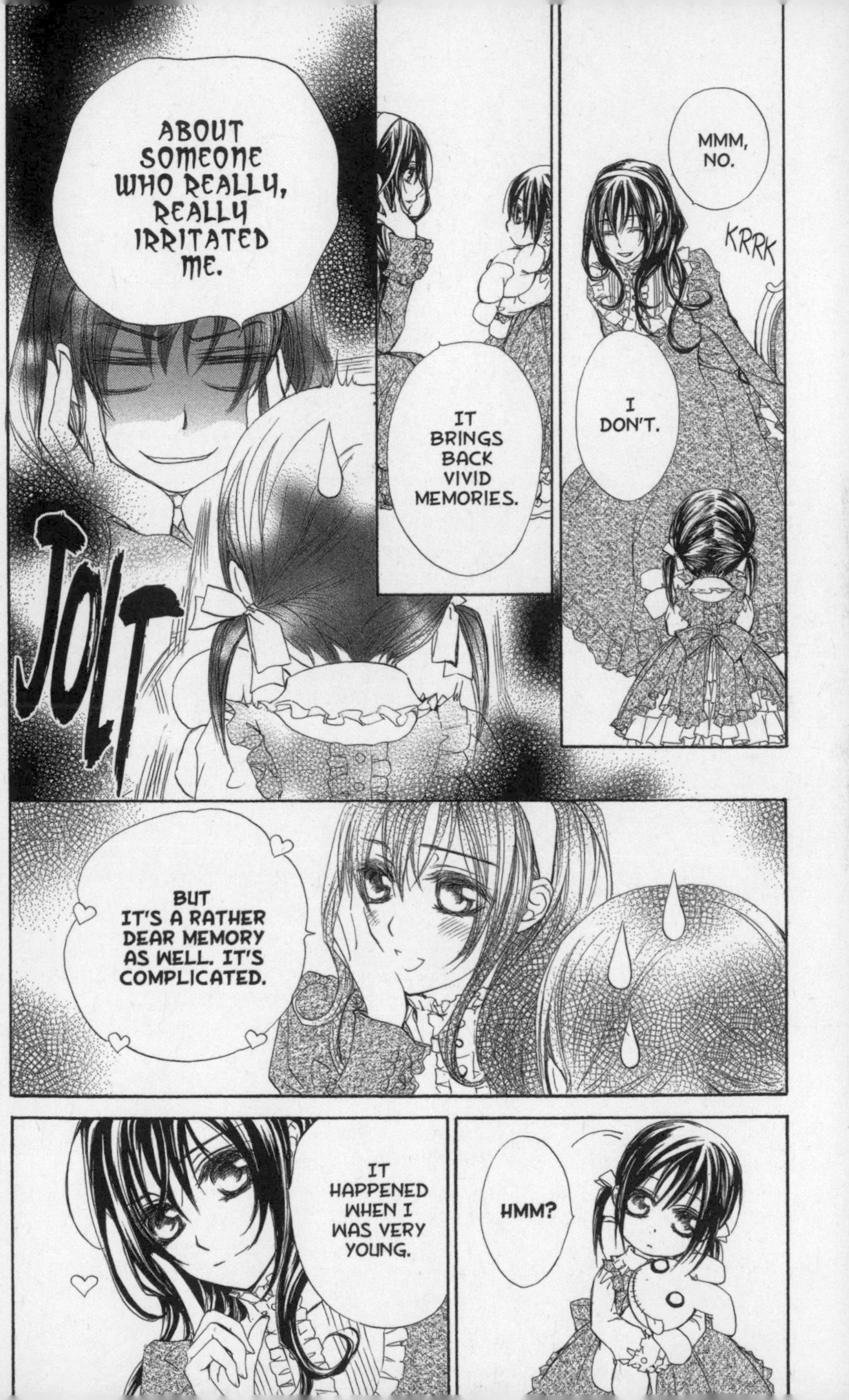
MMM, NO.
KRRK
I DON'T.
IT BRINGS BACK VIVID MEMORIES.
ABOUT SOMEONE WHO REALLY, REALLY IRRITATED ME.
JOLT
BUT IT'S A RATHER DEAR MEMORY AS WELL. IT'S COMPLICATED.
HMM?
IT HAPPENED WHEN I WAS VERY YOUNG.

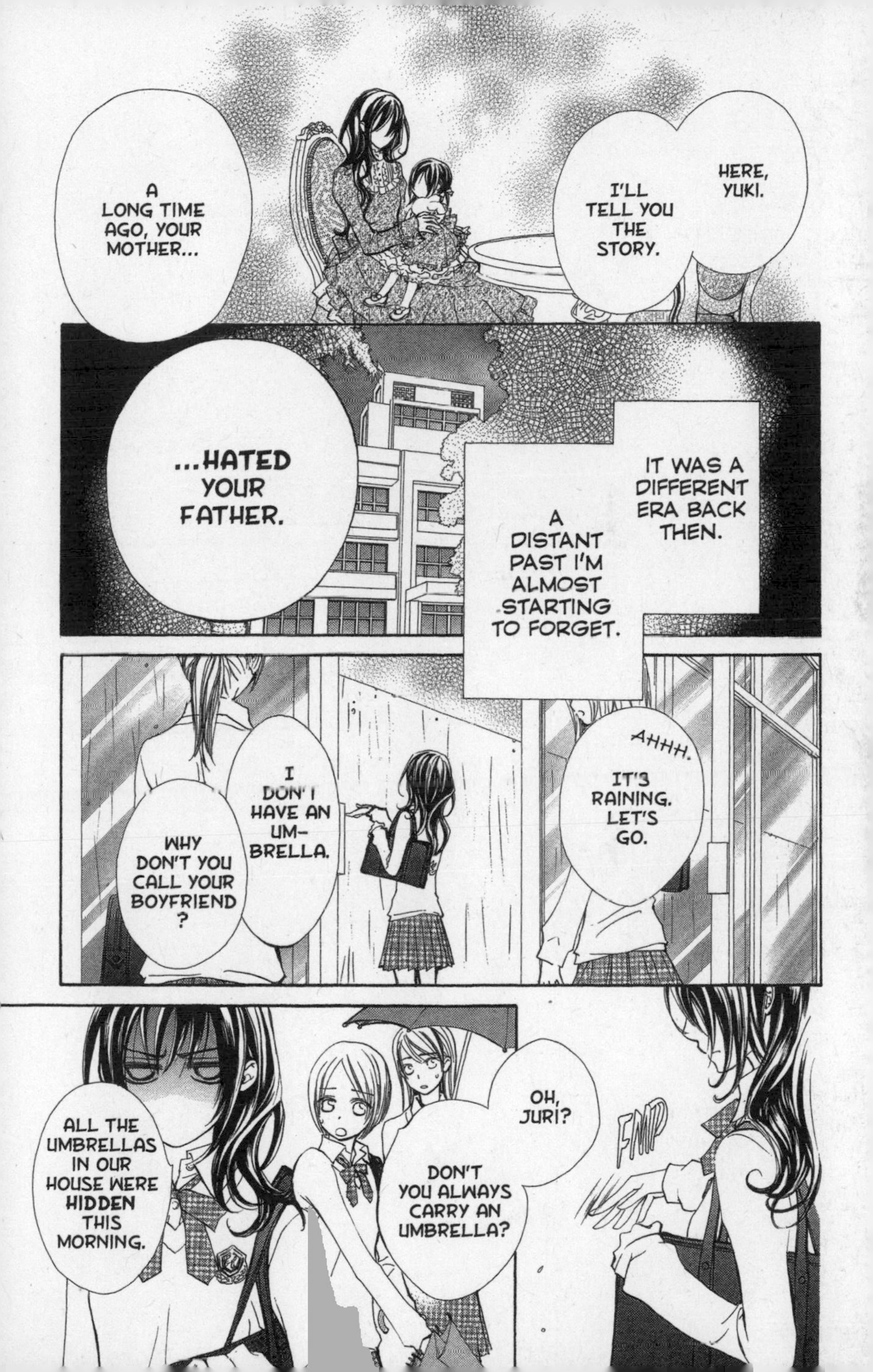
HERE, YUKI.
I'LL TELL YOU THE STORY.
A LONG TIME AGO, YOUR MOTHER...
...HATED YOUR FATHER.
IT WAS A DIFFERENT ERA BACK THEN.
A DISTANT PAST I'M ALMOST STARTING TO FORGET.
AHHH.
IT'S RAINING. LET'S GO.
I DON'T HAVE AN UM-BRELLA.
WHY DON'T YOU CALL YOUR BOYFRIEND ?
FMP
OH, JURI?
DON'T YOU ALWAYS CARRY AN UMBRELLA?
ALL THE UMBRELLAS IN OUR HOUSE WERE HIDDEN THIS MORNING.

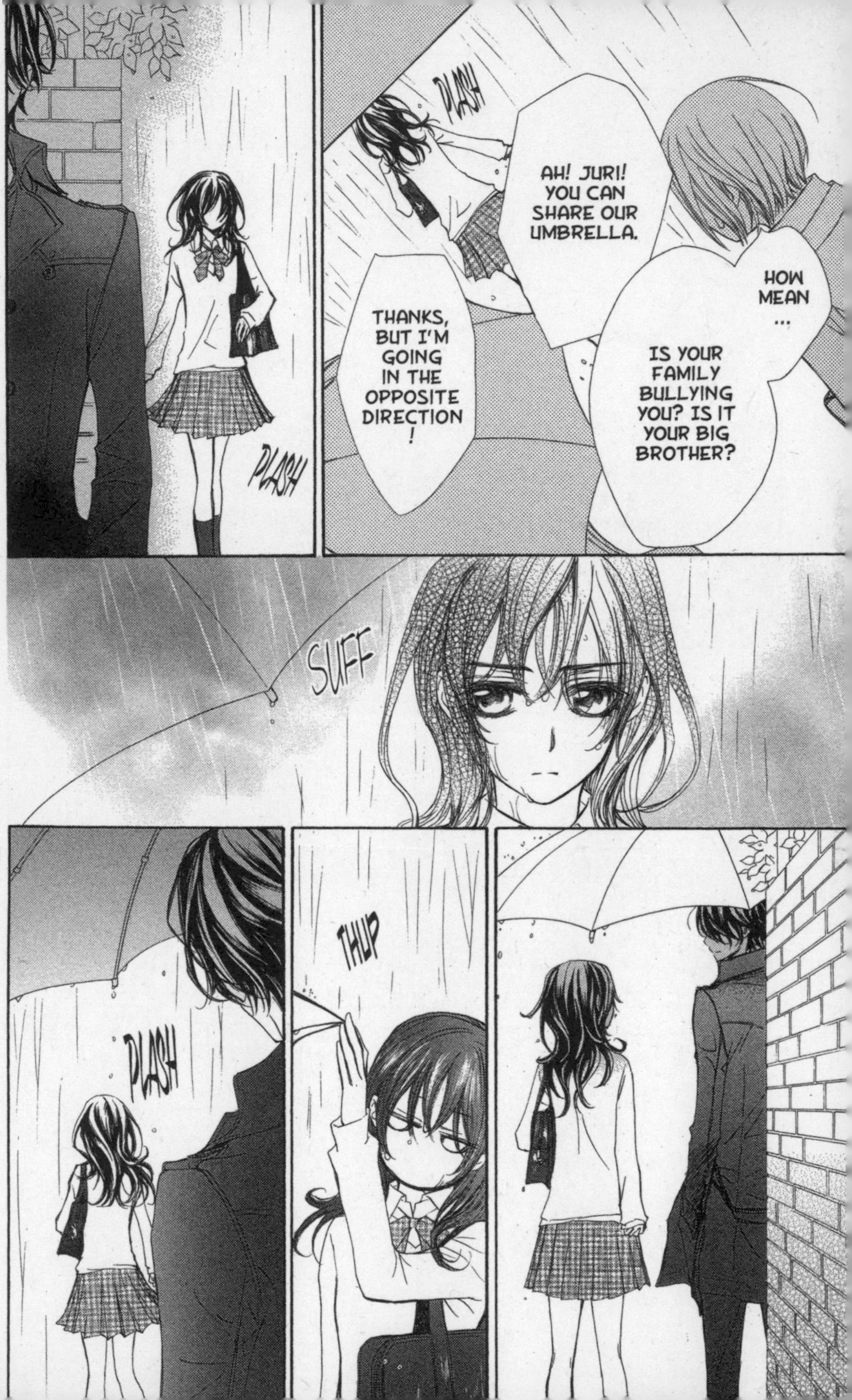
AH! JURI! YOU CAN SHARE OUR UMBRELLA.
PLASH
THANKS, BUT I'M GOING IN THE OPPOSITE DIRECTION!
HOW MEAN ...
IS YOUR FAMILY BULLYING YOU? IS IT YOUR BIG BROTHER?
PLASH
SUFF
THUP
PLASH

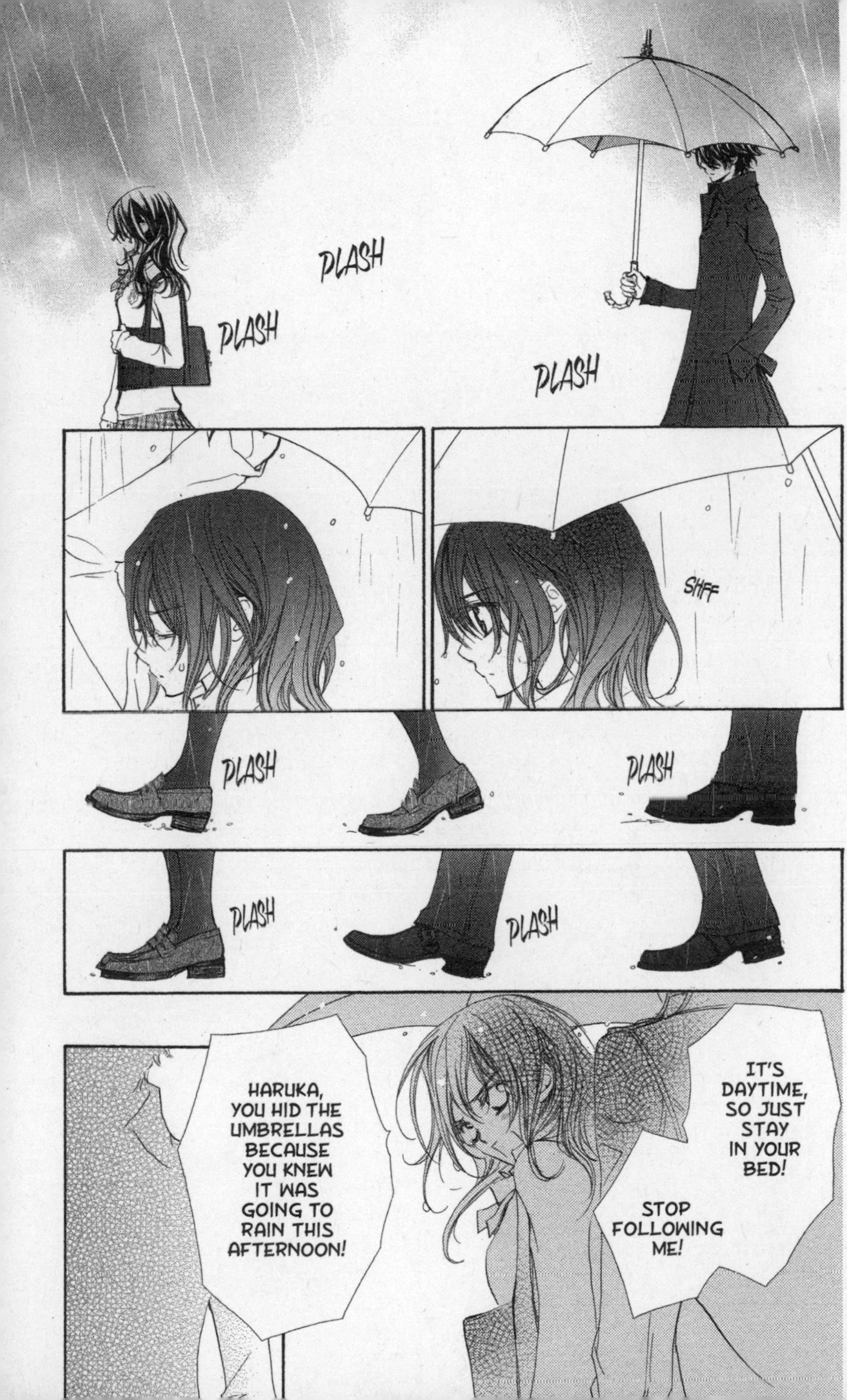
PLASH
PLASH
PLASH
SHFF
PLASH
PLASH
PLASH
PLASH
IT'S DAYTIME, SO JUST STAY IN YOUR BED!
STOP FOLLOWING ME!
HARUKA, YOU HID THE UMBRELLAS BECAUSE YOU KNEW IT WAS GOING TO RAIN THIS AFTERNOON!

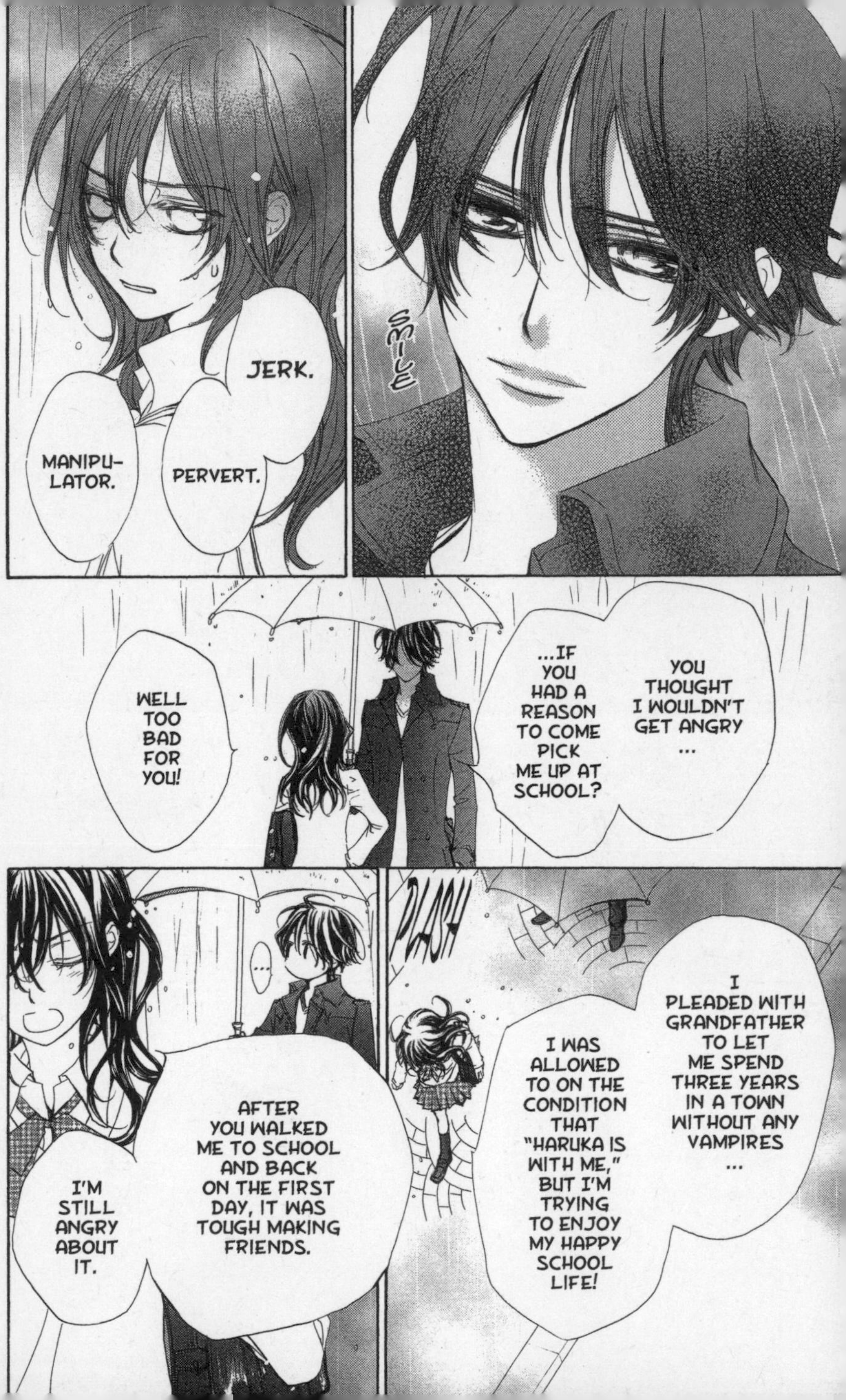
SMILE
JERK.
PERVERT.
MANIPU-LATOR.
YOU THOUGHT I WOULDN'T GET ANGRY ...
...IF YOU HAD A REASON TO COME PICK ME UP AT SCHOOL?
WELL TOO BAD FOR YOU!
PLASH
I PLEADED WITH GRANDFATHER TO LET ME SPEND THREE YEARS IN A TOWN WITHOUT ANY VAMPIRES ...
I WAS ALLOWED TO ON THE CONDITION THAT "HARUKA IS WITH ME," BUT I'M TRYING TO ENJOY MY HAPPY SCHOOL LIFE!
...
AFTER YOU WALKED ME TO SCHOOL AND BACK ON THE FIRST DAY, IT WAS TOUGH MAKING FRIENDS.
I'M STILL ANGRY ABOUT IT.

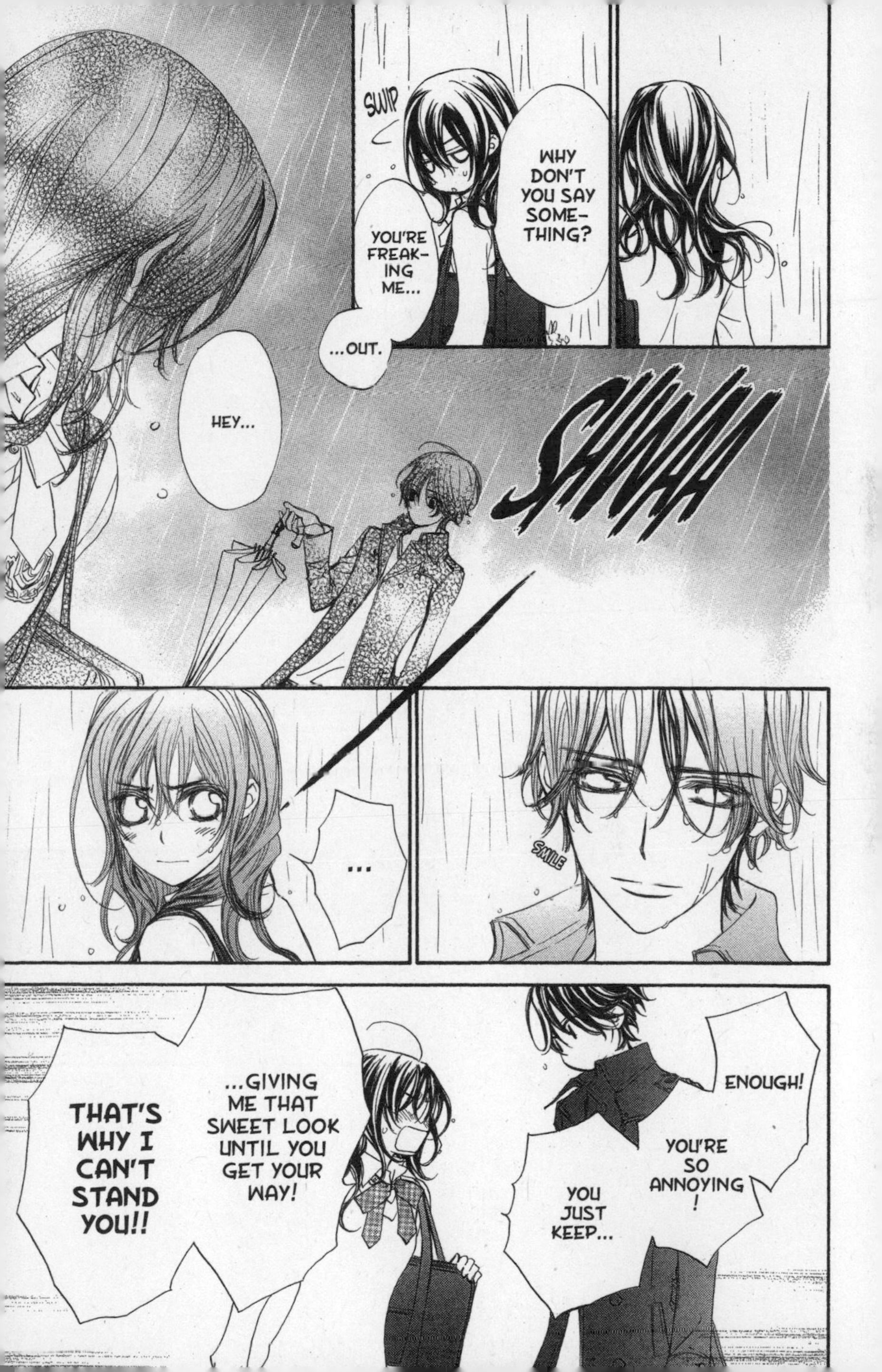
SWIP
WHY DON'T YOU SAY SOME-THING?
YOU'RE FREAK-ING ME...
...OUT.
HEY...
SHWAH
SMILE
...
ENOUGH!
YOU'RE SO ANNOYING!
YOU JUST KEEP...
...GIVING ME THAT SWEET LOOK UNTIL YOU GET YOUR WAY!
THAT'S WHY I CAN'T STAND YOU!!

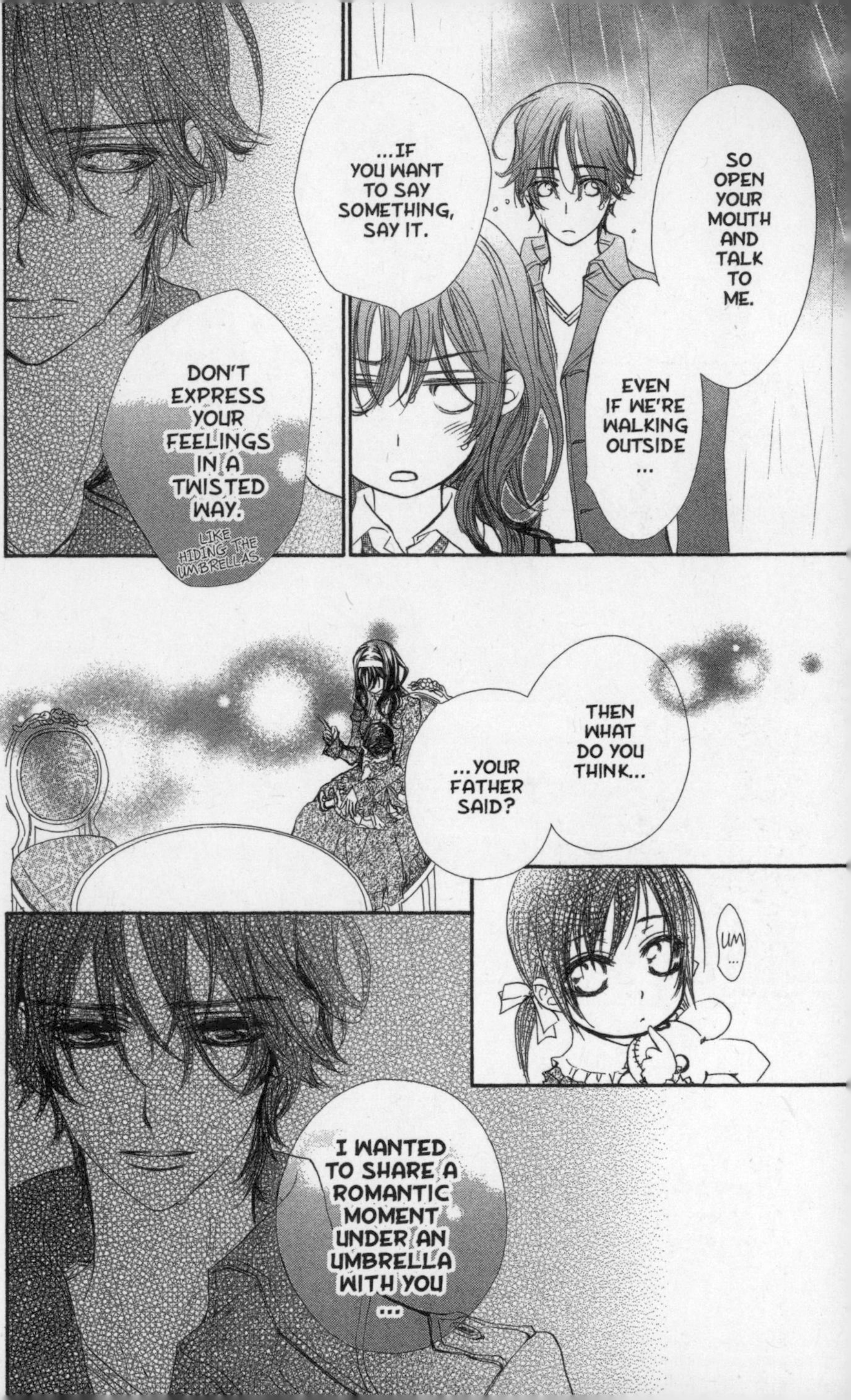
SO OPEN YOUR MOUTH AND TALK TO ME.
EVEN IF WE'RE WALKING OUTSIDE ...
...IF YOU WANT TO SAY SOMETHING, SAY IT.
DON'T EXPRESS YOUR FEELINGS IN A TWISTED WAY.
LIKE HIDING THE UMBRELLAS.
THEN WHAT DO YOU THINK...
...YOUR FATHER SAID?
UM ...
I WANTED TO SHARE A ROMANTIC MOMENT UNDER AN UMBRELLA WITH YOU ...

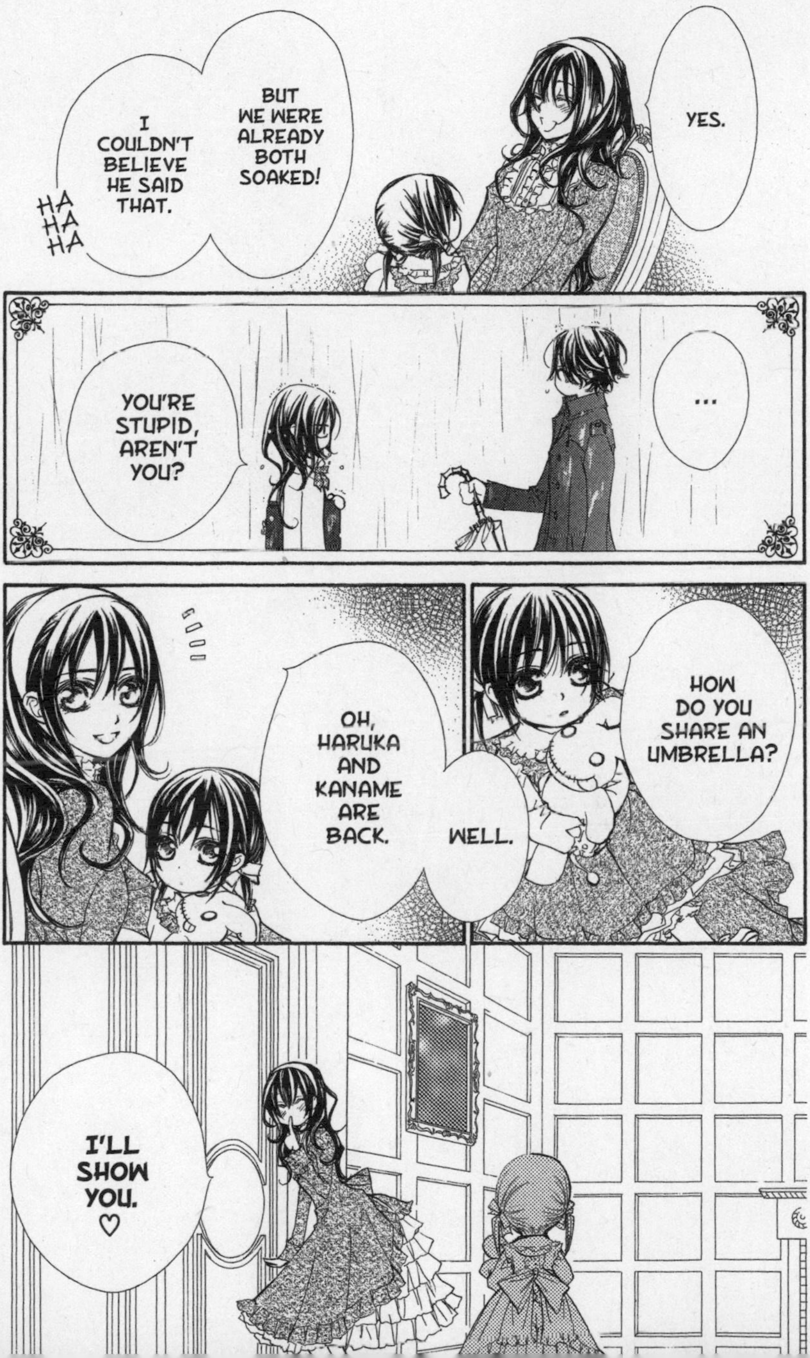
YES.
BUT WE WERE ALREADY BOTH SOAKED!
I COULDN'T BELIEVE HE SAID THAT.
HA HA HA
...
YOU'RE STUPID, AREN'T YOU?
HOW DO YOU SHARE AN UMBRELLA?
WELL.
OH, HARUKA AND KANAME ARE BACK.
I'LL SHOW YOU. ♡

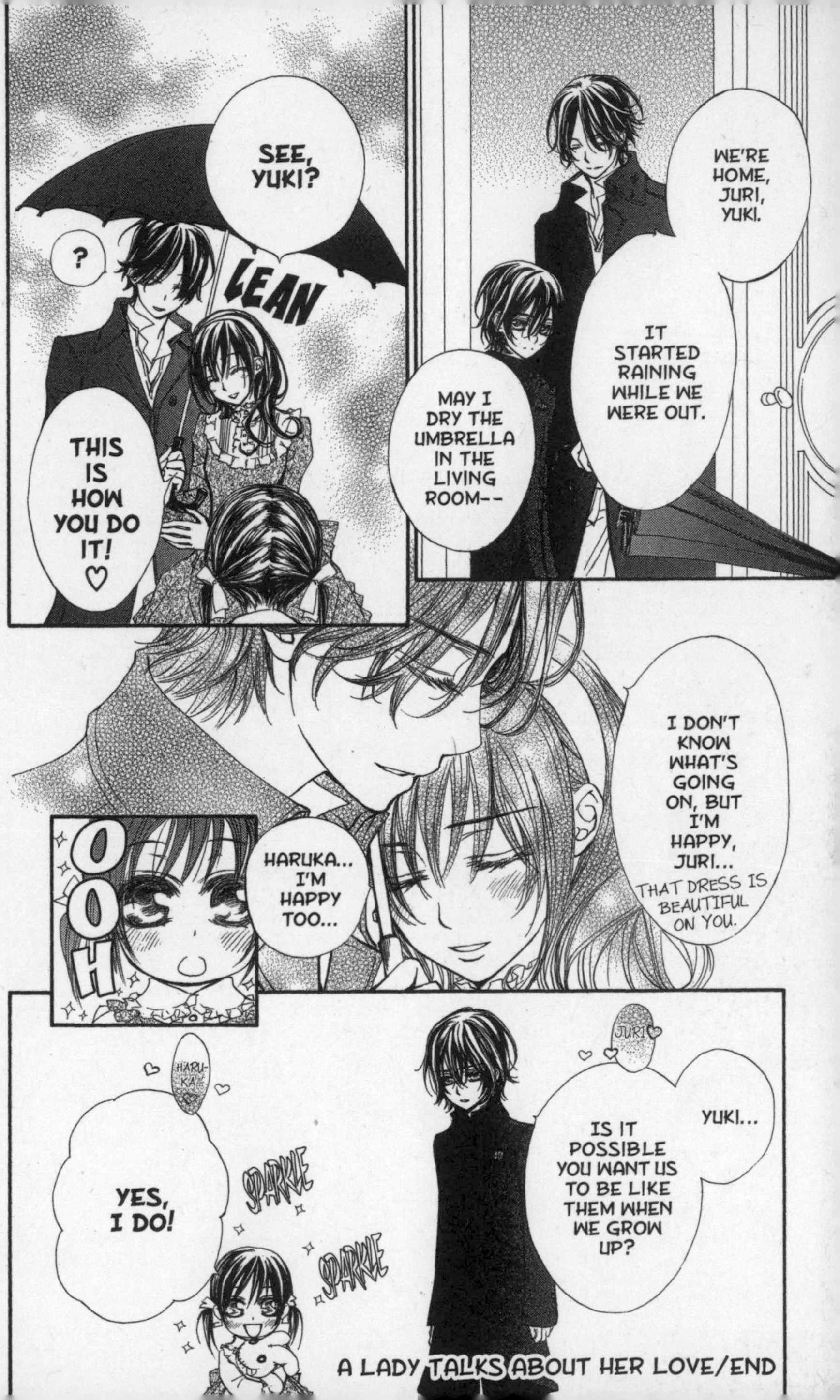
WE'RE HOME, JURI, YUKI.
IT STARTED RAINING WHILE WE WERE OUT.
MAY I DRY THE UMBRELLA IN THE LIVING ROOM--
SEE, YUKI?
LEAN
?
THIS IS HOW YOU DO IT! ♡
I DON'T KNOW WHAT'S GOING ON, BUT I'M HAPPY, JURI...
THAT DRESS IS BEAUTIFUL ON YOU.
HARUKA... I'M HAPPY TOO...
OOH
JURI ♡
YUKI...
IS IT POSSIBLE YOU WANT US TO BE LIKE THEM WHEN WE GROW UP?
HARU-KA ♡
YES, I DO!
SPARKLE
SPARKLE
A LADY TALKS ABOUT HER LOVE/END

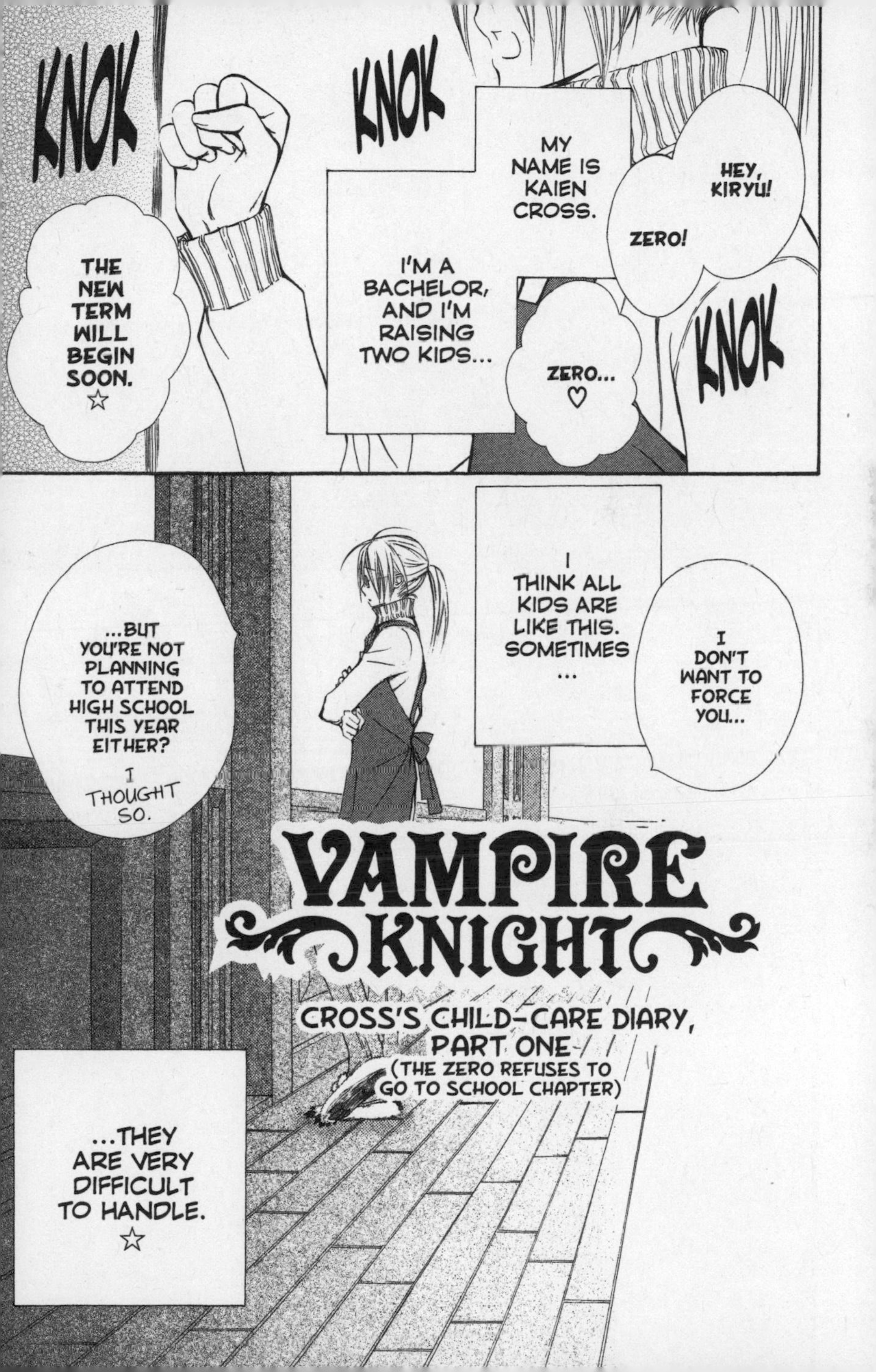
HEY, KIRYU!
ZERO!
KNOK
MY NAME IS KAIEN CROSS.
KNOK
KNOK
ZERO... ♡
I'M A BACHELOR, AND I'M RAISING TWO KIDS...
THE NEW TERM WILL BEGIN SOON. ☆
I DON'T WANT TO FORCE YOU...
I THINK ALL KIDS ARE LIKE THIS. SOMETIMES ...
...BUT YOU'RE NOT PLANNING TO ATTEND HIGH SCHOOL THIS YEAR EITHER?
I THOUGHT SO.
VAMPIRE KNIGHT
CROSS'S CHILD-CARE DIARY, PART ONE
(THE ZERO REFUSES TO GO TO SCHOOL CHAPTER)
...THEY ARE VERY DIFFICULT TO HANDLE. ☆

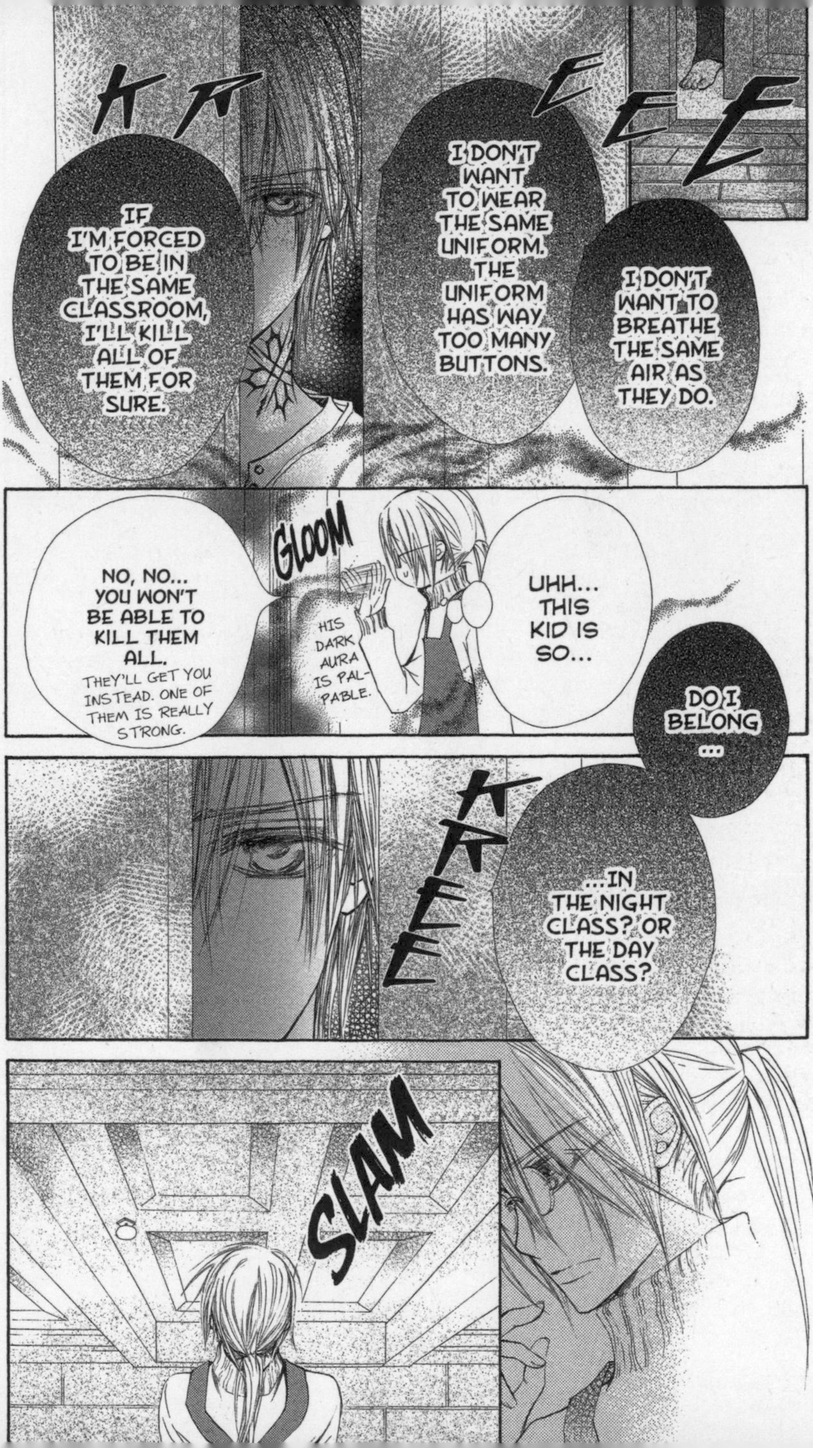
KREEEE
I DON'T WANT TO BREATHE THE SAME AIR AS THEY DO.
I DON'T WANT TO WEAR THE SAME UNIFORM. THE UNIFORM HAS WAY TOO MANY BUTTONS.
IF I'M FORCED TO BE IN THE SAME CLASSROOM, I'LL KILL ALL OF THEM FOR SURE.
UHH... THIS KID IS SO...
HIS DARK AURA IS PAL-PABLE.
GLOOM
NO, NO... YOU WON'T BE ABLE TO KILL THEM ALL.
THEY'LL GET YOU INSTEAD. ONE OF THEM IS REALLY STRONG.
DO I BELONG...
...IN THE NIGHT CLASS? OR THE DAY CLASS?
KREEE
SLAM

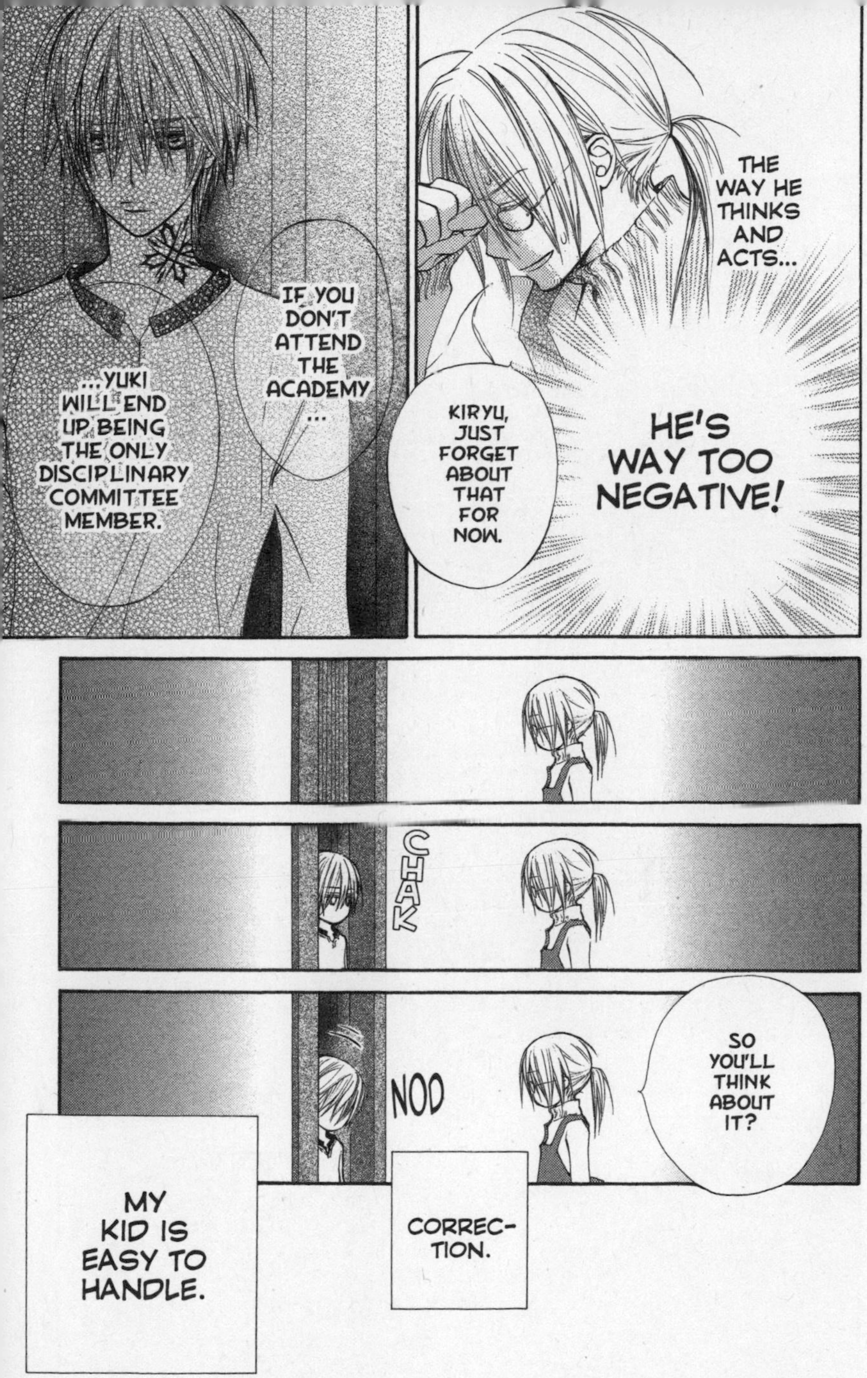
THE WAY HE THINKS AND ACTS...
HE'S WAY TOO NEGATIVE!
KIRYU, JUST FORGET ABOUT THAT FOR NOW.
IF YOU DON'T ATTEND THE ACADEMY...
...YUKI WILL END UP BEING THE ONLY DISCIPLINARY COMMITTEE MEMBER.
CHAK
SO YOU'LL THINK ABOUT IT?
NOD
CORREC-TION.
MY KID IS EASY TO HANDLE.

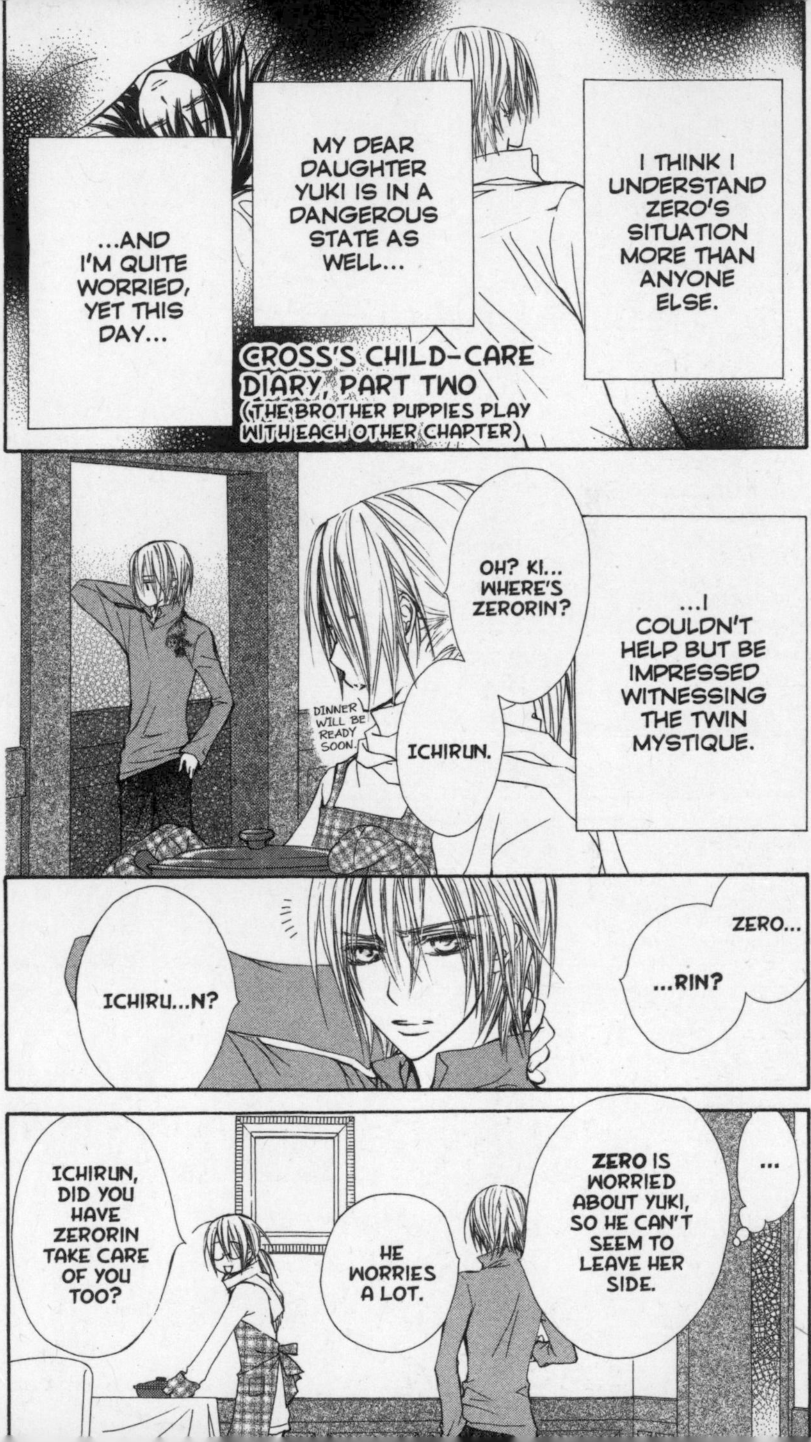
I THINK I UNDERSTAND ZERO'S SITUATION MORE THAN ANYONE ELSE.
MY DEAR DAUGHTER YUKI IS IN A DANGEROUS STATE AS WELL...
...AND I'M QUITE WORRIED, YET THIS DAY...
CROSS'S CHILD-CARE DIARY, PART TWO
(THE BROTHER PUPPIES PLAY WITH EACH OTHER CHAPTER)
...I COULDN'T HELP BUT BE IMPRESSED WITNESSING THE TWIN MYSTIQUE.
OH? KI... WHERE'S ZERORIN?
ICHIRUN.
DINNER WILL BE READY SOON.
ZERO...
...RIN?
ICHIRU...N?
...
ZERO IS WORRIED ABOUT YUKI, SO HE CAN'T SEEM TO LEAVE HER SIDE.
HE WORRIES A LOT.
ICHIRUN, DID YOU HAVE ZERORIN TAKE CARE OF YOU TOO?

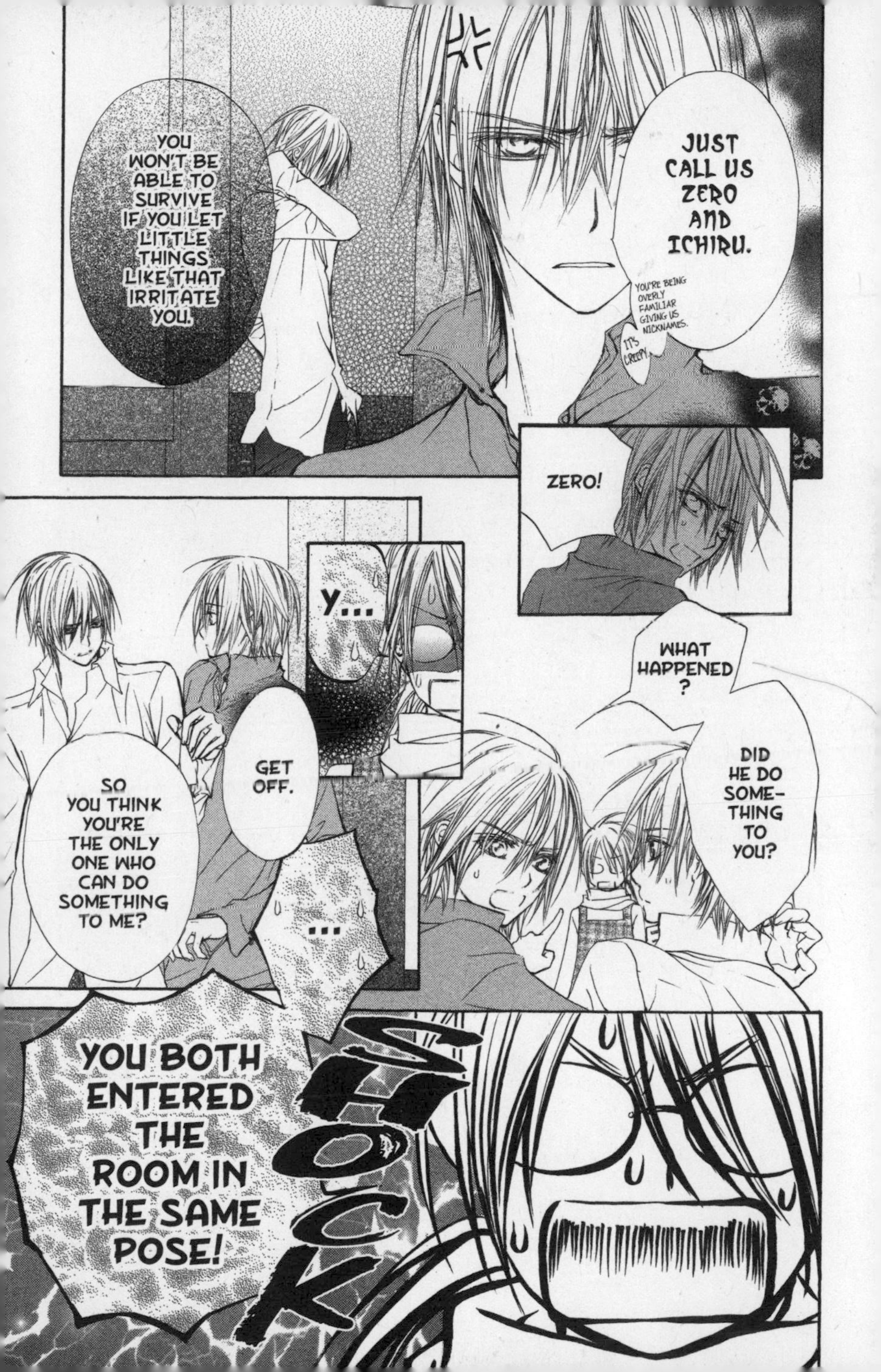
JUST CALL US ZERO AND ICHIRU.
YOU'RE BEING OVERLY FAMILIAR GIVING US NICKNAMES.
IT'S CREEPY.
YOU WON'T BE ABLE TO SURVIVE IF YOU LET LITTLE THINGS LIKE THAT IRRITATE YOU.
ZERO!
WHAT HAPPENED?
DID HE DO SOME-THING TO YOU?
Y...
GET OFF.
SO YOU THINK YOU'RE THE ONLY ONE WHO CAN DO SOMETHING TO ME?
...
SHOCK
YOU BOTH ENTERED THE ROOM IN THE SAME POSE!

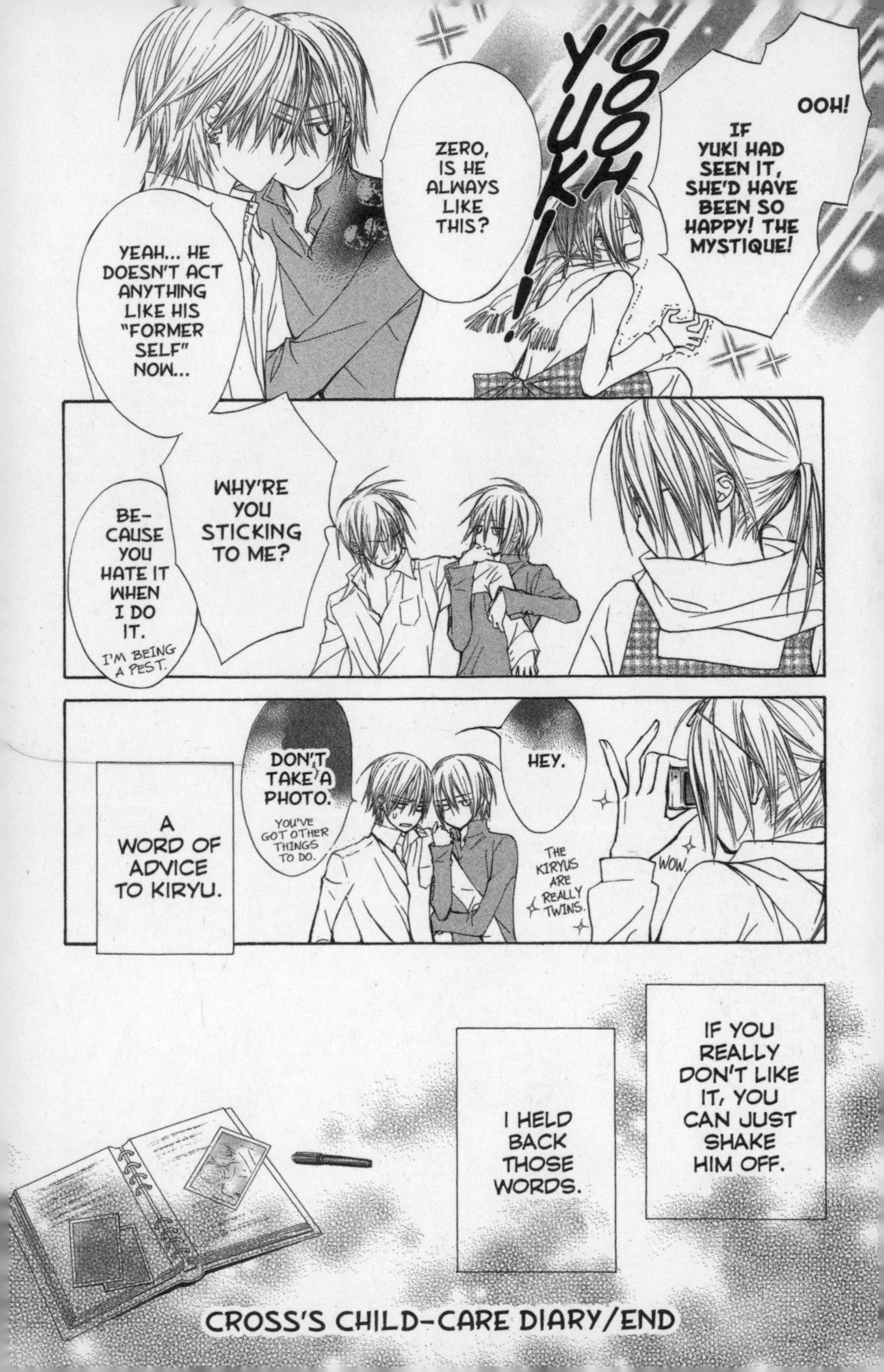
OOH!
IF YUKI HAD SEEN IT, SHE'D HAVE BEEN SO HAPPY! THE MYSTIQUE!
YUUK!!
OOOH
ZERO, IS HE ALWAYS LIKE THIS?
YEAH... HE DOESN'T ACT ANYTHING LIKE HIS "FORMER SELF" NOW...
WHY'RE YOU STICKING TO ME?
BE-CAUSE YOU HATE IT WHEN I DO IT.
I'M BEING A PEST.
WOW.
THE KIRYUS ARE REALLY TWINS.
HEY.
DON'T TAKE A PHOTO.
YOU'VE GOT OTHER THINGS TO DO.
A WORD OF ADVICE TO KIRYU.
IF YOU REALLY DON'T LIKE IT, YOU CAN JUST SHAKE HIM OFF.
I HELD BACK THOSE WORDS.
CROSS'S CHILD-CARE DIARY/END

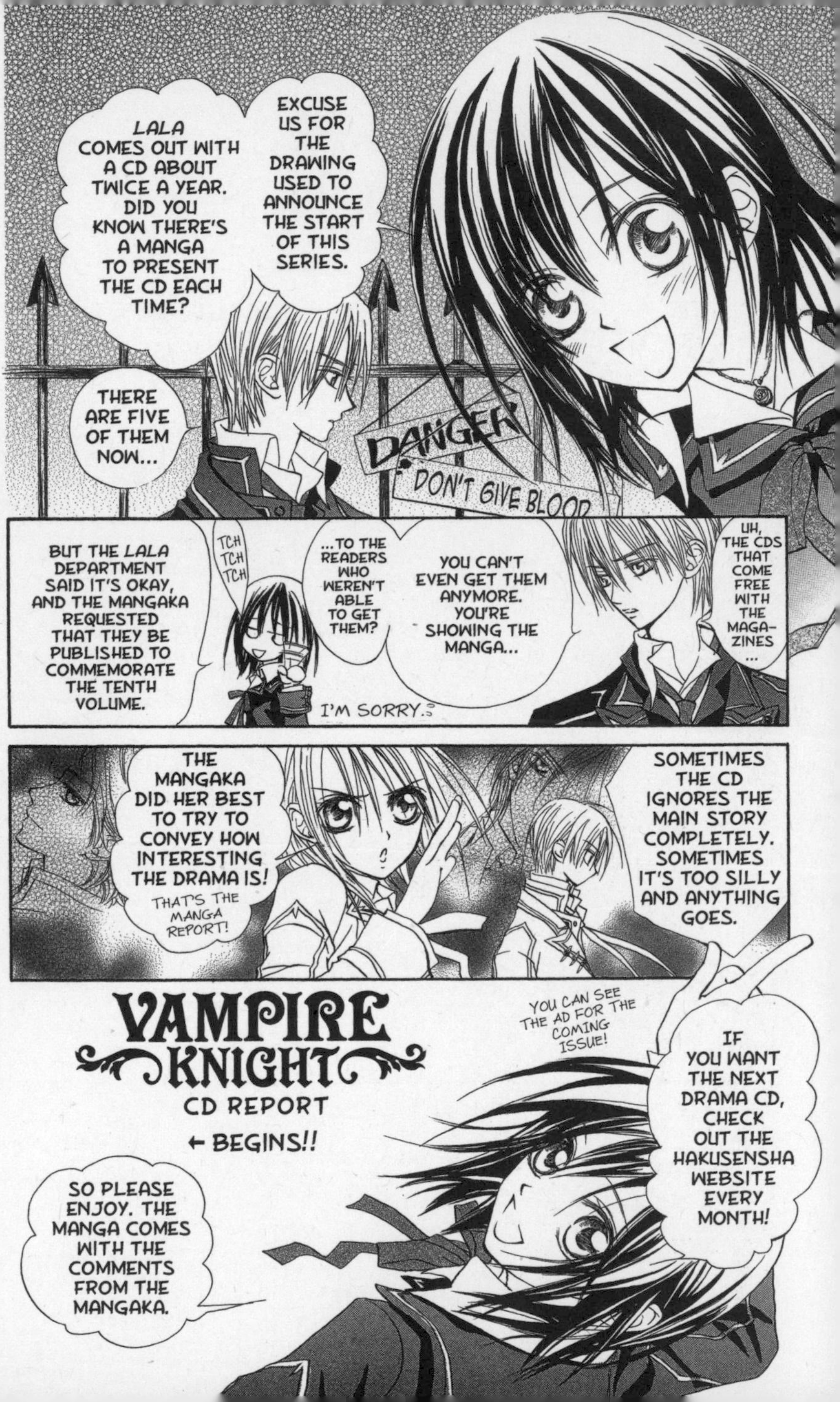
EXCUSE US FOR THE DRAWING USED TO ANNOUNCE THE START OF THIS SERIES.
LALA COMES OUT WITH A CD ABOUT TWICE A YEAR. DID YOU KNOW THERE'S A MANGA TO PRESENT THE CD EACH TIME?
THERE ARE FIVE OF THEM NOW...
DANGER
DON'T GIVE BLOOD
UH, THE CDS THAT COME FREE WITH THE MAGA-ZINES...
YOU CAN'T EVEN GET THEM ANYMORE. YOU'RE SHOWING THE MANGA...
...TO THE READERS WHO WEREN'T ABLE TO GET THEM?
TCH TCH TCH
I'M SORRY.
BUT THE *LALA* DEPARTMENT SAID IT'S OKAY, AND THE MANGAKA REQUESTED THAT THEY BE PUBLISHED TO COMMEMORATE THE TENTH VOLUME.
SOMETIMES THE CD IGNORES THE MAIN STORY COMPLETELY. SOMETIMES IT'S TOO SILLY AND ANYTHING GOES.
THE MANGAKA DID HER BEST TO TRY TO CONVEY HOW INTERESTING THE DRAMA IS!
THAT'S THE MANGA REPORT!
YOU CAN SEE THE AD FOR THE COMING ISSUE!
IF YOU WANT THE NEXT DRAMA CD, CHECK OUT THE HAKUSENSHA WEBSITE EVERY MONTH!
VAMPIRE KNIGHT
CD REPORT
← BEGINS!!
SO PLEASE ENJOY. THE MANGA COMES WITH THE COMMENTS FROM THE MANGAKA.

LALA KIRAMEKI ☆ DRAMA CD

LALA 9/2005 ISSUE

I'M SURPRISED BY THAT SCRIPT, CONSIDERING THE WAY THE MAIN STORY IS GOING...
HYOOO
THE MANGAKA MUST BE INCONSIDERATE, JUST LIKE THE HEADMASTER.
WELL, I HAD A LITTLE FUN THOUGH.
ZERO? WHAT'RE YOU DOING?
ACK
SHINK
DON'T CAUSE TROUBLE!
HUH?! WHY?! YOU HATED IT THAT MUCH?!
WELL, I KNEW YOU WOULDN'T LIKE IT, BUT STILL...
I'LL THREATEN THE CD FACTORY AND MAKE THEM DELETE OUR SCRIPT!
HOW'D YOU COME UP WITH THAT EXPLANATION?
SIGH
DID YOU JUST CALL ME A BRAT?
JEALOUS...
RIGHT?
BRAT...
LOOK FOR-WARD TO IT!!

THE FIRST VAMPIRE KNIGHT DRAMA CD

BUT THE SERIES HAD JUST BEGUN, SO I COULDN'T DELVE DEEPLY INTO THE CHARACTERS ENOUGH TO PLAY WITH THEM. AND THERE WEREN'T ANY CHARACTERS THAT COULD PLAY COMEDY ALL THE WAY THROUGH...SO I HAD TROUBLE WITH THE SCRIPT. BECAUSE ZERO AND KANAME DIDN'T TALK MUCH, I HAD YUKI DO HER BEST.

I REMEMBER FONDLY THAT WHEN KISHIO-SAN ASKED ME, "WHAT'S KANAME LIKE?" I BURST OUT, "HE'S ACTUALLY A PERVERT. HE'S OBSCENE"...

LALA GORGEOUS ♡ DRAMA CD

LALA 11/2006 ISSUE

ZERO AND KANAME DON'T SEEM TO BE ABLE TO KEEP A CONVERSATION GOING, SO I DID MY BEST TO WRITE A SCRIPT TO HAVE THEM TALK A LOT.
IT'S A CD, SO IT COULDN'T BE SILENT...
...
...
SO I APPEARED... I SEE.
I'M SORRY IT WAS BARELY FUNNY. I ALMOST DESTROYED THE CHARACTERS...
MAYBE I DID...
I APOLOGIZE.
I HAD TO DO MY MANGA STORYBOARD AT THE SAME TIME. (I'M A FOOL.)
AND WHEN WE HAD THE VOICE ACTORS SPEAK...
...THEIR CONVERSATIONS WENT ON AND ON, AS I'D PLANNED...
SWEAT SWEAT
WOW!
PINO
BUT MIYANO-SAN AND KISHIO-SAN KEPT THEIR ACTING SUPER LOW-KEY.
CUZ... ...IT'S ZERO AND KANAME.
I WAS WORRIED...
...LAUGH
PBFFT
THEY'RE LAUGHING...
RIGHT?
PINO
GRIP
...BUT I HEARD THE DIRECTOR AND THE VOICE ACTORS GIGGLING IN BETWEEN TAKES...
...AND I WAS RELIEVED... A LITTLE.
VOICE ACTORS ARE AMAZING!
AND MIYANO-SAN AND KISHIO-SAN DID THEIR BEST...
TRYING NOT TO LAUGH
...NOT TO LAUGH AT THE HEADMASTER'S (KOYASU-SAN'S) OVERACTING THIS TIME TOO.
SMILE

ZERO AND KANAME ARE LOW-KEY, PART TWO

...I DID MY BEST. THE GUYS BECAME CREEPY, BUT I COULDN'T HELP IT... THE SCRIPTWRITER WROTE IT AS A GAG. BUT I WAS OVERCOME WITH GUILT, AND BECAUSE I'M A CHICKEN, I FIRST APOLOGIZED TO THE READERS.

LALA TREASURE ☆ DRAMA CD

LALA 10/2007 ISSUE

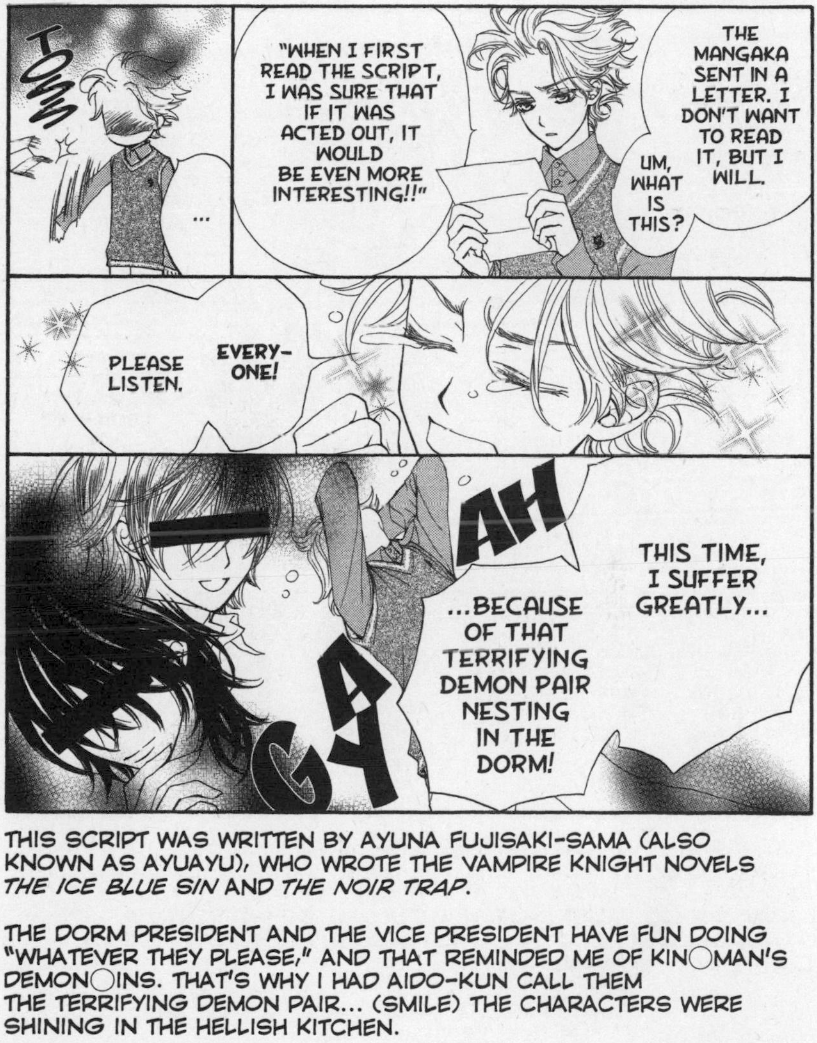
THE MANGAKA SENT IN A LETTER. I DON'T WANT TO READ IT, BUT I WILL.
UM, WHAT IS THIS?
"WHEN I FIRST READ THE SCRIPT, I WAS SURE THAT IF IT WAS ACTED OUT, IT WOULD BE EVEN MORE INTERESTING!!"
TOSS
...
EVERY-ONE!
PLEASE LISTEN.
THIS TIME, I SUFFER GREATLY...
AH
...BECAUSE OF THAT TERRIFYING DEMON PAIR NESTING IN THE DORM!
GA

THIS SCRIPT WAS WRITTEN BY AYUNA FUJISAKI-SAMA (ALSO KNOWN AS AYUAYU), WHO WROTE THE VAMPIRE KNIGHT NOVELS *THE ICE BLUE SIN* AND *THE NOIR TRAP*.

THE DORM PRESIDENT AND THE VICE PRESIDENT HAVE FUN DOING "WHATEVER THEY PLEASE," AND THAT REMINDED ME OF KIN◯MAN'S DEMON◯INS. THAT'S WHY I HAD AIDO-KUN CALL THEM THE TERRIFYING DEMON PAIR... (SMILE) THE CHARACTERS WERE SHINING IN THE HELLISH KITCHEN.

LALA PREMIUM ♡ DRAMA CD

LALA 5/2008 ISSUE

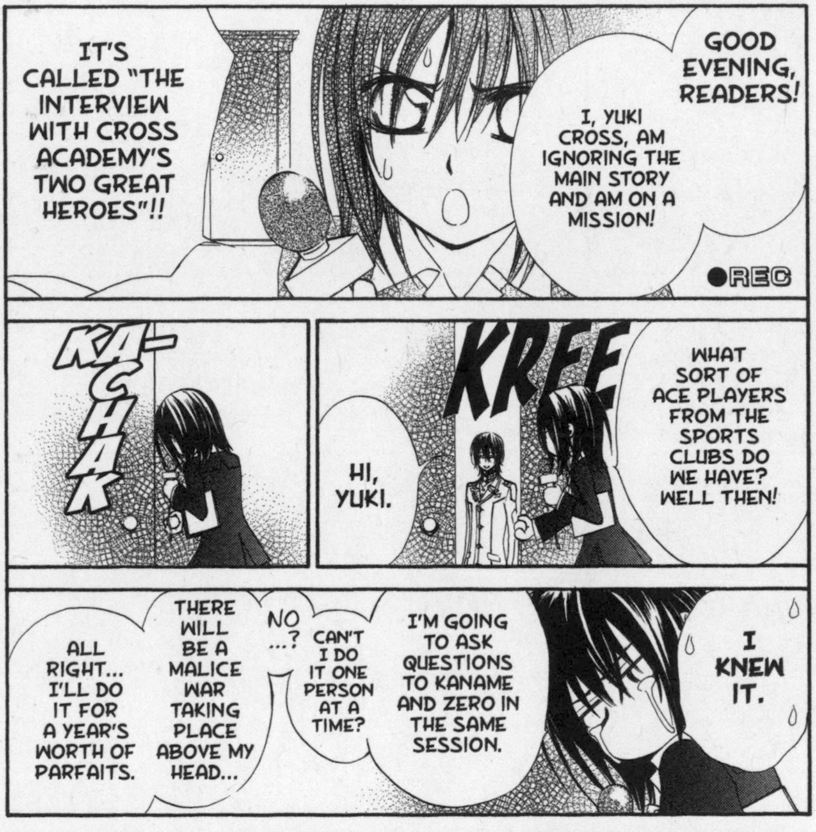
GOOD EVENING, READERS!
I, YUKI CROSS, AM IGNORING THE MAIN STORY AND AM ON A MISSION!
●REC
IT'S CALLED "THE INTERVIEW WITH CROSS ACADEMY'S TWO GREAT HEROES"!!
WHAT SORT OF ACE PLAYERS FROM THE SPORTS CLUBS DO WE HAVE? WELL THEN!
KREE
HI, YUKI.
KA-CHAK
I KNEW IT.
I'M GOING TO ASK QUESTIONS TO KANAME AND ZERO IN THE SAME SESSION.
CAN'T I DO IT ONE PERSON AT A TIME?
NO ...?
THERE WILL BE A MALICE WAR TAKING PLACE ABOVE MY HEAD...
ALL RIGHT... I'LL DO IT FOR A YEAR'S WORTH OF PARFAITS.

THIS SCRIPT WAS WRITTEN BY MORITA MAYUMI-SAMA, WHO WAS IN CHARGE OF THE ANIME SCRIPTS TOGETHER WITH FUJISAKI-SAN.

I DIDN'T THINK "WORD CHAINS" WOULD BE SO INTERESTING! LOTS OF KUDOS TO MORITA-SAN, WHO MADE THE TWO PLAY WORD CHAINS IN THAT FORM.

I COULDN'T HELP BUT QUIP THAT "ZERO AND KANAME...ARE JUST FOOLS WHO LOVE YUKI TOO MUCH...(SMILE)."

LALA DOUBLE PREMIUM ☆ DRAMA CD

LALA 5/2009 ISSUE

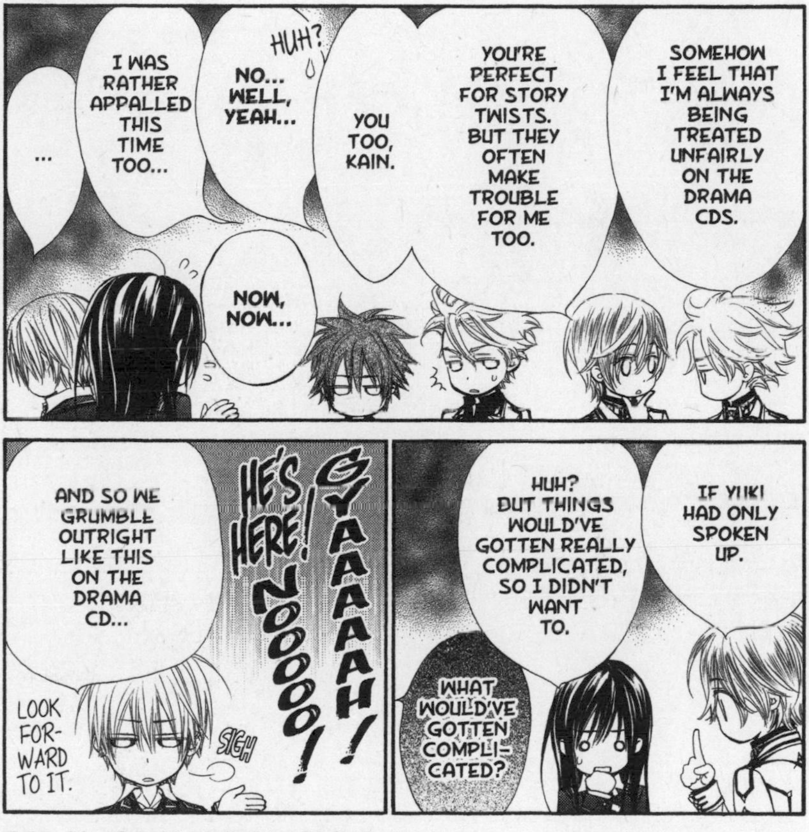
SOMEHOW I FEEL THAT I'M ALWAYS BEING TREATED UNFAIRLY ON THE DRAMA CDS.
YOU'RE PERFECT FOR STORY TWISTS. BUT THEY OFTEN MAKE TROUBLE FOR ME TOO.
YOU TOO, KAIN.
HUH?
NO... WELL, YEAH...
I WAS RATHER APPALLED THIS TIME TOO...
...
NOW, NOW...
IF YUKI HAD ONLY SPOKEN UP.
HUH? BUT THINGS WOULD'VE GOTTEN REALLY COMPLICATED, SO I DIDN'T WANT TO.
WHAT WOULD'VE GOTTEN COMPLICATED?
GYAAAAAAH!
HE'S HERE! NOOOOO!
AND SO WE GRUMBLE OUTRIGHT LIKE THIS ON THE DRAMA CD...
LOOK FORWARD TO IT.
SIGH

THIS CAME OUT PRETTY RECENTLY.

THE NIGHT CLASS MEMBERS APPEARED, SO I HAD TROUBLE GIVING THEM ALL EQUAL TIME.

...IN THE END, KANAME-SAMA BECAME THE STRONGEST (MOST FRIGHTENING?) COMEDY CHARACTER.

...BUT THE MANGAKA HAS GROWN DEFIANT AND HAS NO INTENTION OF APOLOGIZING FOR THAT...

...SO THOSE WERE THE CD MANGA REPORTS! (I ONLY DREW THE ILLUSTRATIONS FOR THE EXCELLENT ☆ DRAMA CD.)

FINALLY, PLEASE LET ME REPORT ABOUT THE ARTISTS WHO WERE DEEPLY INVOLVED WITH *VAMPIRE KNIGHT*, AND WHO EVEN WORE THE SCHOOL UNIFORMS.

HERE THEY ARE!!!

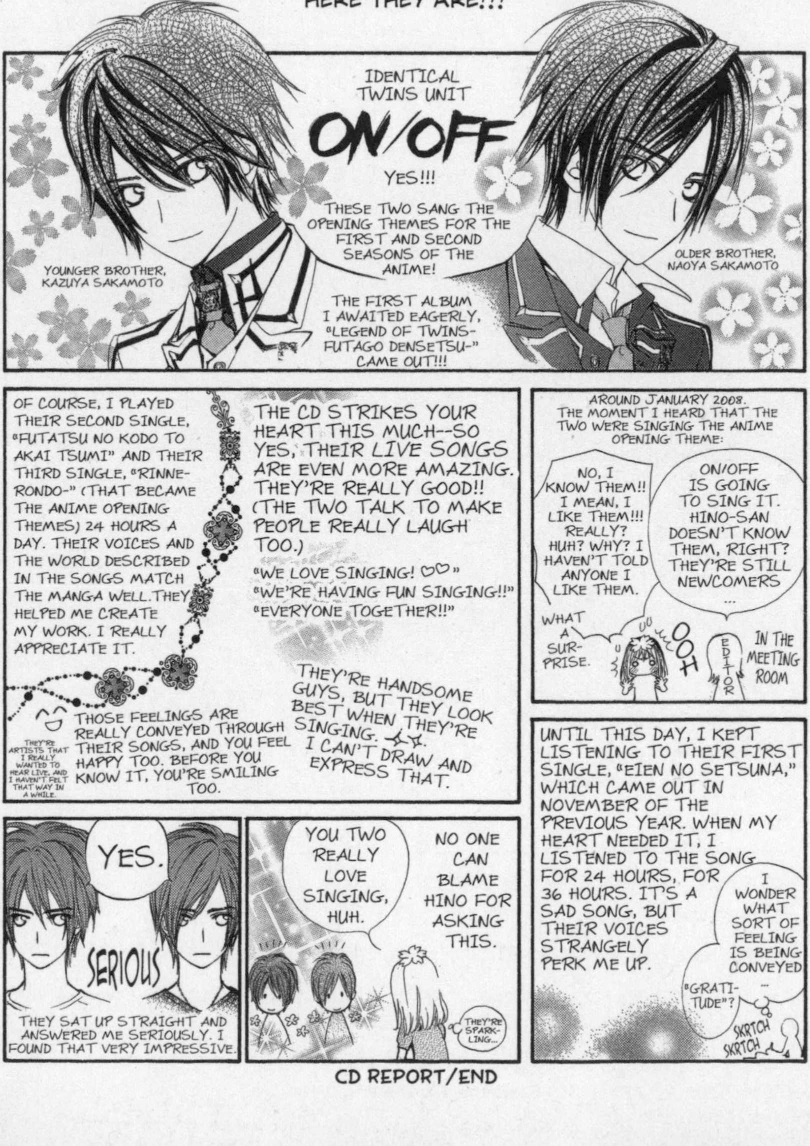
IDENTICAL TWINS UNIT
ON/OFF
YES!!!
THESE TWO SANG THE OPENING THEMES FOR THE FIRST AND SECOND SEASONS OF THE ANIME!
OLDER BROTHER, NAOYA SAKAMOTO
YOUNGER BROTHER, KAZUYA SAKAMOTO
THE FIRST ALBUM I AWAITED EAGERLY, "LEGEND OF TWINS-FUTAGO DENSETSU-" CAME OUT!!!
AROUND JANUARY 2008. THE MOMENT I HEARD THAT THE TWO WERE SINGING THE ANIME OPENING THEME:
ON/OFF IS GOING TO SING IT. HINO-SAN DOESN'T KNOW THEM, RIGHT? THEY'RE STILL NEWCOMERS ...
NO, I KNOW THEM!! I MEAN, I LIKE THEM!!! REALLY? HUH? WHY? I HAVEN'T TOLD ANYONE I LIKE THEM.
IN THE MEETING ROOM
EDITOR
OOH
WHAT A SURPRISE.
UNTIL THIS DAY, I KEPT LISTENING TO THEIR FIRST SINGLE, "EIEN NO SETSUNA," WHICH CAME OUT IN NOVEMBER OF THE PREVIOUS YEAR. WHEN MY HEART NEEDED IT, I LISTENED TO THE SONG FOR 24 HOURS, FOR 36 HOURS. IT'S A SAD SONG, BUT THEIR VOICES STRANGELY PERK ME UP.
I WONDER WHAT SORT OF FEELING IS BEING CONVEYED ...
"GRATITUDE"?
SKRTCH SKRTCH
THE CD STRIKES YOUR HEART THIS MUCH--SO YES, THEIR LIVE SONGS ARE EVEN MORE AMAZING. THEY'RE REALLY GOOD!! (THE TWO TALK TO MAKE PEOPLE REALLY LAUGH TOO.)
"WE LOVE SINGING! ♡♡"
"WE'RE HAVING FUN SINGING!!"
"EVERYONE TOGETHER!!"
OF COURSE, I PLAYED THEIR SECOND SINGLE, "FUTATSU NO KODO TO AKAI TSUMI" AND THEIR THIRD SINGLE, "RINNE-RONDO-" (THAT BECAME THE ANIME OPENING THEMES) 24 HOURS A DAY. THEIR VOICES AND THE WORLD DESCRIBED IN THE SONGS MATCH THE MANGA WELL. THEY HELPED ME CREATE MY WORK. I REALLY APPRECIATE IT.
THEY'RE HANDSOME GUYS, BUT THEY LOOK BEST WHEN THEY'RE SINGING. I CAN'T DRAW AND EXPRESS THAT.
THOSE FEELINGS ARE REALLY CONVEYED THROUGH THEIR SONGS, AND YOU FEEL HAPPY TOO. BEFORE YOU KNOW IT, YOU'RE SMILING TOO.
THEY'RE ARTISTS THAT I REALLY WANTED TO HEAR LIVE, AND I HAVEN'T FELT THAT WAY IN A WHILE.
NO ONE CAN BLAME HINO FOR ASKING THIS.
YOU TWO REALLY LOVE SINGING, HUH.
THEY'RE SPARKLING...
YES.
SERIOUS
THEY SAT UP STRAIGHT AND ANSWERED ME SERIOUSLY. I FOUND THAT VERY IMPRESSIVE.

CD REPORT/END

EDITOR'S NOTES

Characters

Matsuri Hino puts careful thought into the names of her characters in *Vampire Knight*. Below is the collection of characters through volume 10. Each character's name is presented family name first, per the kanji reading.

黒主優姫

Cross Yuki

Yuki's last name, *Kurosu*, is the Japanese pronunciation of the English word "cross." However, the kanji has a different meaning—*kuro* means "black" and *su* means "master." Her first name is a combination of *yuu*, meaning "tender" or "kind," and *ki*, meaning "princess."

錐生零

Kiryu Zero

Zero's first name is the kanji for *rei*, meaning "zero." In his last name, *Kiryu*, the *ki* means "auger" or "drill," and the *ryu* means "life."

玖蘭枢

Kuran Kaname

Kaname means "hinge" or "door." The kanji for his last name is a combination of the old-fashioned way of writing *ku*, meaning "nine," and *ran*, meaning "orchid": "nine orchids."

藍堂英

Aido Hanabusa

Hanabusa means "petals of a flower." *Aido* means "indigo temple." In Japanese, the pronunciation of *Aido* is very close to the pronunciation of the English word *idol*.

架院暁

Kain Akatsuki

Akatsuki means "dawn" or "daybreak." In *Kain*, *ka* is a base or support, while *in* denotes a building that has high fences around it, such as a temple or school.

早園瑠佳

Souen Ruka

In *Ruka*, the *ru* means "lapis lazuli" while the *ka* means "good-looking" or "beautiful." The *sou* in Ruka's surname, *Souen*, means "early," but this kanji also has an obscure meaning of "strong fragrance." The *en* means "garden."

一条拓麻

Ichijo Takuma

Ichijo can mean a "ray" or "streak." The kanji for *Takuma* is a combination of *taku*, meaning "to cultivate" and *ma*, which is the kanji for *asa*, meaning "hemp" or "flax," a plant with blue flowers.

支葵千里

Shiki Senri

Shiki's last name is a combination of *shi*, meaning "to support" and *ki*, meaning "mallow"—a flowering plant with pink or white blossoms. The *ri* in *Senri* is a traditional Japanese unit of measure for distance, and one *ri* is about 2.44 miles. *Senri* means "1,000 *ri*."

夜刈十牙

Yagari Toga

Yagari is a combination of *ya*, meaning "night," and *gari*, meaning "to harvest." *Toga* means "ten fangs."

一条麻遠, 一翁

Ichijo Asato, aka "Ichio"

Ichijo can mean a "ray" or "streak." Asato's first name is comprised of *asa*, meaning "hemp" or "flax," and *tou*, meaning "far off." His nickname is *ichi*, or "one," combined with *ou*, which can be used as an honorific when referring to an older man.

若葉沙頼

Wakaba Sayori

Yori's full name is Sayori Wakaba. *Wakaba* means "young leaves." Her given name, *Sayori*, is a combination of *sa*, meaning "sand," and *yori*, meaning "trust."

星煉

Seiren

Sei means "star" and *ren* means "to smelt" or "refine." *Ren* is also the same kanji used in *rengoku*, or "purgatory."

遠矢莉磨

Toya Rima

Toya means a "far-reaching arrow." Rima's first name is a combination of *ri*, or "jasmine," and *ma*, which signifies enhancement by wearing away, such as by polishing or scouring.

紅まり亜

Kurenai Maria

Kurenai means "crimson." The kanji for the last *a* in Maria's first name is the same that is used in "Asia."

錐生壱縷
Kiryu Ichiru

Ichi is the old-fashioned way of writing "one," and *ru* means "thread."

緋桜閑, 狂咲姫
Hio Shizuka, Kuruizaki-hime

Shizuka means "calm and quiet." In Shizuka's family name, *hi* is "scarlet," and *ou* is "cherry blossoms." Shizuka Hio is also referred to as the "Kuruizaki-hime." *Kuruizaki* means "flowers blooming out of season," and *hime* means "princess."

藍堂月子
Aido Tsukiko

Aido means "indigo temple." *Tsukiko* means "moon child."

白蔲更
Shirabuki Sara

Shira is "white," and *buki* is "butterbur," a plant with white flowers. *Sara* means "renew."

黒主灰闇
Cross Kaien

Cross, or *Kurosu*, means "black master." Kaien is a combination of *kai*, meaning "ashes," and *en*, meaning "village gate." The kanji for *en* is also used for Enma, the ruler of the Underworld in Buddhist mythology.

玖蘭李土
Kuran Rido

Kuran means "nine orchids." In *Rido*, *ri* means "plum" and *do* means "earth."

玖蘭樹里

Kuran Juri

Kuran means "nine orchids." In her first name, *ju* means "tree" and a *ri* is a traditional Japanese unit of measure for distance. The kanji for *ri* is the same as in Senri's name.

玖蘭悠

Kuran Haruka

Kuran means "nine orchids." *Haruka* means "distant" or "remote."

Terms

-sama: The suffix *sama* is used in formal address for someone who ranks higher in the social hierarchy. The vampires call their leader "Kaname-sama" only when they are among their own kind.

Matsuri Hino burst onto the manga scene with her series *Kono Yume ga Sametara* (When This Dream Is Over), which was published in *LaLa DX* magazine. Hino was a manga artist a mere nine months after she decided to become one.

With the success of her popular series *Captive Hearts* and *MeruPuri*, Hino has established herself as a major player in the world of shojo manga. *Vampire Knight* is currently serialized in *LaLa* magazine.

Hino enjoys creative activities and has commented that she would have been either an architect or an apprentice to traditional Japanese craft masters if she had not become a manga artist.

Shojo Beat

Adaptation/Tomo Kimura
Touch-up Art & Lettering/Rina Mapa
Graphic Design/Amy Martin
Editor/Nancy Thistlethwaite

First published in Japan in 2009 by HAKUSENSHA, Inc., Tokyo. English language translation rights arranged with HAKUSENSHA, Inc., Tokyo.

Printed in the U.S.A.

Published by VIZ Media, LLC
P.O. Box 77010
San Francisco, CA 94107

10 9 8 7 6 5
First printing, June 2010
Fifth printing, April 2016

RATED T+ FOR OLDER TEEN

PARENTAL ADVISORY
VAMPIRE KNIGHT is rated T+ for Older Teen and is recommended for ages 16 and up. This volume contains sexual themes and violence.
ratings.viz.com

www.viz.com

www.shojobeat.com